*Friend of
the Library Donor*

Donated by
Terry Bales
SCC Faculty Member

The Entertainers

The Entertainers

Timothy White

BillboardBooks

An Imprint of Watson-Guptill Publications/New York

Photo Credits

AP/Wide World Photos: page 292.

Archive Photos: pages 100, 225; Fotos International: page 90; Bernard Gotfryd: page 241; Saga: page 399.

Corbis: © Lynn Goldsmith: page 116; © Matt Mendelsohn: page 412.

Gamma Liaison Network: Michael Abramson: page 46; David Burnett: page 264; George Rose: page 190.

Annie Leibovitz/Contact Press Images: ©Annie Leibovitz/Contact 1997: pages 136, 204, 336, 367, 384. © Annie Leibovitz 1991: page 308.

© Orion Pictures Company: page 80.

Courtesy Roaring Brook Farm/The Thomas Hart Benton Estate, with special thanks to George Peper of Fort Hill Construction Company; Julianna Flanders Thorpe of Flanders Up Island Realty; and Kathy Rose of The Wooden Tent Studios, who rephotographed the vintage print for reproduction: page 22.

UPI/Corbis-Bettmann: pages 60, 353.

Senior Editor: Bob Nirkind
Edited by Lester Strong
Picture Research: Margaret Sobel
Book and cover design: Jay Anning, Thumb Print
Production Manager: Ellen Greene

First published 1998 by Billboard Books, an imprint of Watson-Guptill Publications, a division of BPI Communications, Inc. 1515 Broadway, New York, NY 10036.

Library of Congress Cataloging-in-Publication Data

White, Timothy, 1952–
    The entertainers: portraits of stardom in the twentieth century / Timothy White.
        p.   cm.
    Includes bibliographical references and index.
    ISBN 0-8230-7606-7
    Entertainers—United States—Biography. 2. Entertainers—United States—Interviews.
  I. Title.
    PN1583.W44 1998
    791'.092'273—dc21
    [B]
                                 97-43767
                                   CIP

Manufactured in the United States of America

First Printing, 1998

1 2 3 4 5 6 7 8 /04 03 02 01 00 99 98

To Charles M. Young

Contents

Home Movies

Foreword:
The Urge to Entertain

IF YOU BELIEVE that America helped teach the world how to entertain itself, then you should know that, even before the American Revolution (1775–83), the public pursuit of our citizenry's hopes and dreams had become interwoven with the ceremonies of show business.

In 1743, American statesman Benjamin Franklin announced to the nation's citizens that "The first Drudgery of Settling new Colonies, which confines the Attention of People to mere Necessaries, is now pretty well over; and there are many in every Province in Circumstances that set them at Ease, and afford leisure to cultivate the finer Arts. . . ."

Thus encouraged, our ancestors set about diverting themselves in ritualized fashion. British and European forms of horse racing and fox hunting, popular in the Eastern, Southern and Middle Colonies since the 1660s, were soon supplemented by theatrical events of the sort the Puritans and Quakers had fled the Old Country to avoid. By the 1730s, cities along the Eastern Seaboard had amateur groups giving public recitals on flute, harpsichord and violin (instruments many immigrants had brought with them, along with their favorite psalmodies and folk hymns).

In Williamsburg, Virginia, a husband-and-wife team of dance instructors raised patronage fees from the town's finest families (the Harrisons, the Lees, the Randolphs) to sponsor a tour by a group of English actors to perform "comedies, drolls, and other kinds of stage plays." Another acting troupe led by Englishman Lewis Hallam visited the non-Yankee colonies in the mid-1700s, and Shakespeare's plays were soon staged throughout Philadelphia, Charleston and New York. Philadelphia had a permanent theater before the American Revolution, although it was common practice to advertise Shakespeare's often bawdy, violent and supernaturalism-stepped dramas as "moral dialogues . . . proving that happiness can only spring from the pursuit of virtue." Secular music was also provided during these plays and between-acts, the strains of fiddles often rising from orchestra pits to accompany some conveniently inserted romantic duet.

Nonetheless, civil writs and church rulings against theatricals remained widespread, shifting many show venues to points outside the town limits. Yet by the mid-1800s, it was usual in all but the most lowly woodland cabins and cottages for an anthology of Shakespeare's plays to share shelf space with the King James Bible. It became part of every father's manly duties to read aloud to his family by evening lamplight, a habit that helped create an appetite for truly adroit doses of the spoken word.

Thus was born the lyceum, or public lecture hall, circuit (the word derived from the Greek *"lykeion,"* the gymnasium near Athens where Aristotle taught). One Josiah Holbrook, friend of educator Horace Mann, started the first American lyceum in Millbury, Massachusetts, in 1826. Within ten years there were some 3,000 lyceums nationally, presenting edifying lectures on science, pseudo-science, literature and social issues like abolition, often with topical songs and skits. The booking of prominent speakers became a business unto itself, with advance fees and a portion of the gate paid out to renowned authors. Ralph Waldo Emerson would arrive by stagecoach for a four-hour discourse on the mystical unity of nature, while British novelist William Makepeace Thackeray would endure freezing railcoaches and lice-ridden roadhouse accommodations to deliver three hours of excerpts from his popular novel *Vanity Fair* to a tavern full of New England tradesmen.

Out of the lyceums grew the commercial summertime chautauqua shows of the early 1900s, these country fair-like educational convocations—featuring wholesome music, and political, travel and religious lectures—having been first proposed at an 1873 Methodist Episcopal camp meeting in Chautauqua, New York.

At the same time, tiny transplants of the one-ring European circus were pausing, at increasingly regular seasonal dates, in crossroads burgs throughout the American heartland. A child growing up in Kansas City or Seattle might wait all year for Circus Day, each numbered square of the kitchen wall calendar meticulously 'X'ed out until the July morning the painted wagons of the Great National Circus trundled into a local meadow.

For city dwellers, master showman P. T. Barnum opened his American Museum on Broadway in Manhattan in 1842 and packed it with midgets, Siamese twins, supposed sea serpents, and the oddments collected by popular explorers like Commodore Charles Wilke. To hook the curious, a band blared all day from an open-air gallery overlooking the spires of St. Paul's Chapel, New York City's most cultivated house of prayer. When Barnum bankrolled the 1850–52 national tour of Swedish songbird Jenny Lind—complete with extensive souvenir merchandizing—it was the forerunner of the modern rock-and-roll road show. And when the glow of that lavish caravan faded, Barnum merged his own traveling circus with his chief competitor's to present the Barnum and Bailey extravaganza, otherwise known as "The Greatest Show on Earth."

The so-called legitimate theater was also expanding in the States, in spite of Old World prejudices. According to Elizabethan laws, actors not accredited by local nobles were subject to all the civil penalties dealt vagabonds. American actors gained little additional stature before the footlights, since most urban theaters of the mid-1800s usually had much unscheduled drama taking place amongst the seated patrons. Relegation to various sections of the auditoriums was according to economic caste and private inclination, the habitues of adjoining gaming parlors, poolhalls and brothels frequently intent on continuing their fun in tandem with any activities onstage. The higher the balcony the more heated the misbehavior, while respectable gentleman and escorted ladies were exclusively consigned to the demure dress circle tier.

High culture was no obstacle to lewdity, as shown by the appearance in the mid-1800s of Italo-French ballet, notorious for its scanty costumes. A basic level of decorum could be expected for theatrical performances by eminent American tragedians Junius Brutus Booth and sons Edwin and John Wilkes, and native or British playwrights like Dr. Robert Montgomery Bird and Tom Taylor commanded audience attentiveness, although an otherwise unengaged John Wilkes Booth did shoot President Lincoln in the head at Ford's Theater in Washington, D.C., during a production of Taylor's *Our American Cousin.*

The 1840s saw the acceptance of another form of stage entertainment, the minstrel show, which took the casual patter-and-sashay modus of the back-country strolling entertainer and grafted it onto a racist lampoon of African-American strivings. Prior to the Civil War, the bigoted crux of minstrel shows was fearful ridicule set to music and played by white musicians and dancers wearing blackface. However, Northern white composers like Pennsylvania-bred Stephen Foster ("Oh! Susannah," "Camptown Races," "My Old Kentucky Home") tried to blend black spirituals and Africa-derived work chants with sentimental parlor songs of the time in an attempt to restore popular dignity to America's otherwise dehumanized slave population. After the Civil War, black performers drawn from freed slaves and their emancipated offspring took back the now-popular "Negro minstrel song" and restored its authenticity.

During the latter half of the nineteenth century, the minstrelsy was the preeminent form of entertainment in the United States, its ranks eventually dominated by African-Americans who disdained demeaning makeup, concentrating on the ticklish rhythmic feats of the music. Many ambitious public entertainers, both white and black, continued to serve apprenticeships in minstrel shows, among them rising boxing champion J. J. "Gentleman Jim" Corbett, famous circus clown Dan Rice, jazz giants Jelly Roll Morton and Lester Young, Broadway musical star George M. Cohan, singer Al Jolson or future "March King" John Philip Sousa, the composer of "Stars and Stripes Forever."

The minstrelsy was the forerunner of the burlesque, follies and Broadway musical forms. Most especially, the routes journeyed by minstrel troupes laid the groundwork for the network of theaters that became the vaudeville circuit—the vast dominant outlet for ordinary Americans until the advent of radio and the movies. When entrepreneurial New England theater owners B. F. Keith and Edward F. Albee graduated in 1886 from freak shows into pirated condensations of Gilbert and Sullivan operettas (with "clean" song-and-dance sketches during intermissions), they sought a spiffier promotional term than the disreputable "variety," and settled on "vaudeville." The word, which originally pertained to songs of the valley of Vire in Calvados, Normandy, had acquired a light-comedy theatrical connotation by the time Charles Dickens used it in *America Notes* (1842). The success of Albee and Keith's composite approach to family entertainment led to the theater chain that America's comics and hoofers had christened "the Keith Circuit." Keith himself incorporated it in 1906 as the United Booking Office of America, and it controlled three hundred theaters east of Chicago, as well as the key New York City playhouses, the jewel in the crown being the Palace. James Cagney began his vaudeville career at Keith's 86th Street Theater in the autumn of 1919, earning $25 a week as a female impersonator in the all-male chorus of a review called *Every Sailor.*

Other circuits of importance were the Orpheum, which covered Chicago and points west, as well as the Pantages, Fox and Shubert circuits—marquee firms that endure in the theater and film industries to this day.

Meantime, Thomas Alva Edison's December 24, 1877, patent application for the phonograph had led to the creation of the North American Phonograph Company. He had competitors, among them Emile Berliner (inventor in 1876 of the microphone) whose gramophone used discs instead of the solid-wax cylinders Edison marketed. The first commercial musical recordings were made in 1889 for coin-operated "phonograph parlors," in which patrons listened through a tubular earpiece to a music cylinder spinning in a basement room. Price: five cents a play.

Columbia Records issued its first record catalogue in October 1890, all the selections being marches from John Philip Sousa's U.S. Marine Band. A trade weekly called *The Billboard* began publication in 1894 to report on the amusement and vending machine industries. Columbia's two-sided disc records—"Two songs for the price of one!"—were introduced in 1908. *Billboard* magazine began including weekly sheet music best-seller sales charts in its 1913 issues, followed by surveys of the biggest vaudeville songs. In 1917, exclusive phonograph record patent rights held by Columbia, Edison and other companies expired, allowing a slew of new labels to emerge.

During 1921–22, Guglielmo Marconi and Karl Braun's 1909 Nobel Prize-winning invention of radio vaulted from novelty item to home entertainment phenomenon, with dance band broadcasts easing over one thousand new stations into prosperity by 1925. David Sarnoff of the Radio Corporation of America (who had monitored the 1912 sinking of the Titanic from a model wireless station in New York's Wanamaker's department store), developed the revolutionary idea of seventy-five dollar home "Radio Music Boxes."

In 1927, RCA and the General Electric and Westinghouse companies began funding experimental television broadcasts, with the National Broadcasting Company moving beyond its radio base to establish a New York City flagship TV station in 1928. That year, Broadway was enjoying a smash with the first important musical to favor storyline and character development over tuneful glamor: Jerome Kern and Oscar Hammerstein II's *Show Boat*.

In October of 1929, the stock market crashed and the Great Depression began, but the entertainment industry showed itself to be relatively secure in the face of hard times. This same year, Edison abandoned the record business for radio.

By 1929, the motion picture technology pioneered in the 1880s–90s by Louis Le Prince, Thomas Edison and Frenchmen E. J. Marey and the Lumiere brothers had catapulted from storefront "vaudefilm" outlets and quaint nickelodeons into the huge North America-wide box office triumph of *The Broadway Melody*, the first "100% All Talking, 100% All Singing, 100% All Dancing" movie. The plot of the picture, which earned the Academy Award for Best Film, concerned two sisters who suffer behind the scenes during the staging of a musical on the Great White Way. Its simple theme mirrored the dogged immigrant values that suffused the scrappy entertainment business: the show must go on.

During the 1930s, Warner Bros. Pictures led the way in the production of movies sparked by the sorrows and pressures of Depression America. The company's policies echoed the spare esthetic, stingy economics and stressful work environment of the era, leading to frequent clashes with its stable of actors. James Cagney appreciated Warner's the-movie-must-get-shot rubric, so long as it didn't sacrifice his personal life for the sake of career— a bold stance at the time.

Modern show business soon introduced a new maxim: the audience must be expanded. New programs and presentations were systematically introduced to satisfy the hungry collective imagination of the American social experiment. Moreover, consumer-oriented firms realized that modern communications could sell products on an unprecedentedly intimate level. With radio, for example, even when audience members closed their eyes, the broadcast was still unfolding inside their heads. Under the tutelage of aggressive advertizers, radio expanded and intensified its broadcast fare with methodically formatted comedy, drama and live music shows that doubled as sales tools.

In 1934, *Billboard* began to survey the most-played songs on network radio. In April 1938, *Billboard* initiated weekly chartings of the most-played jukebox records in America. Moreover, record fans were flocking into stores to purchase the original-soundtrack recording from the first full-length animated movie, *Snow White and the Seven Dwarfs*. Suddenly cinema song writers like Frank Churchill and Larry Morey (*Snow White*) and film scorers like Alfred Newman (*Alexander's Ragtime Band*, *Tin Pan Alley*, *The Song of Bernadette*) were known to the casual observer. And henceforth, all the hybrid products from all the major entertainment mediums—Broadway, Hollywood, radio, TV, records—would gain vast appeal.

On May 5, 1944, the Columbia Broadcasting Company inaugurated *The CBS Television News*, a 15-minute collection of newreels, hosted by Ned Calmer. In the autumn of 1944, NBC launched *The Gilette Cavalcade of Sports*, featuring boxing and wrestling. In 1952, Walter Cronkite was appointed the CBS-TV network's anchorman for political conventions; a decade later he became the anchor for *The CBS Evening News*, holding the post until March 9, 1981, when Dan Rather (in a contract worth a reported $8 million) formally replaced Cronkite as anchor and managing editor of CBS's top regular news broadcast. Ever since, newcasters have rivaled sports figures for special status in the mass communications consciousness.

Over roughly a century, the entertainment industry evolved from a loose assortment of indulgences that enhanced the comforts of community, into a consuming social force unto itself. Yet the average entertainer, regardless of his or her ultimate achievements, remained tied to time-honored traditions of craft, uncomplaining diligence and respect for forerunners. This sense of heritage, of rising up through the ranks of a show business culture created from decades of shared experience, was a potent one. Across generational lines, all of the people in this book progressed and profited by attending the same incremental school of hard knocks. James Cagney's stint as a bellhop at the Friar's Club, Goldie Hawn and Bette Midler's lean times frugging in go-go lounges and Alan Alda's stints as a clown at discount store grand openings are all aspects of the same mettle-tempering climb. The sky was the limit professionally, but only if you had both the talent and the pith to perform well under often pitiable pressures.

Yet the parallels and collegial ties amongst the people in this book run deeper still. Experience in the sportscasting, comedy or melodrama sides of the radio medium shaped the resumes of Dan Rather, James Cagney, Johnny Carson, Bill Murray, John Belushi, Michael O'Donoghue and Julie Andrews (whose fame first derived from her regular role on the popular 1950's BBC series, *Educating Archie*), while Cronkite graduated from announcer in a bookie joint to a broadcasting job in Kansas City. And Cronkite and Rather were not the only figures who both covered and helped create news events—Carson, Aykroyd and O'Donoghue have taken their respective shots at journalism and literature, as well. For her part, Susan Abigail Tomalin was an English major at Catholic University before she met aspiring actor Chris Sarandon and subsequently switched her major to drama (they were married in 1967 and divorced in 1979).

Andrews's English music hall roots and appearances in pantomine and West End musical plays like *Mountain Fire* (1954) link her to the early British stage struggles of Jessica Tandy. Frank Langella, John Travolta, Mark Hamill, Harrison Ford and Carrie Fisher are all descended from vaudeville and Las Vegas nightclub-seasoned forebears. Susan Sarandon has often appeared on the stage in serious and comedic roles, making her theatrical debut in the early 1980s opposite Eileen Brennan in the two-character play, *A Coupla White Chicks Sitting Around Talking* (which she helped finance), and then winning raves portraying the victim of an attempted rape in the off-Broadway dramatic hit, *Extremities*. (Sarandon later formed an improvisational theater company with colleagues Richard Dreyfuss, Peter Boyle, Paul Dooley, Andre Gregory and Carol Kane at the Public Theater in New York.)

Adolescent folk singer Bette Midler rose from bit player in the film production of *Hawaii* (starring Andrews), to lead performer in off-off-Broadway productions, followed by co-starring credits on Broadway, and then pop vocal stardom via cabaret stints at the Improvisation club (where actor Andy

Kaufman often did stand-up comedy) and the Continental Baths. Likewise, Hawn's toil as a Vegas chorine, Marie Osmond's childhood grinds on the county fair circuit, and the Second City sketch comedy experience of Belushi, Murray and Aykroyd each harken back to old-time variety or burlesque show orthodoxies.

The shared sense of craft and risk extend still further amongst this book's principal subjects. Cagney and Hume Cronyn both had the boxing ring in common with Muhammad Ali—who in turn acted off-Broadway in *Big Time, Buck White* and recorded for Columbia Records as Cassius Clay. Kaufman's lifelong preoccupation with the surreal performance aspects of professional wrestling helped shape the aggressive, hoax- and dissimulation-steeped sides of his Tony Clifton lounge lizard characterization and other audience-alienating alter egos he adopted.

Indeed, virtually everyone in this book has had extensive involvements in the mediums of others. Most have appeared on recordings of one sort or another, most have done live television and Hollywood films, most have danced and sung and taken pratfalls on the boards, and all have constantly made themselves vulnerable in the service of their art. Travolta sought James Cagney's professional counsel at the same juncture that Cagney was preparing for his role in the film *Ragtime*.

Travolta also illustrates the intersecting realms of the lyceum and science fiction, since the controversial Scientology creed of which he is a devotee was devised by the late sci-fi writer L. Ron Hubbard, a practiced speaker on the pseudo-science/pulp cosmology lecture circuit of the 1950s. *Star Wars* director George Lukas's Zen-derived science fiction concept of "the Force" would ultimately become a casual show business metaphor for all things honest and intuitive in the industry.

To be sure, there has been overreaching in the efforts by those profiled here to build an ethos out of their urge to entertain, yet each artist has also shown a willingness to expose failings, flaws and limitations, being regardful of the show business precept that perfectionism should take a back seat to sincerity. As such, they may well form the ranks of a fading breed.

Although Walter Cronkite and Dan Rather both bristle at suggestions that their camera-booth coverage of political conventions, presidential elections and NASA space shots has been theatrical, there is little doubt of that precise aim in the minds of the pols and government agencies who mounted such spectacles while courting/contouring media access.

In the days since Cronkite and Rather made their reputations, there are less guarantees that a television anchorperson has acquired extensive practical reporting experience. Instead, it's more customary for news coverage to be dispensed by videogenic "talking heads" (in *TV Guide* parlance), who are often neither the source nor the editor of the information provided.

Which brings us to an intrinsic aspect of this book, namely, the evolving nature of arts and cultural journalism itself. Much of modern entertainment reporting, including accepted practices like weekly reviews of music and musical recordings, was pioneered by *Billboard*, which regularly critiqued sheet music, early Columbia, Edison and Berliner recordings and popular songs introduced in vaudeville and musicals. *Billboard*'s seminal coverage of circuses, carnivals, stage drama, musical theater and film fare both here and overseas was comprehensive enough to have enlisted the talents in the 1920s of James Albert Jackson, the first regular African-American columnist/featured reporter in a national magazine—and the man who became one of the leading chroniclers of the Harlem Renaissance.

America has since produced innumerable trade and consumer publications covering the arts, among them publications as diverse as *Crawdaddy*, *Rolling Stone*, *Harper's Bazaar*, *The New York Sunday News Magazine*, *Cosmopolitan* and *The New York Times Magazine*—each of which initially published material contained in this text.

Hopefully, the informing principle in all good journalism is that no one, least of all a responsible reporter, should ever try to understand any person too quickly. None of the profiles here is based on a single encounter, and most reflect time spent with performers over the course of weeks, months, or a year or more. Many of the people portrayed herein were uncommonly shy in face to-face encounters. "My goodness, you dig deep," Jessica Tandy remarked one afternoon, unconsciously reaching for her husband's arm for support during an interview for the joint profile with Hume Cronyn. The question posed was not terribly probative; Tandy had merely been asked about the London neighborhood in which she grew up. However, the topic evoked painful memories of Tandy's early poverty, and her impulsive, trembling gesture to her spouse underscored the candor she summoned in answering.

It took four years of letters, phone conversations with Johnny Carson and tentative assents before I finally interviewed the acutely reticent comedian/television host. In my first five-hour brunch interview with him in his Bel Air home, he struggled mightily to conquer his own reserve and explain himself, and seemed enormously relieved when we were done. Yet one week later, he phoned *Rolling Stone* from his suite at the Sherry Netherland Hotel on Fifth Avenue and asked if I'd like to come over to chat some more. The talk-show superstar said the chance to explain himself at length had been more liberating than he realized, and he wanted to take an "additional stab" at the one freedom he had never previous allowed: discussing himself.

Facts are details confirmed by diligence, but the truth is a series of connections made that disclose the bolder shape and substance of the business of living. The worthiest goal in entertainment journalism is to be accurate in one's portrait while disappearing behind the process, in order to eliminate the distance between the writer and the subject.

One hopes that aim has been attained to some extent in these profiles (all of which now contain additional, previously unpublished material) because, sadly, some of the people in this book have passed on, leaving legacies that defy easy categorization or current equivalents. The tragic death of John Belushi in 1982 due to a drug overdose left an unfillable gap for a brilliantly instinctive comic talent, with both Hollywood and television still searching in vain for another mischievous but lovably "Belushi type" to beguile the public.

Someone less approachable though equally irreplaceable was Andy Kaufman, a frequent and always unpredictable guest on *Saturday Night Live* who expired from lung cancer in 1984. His last involvement with *SNL* was in a staged altercation with producer Dick Ebersole in 1982 after he was "cut" from the show just before airtime, the fight actually being a stunt to set up a subsequent call-in vote, asking viewers to decide if Kaufman should be invited back or barred from future appearances. When viewers voted for the latter, Andy elected to abide by the results of his conceptual "joke," and never returned to the program.

Also gone is Belushi mentor Michael O'Donoghue, the witty and inspired actor/songwriter/author/poet/broadcaster and television and film writer who in the early 1970s assembled virtually the entire roster for what later became *Saturday Night Live* while overseeing the infamous *National Lampoon Radio Hour*. O'Donoghue, who died suddenly in 1994 of a cerebral hemorrhage, was the spiritual father of the sophisticated, often ironic/sardonic but always unfliching style of modern wit that came to be called "The New Humor."

The athletic, risk-taking code of the hoofer and the song-and-dance traditionalist in the Cagney mold has been diminished in recent decades, with the "dance" sequences in music videos often consisting of artfully jump-cut vignettes of pose-striking non-dancers. Travolta, however, is a link to a time when the excitement of drama-*cum*-choreography was still a strong box office lure, with audiences well aware that the challenges shown on-screen were synonymous with the demands of the actual role. In September 1979, I quietly slipped onto the closed set for *Urban Cowboy*, the vast Gilley's saloon off dusty Spencer Highway in Pasadena, Texas, and I watched beside the camera crew for several days as Travolta worked through both his intricate dance sequences and his mechanical bull-riding sessions, demanding tasks for which there were no short-cuts.

As with Travolta, everyone in this book was captured at a moment that would come to represent a critical turning point in their work, whether it was a time of validation for their emerging gifts, a peak moment when they revealed previously unperceived depth and facility, a unique opportunity they were able to maximize to unsurpassed effect, or a period of transition whose components would prove to be defining factors in their overall careers. Indeed, the *Star Wars* portion of the text displays a convergence of fame, frustration and uncertainty of an individual degree unique in the annals of popular culture. And in each case the people in this book would never again be so vulnerable or accessible.

Entertainment, arguably America's chief export to the rest of the planet, has now become the stuff of multi-national corporate strategies and simulated creative bursts. Its output is increasingly intended to engender a satisfying distance instead of a challenging proximity. In the near future, much mass-marketed screen drama could originate from desktop animation workstations patched into audio-visual libraries, each dramatic cry and whisper refined and recycled to an infinite fare-thee-well.

Is the simulated side of show business's destiny an odious one? No one really knows. Alarm over technology has often proven misplaced, since innovation often carries its own exciting aesthetic dimensions. Sometimes it's simply the potent marketing of the new that spells the popular decline of the old. But if the merits of human exertion are decisively undercut by technology, the alterations in our definition of creativity could be disturbing. Where will the integrity of an artistic statement reside? And how touched will any of us still be by the ordinary, flawed effort of those who actually tried, without trickery, to see beyond their own eyes, run beyond their own legs, feel beyond their own hearts?

In America, entertainment became integral to the cause of freedom and self-knowledge, the democracy of its presentation apparent in stage bills from the early 1800s that listed a Shakespeare play, acrobatic displays, dance routines, balladeers and a farce in a single evening's proceedings.

Even full-scale operas in the nineteenth century were regularly presented on the same programs as minstrel singers, trained animal troupes and comedic skits, the opera itself regularly interrupted with popular songs—a widespread practice for which composers like Antonio Rossini (1792–1868) actually made formal structural allowances.

Thus, the custom of mingling so-called high art and low art has long been characteristic of our culture, with patrons in the expensive boxes or the cheap balconies all passing judgment on the same artistic panorama. This casually democratic vantage point on transcendence is valuable. If entertainment should someday become a dodge, losing its charter of effort and code of ideals, then we may forfeit our common capacity to name and appreciate the specialness of our self-expressive strivings in its arenas.

The future is close and often appears disquieting. As our world grows smaller, our illusions seem to increase. If or when the frank and inclusive world fostered by the entertainers in this book finally disappears, should anyone take the time to reflect on its bygone precepts, they will marvel at the passion with which these performers tried to summon up and share some part of their better selves. And they'll discern the simple, unadorned truth: nothing this real could have lasted forever.

Vestiges of Vaudeville

James Cagney:
An American Original

T aking up film acting at a juncture when the profession was just beginning to show a measure of procedural and artistic maturity, James Cagney quickly burst the tender bubble of its tony sense of glamor and made the form raw and unsettled once again. He accomplished this because he knew how to inhabit his roles with unnerving clarity, using a vivid medium to enforce an unprecedented level of ordinary vulnerability.

"He had an energy about him," said fellow screen star Pat O'Brien, Cagney's closest friend for 60 years. "As an actor he could play musical comedy, farce, tragedy, drama—and his range was instinctive, not ambitious."

Cagney lived his life much the same way, seeking out a close circle of friends and several private realms of respite with equally cogent powers of intuition. In the summer and fall of 1981, I visited Cagney on the set of his last feature film, *Ragtime*, and interviewed him at his suite at the Carlyle Hotel and at his working horse farm in Dutchess County, New York, as well as talking with his oldest chums (O'Brien, Ralph Bellamy, Frank McHugh) and youngest associates (John Travolta). As with many of the stories in this book, not everyone I spoke to was quoted in the finished piece; indeed I talked to many people simply to gain a basic understanding of Cagney, his emotional core, and the few things in his long life that had truly claimed his heart.

It was at Cagney's gentle urging that I made a side trip from another story-in-progress and visited Roaring Brook Farm, the rustic Hillman Homestead estate on Martha's Vineyard he'd owned until the late 1970s. "Loved that place," he confessed. "If you ever go there, you'll see why."

Walking around the high grass of the 78-acre grounds and peering into the simple cottages at its center, one was struck by the resemblance of the estate to the Irish coast Cagney briefly left this very retreat for in the late 1950s to film *Shake Hands with the Devil*. Cagney beamed when later told about this writer's walking tour of Roaring Brook Farm's open pastures and wooded trail to the ocean, peeking into the old barn, the colonial-era main house, and the small gray saltbox studio he built behind it, where he had once painted in solitude and installed a hardwood floor in late summer, 1941 to practice the dance numbers for *Yankee Doodle Dandy*.

"It was beautiful then," he said of the Vineyard in the late 1930s and early 1940s. "Same look of the wind on the grass that you see in Ireland. Now it's getting too fancy, with the whole celebrity angle. I remember an old farmer up there saying to me one day—I was about 35 at the time—that he wanted to put an ad in the paper to get some young boys to help him for the summer.

"I looked at this old guy, who was plowing his field with oxen, and I thought, 'I would have *killed* for a summer like that when I was a kid.'"

Cagney put that same fierce depth of feeling, that surpassing sense of mingled appreciation, amazement and regret, into his acting. But he admired other people's mysteries as much as their more accessible traits, whether they were colleagues, companions, or characters whose screen destinies he was temporarily empowered to depict.

"Angels with Dirty Faces is my favorite of the films I did with Jim," said O'Brien, who played parish priest Father Jerry Connelly opposite Cagney's hoodlum character Rocky Sullivan in the 1938 crime drama. "One of the reasons is the ambiguous ending: Did Jim's character go yellow as he was led to the [electric] chair, or was he faking it for his pal, the priest? We talked about it during filming in London for *Ragtime* and Jim admitted he never made up his own mind, either. 'That's why the scene was so powerful,' he told me."

The last time I saw Cagney was at his horse farm in upstate New York during the extensive, concluding talk detailed in the profile that follows. He had grown increasingly frail during the months of shooting and postproduction work for *Ragtime*, and seemed like he was gradually, gracefully preparing his ultimate farewell. On the evening before our final meeting in 1981, I spoke at length with Cagney's aged crony Frank McHugh, checking several specifics in my emerging portrait and ultimately asking if my overall sense of Frank's old cohort seemed an accurate one. At this question, McHugh, who starred opposite Cagney in *The Crowd Roars* (1932), began to cry.

I asked McHugh if any aspect of the conversation had hurt or offended him in some way, and he said no, explaining that he'd recently lost his longtime wife and that he was still grieving. "I try to be religious, and be accepting," said the 83-year-old actor, "but the way we've discussed Jim tonight, it makes me realize how much I could still lose."

Cagney would outlive Frank McHugh, who passed away in September 1981, several weeks after our conversation. Pat O'Brien, who was to die in 1983, suddenly added at the end of my interview with him about Cagney: "I've got to tell you a simple feeling I have about that man. I think he glows the way he does because God has got his arms around him."

Cagney himself succumbed to a heart attack on March 29, 1986, while on his Dutchess County farm. Born in 1899, the year songwriter Chauncey Olcott published "My Wild Irish Rose," James Francis Cagney, Jr., was 87.

THE INTERVIEW

THE WINDOW SHADES ARE DRAWN against the late-summer sun, transforming the suite in Manhattan's genteel old Carlyle Hotel into a lonesome oasis of resignation not unlike the sitting room of a sanitarium. It is perfectly quiet within—no, there is the faint wheeze of labored breathing. Hunched in a stuffed easy chair at one end of the long living room is a pillowy mound of a man dressed in crisply pressed cotton pajamas and a linen bathrobe, his small feet reposing in scuffed leather slippers, his thin hair neatly combed. He appears to be asleep, his round, pink head pitched forward, chin upon the barrel chest, plump arms lying against his thick waist. If not for his size and the silvery stubble that coats his jaws, he might be one of Maurice Sendak's man-faced infants, dreaming inside the frames of the illustrator's pleasantly baroque picture fables.

How does one awaken James Cagney, one of the finest and most versatile talents in the annals of cinema? Surely, at the age of eighty-two, with half a century of stardom (and twenty years of retirement) behind him, he desires and deserves his rest. But the consequences of living so long and rising so high in his profession have conspired against him.

"Jamesy, Jamesy, wake up, you old so-and-so," whispers Marge Zimmermann, Cagney's sixtyish aide-de-camp, who has been a close friend of the actor and his wife, Willard ("Billie" to insiders), for a dozen years.

The small, piercing blue eyes pop open with comic suddenness. "Ho!" he shouts. "Falling down on the job, am I? Get with it, Cagney! You're on!" He extends a large hand with glee and gives what proves to be an absolutely crushing handshake, confirming what his old acting crony Ralph Bellamy recently told me:

"Whenever Jimmy is suddenly afflicted with emotion, he has one of two reactions: he either falls silent and tears appear in his eyes, or he explodes with a distinctively sharp round of laughter to clear the air. They're the two ways he's devised for revealing but protecting himself—and he uses laughter the most."

Such has been the venerable star's public demeanor over the last fifteen months as he emerged from self-imposed exile to appear in *Ragtime*. Reviews have been mixed for director Milos Forman's interpretation of E. L. Doctorow's best-selling novel-cum-travelogue of turn-of-the-century New York City, its arabesque of fact and fiction intertwining the lives of a middle-class New Rochelle family and a ragtime piano tinkler named Coalhouse Walker. The negative notices focused on the truncated transferral to the screen of the book's rich tapestry of famous characters—Harry Houdini, Henry Ford, Booker T. Washington, Emma Goldman, architect Stanford White, moneyed dissolute Harry K. Thaw and his lovely, unfaithful spouse, Evelyn Nesbit, et al.—while the positive reviews hailed the return of a historic figure no less fabled: James Francis Cagney, Jr.

For a time, it seemed as if the country were going Cagney-crazy, with New York City Mayor Ed Koch giving the actor the key to the city, the Yankees inviting him to toss out a ball during the World Series, President

Ronald Reagan bestowing grandiose kudos, and life-achievement award dinners springing up across the country like four-leaf clovers. Tributes are much deserved (Cagney earned an Oscar for his song-and-dance sagacity in the 1942 *Yankee Doodle Dandy* and an honorary Best Actor award from the American Film Institute in the late Seventies). He virtually invented the modern antihero with his portrayal, in *The Public Enemy* (1931), of Tom Powers, the rum-running slum pug who gets shot down by underworld gunmen after avenging the gangland execution of his buddy.

"He created an entirely new character in film, a villain who was never too simple or entirely repellent," says Milos Forman. "And he allowed you to like and enjoy such a person without feeling guilty. He never sacrifices personality for craft, or vice versa, and that's a very rare quality that only a few actors— Bogart, Gable, Spencer Tracy—had. Drawing from things that are deep inside him or simply integral to who he is, Cagney is always a character, but always Cagney."

"Frankly," says the man himself, shifting in his seat at the hotel, "I always felt I was doing what was fashionable at the moment. I was giving them what *they* wanted but trying to keep it pleasant, at least for me."

Cagney never intended to become a career actor. "Back in the days when Jim worked as a bellhop in the Friar's Club," says Bellamy, "he used to see these actors coming through the doors in flashy suits, telling him, 'Last week, I earned *fifty bucks* dancing and singing in a show!' Jim used to tell me how amazed and jealous he was, thinking, 'Hell, I can hoof and carry a tune as well as these guys.' He was driven into show business by the desire to earn money for his family and to escape the poverty of his youth in New York City. I don't think—and I've known him for fifty years—that he ever intended to spend almost his whole life acting. He would have been happier remaining a song-and-dance man, so long as it paid his bills."

Cagney's first job in the legitimate theater was a stint as a female impersonator in a revue called *Every Sailor* at Keith's Eighty-first Street Theater. Most of the cast were fresh off the U.S.S. *George Washington*, where they'd entertained World War I sailors with a drag sendup of naval life. Female impersonators were the rage at the time, and every vaudeville show had one on the boards. ("My dear mother was a little surprised when I showed up onstage in a dress," says Cagney, "but she got the family to applaud—gave 'em a nudge in the ribs.")

He was thirty-one before he made his first film, *Sinner's Holiday* (1930), a sizzling, sixty-minute melodrama based on a New York play called *Penny Arcade*, in which he and friend Joan Blondell had costarred. Al Jolson was good enough to buy the screen rights and sell the project to Warner Brothers with the stipulation that Cagney and Blondell repeat their roles in the movie.

And so began a career marked by some of the finest films ever fashioned: *Taxi!*, *Winner Take All*, *Footlight Parade*, *Ceiling Zero*, *Angels with Dirty Faces*, *The Fighting 69th*, *Yankee Doodle Dandy*, *The Time of Your Life*, *White Heat*, *A Lion Is in the Streets*, *Love Me or Leave Me*, *Mister Roberts*, *The Seven Little Foys*, *Shake Hands with the Devil* and *One, Two, Three*, to name a few of his sixty-odd feature-length performances.

To talk with James Cagney over the course of the last few months was to travel back in time inside the mind and heart of one of the most remarkable people this country has produced. Through sepia-tinted photos he tapped with his index finger, intensely rendered oil paintings he singled out from his own workshop, and recollections that he unfurled in careful, halting conversation, he endeavored to provide someone close to one-third his years with at least a preliminary understanding of what it was like to grow up poor, frightened and fired with a determination that transcended ambition, during a time when America was careening around a blind curve and into the twentieth century.

"The whole nation was wide open—*wide open*," he says. "So many professions, including film acting, were in their inception. You knew it was a chance to get a big stake that would probably not come again. Big dreams everywhere, but most people had nothing. So you rolled up your sleeves and charged at *anything*. And [*laughing*] you prayed."

Cagney was born on July 17, 1899 (Warner Brothers publicists would later adjust that date to 1904), the son of a bartender whose forebears had traced his ancestry back to the O'Caignes of County Leitrim in Ireland, and one Carolyn Nelson, the half-Irish, half-Norwegian daughter of a sailor. His first home was a brownstone at 391 East Eighth Street, in a poor neighborhood on the Lower East Side, but the Cagneys soon moved to East Seventy-ninth Street and then to East Ninety-sixth Street.

"My father had a saloon at Eighty-first Street and First Avenue, just a little place," Cagney recalls, sipping a glass of orange juice, "and he was known as the 'two-for-one' bartender, meaning that he drank two for every one he served. Not a wise way to make a living. In those days, my father thought he had something going simply by running the place, but he was wrong, unfortunately.

"He was a bookkeeper, originally—that was the irony of it. He also liked to play the horses and ran through a lot of what little money we had. He died in 1918 after a quick bout with the flu. His alcoholism had weakened him to where the bug took him like *that*. He was irresponsible but very good-natured; he had the gift of gab and told a damned good joke. And he had been a good boxer and also a baseball pitcher. People nicknamed him 'Jimmy Steam.' But it was my mother who raised us, and she gave us her values: fair play, hard work, a strict Catholic upbringing. We all loved her so."

Cagney, a teetotaler, forgave his father's failings and excelled at pursuits that embodied the best of his parents' traits. A natural boxer, albeit with a streetfighter's abandon, James trained in his teens with local pros like Arnold "Jimmy" Kelly and Patsy Cline ("He was Italian," Cagney instructs with a smile). And while he held jobs that ranged from working as a custodian at the New York Public Library to waiting tables in a tearoom, he often found that his greatest currency—literally and symbolically—could be won in a sidewalk slugfest. Red-blooded as well as red-haired, he never flinched from the opportunity.

"I was sitting on a curbstone one day as a boy," he says in his gentle rasp, "playing this matchbox game for pennies, when a fella came along and said, 'Cagney! Red! I got a guy here who'll put up a quarter to fight you!' I stood up, threw a punch at my opponent, and we were at it. Money was where you made it, eh? I won the fight, by the way.

"I'd been fighting since I was six," he notes, "and I practiced often. Years later, it helped my dancing. One time I was in a fight that had been going, off and on, for three days with this guy, and somebody yelled out, 'Where are these boys' mothers?!' Well, my mother was standing there watching, making sure it was square."

That particular marathon match was with a scourge named Willie, whose merciless punishment had sent James' brother Eddie into a convalescent bed. Cagney had gone looking for the mug, and after challenging him, they went at it.

"Things calmed down by the third night, when I broke my hand," says Cagney, "and we agreed to a rematch once it healed." Shortly afterward, Willie landed in jail on some since-forgotten offense, bouncing from there to Sing Sing and then Dannemora prison.

"Never saw him again, but he wrote me once," Cagney says. "Last I heard of him, he had slit some poor inmate's throat. But this was my environment, these were my neighbors and friends."

Ragtime is still a month away from its premiere when I visit Cagney one day at his quaint stone farmhouse, which perches on a bluff overlooking a glassy pond in a lightly wooded corner of his Dutchess County estate in upstate New York. Casually dressed in a light-blue work shirt and baggy black slacks, he begins to talk of the battles he fought once he'd made it to Hollywood. He wanted to ensure his fair treatment by the architects of the notorious "studio systems" that severely restricted the salaries and creative motives of actors under rigid multipicture contracts. Signed to Warner Brothers, Cagney's chief adversary was Jack Warner.

"Want to know about Warner, eh?" he says with a grin. "Well, he was a good-looking young producer who was in charge of the actors as far as the studio was concerned. Not much older than I when we first shook on our deal, but acted like he was my old man. A hard fellow, very hard. A tough nut.

"I used to like to walk out on him, frankly, whenever my contract didn't suit me. I'd cuss him out in Yiddish, which I had learned from Jewish friends in my days at Stuyvesant High School. Drove him wild. 'What'd he *say*?!' he'd yell. 'What'd he just call me?!'

"People now see me as being tough, but it had nothing to do with being tough and *everything* to do with being stubborn. The point in life is to get what you want. There's no gain in getting things you don't want, and there's no gift in settling for something."

Cagney's problems with Warner Brothers were not so different from the ones other actors were having around town. "When the Screen Actors Guild got started in 1935, I joined right up, because I knew most actors were getting less than a hundred bucks for six- and seven-day weeks. People think all the movie people were rich, but it just wasn't true. The *producers* were rich. The top actors either got a fortune—$100,000 or more for a picture—or they got $400 a week because the studios had them sewn up. All we wanted was an eight-hour day and payment that reflected our talent and our box office. Years later, when I first heard that Steve McQueen was offered 3 million bucks for a picture, I almost fainted. He was a helluva actor, but *3 million bucks! That's nuts!"*

The harder Cagney worked, the more intransigent he became in his attitude toward the people he perceived as his exploiters. By 1936, he was one of the top-ten box-office attractions in the country and expected to be compensated accordingly. Few other actors had the moxie to follow in the footsteps of the "Tough Guy" when he refused to work under existing conditions, and the practice became known in the film community as "doing a Cagney." But, as he is quick to remind: "I never left in the middle of a picture; I finished up the job first. And I usually split because of a violation of my contract."

Whenever he could brush Hollywood aside, his focus usually shifted to the bucolic life of leisure he had sought since boyhood. His first exposure to rural living had come at the age of four, when his father hired a horse-drawn rig to take the family out to a relative's house in Sheepshead Bay, Brooklyn, for a two-week summer vacation. James never forgot the lush property, with its morning glory-draped fences and flowering shrubs. In 1936, he bought a farm in Martha's Vineyard (now deeded to his son), and in 1955, he purchased the property in Dutchess County. He made similar attempts to secure rustic hideaways in the West, although with mixed results.

"Jim hates this story," says Ralph Bellamy, "but I'm going to tell you it anyway because it says so much about the earnest nature of the man. He loves the outdoors and is an accomplished naturalist and an informed conservationist, right? Well, back in the mid-Thirties, he got himself eleven acres in Coldwater Canyon, just over the hill from Hollywood, in a place that had no house near it for a mile in any direction. He was going to create a paradise. He builds a stable for trotting horses, including a track, and buys ducks and geese and makes a pond for them. Then he gets some goats to run up and down the hillsides, and he puts up a chicken coop and fills it with twenty-six hens and four roosters! He goes up one day to check everything out, but he's still not satisfied. It's not quite right, and he wants to find a way to improve it. He goes down to the henhouse and sees that he's got just four roosters and figures, 'Well, *this* won't do,' so he goes and gets another twenty-two of them, so that every chicken will have a mate. The next thing you know, there's a commotion you wouldn't believe, with every chicken in the place on the roof of the coop and the roosters diving at them from the sky. It was hilarious! There were feathers all over every *inch* of Coldwater Canyon. The story spread around town, and he still isn't over the embarrassment."

This agrarian indiscretion notwithstanding, Bellamy has nothing but respect and deep affection for his pal.

"He's a very retiring person," says Bellamy, "and he's inclined to a kind of melancholia that he's had to strain to overcome. Crowds, I think, have always frightened him, and they were an aspect of this business that he always hated. He never really liked the business much, especially the corporate side. 'They can't *level* with you!' he'd always say, very hurt. But show business has kept him in touch with the outside world. He's always there for his close friends, but he's not outgoing."

Slowly, Cagney cultivated a support system of intimate male-actor companions consisting of Bellamy, Pat O'Brien, Frank McHugh, Spencer Tracy and Frank Morgan, all of whom had known one another from their days on the New York stage. Whether working or not, they found time each Thursday to meet at Los Angeles restaurants like Chasen's, Romanoff's and

Lucey's, or at one another's homes. They dubbed themselves the Boys Club, but director Frank Capra preferred the Irish Mafia, even though Bellamy was English and Morgan was German. In time, the clique expanded to include Lloyd Nolan, Harvey Perry, William Frawley, Allen Jenkins, Lynne Overman and others.

Of the bunch, Pat O'Brien became Cagney's chief confidant. They had met in the Twenties while appearing in stock companies in Asbury Park and went on to make some eight pictures together, the first being *Here Comes the Navy* in 1934, and the last (prior to Cagney's asking O'Brien to be cast as Harry K. Thaw's lawyer in *Ragtime*), *The Torrid Zone* in 1940. They still speak with each other at least once a week.

"Pat and his wife, Eloise, always liked the nightclubs and the parties," says Cagney. "They loved to stay out to all hours, and as a matter of fact, they still do. He and I were direct opposites, but there was never a problem. He always called me the Faraway Fella, and I always called him the Bull of the Woods. I called him that because when he got started on a project, you had to get the hell out of the way or be run over by him, he was so wildly determined.

Why did O'Brien call him the Faraway Fella?

"There was a party given by the Masquers' Club for Frank McHugh in the Fifties. Pat knew I didn't like parties, so he calls me up and says, 'You're gonna be there, *aren't you?*' I said, 'Hell, yes!' He said, 'Don't gimme that. Just be there. It's for Frank.' I said, 'Why do you doubt me, my boy?' He said, 'Well, Jim, you're one of those faraway fellas.'"

"The kindest thing he ever did for me was to get me into *Ragtime*; I hadn't done a picture in forty years," says O'Brien. "Jimmy doesn't go out and make friends haphazardly. He has to know you pretty darn well before he decides to stand by you. But once he crosses that line, you're his man forever."

"I like friends who last," Cagney confirms. "There's an art to picking them, and I'm not a casual person. I'm the kind who needs to go his own way; I'm not one who feels the need for much attention. Now some say Cagney's aloof. I don't think so, really [*chuckling*]. I wrote a little verse about it one time. It went:

Mine not the searching eye
Mine not to ask the why
Mine not to vie with wit
Mine not to give a—

"I think you can guess what the last word is," he says with a booming laugh.

Enigmatic on a personal level, Cagney the professional is equally elusive, and the few anecdotes that are now trickling out about his on-set demeanor reveal an utterly serious but often insecure man who occasionally seemed disoriented by his station in life.

"We were three days into shooting *Boy Meets Girl* in 1938," says Bellamy, "when Jim decides to go to see all the rushes, something he *rarely* did. Afterward, he comes back, a frown on his face.

"'What's wrong?' I ask.

"'You know that I'm a fast talker,' he answers in his rapid-fire way.

"'Yeah, I know.'

"'Well,' he says, 'I just saw three days' rushes, and I can't understand a single word I spoke!'

"Before I could really sympathize, Hal Wallis [the studio executive] sent out a note telling us to start the picture over and make it louder, *faster* and funnier!

"Incidentally," Bellamy confides, "Jim was never really happy with his work beyond *Yankee Doodle Dandy* [1942] and the other few pictures he danced in. He was a severe critic of his own work, and he also had a serious weight problem that runs in the whole family. He used to spar with a prizefighter for a few weeks before each of his films to try to lose weight. On the dancing films, it usually wasn't necessary, because he dropped the weight in the course of rehearsal."

A slam-bang flag-waver that galvanized the country's patriotic war time resolve, *Yankee Doodle Dandy* can be viewed in retrospect not only as the idealized film biography of showman George M. Cohan but also as a haunting reflection of Cagney's own picaresque professional unfolding. True to the script, the film star himself had risen up through the vaudeville ranks to embody the best showmen of his age; like Cohan, he was a traditionalist who drew his family closer to him with each success; he had also married a showgirl, whom he immediately coaxed into retirement. And the time would come when Cagney would follow Cohan's example and abruptly withdraw from the spotlight.

Whether or not Cagney was conscious of the personal correlations in the Cohan role, he says that he was always "looking for a personal touch," something derived from his own experience, to flesh out his characterizations. "I always planned it so that people would leave the theater with vivid memories of the characters, some detail to nail them with. In the case of *Angels with Dirty Faces*, for instance, I thought back to this pimp, this cokey

I used to know in Yorkville, who was forever hitching up his pants, and I stole that from him to enhance the role."

"One of the keys to Cagney's superiority as an actor is that he's a master of observation," says Jack Lemmon, who starred opposite him in *Mister Roberts* (1955). "Every actor who's worked with him has a Cagney-on-acting story, but I think mine has got to be one of the best. Back in the early Fifties, when I was doing a lot of live television, I did a Kraft Theatre show where, as an exercise in discipline, I did everything left-handed. It took weeks of practice, but when I did the show, no one noticed it; not my wife, not even the director. I considered it a big achievement. About two years later, I meet James Cagney as we're beginning to start work on *Mister Roberts*, and he says to me, 'I've seen kinescopes of some of your stuff with the Kraft Theatre. You were very good.' I was completely thrilled with the compliment. Cagney turns to go, and then he looks back at me and says, 'By the way, you're not still pretending you're left-handed, are you?'

"I almost shit. That marvelous son of a bitch was *that* observant."

Naturally adept at his job, Cagney was disinterested in reviewing the finished product once he'd fulfilled his responsibilities. "I've never seen seventy-five percent of the films I've done," he says bluntly. "Good or bad, I knew in my heart that I had always given it my best shot, so there was no point in watching myself make the effort."

Considering his attitudes on acting, it's not surprising that he expected a similar perspective from his coworkers, especially directors. For Cagney, a good director was both decisive and unobtrusive on the set, and his favorite, Lloyd Bacon, possessed both of these qualities.

"Lloyd Bacon, son of Frank Bacon, the old stage actor, would get a script, like the one for *Footlight Parade* [1933], and he would *never* read it. The day we'd start shooting he'd open the script, mark out our lines for the day; he might change the setups from a long shot to a close-up, or vice versa; that was the extent of his commitment to the script. His technique was to *trust* the actors, and it worked. Bacon once said to me, 'I tried for two years to make a go at acting, and I couldn't figure it out. How the hell am I going to tell *you* how to do it?' Sounds funny, I know, but he wasn't joking. He knew enough to keep a simple thing simple.

"I also loved Howard Hawks. He had a wide-open personality. When we were doing *Ceiling Zero* in 1935, I played a footloose airplane pilot. He came to me with a few ideas about the role, and after we discussed them he said, 'Your ideas are better than mine. Let's shoot it.' And that was the extent of it. No haggling, no nonsense."

"Jimmy hated directors who constantly gave orders instead of directions," says O'Brien. "He felt that if you were shouting orders all the time, it was because you'd chosen the wrong cast."

But it was Billy Wilder who drew his outright disdain.

"Billy Wilder was more of a dictator than most of the others I worked with," Cagney explains. "We worked together in 1961 on *One, Two, Three*, and he was overly bossy, full of noise—a pain. Still, we did a good picture together. I didn't learn until after we were done that he didn't like me, which was fine as far as I was concerned, because I certainly didn't like him. He didn't know how to let things *flow*, and that matters a great deal to me."

One, Two, Three was Cagney's last picture until *Ragtime*. After beefing for three decades about the dull rigors of acting, he nonetheless astounded even his closest friends with the firmness of his decision to quit.

"He was not happy with Wilder at all," says Bellamy, "and the pace of the film got to him, too. He was not a young man at the time, and it was a nonstop picture in which he had long speeches and was on camera for almost the whole time. When he finished, he came back and told me the experience had disturbed him, but he wasn't all that specific."

Bellamy was visiting the Dutchess County farm in the late Sixties when a letter arrived from Charles Bluhdorn, head of Gulf and Western, Paramount Pictures' parent company. Enclosed was a blank contract and a request to fill it in for any amount the actor wished. Cagney showed it to Bellamy.

"I asked, 'What are you gonna do, Jim?'

"He said, 'I'm gonna forget it. I'm through, but these people refuse to believe it.'"

But now that his career has become the grist for innumerable film festivals and college-level cinema courses, James Cagney has a certain desire to clarify, correct or even critique the private processes that informed his final public product. "If you want me to attempt to set the record straight on anything else, I'm willing to try," he invites with a laugh. "Don't be shy. It may be now or never."

Let's see, Al Jolson truly did give you your big break in the movies with Penny Arcade, *didn't he?*

[*Nodding*] He saw Joan Blondell and I in the stage play and bought the screen rights. Pitched the picture deal to Warner Bros. with the stipulation we both appear in it. Very square of him, I thought. Joan was marvelous in our first picture together. She was a wonderful woman, and a natural comic on- and off-camera, but very careless of ordinary things. Maybe it was because her parents were show business people, too, always living by their wits. It gets in the blood, that attitude. Her father, a good comic himself, was about fifty years old when I first met him, and he still wore the little boy's clothes he'd used in his act on the street. He had a remarkable disregard for certain realities.

How bad did things really get in Hollywood in the '30s with the rigid studio system?

Everyone was *"under contract."* That was the phrase that rang in our ears. If anyone had any talents they were signed up tight and told what to do. It was a racket. But some people were wise to it from the start. When Clark Gable signed with MGM, he said to Ralph Bellamy: "I'm not buying *anything* I can't put on a train." He was the King, the top man in town, but regardless of any contract or any salary, he didn't originally have any plans whatsoever to stay there.

Hollywood was just a small town back then, if you'll remember. Most actors just wanted to do their work there and get on back to New York immediately. The contracts were more so the so-called stars would always be on hand, to be used when they were needed. The town itself had little to offer beyond work.

My walkouts on Jack Warner, I know this stuff is notorious now, but back then I was doing it without fanfare, contrary to what the newspapers said. However, I did do it with *flair*. The first time came after a conference in the early '30s. The business manager of the studio told me, "We're doing too much now with the limited resources we have and we can't give you a raise!" I said calmly, "Well, you can't blame a man for trying, right?" He said, "Why, no," equally civilized. I went out of the office, called my wife Billie on the phone and said, "Meet me at the train station with our bags. We're going East." We got on the train and stayed East for six months, doing nothing. Finally Jack Warner called another conference "to clear the air," as he put it, and we made a new deal. Very smart of him, I thought. [*Laughter*].

I went through this every two years or so at Warner Bros. because I was doing five and six pictures a year, becoming a top draw, and watching them take advantage. So I simply moved to prevent that. I'd hop on a train, and when they'd make the call with the right salary, I'd go back to work.

How did Jack Warner view all this?

He was plenty annoyed, naturally. [*Chuckles*] But these pictures were being made for $120,000 and bringing in millions. The fact of this softened their view of my actions, but it was all a damned game, you know? And Jack loved to play it.

Depending on the deal with the studio, most of the directors did well. The actors were often near the bottom of the scale. The problems I was having at Warners were not so different from the ones the other actors were having around town. Many people soon woke up to the fact that my troubles were their troubles. Bette Davis told me that; Boris Karloff, Gable, a lot of 'em. My brother Bill became my business manager-advisor in the '30s and looked out for me; later he became a good producer.

You began to dislike your image at Warners, too.

[*Nodding, sour-faced*] All this business of cuffing women all the time, I was tired of it. It was uncalled for, and people don't need to see that stuff. But you know that grapefruit scene with Mae Clark in *Public Enemy*, that came from something this hood in Chicago once did to his gal. He pushed an omelet in her face one morning. Man's name was Hymie Weiss.

I get sick of talking about that stuff, though, all the slugging and getting slugged. Donald Cook, the actor who played my brother in *Public Enemy*, accidentally punched me in the mouth in one scene and he broke one of my teeth. Served me right for not ducking, really.

There were some other unique hazards in Hollywood's early days, like you dodging live ammunition in The Public Enemy.

My God, the man was firing a machine gun at me, while I ran behind this wooden wall! But people don't realize that that was *not* the only time they shot real bullets at me. They did it in *Taxi!* in 1932, in *G-Men*, and they also used the real thing in *Angels with Dirty Faces*.

In *Angels*, I stepped off the set while they fired, and a bullet put a hole in the wall where I'd just been standing. In *Taxi!*, a bullet riccocheted all over the place and landed in some guy's coat pocket. Nobody knew how to fake bullet holes and gunfire back then. Looking back, I don't know why I went through with it.

Professional innocence, maybe?

Innocence? Ho, son, you are too kind, much too kind. It was plain fool-hardiness!

You held a lot of jobs as a young man before acting began to pay off.

When I was a kid you did anything, so long as you worked. I worked as an architect's assistant, sold tickets for the Hudson River Day Line boat. Five, then fifteen bucks a week—any salary was a good one. Truthfully, once I got into show business, other kinds of work seemed distant to me. Still, there were many times I wanted to quit early on, because my wife and I were struggling, even destitute. I said, "Billie, we're not getting on, I have to stop," and she'd say, "Nothing doing. I'll take extra jobs before I'll let you stop acting." In 1923–24, I put together nine different acts to try and make a living on stage. Didn't land a single job.

Why was your very first legitimate theater job as a female impersonator?

Female impersonators were the rage at the time; every vaudeville show had one. It had no stigma. I knew some queens in my day. One fella I worked on a bill with was a fine acrobat, juggler, tight-rope walker, you name it. So what if he as a queen? He had a damn good act.

Tell me exactly how you met your wife, back when she was in the 1920 vaude-ville revue, Pitter Patter.

She was just a little country girl and I was a New York hick. I was hanging 'round the stage door one night as she was coming out and her date hadn't shown. The doorman says, "Why don't you take her to dinner, Cagney?" He tells Billie, "Cagney hasn't got a date, either. Why don't you let him take you to dinner?" But I was flat broke and I said so. Billie said, "Well, then I'll take you." We were married within a year or so. I'm no fool.

Didn't you and your wife run a dancing school, the Cagné School of Dance, in Elizabeth, New Jersey, in 1927?

[*Coyly*] That was a shrewd venture. I taught myself to dance, right? So I decided that I'll teach the younger ones. They learned fine but they never paid their bills. They were all hoofers, professionals, smart enough to learn and smart enough to walk when they had. Kind of a bad idea for a business. My wife worked all day with me at the school and then did a show at night to cover our keep.

I should have known better. I tried to teach hoofing years before; put an ad in the paper: DANCING TAUGHT. A young Scotsman arrived, got up and did moves I couldn't even approach, clog dances and jigs. I wasn't even equipped to learn from *him*. I stared and then I surrendered. In Hollywood, I learned a lot of my best dance steps from a chap named Johnny Boyle and another named Harland Dixon, both old vaudeville hoofers and dance stars in their own right.

How did you come to do that guest shot as George M. Cohan in The Seven Little Foys *in 1955, dancing with Bob Hope as Eddie Foy on the table at the Friar's Club?*

It's generally been said that I did it as a favor to Bob, but to tell you the truth I wanted to take off some weight at the time. I was 56 and a little stocky. So when Bob asked me, I said, "Sure!", practiced with him for three weeks, and took off 15 pounds. Worked out nicely, although my knees were all swollen from the stress.

As for the routine itself, a lot of people called it the highlight of the film but I'll tell you a little secret: I had done that dance since 1922, in a show called *Lew Fields' Ritz Girls of 1922*. It was one of the original soft shoe dances done in America—and I don't say that casually. I taught it to Bob, who was a quick learner, and we snuck it past them.

Didn't you meet Cohan as a boy while working as a bellhop at the Friar's club?

Well, I needed a job—as usual—so I tagged along with a friend one day and we both got jobs there. I carried Geroge M. Cohan's bags a couple of times. As I recall, he was an okay tipper. Years later, Chamberlain Brown, a New York agent, called me up to audition for a part in one of Cohan's shows. I went up to Brown's office and Cohan was there leaning against a desk. "You're not exactly what I had in mind, son," he said as soon as I came through the door. I said, "Fine, sir," and left again. No job.

When *Yankee Doodle Dandy* came up, I heard that he had me in mind but I'm not so sure that's true. In time, he sorta aimed the project at me but he had gone to a number of studios with the basic script, asking $100,000 for it. A few people had turned him down before he sold it to Warner Bros., and I think it's fair to say that all he wanted initially was the money.

He knew I'd been a hoofer when he clinched the deal with my studio and my name was brought up in discussions, but it was never tailored for me and could have conceivably gone to another actor. I was at the right place at the right time when Cohan got what he wanted in the first place—the money. By the time I got the part in the picture he was seriously ill. I never saw him again. But I was grateful for the part because I admired him, and it remains my favorite film. Any actor who gets the chance to act, sing *and* dance in the same production, working with first-rate material, has to be grateful.

What was the Yorkville section of New York like when you were growing up?

It was a typically tough New York neighborhood, full of sorrow, poverty and happiness in the face of both. There was crime and arguments and fights— all of that was normal. I had my nose broken once. When I heard the *crack!*, I asked the guy, "Hey, you had enough?" He nodded and we stopped. He didn't even know he'd slammed me.

But there was sweetness, too, in my neighborhoods—East 79th Street, East 99th Street—if you knew where to look for it. I'll never forget the time the Yorkville Nut Club, my baseball team, was invited up to Sing-Sing to play a game with the prison team. I go out on the field, and everybody on the other team is yelling, "Hey Red! What's new?" I knew half of the inmates!

One of the players on the other team, we always called him Bootah, he later died in the electric chair. I remembered that when I was doing my chair scene in *Angels with Dirty Faces* with the Dead End Kids. Remember them? Nice enough boys, but a little smart-alecky at times. They did a picture with Bogart [*Crime School*, 1938] where they ganged up on him off-camera and pulled his pants down. Truly. During the filming of *Angels*, I cuffed a couple of 'em, just a love tap, to let 'em know that stuff didn't go with me.

As an actor, did you have a tendency to improvise?

[*Smiling impishly*] I had a tendency to *act*. If a line didn't fit, didn't feel right, I'd say, "What are you doing about this?" Most directors would say, "Okay, try it." No arguments; there instead was a willingness to explore a bit. Without that, you've got a stale task ahead of you, and it shows on the screen.

And that "dirty rat" stuff all the comics put on me, I never said that, of course. But I did and do still have a style of walking and talking. You'll notice my arms don't hang at my sides like they should; they hang *forward*. That came from too much weightlifting in my youth. Some of the comic impersonators pick that up but most of 'em don't.

Was it customary in those days for an actor to be on his own a lot, getting only minimal direction?

It was all mixed up. One director who took his title too seriously would generate a lot of lively, pointless activity, while another would just let the actors invent things, offering some low-key encouragement. But generally speaking, they just let the actors go because we were inevitably the most experienced people in a very young business.

I must say that H. C. Potter, the director of William Saroyan's *The Time of Your Life* [1946], was nothing much. He stuck to the script like glue because he had to. If it wasn't there in front of him in rigid black and white he couldn't see it. I hate that. In the end, the actors made that film. We had started shooting the first morning when Bill Bendix [who played Nick, the owner-bartender of the pivotal saloon] says to me, "Where the hell's the Armenian?" [*Winking*] Saroyan was there at the time, and we both knew it. I said, "Oh, I don't think he's here yet, but you know those Armenians. He'll show up to cause trouble!" Eventually we let Saroyan in on the gag, though. And I liked the man. He was easy-going.

After the picture came out he sent me a kind telegram, saying he had gone to see the picture in a California theater and liked it so much he forgot he'd written the play it was based on. Quite a compliment.

Saroyan was an interesting man. I took him to the Player's Club in Gramercy Park for lunch one day, and as he came down the steps—with that white face, those bulging eyes, and that absolutely immense moustache of his—he seemed distant, I couldn't get his attention. Finally I said, "What are you thinking about?!" And he said, "*Sssh!* I'm listening to the pool balls clink on the table." He was, you see, a gambling man. Won and lost a fortune or two. It was a shame, actually, but the sounds were like music to him.

Getting back to directors, how do you feel about them in general?

I directed one picture, *Short Cut to Hell* in 1957, but it bored me to sit and watch, to move people around. Most directors have their work done already by good cameramen and the actors themselves, and they get payed to yell, "Cut!"

Like Billy Wilder. We worked together in 1955 on the Ruth Etting story, *Love Me or Leave Me*, with Doris Day. He and other people on the picture were trying to make my character of [racketeer Martin] "The Gimp" [Snyder] too technical. They had all sorts of devices on hand that they felt would aid me in affecting the character's limp, and so forth. All this junk to make sure I bent my knee when I walked. I said, "Get rid of it."

Do you know what pre-natal paralysis is? There's not much play in the leg afterwards. I just tightened my leg and stooped, and that was all. It was a snap.

Funny thing about Wilder: most of the time he was quiet, and all the fuss was behind the scenes. [*Shrugs*] Maybe he was afraid of me.

Do you have a favorite leading lady? Mae Clark, Joan Blondell, Doris Day, Bette Davis, Loretta Young?

Doris Day was marvelous in *Love Me or Leave Me*. She could sing and act without any strain. She had a nice naturalness to her that put me at ease. I respond to that.

Are there any roles you would like to have played, parts that eluded you?

Largely there were parts people wanted me to play that I didn't care for. George Cukor offered me the role of Eliza Doolittle's father in *My Fair Lady*, made a big pitch, but I passed. Francis Coppola paid me a visit to ask if I'd do something in *Godfather II*, but I was busy doing nothing, didn't care. Always wanted to play Teddy Roosevelt, though; I greatly admired that man. But I could never find a script worth a damn.

Do you have any other films you're particularly fond of besides Yankee Doodle Dandy?

Yes, I really enjoyed *Man of a Thousand Faces* [1957], the Lon Chaney story, and *Mr. Roberts* [1955]. I loved that Lon Chaney role, with all the gruesome makeup. It used to take about four hours to be made up for each character: the Hunchback of Notre Dame, the Phantom of the Opera, and so forth. Once I had it on, it had to stay on 'til the day's shooting was done, and when I'd take my lunch break nobody would sit with me in the cafeteria at Universal, I was so awful looking. And yet, when my son visited the set one day while I had the Hunchback's face on, he just walked into the dressing room, didn't blink, and said, "Oh, hi Pop." Go figure it.

Hank Fonda was also in the original cast of the Broadway play of *Mr. Roberts*, of course, but I was thrown in the film as the captain. They had somebody else as a first choice, and when that didn't pan out, Jack Warner said, "Get Cagney, he'll handle it." Jack Lemmon turned out to be the star of the picture, winning the Oscar for best supporting actor.

As for me, I liked the nautical thing about it, being an informal sailor myself. Incidentally, there's a story going around that I apppeared as an extra in the original film production of *Mutiny on the Bounty* [1935] but that's not true. I took my sailboat over to Catalina Island one day while they were filming to say hello and have dinner with the crew, but I kept my nose out of the actual project. We all fight the impulse of being a ham. And laying somebody else's egg.

Your first film with your buddy Pat O'Brien was Here Comes the Navy *in 1934, right?*

Yes. I met Pat just before I went into pictures, and we've been best friends ever since. We'd sit around Chasen's in Los Angeles and shoot the bull, often picking on Spence [Tracy] for some item that had just appeared in the papers, and he'd try to bear down on us with that malevolent eye of his, but we weren't buying it and eventually we'd all burst into laughter. Spence was a good sport, but there was always something restless, unsettled about the the man.

Mostly, we hung out at each other's houses, talking about our youth. We were a sentimental bunch, really. There was a lot of fooling around with our crowd. One time a fella came over to tell me, "Cagney, your pal Ralph [Bellamy] is very sick!" I split instantly, and ran four blocks, full speed, to his dressing room. I burst in and the guy's sitting there, full of smiles, sipping Scotch. I say [*angrily*], "Say, what the hell is this?" He says, "Since everything's alright, why don't you have a drink?" We had a good laugh. But no drink together. I didn't drink. Still don't.

How did a boy from Yorkville get into farming in '36, being a country gentleman?

Very easy, very easy. The smartest thing I ever did after buying property on the Vineyard was getting this acreage in Dutchess County. We raised oats, hay, and horses: Morgans, a beautiful, all-purpose horse you could ride or work. A Vermont-based breed; small heads, tiny ears, big chests, a snappy way of going. I've got about a dozen of them. An easy horse to break, although I had a mare who was a helluva bitch [*Laughter*]. I loved the trotters, loved to ride; it was no great stunt, really, not a difficult sport.

How did you acquire the hobby of painting?

I used to sketch caricatures for relaxation. Then in the 1950s, a friend hooked me up with a wonderful Russian, Serge Bongart, who took me on as a student. I've painted a lot of sad scenes, like one of an old man who later died of malnutrition, and a crippled boxer. When Bongart saw the boxer's portrait he said it was too spooky. "Did you use a model?" he asked. I said, "No, he's a combination of every brutalized fighter I've ever seen." The title [*The Victor: Chronic Progressive Fibrotic Encephalopathy*] is the medical term for being punch-drunk; the winner who loses everything.

When you've got to fight, fight. But if you make it a habit, you destroy yourself instead of the opposition. As a boy, I fought for prestige; it was a form of entertainment. I'm amazed at the stupid, wild things I did as a kid, without thinking, senselessly. I'm a product of my background, a poverty-stricken one that I was oblivious to, but it left its mark.

These days, I take fewer chances—no flying, for instance. I had an experience one time when the damned plane actually turned upside down, and that was it, pal. This was during the '40s, on a flight from Florida to New York. Our plane got caught in an electrical storm and it flipped us over. When we got off the plane in New York, my wife turned to me and said, "Jim, promise you'll never, ever fly again without me." I said, "Yes, but—" At first I didn't understand her, and then I realized that she *never* intended to fly again and wanted to keep us both well-grounded!

Which brings us back to acting. What do you think your best quality as an actor is?

[*Long pause*] Damned if I know, honestly. Even when I had the freedom to add and remove things from my scripts, it only succeeded some of the time. I kept my thinking to a minimum.

As the sun dims in the slate-colored sky, the conversation shifts from breezy chatter to contained contemplation as the actor ponders his future.

Cagney expects his next film project to be *Eagle of Broadway*, a script about the last three months in the life of the gunslinger-turned-newspaperman Bat Masterson and his friendships with Damon Runyon and Louella Parsons.

"He was a sensible man, Bat," Cagney muses. "Very sensible. And he wasn't the crazed killer the lore has made him out to be. He killed only when necessary. Although, when he'd add up the number of men he'd killed, he never counted Indians or Mexicans, which doesn't speak too well of him.

"He was a kid, a young buck, when he killed his first man. And by the time he went to Dodge City and helped Wyatt Earp clean up the town, he was used to killing. It was a fact of life in the Southwest that he had utterly accepted. In later years he became a sportswriter, of all things."

The description of Masterson sounds tinged with a double-edged fascination—not just with the character but also with the idea that Cagney's actually readying *another* performance. There is general agreement among family and friends that aide Marge Zimmermann was crucial in creating the climate that got Cagney involved in his craft again. (Although some mutter that Marge's custodial wherewithal regarding Cagney's private affairs seems excessive, a judgment Cagney himself dismisses with an impatient shrug.)

Zimmermann and her husband, Don, became part of the actor's tiny inner circle in the late Sixties. Neighbors of the Cagneys, the retired restaurateur and her civil-engineer husband met the couple while antique hunting. A casual social acquaintance was solidified when Marge, concerned about the actor's faltering health, insisted on escorting him to a doctor, where he was diagnosed a diabetic. Shortly thereafter, a stroke shook James to his foundations, "scaring him into giving up," as Zimmermann puts it. She conferred with his wife* and physician and then took it upon herself to get him "back into the land of the living." Her husband oversaw the building of a swimming pool next to the farmhouse to augment his fair-weather exercise, and he was gently coerced into resuming his habitual strolls. The next logical step was the selection of a film role that would befit his time-honored status but not overtax him.

Cagney had met Milos Forman while the Czechoslovakian director was working on *Hair* with Treat Williams, and all three became quite chummy. In the meantime, the task of directing *Ragtime* had shifted—amid controversy fired by producer Dino De Laurentiis' misgivings with Robert Altman—to Forman.

"My wife and Marge asked if I would come out of retirement to appear in the film," Cagney explains. "First I said no, then they talked me into it with Forman's help. They offered me the part of Grandfather, then the part of Police Commissioner Rhinelander Waldo. I spoke to my doctor, and he said, 'Do it. You need the activity. It'll keep you going strong.'

"I want you to realize," he emphasizes, "that the murder of Stanford White by jealous Harry K. Thaw, which opens the picture, was the first really major murder case in New York when I was a kid. It was 1906. In 1920, Evelyn Nesbit, Thaw's ex-wife and White's old mistress, was on a vaudeville bill with me! She had a song-and-dance act with her then-current hus-

---

*Frances Willard "Willie" Cagney died October 10, 1994, in Sharon, Connecticut.

band. She seemed okay, nothing special. But everybody knew her reputation, all right."

Near the end of my visit, I ask Cagney to clear up the mystery concerning his decision to retire in 1961.

"I've never fully explained that to anyone," he murmurs, bowing his head as he leans forward in his chair. "It was a very personal decision. I had had it, but I'll tell you exactly what I meant by that. Most of the shooting took place at Bavaria Studios outside of Munich, right in the middle of the German countryside. Being a city boy, I've always loved the country, and this landscape was magnificent. I began to realize that I was happiest when I was outside, roaming around the hills. One day, after finishing a scene, I walked out of the studio to get some exercise. A few moments later, one of the crew yelled, 'Ready, Mr. Cagney!' They were ready to light the set again. I walked back into this cavernous studio, which was pitch black, and on impulse, I turned back to look at the sunshine I had left behind. I stood there, very upset, thinking, 'Darkness before me, sunlight behind me. This is it; no more. I want to be in that light.'

"That was the whole point, son," he says, gripping my hand firmly. "A man can't earn his living walking into darkness, separated from the real world and its beauty. I followed my heart, away from acting. I love to make people happy, of course, but Cagney has to come first, right?"

"Why did you return to acting?" I ask.

"Those closest to me told me that my chief occupation had become daydreaming, which is true," he says with the small, shy smile of a child. "I'd become a daydreamer and a spectator, the faraway fella Pat O'Brian always accused me of being."

"Ever think you'd still be acting at your age?"

"My God, no! That's the wonder of this business: people constantly coming and going and coming back again, each having a particular thing to offer at a particular time. People billed over me disappeared the next year, and extras later became costars. It's all a little nutty."

"However, you've been a box-office star for virtually your entire film career."

"For the first two years, 1930 and 1931, I was just making a living doing nothing significant. Near the end of '31, I did *Public Enemy*, and that was the turning point. I became a draw."

"Well, that's fifty solid years of stardom, by my count."

"Let's just say," he says, chuckling softly, "that I think I might do all right in this business."

Hume Cronyn
and Jessica Tandy:
Theater's Final First Couple

"**W**e've had a lot of adventures but we've paid a big price,"
said Hume Cronyn, seated beside wife Jessica Tandy in
a lower Manhattan rehearsal studio one afternoon in the early
autumn of 1982. "I have a lot of great friends that I rarely ever
see. Sometimes Jessie and I can go for as much as two years
without being in touch with people. We can often lead a relatively monastic existence."

That there was no one so close to them as they were to each other may sound like a common description of a lasting marriage, but after spending time with the most celebrated theatrical couple since Alfred Lunt and Lynn Fontanne, directly observing the extent to which their distance from loved ones had been a source of dismay, an often poignant picture of life's trade-offs emerged.

At one point Hume Cronyn made the somber, almost solemn declaration that, for him and his wife, the grand total of missed performances between them "doesn't bust two dozen," despite often-serious illness and other obstacles.

The professional task at hand as we talked in the drab rehearsal space was their co-starring roles in *Foxfire*, a dramatic play due to open in two months at the Ethel Barrymore Theater (the site 34 years before of Tandy's initial career triumph in *A Streetcar Named Desire*).

Named for a nocturnally glowing lichen found on fallen trees in the forests of Southern Appalachia, *Foxfire* was the story, with songs, of the fictitious Nations family and its waning will to hold onto its mountain homestead.

"This is a play about the inevitability of change, and what change does to family structure," explained Cronyn, who spent six years developing the property with the Buckinghamshire-born author/journalist Susan Cooper. "It compares, by implication, the values and concerns of an earlier age with contemporary values, mirroring what's been gained and what's been lost along the way."

Minutes later, as Cooper, the Cronyns' actress friend Sigourney Weaver, noted agent Sam Cohn, the Cronyns' eldest daughter, and a few other guests looked on, Cronyn and Tandy stood alone in the center of the hall amid substitutes (coat racks, etc.) for trees and scenery, embodying a deeply shy and anxious Annie and Hector Nations in a flashback from old age to the Appalachian couple's first romantic encounter as teenagers. The transformation from old codgers to callow youths was stunningly convincing, particularly the moment where the timid Hector attempts a pristine kiss.

Treading up behind her, touching her hand, awkwardly steering her into the gesture before impulsively proposing to her, Cronyn was an uncanny picture of adolescent qualmishness. And a girlish glow flooded Tandy's features as she quavered in his arms, prudish bashfulness blossoming into a vivid blush.

The sum effect was so spellbinding that it left Cooper, the rest of the cast, and other observers in tears.

"Hume and I have been writing *Foxfire* since 1975," Cooper later explained in the hallway, "and whenever Hume and I have gotten uptight with work or with each other, Jessie, who has great natural patience and gaiety, would say, 'Darlings, it's only a play.' But to see Jessica twirl around in that scene just now and drop all those years, so she *is* 16 again. . . . It's something I'll never forget."

After *Foxfire*, for which Tandy won a Tony Award, she and Cronyn, as well as Cooper, who had become a close friend of the couple, were all in considerable demand in Hollywood and television.

Besides appearing in the already-completed *The World According to Garp* with her husband, other subsequent motion pictures in which Tandy starred included *The Bostonians* (1984), *Cocoon* (1985, with Cronyn), *Batteries Not Included* (1986, with Cronyn), *The House on Carroll Street* and *Cocoon: The Return* (both 1988, the latter with Cronyn), *Driving Miss Daisy* (1989, for which she won an Academy Award as Best Actress), *Fried Green Tomatoes* (1991, which gained her an Oscar nomination as Best Supporting Actress), *Used People* (1992), and *Nobody's Fool* (1995).

Cronyn also would later be featured in such movies as *Impulse* (1984), *Brewster's Millions* (1985), *The Pelican Brief* (1993), and *Horton Foote's "Alone"* (1997, Showtime). He won three Emmys between 1989 and 1994 for his acting in *Age-Old Friends* (HBO), Neil Simon's *Broadway Bound* (ABC), and the *Hallmark Hall of Fame*'s "To Dance with the White Dog" (CBS).

Meantime, Cronyn's collaboration with Cooper on the script for the teleplay "The Dollmaker" resulted in a best actress Emmy for Jane Fonda when it premiered during the 1983–84 season as an *ABC Theater Presentation*.

Jessica Tandy died of ovarian cancer on September 11, 1994, at the age of 87. Two years later, Cronyn, 85, married 61–year-old Susan Cooper, whom he and Tandy had originally met in the British Virgin Islands in 1974. Having worked with Cooper for over 20 years, she was the only woman besides Tandy to have shared a sizable measure of Cronyn's professional life.

THE INTERVIEW

M ENTION THE REMARK that many make about them—that they've been side by side for 40 years and are still in love—and Hume Cronyn grimaces and Jessica Tandy looks as though she's just swallowed a doorknob.

"Say now, just don't go believing the hearts-and-flowers routine about Jess and me, the syrupy stuff that's served up whenever our relationship is recounted in those glossy theater profiles," Cronyn counsels with mock seriousness. "That's not the strength of our marriage."

On a recent sun-splashed afternoon, Hume Cronyn and Jessica Tandy are reflecting on their lives together. The elfin, jug-eared Cronyn seats himself next to the regal Miss Tandy on the couch in the living room of their cozy suite in Manhattan's Wyndham Hotel, where they have lived since 1980, after they sold their lakeside house in Pound Ridge, N.Y.

The décor of their suite is a cheerful, lived-in combination of Palm Beach sun parlor and suburban Connecticut den. The upholstery is bright with citrus colors or stark white and fresh potted flowers enhance the tropical mood, but a cozy clutter of books, magazines, subdued prints and weathered knickknacks keeps it within bounds.

True to their disavowal of the hearts-and-flowers routine, they spent their 40th wedding anniversary in late September on the road in Baltimore, honing yet another Broadway-bound play. For this couple whose lives have been inseparable from the theater for a half-century, *Foxfire*—which opened at the Ethel Barrymore last month—marks the 11th time they have appeared together on stage.

The electrifying impact of Hume Cronyn and Jessica Tandy has become the stuff of theatrical legend—from their first Broadway appearance together in the huge 1951 hit *The Four-Poster* to *The Gin Game* in 1977, in which their performances as two contentious old sanitarium card sharks were a ferocious tour de force, so steeped in deft timing, nuance and emotional coloration that it resonated as an example of dramatic acting's capacity to own and consume the moment. The Pulitzer Prize-winning play earned Jessica Tandy a Tony Award.

Foxfire, which was inspired by the popular series of books on Appalachian folkways and which Hume Cronyn co-wrote with the British writer Susan Cooper, is a quiet evocation of the life of Appalachian farmers working the poor mountain soil. Miss Tandy is Annie Nations, widow of Hector—played by Cronyn—who has been dead these five years but who is still very much alive to her. While the play itself has received mixed reviews, critics have invariably noted the towering craft of these two veteran actors. "Everything Miss Tandy does," wrote *The New York Times*'s theater critic Frank Rich, "is so pure and right that only poets, not theater critics, should be allowed to write about her." One critic likened the Cronyns onstage to chamber musicians, "each anticipating the other's moves."

Both members since 1979 of the Theater Hall of Fame for their outstanding contributions to the American stage, the Cronyns have long shouldered the honorific title of First Couple of the American Theater. She had first taken Broadway by storm in 1947, creating the Blanche du Bois persona in *A Streetcar Named Desire*. He was nominated for an Oscar for his role in the 1944 film *The Seventh Cross*, winning a Tony in 1964 for his lead role in a *Hamlet* directed by John Gielgud.

Because of their fame in tandem, the Cronyns have come to be seen almost as a single talent instead of two very different actors from very different backgrounds: Jessica Tandy's childhood was one of grinding poverty in London, England; Hume Cronyn, on the other hand, grew up in a London, Ontario, mansion with nannies and servants.

Of the Cronyns' differing but exquisitely compatible acting styles, the director Elia Kazan, a close friend who has worked with them both, says: "Both Jessie and Hume have that extraordinary ability as actors to express the dimension of a character through a natural discovery process that doesn't involve a lot of neurosis. Jessie explores the role from the inside out, while Hume likes to do a lot of research and to come to inhabit the character, getting at him from the outside inward. Either way is fine if it works, but what's most significant is how immaculate the characterizations are! With Hume Cronyn and Jessica Tandy, there's no sloppy, self-indulgent spill-over into their personal life. It's the miracle of great acting: *They* don't get taken over by the characters; *you* get taken over by the characters!"

On this sunny afternoon, the atmosphere in the Cronyns' living room is at times palpably charged. Both in their early 70s, they are in a fragile transitional time: The dilemma posed in *Foxfire* has strangely dovetailed with the dilemmas in their own lives.

Just as the 79–year-old Annie Nations is confronted with a seemingly rootless son, who is asking her to wrench herself away from the past, the Cronyns are deeply concerned about their two children who are still unmarried: Chris, 39, who works in film production, and Tandy, 37, an actress. (Susan, 48, Miss Tandy's daughter from a previous marriage, is a teacher who is married with four children.)

While their hotel residence is a forced circumstance ("We can't seem to find the time to look for a house," says Cronyn), their permanent haven is in their attachment to each other—and it is that kind of safe place that they want their children to have.

But what is also obvious to anyone who spends time with the Cronyns is that their sufficiency in each other has created a remoteness from loved ones that is a source of pain and perplexity for all parties involved.

"We've had many wonderful family holidays," says Cronyn, an ever-present glowing pipe cocked in his palm, "but at our age we're bound to our theater schedules: early meal, no lunch, an hour sleep, go to the theater, supper, bed."

It is also a kind of life that has taken a toll on the Cronyns' relationship with their children.

Several days earlier, their son, Chris, had said, "It hasn't been front row, center stage with bouquets, for me and my sister Tandy. We didn't always see a lot of our parents when we were growing up. My father went to boarding schools at an early age, which he disliked, but we wound up in them, too.

"My mother is very gracious and very retiring next to my father, who tends to be a compulsive organizer and taskmaster. He never let either my sister or me forget his overall prowess in his chosen path, and so my sister and I could never quite please him by comparison. Consequently, I, at least, grew rebellious toward him as a teen-ager and for some time beyond that, too.

"The first time I ever made contact with my mother was when I was asked at the age of 8 to assume a small role in a Broadway play. It never happened, and one weekend morning before the thing fell through, my mother called me into the living room and said, 'So! Let's chat about this acting business.' I'm thinking I'd rather be out playing with my friends, but I sit next to her on the couch. She suddenly begins to cry.

"After a few moments, she says, 'Now, you may not think I'm crying, but anybody in the third row will.' It was a terrifying moment which stays with me to this day. Nothing could have convinced me my mother wasn't genuinely upset, and so when she turned it off like a TV I was stunned. It was very disorienting; children have no equipment to deal with that stuff.

"It took a lot of time and energy for my parents and me to get in touch and stay that way—which we have. I had to forget the lonely times. They've always been there for each other, but I was often removed from that."

The Cronyns gingerly acknowledge their estrangement from their children in former years, handling the topic like a piece of delicate crystal, saying they hope they have made inroads toward amending the situation.

"My children saw more of their parents than I ever saw of my mother and father," says Cronyn, clearly uncomfortable. "But that was a different time and a different convention. One of our problems in terms of the children was the touring, but we tried to correct that by spending summers and most holidays together. They're wonderful kids."

"There have been times when Jessie couldn't abide *me*," Cronyn notes, changing the subject. "When she was doing well in *Streetcar* and I wasn't getting much work, we put a whole country between us for weeks until I got adjusted. And then there was the time during *Gin Game* when I moved out and got my own hotel room for a few days so we could both breathe freely. I'll tell you a little secret: The first time we spent any time together we didn't exactly bill and coo. Fact is, she thought I was a perfect jackass!"

He stands up and suggests I change seats with him, so that I'm on his right.

"Glass eye," he explains, sharply tapping his pipe stem against the replacement—an impish but bizarre gesture. He mutters that he lost his left eye to cancer in the spring of 1969. "Obviously, I can't comfortably see anyone whom I'm speaking to if he's on my left."

He settles into what appears to be his favorite piece of furniture, an overstuffed chair, frayed at the arms.

"Hmmm, O.K., now, ahhh. Very well, then. Er, what were we talking about?"

"How we met, darling," Miss Tandy says, propping an elbow on the back of the low couch and resting her head upon her hand, so that the afternoon sun catches her profile.

"Yes, yes! Boy, I'm quick today, aren't I?" he laughs, and pauses, staring at his wife as the light bathes her. "You were so beautiful then, and still are, Jess," he whispers, then glances back at me, his face reddening slightly.

Jessica Tandy was born on June 7, 1909, the daughter of a one-time traveling salesman and a mother who was headmistress in a school for retarded children. Miss Tandy grew up (along with two older brothers) in threadbare circumstances in a five-room brick flat in unfashionable northeast London.

"When I was in my teens," says Miss Tandy, "and going home in a cab with friends after my acting classes, I'd tell the driver where I lived and he wouldn't even know where that was, which is highly uncommon for a London cabby. I was so mortified."

Jessica's father died of cancer when she was 12 and her mother scrimped and saved, moonlighting at clerical jobs and teaching adult school at night, to pay for Jessica's private-school tuition. At 15, Jessica began her studies at the Ben Greet Academy of Acting in London. Her interest in theater had been aroused two years earlier when, being too young to be left home alone in the evenings, she accompanied her mother to adult school and enrolled, along with students 20 years her senior, in a Shakespeare appreciation course.

"My mother, being ambitious for all of us, endorsed the stage as a dignified way for me out of our bleak life," says Miss Tandy. "It sounds terribly snobbish, but she raised us to be intellectually above our neighbors. She read to us, took us to plays, the pantomime, museums. I didn't date, ever. By the time I was in acting courses, both of my brothers had gotten scholarships to Oxford."

When she was 23, in 1932, she caused a sensation in Europe with her portrayal of an impetuous schoolgirl in *Children in Uniform*. That same year, she was married to the British actor Jack Hawkins ("A fine actor, a poor husband; it was not a good marriage") and became the toast of the West End. An acclaimed performance in John Gielgud's company as Ophelia in *Hamlet* further established her reputation, as did her work opposite Laurence Olivier in his Old Vic production of *Henry V*.

In 1940, she journeyed to New York City (with her daughter, Susan, then 6 years old; Hawkins was then serving in the British Army) to appear in a play called *Jupiter Laughs*, which was notable only for a backstage visitor after the curtain one night who would help persuade her to remain on this side of the Atlantic—Hume Cronyn.

"It's not easy to say how I decided on an acting career," says Cronyn. "As a child, I'd played theater games, and I was sent to McGill University to study law and art. Everything seemed to be frowned upon by my family as being socially unacceptable, and I grew to *detest* that. My poor mother had to fend off the family dismay when I went public with my decision."

In 1932, at the depths of the Depression, the handsome, natty Cronyn arrived in New York City to enroll at the American Academy of Dramatic Arts. He drove an air-cooled Buick roadster and, with a princely allowance of $173 a week, was the dandy of the speakeasies.

Hume Cronyn was born on July 18, 1911, the fifth child of Hume Blake Cronyn and the former Frances Amelia Labatt of the Labatt brewing family. The senior Cronyn was a member of the Canadian Parliament and chief executive or director of several companies. Six-foot-two and charismatic, "he had the equipment to be an actor," says his youngest son.

Young Hume spent his first seven years at Woodfield, a magnificent Edwardian mansion in London, Ontario, that was the family seat. His enrollment in a boarding school was painful. He missed his parents terribly and, being short, he was the target of much bullying by older boys. (He later took up boxing, becoming a lightning-fast featherweight at 127 pounds; he is still a sinewy 128.)

He became quite close to his mother, but by the time such a thing might have been possible with his father, Sir Hume was suffering from cerebral sclerosis, a hardening of the arteries of the brain. The young Cronyn's strong dislike for his regimented upper-class upbringing was woefully accentuated every time the family was dressed for dinner and his father suffered one of his "epileptic-like" seizures.

"So long as I live," he recounts gravely, "I will never forget that night at the dinner table when my father had a spasm and his hand was involuntarily *slammed down* into his steaming hot plate of golden buck—a dish of eggs and cheese. He was rendered unconscious and we all had to keep our places while the butler came over and righted my father, wiped him off carefully and served him a fresh plate.

"After a bit, he regained consciousness. He looked around at all of us, bewildered, and then moved to pick up his silverware as we resumed the conversation exactly where it had broken off. But as he went to grasp the fork he stopped, staring at his hand, which was scalded. He had no idea why."

When he reached McGill University, the young Cronyn broke loose "with a vengeance" from the social strictures of his boyhood. By the time he had made his Broadway debut in 1934, he was quite the social gad-about.

Things, however, were not going well when he and Miss Tandy first met. She was broke, and so thin that her last $100, which she kept tucked in her girdle, had somehow slipped out and been lost during an audition. He, at 29, "had been married for one year to a marvelous girl," but there was a mutual decision to divorce. "When I met Jessie," says Cronyn, "I was engaged to be married to someone, but never expected to be in love again, which is a conclusion you come to easily at 29.

"Anyhow, so I took Jessie to supper—she insists it was lunch—and it was *not* an enchanted encounter. I was making all these jokes about the English and she thought I was a pompous fool. It didn't start well, but I pursued her. She was very slow in responding. *Very.*" She was, after all, still married to Jack Hawkins.

About this time, Cronyn's mother was diagnosed as having terminal cancer, and the family thought a wedding would be inappropriate just then. The nuptials were postponed. And postponed. Cronyn's intended became uneasy, but he continued to straddle the fence, wooing the mildly recalcitrant Miss Tandy, placating the flustered fiancée. By the time the errant groom finally decided he did indeed want to be wed again—to Miss Tandy— the family of his betrothed had thrown in the towel.

Cronyn then wooed Miss Tandy in earnest. Evenings, he wined and dined her, turning up at her front door in white tie, tails and top hat, his Buick roadster humming at the curb. They would go dancing, to the theater, and to night spots with friends.

Cronyn was almost incorrigibly jealous of the men in Miss Tandy's life, past and present. Finally, says Miss Tandy, "I told Hume, quite firmly, 'What I am is also what I've been, and if you truly love me as you say you do, you will love the sum total of what I am and who I am, and just leave it at that. *So just stop it!*'"

"And I only stopped it," he says with a wink and a jaunty puff of his pipe, "because the lady agreed to marry me! So you see, the strength of our relationship from the start has been that I agree to listen to her as long as she promises to pay no attention whatever to what I blabber."

In 1942, Alfred Hitchcock (who had stumbled on a screen test that Cronyn had done for Paramount some years earlier) invited him to try out for a part in the film *Shadow of a Doubt* (which he eventually got). Traveling together to Hollywood, Cronyn and Miss Tandy decided upon arrival to take the plunge. After waiting out months of divorce proceedings, they were married on Sept. 27.

While Cronyn, who was initially under contract to MGM, became a character actor in demand, appearing in some 16 films over the next 10 years, Miss Tandy landed mostly small parts in half as many pictures during her indenture with 20th Century-Fox. "Nobody out there really took me seriously as an actress," says Miss Tandy. "Hume really engineered my first significant parts in movies."

Their first film appearance together was in *The Seventh Cross* in 1944 with Spencer Tracy. Asked on the set how he was getting along with Cronyn—who was already notorious for his obsessive attention to detail—Tracy quipped, "The son of a bitch would fix the damned lights if they'd let him."

Cronyn turned to screenwriting after the picture with Tracy in order to keep from going stir crazy during the months he waited for his next role. He was fortunate enough to have hooked up with Hitchcock, who cast him in *Lifeboat* in 1944. Cronyn went on to write screenplay treatments for the portly, eccentric genius.

"It's all true about there being no film to speak of on Hitch's cutting-room floor," says Cronyn. "He'd frame every shot in advance and that was virtually it, with no backup master shots, experimental closeups or things from 10 off-hand angles. He'd be so bored during the actual shooting of the exhaustively prearranged pictures that he'd engage you in long conversations about the wonders of the British railway system, which he knew backward and forward. And he always kept a phone at hand on a little table to make random long-distance calls.

"'Hume,' he'd say, 'do you have any friends in Beirut? Let's ring Beirut and see who's awake over there!' And so he would."

Hitchcock was also "an avid collector and teller of long, involved jokes and humorous anecdotes," says Cronyn. "Many times, in the midst of intense script conferences, he would interrupt out of the blue to tell one. Finally, I couldn't prevent myself from asking him why the hell he always picked these critical moments to begin these rambling tales.

"'It's because we've been pressing too hard,' he said calmly. 'You never get it right when you press.'"

In the meantime, Miss Tandy was concentrating on the raising of Susan, Chris, who arrived in 1943 and Tandy, born in 1945. Outside recreation centered on the Hollywood version of charades known as "the Game"—the marathon sessions held in Gene Kelly's house, with Keenan Wynn, Paul Draper and Van Johnson joining in, and Judy Garland often dropping by to sing a few songs by Hugh Martin and Ralph Blane, who would be there at the piano. There were also the seven-course banquets at Bob Nathan's mansion, which might be followed by brandy in the drawing room with Thomas Mann or Artur Rubinstein.

It was Cronyn who finally rescued his wife from the jobless quagmire by directing her in 1946 in *Portrait of a Madonna*, one of nine one-act Tennessee Williams plays he had optioned over the years.

Joseph L. Mankiewicz, a director at 20th Century-Fox, fired off a memo to Darryl F. Zanuck after seeing Jessica Tandy's performance in *Portrait of a Madonna*: "I have rarely seen acting to equal hers, and even more rarely seen a very tough, invited professional audience brought cheering to its feet as spontaneously. By the way, she does not play an Englishwoman."

"The 'Englishwoman' line summed up the mentality Jessica faced then," says Mankiewicz. "The narrowness of most people in Hollywood in the mid- to late 1940s was beyond imagining. If you had, for instance, an English accent you were like a piece of furniture that might or might not fit in a certain scene. That was it.

"Still, a lot of people saw the enormous potential in Jessica because of *Madonna*. I remember Sam Goldwyn coming up to me after seeing Jessica and saying, 'Joe, that play has got the mucus'—he meant 'nucleus'—'of a great story. I'm tellin' ya, Joe, with Tandy the mucus is there.'"

Predictably, it was Broadway that took affirmative action. Elia Kazan and Irene Selznick flew in from New York to catch *Madonna*, and their interest led to Miss Tandy's being cast as Blanche du Bois—opposite Marlon

Brando—in the 1947 production of Tennessee Williams's *A Streetcar Named Desire*. In making the character of the mad nymphomaniac one of the most renowned in the American theater, Miss Tandy established herself as one of the finest actresses in the world.

"I've always felt that one of the most fascinating things about Jessica's performance in *Streetcar* was that she made me realize what a lady the tramp character is," says Kazan, who was director of the play. "It was brilliant, totally intuitive acting. That is what great acting is all about, but Hollywood, then and now, has always had trouble getting that through its thick collective head."

As Miss Tandy found out for herself.

"I was back in Hollywood for two weeks after *Streetcar* when the Fox casting director called," says Miss Tandy, who would soon lose out to Vivien Leigh the movie counterpart of the role she had created on Broadway. "I get on the line and he asks, 'How tall are you?' I say, 'I'm 5 feet 4.' He said, 'Fine, that's all I wanted to know.' He never called back. It was good for both Hume and me, though. We learned in this short life where we truly belonged: in the theater."

With *Foxfire* playing on Broadway, a measure of the Cronyns' creative anxiety is now directed elsewhere. Cronyn is collaborating once more with Susan Cooper, on the script for *The Dollmaker*, a teleplay adaptation of the novel by Harriet Arnow that was commissioned by Jane Fonda. The setting is again Appalachia, and filming for the three-hour ABC-TV movie begins in the spring with Miss Fonda in the lead.

Miss Tandy also appears in two new movies, *Still of the Night* (a suspense thriller starring Meryl Streep and Roy Scheider) and *Best Friends* (a romantic comedy with Burt Reynolds and Goldie Hawn in the lead). In both cases, Miss Tandy's roles are small ones. "My parts are never big in films, it seems," she says, "but that's all right. I'm no longer willing to devote time to developing myself as any sort of presence in Hollywood. Films aren't as satisfying to me as the theater."

Through the years, the Cronyns gathered many like-minded people around them, such as John Gielgud, Laurence Olivier, Gene Kelly, Elia Kazan, Tennessee Williams, Alec Guinness, Alfred Hitchcock, Joseph Mankiewicz, Jose Ferrer, Robert Whitehead, Zoe Caldwell, Arlene Francis, Henry Fonda, Thornton Wilder, Mike Nichols, Karl Malden, Sean O'Casey.

But they have reserved the lion's share of their inner selves for each other. One proud, inquiring woman, bent on escaping the doleful essence of poverty, meets one proud, curious man, intent on fleeing from the loneliness and isolation of privilege. One obsessive man, who seeks to figure out the world, falls in love with one driven young woman who longs to express all she knows.

One wants to fill the cup, one wants to drain it, and vice versa, in gentle sequence, on and on.

Setting aside his spent pipe near the close of our talk, Cronyn begins to contemplate the enormous differences between his and Miss Tandy's background. Chopping the air with his hands, he says in exasperation: "Look at our pasts! You had so much struggle in yours and I was so fortunate, yet you have all the cheer and I'm the one who gets so broody and anxious and cha-grined. It doesn't make sense!"

"No, it doesn't really," says Miss Tandy, "but it's O.K., Hume. We each knew our needs."

The sun is nearly gone, the darkening room lit by one lamp. Chris and Tandy are on the way over to meet them for an early dinner. The Cronyns say that their "deepest fear" in life now is that their children won't find the safe place that they have somehow located for themselves; that they won't discover a purpose in the world they can share with someone else.

The atmosphere in the living room is suddenly tense.

"If Chris and Tandy just each had someone they could hold fast to," says Cronyn, leaning forward, his voice trembling. He looks angry, frustrated, largely with himself. "If they each had someone—"

"Now, Hume," says his wife, very softly, and turns to me.

"The children show no signs of wanting to be married. We're getting on in years. It's a sore spot with Hume, and perhaps a sorrow with me. But they'll be fine."

"I'm sorry," Cronyn apologizes, thinking out loud. "When I became an actor, coming from my background, well, a lot of things were not allowed. It was not good form to show emotion; you did not impose your feelings on other people. I was so taut inside."

"And I gradually learned," says Miss Tandy, "that in my best work I remember to withhold things emotionally, so that the audience can feel them."

"We've both had inhibitions we had to conquer," says Cronyn.

"And we did, darling," says Miss Tandy, her voice scarcely above a whis-per. "We've done it together."

"I don't understand life," says Cronyn, "but I think the key, if not the answer, to it is affirmation. We can't figure it out, any of us, but if we can embrace the mystery, it can be quite wonderful."

There is a smattering of quiet talk. Then the Cronyns rise to their feet; goodbyes are exchanged.

My host walks me out to the elevator, and then he returns to the apartment, leaving the front door wide open to receive the children, due any moment.

Miss Tandy is standing near the doorway with her back to her husband, gazing out at the twilight, a light breeze playing upon her white hair. Cronyn walks up behind her and touches her finger, the one with her wedding ring.

She grasps his hand tightly. Then, as the last traces of daylight vanish from the horizon, he embraces the mystery.

Interviews with the Vampires

"**B**ella Lugosi introduced Dracula to a mass audience," explained actor Frank Langella over a deli lunch backstage at the Martin Beck Theater in 1978 following a matinee installment of his starring role in the Broadway production of Dracula. "He was the first person to truly embody Dracula so he became the standard; his own personality set the tone.

"This country in 1927"—when the first Dracula stage play opened at what is now Manhattan's Helen Hayes theater—"was much younger emotionally. And the original play, according to people I know who've seen it and one actor who was in it, had no laughs. They took it very seriously.

"But onstage now, when he says, at the nearness of his demise, 'Thank you for reminding me of the time,' it's oneupsmanship on the mere mortals. The audience adores him for it. Dracula is a king who loves being a king, would be nothing else, would rather die than reduce himself to the level that most of us have to live on.

"Lugosi's Dracula never joined in the fun," added Langella regarding his colleague's immortal role, "but there's no reason why he can't now!"

After reprising his stage Dracula for Universal Studios' film in 1979, Langella starred in a number of other movies: *Those Lips, Those Eyes* (1980), the murder mystery *Sphinx* (1981), *The Men's Club* (1986), *Masters of the Universe* (1987), *And God Created Woman* (1988), *True Identity* (1991), *1492* (1992) and *Dave* (1993).

Meanwhile, the Dracula cinema sweepstakes stalked on, offering up Werner Herzog's *Nosferatu, The Vampire*, starring Klaus Kinski (1979); *Love at First Bite* (1979), starring George Hamilton; *The Hunger*, featuring Susan Sarandon, Catherine Deneuve and David Bowie (1983); and a mixed body-bag of vampire vehicles such as *Transylvania 6–5000, Fright Night, Once Bitten* and *Return of the Living Dead* (all in 1985); *The Lost Boys, Evil Dead 2: Dead by Dawn, Return of the Living Dead, Part II* (all in 1987); *Fright Night Part II, Return to Salem's Lot* and *Vampire's Kiss* (all in 1988); *To Die For* and *Daughter of Darkness* (both in 1989); *Dark Shadows* (1990); *Children of the Night* (1991); *Buffy the Vampire Slayer, Innocent Blood,* and Francis Ford Coppola's *Bram Stoker's Dracula* (all in 1992).

Two decades later, Langella was back on Broadway as the leading man in another successful show, a 1996 revival of Noel Coward's *Present Laughter*, followed by the starring role in the off-Broadway production of *Cyrano de Bergerac* in 1997–98. *Dracula* was resurrected in 1997 for the centenary of Bram Stoker's novel; New York's Museum of Modern Art mounted a retrospective salute (co-curated by distinguished Dracula author/scholar Leonard Wolf, father of novelist Naomi Wolf, whose latest book *Dracula: The Connoisseur's Guide*, was published to wide acclaim) that included screenings of 40 vampire films from 12 countries. The centennial also coincided with the 20th anniversary of Anne Rice's *Interview with the Vampire* (whose film version starred Tom Cruise and Brad Pitt), an occasion Rice commemorated by issuing a new edition of her modern classic. The Houston Ballet also unveiled a well-received *Dracula*, set to the music of Franz Liszt, which *The New York Times* adjudged "a haunting extravaganza of neo-classical dance."

Trent Reznor of industrial-rock outfit Nine Inch Nails borrowed liberally from Coppola's 1992 *Dracula* for his 1997 video depiction of the song, "The Perfect Drug." Meanwhile, the 1992 movie *Buffy the Vampire Slayer* (about a cheer-leading Valley girl turned nemesis of the undead) was adapted in 1997 as a pop-ular television series—a development that seemed to up the ante, both onstage and off, in the eternal tug of war between bloodsuckers and their victims.

Actor Louis Jourdan followed his own superb three-part PBS performance in *Count Dracula* in 1976 with a supernatural turn as a camp villain in the title role of *Swamp Thing* (1982) and *The Return of the Swamp Thing* (1989), besides being featured in *Octopussy* (1983), *Year of the Comet* (1992) and other films.

Christopher Lee, the preeminent modern-day portrayer of princes of the undead, diversified in the 1980s and 1990s, appearing in the Chuck Norris movie *An Eye for an Eye* (1981), as well as *The Salamander* (1984), *Howling II . . . Your Sister Is a Werewolf* (1986), *Jocks* (1987) and *Gremlins 2* and *Blood Sacrifice* (both 1990), among dozens of other adventure and horror films.

"A good 'heavy' will usually eat his opposite alive," assured Lee during our interview in 1978, speaking during a break from his embodiment of a vampire killer in a skit while guest-hosting *Saturday Night Live*. "That's one of the reasons why many actors would not, and still will not, play straight roles opposite a strong villain. A lot of them are afraid to even try." Lee showed the sinister grin that made him one of the most memorable Draculas of all time. "Frankly, they're scared to *Death*."

Forewarning: How this story has been learned will be made manifest in its reading. All needless matters have been eliminated, so that an account almost at variance with the possibilities of latter-day belief may stand forth as simple fact. There is throughout no statement or detail wherein the reportage may err, for all records chosen are exactly con-temporary, given from the standpoints and within the range of knowl-edge of those who made them.*

An Excerpt from Lina Westenhark's Journal
(Courtesy the family of the deceased)

April 23, 1978—The lingering, unseasonable chill of the night air only

---

*With acknowledgments to Brain Stoker's original introduction to the 1897 edition of *Dracula*.

serves to redouble my strong feelings of loneliness and ineptitude. And something else—I am deathly afraid; sick with the sensation, as I was as a girl of 12 on the summer evening that my parents were detained in Budapest by bad weather and I was left to spend an entire night alone in the gloomy, rundown Romanian country house my father had then just purchased as a family vacation retreat. We sold the place only a month later and returned to good old Philadelphia. None of us had felt comfortable in that house, and Dad was mystified how, in the midst of a sweltering July, certain of its rooms (or only sections of some) could remain freezing cold. The last, eerie straw came on a trip to a small shop several miles away in the village of Bistrita. Growing accustomed to seeing us, the owner asked if we were newcomers to the area, and when we told him our address, he and his wife made the sign of the cross, pointed pairs of fingers towards us symbolically, and mumbled the queer words, "ordog" and "moroi." Later we looked up their meanings in a Hungarian-English dictionary: "Satan" and "undead." The following morning my family and I packed our luggage and left the Carpathians forever.

After being buried in my memory for over a decade, I heard those upsetting words again last night, on the lips of an elderly couple leaving the Little Platzel tavern on East 84th Street and Second Avenue, just before I boarded the bus Mr. Dracul had suggested I take to reach his home. Being new in New York City and on the first night of my late-shift assignment as a novice practical nurse, I had left the stop at the corner and approached the kindly-looking strangers, asking if they could advise me about the frequency of the buses. At 11:30 p.m. the street was unsettlingly empty and I was grateful for any company. The couple eyed me with curiosity, wondering why I had just allowed a blue N15 bound for South Ferry to go by. Impulsively, I showed them the note left in my office mailbox along with my work schedule:

Dear Miss Westenhark:
Welcome to New York City. I am anxiously expecting you this Saturday. A person of my age and condition does not get many visitors, as you can well understand. Since you are living on the East Side in the Germantown area and I reside in the Village, I recommend that you travel to me on one of the downtown buses at Second Avenue. Take care that you board only a black bus, lest you become disoriented or lost. They run less frequently, but if

you look for one around 11:00 p.m., the wait should not be too
long.

Your friend,
Mr. Dracul

The old Hungarian gentleman's brow furrowed as I explained my
predicament, and he shook his head. He was telling me that he knew
of no black bus that ran on the avenue when his wife reached the end
of my note and read my patient's name aloud; then she murmured, as
if it were an epithet, the word "nosferatu." I was surprised to see her
begin trembling, but at that instant a bus snarled to a halt behind me.
Glancing, I saw that it was jet black and made haste to gather my
things and jump on.

Suddenly the old couple began to shout at me ("Moroi! Moroi!
Ordog!") and the woman clutched the sleeve of my raincoat. "There's
no need for you to take this bus," she whispered, almost begging. "You
must not; there will be others."

I told her I didn't understand what she could mean and that I had
to go to work.

"Do you know what day it is?" she pleaded. I answered patiently
that it was Saturday the 22nd, suspecting she might be intoxicated
although she didn't look it. Her head bobbed as she replied: "Oh, yes!
I know that! But do you know what day it is? It is the eve of St.
George's Day. We have a belief that tonight, when the clock strikes
midnight, all the evil things of the world will have full sway! Do you
know where you are going, and what you are going to?"

She was in such distress that I tried, hastily, to comfort her, but without effect. Exasperated, I hoisted my bags to the second step of the bus,
and had dropped my token into the meter when I felt the woman thrust
a little necklace of some sort into my coat pocket. It was not until I took
my seat on the empty bus that I realized what it was: a rosary.

I thought it odd that no other passengers were taken on during the
long ride downtown, not that the driver ever slowed to allow such a
thing. At length, we came to a stop before an ancient, battered brownstone deep in Greenwich Village. Stepping off, I looked quickly at the
driver, himself in a uniform that matched the funereal decor of the
vehicle, but the visor of his cap hid his face. The doors snapped closed
the moment I alighted and the bus sped away.

I stood at the heavy oaken front door for a long time, knocking to no avail, and peering for any sign of light or life in the brownstone's many darkened windows. I turned after a last, extended assay to find a hoary man, dressed entirely in black, standing before the now-open door with outstretched arms. He lifted my heavy bag with ease and deposited it in the dimly lit parlor.

"Welcome to my house!" he said with a peculiar foreign intonation, moving aside to admit me in a courtly manner. "Enter now and of your own will! Come freely, go freely, and leave something of the happiness you bring!"

Treading cautiously, I asked if he were the man of the house, thinking that he didn't fit the description of the feeble invalid I was there to attend.

"Oh yes, I'm Mr. Dracul," he said after the great door had been bolted shut behind me. He smiled and held out a long white hand in greeting. I don't know which startled me more—the stone-cold touch of his fingers or the sight of the large, sharp canine teeth revealed by his rigid grin. As my patient leaned forward I could not repress a shudder. It may have been that his breath was rank, but a horrible feeling of nausea came over me as his pointed nails gently touched my cheek in an awkward attempt at paternal charm. Looking over his shoulder at the reflection in a tarnished silver plaque upon the wall, I almost screamed to see that it showed me to be standing alone without his withered figure in front of mine. What sort of a man is this, that has no presence in mirrors and looms over me with an awful glare?

Very late in the evening, as I dozed in the musty den beside his locked room, I had a ghastly dream that he had come to me in my sleep, his eyes as red as blood, and performed an unearthly seduction. I felt helpless in his powerful arms and he seemed to grow younger, almost handsome, as his dark form slipped over me, pulling my frock away from my chest and pressing fetid lips to my neck.

Now, this morning, as I watch the first traces of daylight creep in through the heavy gates on the upstairs windows, I feel somehow unclean and abandoned, missing desperately my friends from school, Mom, Dad and dear Jonathan. During the frenzy of my nightmare, I must have accidentally pricked myself with my graduation pin, because I've discovered two tiny cuts on the side of my neck. The sun can't come swiftly enough for me, and yet I dread it worse than the images of last night's terrible vision, because I cannot shake the notion that I am a prisoner in this house.

THE INTERVIEW

S EEMS LIKE EVERYWHERE one turns nowadays, the fabled old vampire count is within biting distance. Across the nation, he's the subject of, or inspiration for, a glut of best-selling books, sold-out stage productions and feature films, with many more on the way. After a heinous six-century reign, how does the undead Dracula, Master of the Night, king of warlocks, werewolves, rampaging bats and bloodthirsty cadavers, manage such staying power?

Frank Langella, the magnetic, princely leading man who incarnates the current craze in the Broadway smash, *Dracula*, has logged a lot of pensive hours in his counterpart's coffin, and he thinks he's finally divined the cryptic truth.

"I don't think there's anybody who hasn't wanted to be Dracula," he contends. "By that I mean there isn't anybody who wouldn't like immortality, and wouldn't sign a contract quick if there could be a way to have it. Certainly everybody wants to be the best of their breed, the top, No. 1—and if you take Dracula at his own words, he is the king of his own kind. At the end of the play, when the men who've come to destroy him are holding him at bay, he says, 'You do not know how many men have come against me! In these veins flows the blood of a conquering race!' Dracula is a *boyar*, a nobleman, a glorious victor over Death. Emotionally, he lives on a scale far greater than any other of the measly mortals around him.

"I decided to play him as I felt he was: a lonely, troubled monarch with a sense of humor and a unique and distinctive social problem—he is compelled to subsist on the blood of innocent victims. If he can get his daily dose and be back in his box by sunrise he's fine and can go on for centuries more, fearing only the stake. Who else lives like that?

"I think a singularity of lifestyle can produce a certain type of grandeur, poise—identity—and Dracula's got it. All legendary characters have these qualities; it's what makes them special, so that when they walk into a room everybody backs off. I'm not gonna make Dracula out to be a hero, but he can be a positive force in certain ways. He demonstrates, for instance, that if you set out to do something with integrity and strength of purpose, allowing nothing internal or external to get in your way, you can conquer anything, even the grave.

"There's another reason," adds Langella, "why audiences love Dracula: He's sexy. Certainly it's obvious why he's appealing to women—because it's nice to fantasize having a tall, dark stranger appear in your bedroom, pick you up flamboyantly and do it to you in a whole new way. If you're a man,

I think that the nicest fantasy love session would combine the same strength, tenderness and mutual fascination.

"All of this takes style and that's something I've always seen in Dracula, occasionally in film but mostly as he was originally pictured in Bram Stoker's book. I never thought he was a guy with a mouth dripping blood all the time. If anything, I think he'd have found that abhorrent. It would be totally out of character for him to want blood spurting everywhere, with throats ripped open and all that messiness. He would have been neat, clean, gentlemanly about his bloodsucking; a nice, tight *fuck*—if you'll pardon the expression—of the neck is what he'd be after. Listen, this man is of royalty! He's got hundreds of years of majesty behind him!"

Sound like any Count D. you've ever encountered? Well, the facts are wilder than the fictions.

The mythic Dracula of the '80s derives no small portion of his infernal nocturnal habits from the historic legacy of carnage orchestrated by one Vlad Tepes (the Impaler), *voivode* of Wallachia, a fierce warrior and tyrant who dominated his woeful vassals on and off between 1448 and 1476. In his own time, Prince Tepes (*tsep-pesh*) had another nickname: Dracula, a Romanian term meaning "son of a dragon" or "son of a devil." The two were interchangeable, since his father, Dracul, was himself a mean mistreater not coincidentally appointed to the monastic/militaristic Order of the Dragon in 1431 by the Holy Roman Emperor Sigismund.

While both father and son excelled at the art of fighting Turks, Dracul Jr. reserved a generous portion of his bloodlust for the folks back home. A fond peacetime amusement for the scion was the torture and execution of anyone he deemed wicked or stupid. Targets were universal, encompassing men, women and children of all ages and stations, while the favorite method of cruelty was impalement. There is no evidence that the real Dracula was a vampire, but he did enjoy a stake dinner. Often he would sit at a groaning board in the center of the ongoing mutilation, nibbling while numberless unfortunates were skewered in geometric patterns (precise rows, concentric circles). Some were impaled upside down, others heads up; either lengthwise from crotch to neck, through the heart, or at the navel. For variety's sake, there were also strangulation, skinning, boiling, disembowelment and nails through the skull. All of it, of course, while the poor wretches were alive and kicking. On one red-letter day, Vlad massacred 30,000 in the village of Amlas, cutting them up "like cabbage." Small wonder this man was rapidly accepted into folklore as an offspring of Satan.

Bad news travels fast, and far. Accounts of the Impaler's inhumanity survive in German and Russian literature, notably a 15th-century Russian manuscript entitled *Story of Dracula*. These or similar texts would long afterwards come to the attention of a minor Irish novelist by the name of Abraham "Bram" Stoker. While attending Trinity College in the mid-1860s, young Stoker's aim to seek a prestigious post in the civil service waned as he became entranced by the theater, due largely to the ominous charisma of famous actor Sir Henry Irving, whom he first saw in Dublin in 1867.

After graduating with a degree in mathematics, Stoker began to concentrate on writing and drifted into drama criticism before becoming, in 1878, the secretary, theater manager and symbiotic confidant of his idol, Henry Irving. Simultaneously, he indulged a zealous interest in the development of a popular contemporary novelistic form, the Gothic romance. *Camilla*, an early work by Irish author Joseph Sheridan Le Fanu, drew special inquiry, since its focus was vampires. If Stoker's first published work was a dry offering called *The Duties of Clerks of Petty Sessions in Ireland*, it must have been a temporary lapse into reality/responsibility, because he subsequently began turning out titles like *The Lair of the White Worm*, *The Lady of the Shroud* and *Under the Sunset*, the last featuring the King of Death. His investigations into vampire chronicles continued apace in the recesses of the British Museum and in correspondence with Romanian savants, until he ultimately produced in 1897 one of the August horror novels of English letters.

Stoker unquestionably was influenced by previous works such as John Polidori's *The Vampyre* (1819), Thomas Peckett Prest's *Varney the Vampyre* (1847), and an 1888 travel book exhaustive in its scrutiny of Hungarian peasant superstition, Emily Gerard's *The Land Beyond the Forest*. Even so, *Dracula*'s prose rang with Stoker's own studied flair for the macabre.

Briefly, the storyline of Stoker's immortal tale unfolds in the journals of young English solicitor/real estate agent Jonathan Harker and his fiancée, Mina Murray; epistles between Mina and dear friend Lucy Westenra; an assortment of other diaries, transcribed newspaper accounts, and even the oral documentation of a Dr. John Seward, preserved on the newly invented Edison phonograph!

What may sound disjointed and choppy to the unacquainted is in fact a strikingly clever and absorbing narrative, wherein Jonathan Harker journeys to the Transylvanian castle of a mysterious Count Dracula to settle the arrangements of Dracula's purchase of a British property in Carfax Abbey. The trip proves a frightful one, the sense of foreboding intensified when Harker finds his host to be a menacing crone who takes a terminal rain check on mirrors and square meals, traverses sheer stone walls like a bat, and keeps a harem of ravenous vampiresses happy by feeding them new-born babies. A prisoner in the castle, the panic-stricken solicitor learns the Count plans a voyage to England, complete with a cargo of 50 coffins of hallowed soil, presumably to conquer the country from the neck down and spawn a race of undeadbeats.

Harker escapes on the heels of the monster, suffers a nervous breakdown, but makes it home to find that his bride's buddy Lucy, and then Mina herself, have fallen prey to Dracula. Lucy joins the ranks of the *nosferatu* (a Romanian term translated as "not dead"), attacks tykes, and gets spiked in the aorta by Dr. Abraham Van Helsing, an ever-ready authority on metaphysics from Amsterdam. With Jonathan back, the race is on to save the lovely Mina from Lucy's fate. And Dracula pulls out all the stops, enlisting the aid of a lunatic under Dr. Seward's care named R. M. Renfield. It's a close shave, but virtue triumphs with shivers to spare.

All this first-rate phantasmagoria notwithstanding, what separates Stoker's masterpiece from the rest of the undertakers' essays then in vogue was its topical, realistic mode. His fiendish Count was no museum piece or illuminated yarn, but a latter-day incubus who stalked the boudoirs and cemeteries of Victorian England. The utter immediacy of the tale fired the imaginations of readers and made it an entertainment must for all who could stomach its licentious portents.

As a result, the book lends itself easily to periodic updates. When a Hamilton Deane-John L. Balderston stage adaptation of Stoker's novel (the first such production was the 1897 British *Dracula or the Undead*) opened at New York's Fulton Theater in 1927 with an unknown named Bela Blasko, a.k.a. Lugosi, in the lead, its protagonists were current enough to have walked in off the street. Capitalizing on the press reports of genuinely alarmed patrons, the Fulton provided curbside first aid service for the overwhelmed. Superior film versions date from German director F. W. Murnau's 1922 *Nosferatu*, and the release on St. Valentine's Day, 1931, of Tod Browning's *American Dracula* with Lugosi duplicating his stage triumph.

Can't keep a ghoul man down, apparently, for no matter how often Dracula gets pinned by a pointed instrument, he rises again, unfettered, in a fertile location. A sampling of vintage screen entries include Gloria Holden's *Dracula's Daughter*; *Son of Dracula*, starring Lon Chaney, Jr.; *House of Dracula*, with John Carradine as the Count; an array of Christopher Lee outings—*The Horror of Dracula*; *Dracula, Prince of Darkness*; *Taste the Blood of Dracula* and the Spanish *Vampir*—plus a spate of bone-yard aberrations like *Dracula vs. Frankenstein*, *Billy the Kid vs. Dracula*, *Dracula's Dog*, an all-black inner-city exploration called *Blacula*, Andy Warhol's avant-gory *Dracula* and Roman Polanski's inspiration to youth, *The Fearless Vampire Killers*. In all, there are over 200 such movies waiting to be re-released/resurrected, and the latest obsession is just beginning to take hold.

Memorable among present brisk-selling tomes are the delightful *Dream of Dracula* and *The Annotated Dracula* by professor Leonard Wolf; Raymond T. McNally's and Radu Florescu's scholarly *In Search of Dracula*, not to mention *Dracula: A Biography of Vlad the Impaler*, *The Dracula Scrapbook*, *Hotel Transylvania*, *Children of the Night*, hot new novels like Anne Rice's *Interview with the Vampire* and sci-fi offshoots, *The Space Vampires* by Colin Wilson and A. E. van Vogt's *Asylum*, for starters. And there's a hit record to turn pages to—Warren Zevon's "Werewolves of London."

"Dracula," as Frank Langella exclaims, "is a million-dollar name!"

Thankfully, I have arranged to face Frank Langella in the warm light of day, entering his lair in the bowels of New York's Martin Beck Theater by traversing the now-lifeless set of Dracula, an awesome, saturnine construction of illustrator/designer Edward Gorey's most dour, skeletal nasties. Embedded and camouflaged everywhere in the thin-lined maze of black, white and gray are batsbatsbats—etched in the wallpaper, moulded between the bedposts and encrusted in the huge sarcophagus that lies empty opposite the two trap doors by which Frank/Dracula eludes his enemies.

Langella's dressing room is guarded by a suspicious-looking wench who vanishes silently as I arrive. Predictably, Frank follows the Devil's dictum that he may only ensnare willing souls, and bades me to enter freely and of my own volition. I am no sooner across the threshold than, with a flourish of his azure terrycloth bathrobe, he orders me to sit across from him as he reclines regally on his couch. I watch as he finishes a glass of fruit juice, then places it upon a crumb-strewn Sesame Street place mat emblazoned with the image of The Count, a Muppet doomed to the timeless task of teaching tots their numerals.

Despite the gray eye shadow, pale pancake and his imposing stature, I am at once taken by Langella's nonchalant demeanor and hearty, melodic laugh. But as I survey the multitude of Dracula merchandise and mementoes crammed into his cozy haunt (plastic/plaster busts, dolls, danglements, puppets, paintings, pendants, a *Dinner with Drac!* lp), I am reminded of the many wily ways of the mighty vampire himself: He can not only transmogrify into a bat and werewolf, but also a mist or phosphorescent dust which can steal through the merest crack or cranny. Recommended defenses against his intrusions are garlands of garlic and crucifixes. A branch of wild rose will confine him to his casket, a blessed bullet fired into the occupied pall will undo him, but the surest procedure is the venerable stake through the heart, accompanied by a severing of the head.

Fair enough, but how can one deter the burgeoning commercial multiplications of his unholy name?

"Why fight it?" Langella chuckles. "What's the phrase? 'There are some things man was not meant to understand'?

"Look, just take the bare frame of the story, as if, for example, this was a brand-new play and we had not grown up on Dracula stories. The show is about a thing called a *vampire*, an immortal man who sleeps in a box, wakes at dusk and roams the earth, having a fine time. He's a rugged individualist and people, young and old, respect him—as I do—for it! If you took a packet of my mail and read it, you'd see that audiences feel just that way."

When Langella's oratory is interrupted by a phone call, I take his advice and pick up a note at random from the frondage of mailgrams and letters taped to the walls ("Break a tooth!", "Bloody good luck!", "May your sucking bring happiness to millions. Love, Annie and Mel Brooks"). Set down on stationery decorated with pussycats and birds, in a child's deliberate scrawl, is the following:

> For my birthday party we went to see Dracula. One of the spots I like was when you bit Lucy in the neck. I also liked when one of the guys stabed [sic] you. Can you please write back and tell me how you could be alive when he stabed you. Also, how come you were so friendly in the beginning?
>
> Judith

"I'm not certain what effect I have on children," Langella concedes. "For the most part, they seem to adore Dracula—not me; ten years from now they won't remember the actor, just Dracula.

"Now, I think to myself, 'Am I doing something terrible to these children? Am I making evil pretty to them?' I really don't believe so. There's nothing wrong with them finding Dracula attractive and interesting, since he does get his just desserts in the end. When kids go home, asking their parents, 'Why did Dracula have to die?' they can say it was because he was a man who took blood and that's wrong, bad. Besides, in many ways, Dracula's death is a mercy killing. I always wanted to have him scream out, 'Yes! Do it, do it! Set me free!'"

One of three children born to Frank and Angelina Langella, Frank Jr., 38, grew up in Bayonne and South Orange, N.J. His older brother, Andrew, works in his father's business, described as "refinishing oil drums for industrial use," but the younger Frank had other ideas. He landed his first role at 11—an 85–year-old man in an Abraham Lincoln pageant at School No. 3 in Bayonne. Since then, he's had a creditable film and stage career, appearing in Mel Brooks' hilarious *The Twelve Chairs*, Rene Clement's *Le Maison sur les Arbes*, and *Diary of a Mad Housewife*, for which he won the National Society of Film Critics Award. He's captured several Obies for his off-Broadway activities and a Tony for his Broadway debut in Edward Albee's *Seascape*. The revival of the Deane-Balderston dramatization of *Dracula*, however, vaulted him to stardom. Looking back to when he was an 11–year-old, would he have been appalled by his character?

"When I was a kid I had all kinds of crazy fears, dreams about people coming in the night to get me, tigers and ghosts, but no vampires. Mostly it was the Mummy; that film scared the living shit out of me.

"I don't enjoy being scared anymore. I don't see any reason for putting myself in such an uncomfortable position, to plague my mind with all that stuff. But I don't believe in mysticism of any sort. I'm very pragmatic; I don't believe in spooky things. Dracula to me is glorious to perform, but not for a moment do I believe he does or could exist."

Actually, Langella's Dracula (a very loose variation on the book's) is exciting and fun but never fearsome. Claiming he can be dispassionate about him, we discuss the celebrated vampire's broad appeal.

"I didn't research him heavily," Frank confesses in his calm, smooth-spoken tone. "Whenever I'm playing a famous character who has either lived or been known widely, I find that researching him too heavily can stifle my imagination. I purposely didn't see any of the movies. I wanted to do something with him that would be, if not completely different, then unique. So I didn't steep myself in the book or how Lugosi or Christopher Lee did him."

"How do you feel onstage, in the Dracula persona?"

"You very rarely get an opportunity to play someone who's totally omnipotent, and that's what he is," Langella says with pleasure. "There is an extraordinary feeling about playing a character who is all-powerful. I can think about this now, but when I'm onstage I never consider it. We're used to seeing Dracula taking himself terribly seriously and I try not to. God knows, when somebody comes at him with wolf-bane, or when he wants to screw Lucy, that's serious. But the rest of the night I think he's having a rather cheerful time. It's everyone else who feels uneasy.

"What I am constantly aware of is that I'm maneuvering, going after my needs, and my need there is Lucy. I have a great desire, passion, *lust* for her on all kinds of levels."

"Throughout the play," I observe, "Dracula seems to tower over the rest of the characters. He has a grand purpose in life and death, a resolve they only aspire to."

"These are puny, tiny people as far as he's concerned," Langella nods with relish. "They are *nothing*; to be used and gotten out of the way—except for Lucy."

"What's so special about Lucy?"

"He's in love with her," he exults. "That's the answer! She's his queen. 'The blood is the life!' Dracula says (quoting the Bible—Deuteronomy 12:33], but here he's found something more important. Why did he fall for one being and not another? What draws *him* to the point of irresistibility and carelessness? Love, of course—what else?"

"Your *Dracula* is a true Gothic romance," I tell Langella. "The bedroom scenes with Lucy are unexpectedly amorous, and I think I see a terroful ambivalence in her eyes. The idea of being ravished by the Count is not altogether unpleasant to her."

"We had long talks in rehearsal about Lucy's complicity in the erotic love scene," he recounts. "She had to be at Count Dracula's mercy but not totally a victim. After all, you, me, everybody falls into evil so often that's it's got to be pretty nice or we wouldn't be so prone to it. We're always doing things that aren't good for us, always eating, or smoking or screwing around too much, or whatever it is that everyone says is wrong; and then repenting and feeling guilty, saying, 'I won't do that again . . . for a while.'

"The idea of evil as always being painted black, being hideous with horns—that came from the Church and social guilt. It's especially apparent in the Victorian setting of the play. If somebody went out and did something wonderfully naughty at that time and openly enjoyed it, it was decried as awful. Guilt crept in and that's how things like sin were created, whatever *that* is."

Louis Jourdan, outlining his acclaimed performance in the chilling three-part Public Television production, *Count Dracula*, says that he "tried to make him as attractive as possible. Like so many evil people, Dracula really believes he is doing good. He claims to give his victims eternal life." From Langella's perspective, what is the kindest thing Dracula does?

"Well, it's not in the script as written, not in the dialogue, but I have always felt he had a great affinity for Professor Van Helsing, the man who ultimately destroys him. He realizes that Van Helsing is a man of bearing and lofty impulses, a fighter. When Van Helsing accidentally cuts his finger in the second act, Dracula could very easily swoop down then and there and kill him. Instead, he warns him to 'Take care how you cut yourself. It is more dangerous than you think!'

"In his battle of wits with the Professor, Dracula plays by the rules. He's not a vulgar man and yet he's been portrayed with so much vulgarity. What happens very often with characters of greatness is that we worship them and then, when we can no longer stand our feelings of inferiority, we pull them down. Dracula is a king who revels in being a king, and he would rather die than reduce himself to the level most of us must live on."

Granted, Dracula may be exalted and principled, but surely he's capable of a measure of insensitivity. What's the unkindest thing Dracula does?

"What an *interesting* question," says Langella, mulling it over. "Hmmmmm; you know, I guess I'm so sympathetic towards him, I can't think of a single unkind thing that he does. It's not very nice to break a mirror, as he does in Lucy's house, but I wouldn't call that unkind; just rude. I just ran through the entire script in my mind and he never does one mean thing—he's got perfect manners."

"How about his treatment of the mental patient, Renfield? Dracula brutalizes him in the third act."

"*No.* That wasn't an unkindness. He vowed to Renfield that if he did as his master said, he would have power and life through eternity. And, like the rest of us mortals, Renfield lets Dracula down. I tell you, I'm speaking very much in the presence of my own character, since I'm wearing his make-up," Langella admits sheepishly. "But no, he wasn't unkind to Renfield. I think Renfield's been pretty shitty to Dracula, going off and telling people where he's hiding out!

"He's the Judas of my life, that Renfield! He'll get his tonight!"

The phone rings for the umpteenth time.

"Aw, there's no rest for a vampire," says Langella with a vexed grin. "They should know better than to call me before sundown."

"When I went, I had no idea what to expect, but seeing Frank in the play and seeing his effect on the audience was spectacular; beyond anything I'd anticipated. He created a completely different character; one with charm, sex appeal—and, most important of all, he endeared himself to the crowd. Gained their sympathy! No doubt of it, Frank's performance made my mind up for me. I decided right then to make the film."

The speaker is Walter Mirish, the man who will produce the forthcoming Universal production of *Dracula*, starring Frank Langella, directed by John Badham of *Saturday Night Fever* fame, from a script by W. D. Richter, to be shot (tentatively) in Los Angeles and London. Production is scheduled to start in October, concluding at Christmas. Divulging his hopes for the film, Langella says that if he had his druthers he "would like there to be a shade more knowledge in the movie as to how and why Dracula became what he is.

"It would make him a man of even greater weight," he feels. "I try to play him now as if he's carrying all that history around with him, but it would be nice if we could share a bit of his ancestry. It would add to the epic tragedy."

Speaking of epic tragedies, if these splendid plans have a vaguely familiar ring, they should. Universal mounted the 1931 *Dracula*, putting the actor who rose to prominence in the American stage version into the title role . . . where it devastated his prospects for ever doing anything else. From the onset, the name of Bela Lugosi was synonymous with the character he came to personify, until it looked as if Dracula were playing Bela. It's entirely possible that Lugosi could never have excelled in any non-vampire parts. He was a sullen, mistrustful man who never quite overcame the language barrier and was dismayed that many feared even his offstage visage. He made and lost a tidy fortune and was eventually obliged to undertake a perpetual calendar of summer stock stints as the Count to pay his bills. After five wives and a 17-year bout with a morphine habit (begun while filming *Dracula*, to combat sciatic pains), he expired in 1956 at the age of 73 and was buried, as requested, in his familiar tails and red-lined cape.

An apprehensive Langella turned down the stage role the first time it was offered. Now, he's the fellow so many vampire addicts will take with them to their fitful dreams. If Bela returned today from the tomb, it's doubtful his stilted, humorless aspect would outshine Langella's suave, sprightly ways. The new *Dracula* probably would not have been a sensation without Langella, who managed the knotty feat of drawing unanimous popular and critical praise in an arena where entertainment is either high or low brow. Langella swears that his involvement with the character will cease the last day of filming. For him, there will be no revivals. Ever. Still, if the movie's half good it will have a life of its own.

The secret of Dracula's reacceptance likely lies in the strong favorable response to recent erudite studies of the Bram Stoker work and its historical underpinnings. Once the book earned classic status, taking a place beside Mary Shelley's *Frankenstein* (1817), it simply remained for a modern embodiment to galvanize the receptive public.

That's one theory. Leonard Wolf shares it, but insists there are deeper, grimmer reasons for the furor that has yielded nationwide Dracula parties and $10.75 T-shirts complete with red fang stains at the collar. The San Francisco State English Lit professor and authority behind *The Annotated Dracula* takes time out from Chaucer, work on *The Annotated Frankenstein* and his own Dracula film project to give me a sobering analysis. Incidentally, unlike others (Roger Vadim, Ken Russell and George Hamilton, to date) hopping on the Hollywood hearse, Wolf's preoccupation with vampires is in his blood—he was born in Transylvania.

"The Deane-Balderston play is a low-grade spoof of Stoker's book," Wolf states flatly, "but Langella does a miraculous job of not spoiling the fun and still giving an electrifying rendition. Frank caught the thematic core of the complex Count—a lust for life. If you examine Stoker's *Dracula* you begin to see the Atomic Age anxieties it covers. Langella understands the many lusts—not only sexual but also for violence—inherent in the book and now mirrored in our culture. He knows his audience and simply plays to them.

"There are four elements central to the symbol of the vampire that help to explain its enormous new appeal in this country:

"The first is a *fixation on violence*—an American way of life, part of its frontier tradition. People love the bloody action.

"Next is the *refusal to acknowledge death*. This is very American. In our funeral parlors, we hide our deaths or almost refuse to admit that the bodies are dead. The corpse is either shut into a closed coffin or dressed in special costumes and worked on with cosmetics so that he or she resembles a living, sleeping person. The dead are always referred to as 'the departed,' for instance, as if they were on vacation. Not many modern Americans have ever smelled death, unless they've fought in a war. Dracula *denies* death. Period.

"Then there's the *fixation on youth*. In the book, Dracula is introduced as an old man. It's clear we're starting with an impotent vampire who feels himself getting feeble and senile and decides to give it one more valiant try. The key is that blood makes vampires young and vital, but American versions of the story almost always skip over that detail, preferring to cast as Dracula romantic leading men who are mature, if not downright youthful. America is stuck on being between the ages of 18 and 32. Dracula, you see, is a Faustian figure; moreover, as he initiates women into his service they grow more beautiful, sensual, robust. Our culture has always said no to Nature by splitting atoms, inventing organisms, building dams, even cloning; always encroaching on the space reserved for God. Dracula helps us say "No" to uncertainty and aging.

"Finally, there are in the story an infinite number of *sexual confusions that erase responsibility*. America's evolving liberation from sexual constraints has created a lot of bewilderment. Now that nearly everything is allowed, what are the sexual imperatives? Which sexual unions are most desirable or morally right? Man and woman, woman and woman, mother and son? In our culture, in the real world, sexuality carries with it many big responsibilities. For the vampire, though, there is no conscience involved, and the consequences sort of take care of themselves. All that's required for shared fulfillment is a bite on the neck. There's no genitalia necessary, so there's none of the depressing failures. For victims, nothing is important but to lie still. It's all *gimme*—and no pregnancy. Matter of fact, not only is sex made easy by Dracula, but so is religion.

"It gets extremely weird when you delve into it. Any culture that would feed its children a cereal called Count Chocula has got to be obsessed with something."

Frank Langella should take care how he casts himself; it is more dangerous than he thinks. Or is it happenstance that the only man not sitting up nights devising ways to capitalize on the Dracula stampede is the Count's most prolific living avatar?

"Dracula?! Five years ago I made a decision not to discuss my role as Dracula ever again!" Christopher Lee roars, nervously petting his flowing, silver-streaked mustache. We are seated together in NBC-TV's Studio 8H, the New York base of operations for *Saturday Night Live!* Around us, cameras are being jockeyed, scenery is being sawed and screams are being rehearsed by Laraine Newman and Jane Curtin in preparation for Lee's appearance as a guest host.

The cast had supposed that Lee would consent to a few bloodsucking sendups for their special horror extravaganza, but no dice. Christopher doesn't go that route anymore. Instead they have to settle for his depiction of elocutionist Henry Higgins instructing Baba Wawa in the rudiments of correct discourse. He does agree, however, to square off against Dan Aykroyd as James Bond's latest arch-foe, Dr. V-Neck, but that sketch gets axed just prior to airtime.

Ironically, Lee is just now about to try his hand as a vampire killer, hunting down the undead *Memoirs* of that contemptible nightstalker, Richard (Aykroyd) Nixon. A rival irony is the fact that, with his bushy mustache and snow-capped widow's peak, Lee more than ever resembles the Stoker's-eye Dracula from whom he is desperate to distance himself.

"It's not out of dislike or regret that I refuse to speak about Dracula," he emphasizes. "I simply decided—promised myself—to move on, and forever disassociate myself from the role. I guess I grew into a lot of those demonic parts because of my tall, dark appearance. What you would call a sinister look."

"You call it sinister," I say. "But I'd call it seasoned, or distinguished."

"Ah yes!" Lee submits, smiling. "Class! It's instinctive, part of the thing that drives a successful demon. Playing the villain is the most fun because it has the most impact, the most energy. There's the undying struggle between good and evil. With the demon parts I played, I always tried. . . ."

His voice trails off; he's struggling with the topic, perhaps longing to recall his gory days as You Know Who. But a promise is a promise.

"A great villain, a truly demonic one, has a heroic quality," Lee concludes. "He's propelled by horribly evil forces, but there's also a sadness there." He becomes wistful. "The great demon always seems to achieve more than the other guys, doesn't he?"

Moments later Lee and John Belushi are in caps and somber overcoats, huddled before a fog machine, making clandestine plans to pounce on the Vampire of San Clemente . . . when a hellish voice bursts from the studio PA system.

"HOLD IT GUYS! SORRY CHRISTOPHER, BUT THE BLACK HAT YOU'RE WEARING IS WRONG! NO GOOD! LOOKS TOO COSSACKY! NO HAT!"

Wounded, Lee removes the headgear. "I thought it was appropriate for the scene," he murmurs. "It comes from Romania. Really."

Funny thing about impersonating the Devil's son: You're damned if you do and damned if you don't. The weight of this world *and* the next is on Frank Langella's broad shoulders each time the curtain goes up at the Martin Beck Theater. Many observers perceive the perils posed by the new rage he represents as being odious in nature, far-reaching in scope.

A hint of the impending turpitude surfaces at a Wednesday matinee of *Dracula*. During the normally steamy but restrained love scene, the deft Count falters in his scrupulous affections, inadvertently catching the strap of

Lucy's clinging nightgown pulling it downward to expose her sculptured left breast. There is no discernible outrage in the rapt house of senior citizens and small fry, just modest sniggering and communal shock.

"That happens about twice a month," Langella reveals afterward.

"It's entirely accidental. The scene is exciting because of its simplicity, timing and purity, and I don't wish to embroider it. I think the fact that the breast was bared was too *real*—and that ruins things for the audience. All that went through my mind was 'Damn it! I hope I'm not poisoning any sweet young minds.'"

Suddenly Langella is summoned from his dressing room by his *valet de chambre*. "There must be 80 people at the stage door," she sighs, "and they all want autographs. Could you c'mon out?"

A thunderous whoop goes up when Langella materializes in the entrance-way. Squinting into the late-afternoon light, he scribbles with abandon and the throng presses in. One wispy cherub with a blue flower in her hair emerges from the turmoil and softly announces: "I like the way you handle your cape." She is no more than five. Frank/Drac gapes, then howls with glee. He is signing the little one's program when a raven-tressed teenage nymph in taut jeans and fatigue jacket shoves her way to his side. There is an enigmatic fire in her hazel gaze, a dire urgency to her request. "Please," she entreats him, looking deep into his painted eyes, requesting his private ear. "I want to tell you something."

Langella tenses. "No you don't," he says with finality, gently but firmly forcing her back with one hand. She lingers, hesitating, on the outskirts of the inner circle, staring anxiously, straining to regain his attention. He cool-ly ignores her, but she will not be daunted.

A corridor opens up in the crowd and she hurries through it. "Please. I have to tell you. . . ." She catches Langella off-guard. His hands are not free to hold her at bay, and as she lunges forward he can feel her hot breath upon his neck. . . .

"Your fly is open."

Dudley Moore:
Still Not Beyond the Fringe

Dudley Moore had something to prove. It was the sweltering summer afternoon of final shooting for the conclusion of 1981's film comedy phenomenon, Arthur—specifically the scene in which would be settled the questions of who the wealthy, irresponsible Arthur Bach (Moore) planned to marry: his fiance (played by Jill Eikenberry) or his ditzy new girlfriend (portrayed by Liza Minelli). Arthur's decision would in turn determine whether he'd retain his vast inheritance (roughly, the difference between $750 million or several soggy tuna fish sandwiches).

Moore, a squat elfin sort with a haystack hairdo, had just walked over from his Waldorf-Astoria suite to the on-location set at the steps of St. Bartholomew's Church on Park Avenue. Costumed in tattered tails and made up with grime and bogus lacerations, he had caused quite an indignant stir amongst the guests in the lobby, who took him for a retrobate.

"Watch how professionally, how maturely I behave on the set," he whispered, alternately amused and annoyed by the miscomprehensions of judgmental New York passersby. "I'll show them, set an example!"

The call came for the actors to take their places and Dudley and Liza descended the steps, posing before a gleaming Rolls Royce. Behind him shifted a mountain of unruly spectators, swaying on the tops of cars and scrambling over each other as police struggled to impose decorum. Somebody yelled "Quiet!" and miraculously, the Big Apple's ritual honking, talking, and pushing seemed to cease as all watched stiffly.

A makeup woman rushed up to the little man in the tux to doublecheck his dishevelment. Satisfied, she moved out of camera range, but Moore politely pulled a large, square utility mirror out of her grasp. He lowered the looking glass to a point beneath his belt, and his was the only voice audible above the hush as he gazed downward.

"Ahhh, yes, people," he said. "Everything is in place."

The gathered throng responded with a big laugh, and there was much genial nudging and controlled exasperation exchanged between the cast and crew as filming resumed. Afterward, co-workers for the Orion Pictures project compared Moore to Dennis the Menace or a character out of *Tom Brown's Schooldays*. But to get the full picture one would have to toss in equal helpings of the club-footed Philip Carey of *In Human Bondage* and the hopelessly horny George Weber, the role he played in quest of Bo Derek in *10*.

In the years after he achieved international stardom as the inebriated focal point of *Arthur*, Moore would become a staple in the tabloids for his on-again/off-again relationships (including marriages to Brogan Lane and Nicole Rothschild) following his breakup with former Miss America Susan Anton.

Moore also kept busy as a well-regarded concert pianist, had open-heart surgery in September 1997, and made a steady string of artistically tepid movies, often with seemingly autobiographical titles: *Lovesick* and *Romantic Comedy* (both 1983); *Unfaithfully Yours*, *Best Defense*, *Micki and Maude* (1984); *Santa Claus: The Movie* (1985); *Like Father Like Son* (1987); *Arthur 2: On the Rocks* (1988); *Crazy People* (1990) and *Blame It on the Bellboy* (1992).

"We all go through patterns," noted Anton in 1981 in reference to Moore's psychotherapy-suffused outlook on life, "but nothing is ever that serious or tragic with Dudley."

Indeed, Moore found a new audience in the 1990s, capturing a generation of pre-teen devotees as the voice of Spin, the animated globe who makes quasi-salacious quips about "all those bathing beauties down by the coral reefs" (i.e., tropical fish) as he narrates "Deep Sea Dive" and other episodes of National Geographic's "Kids Video" series, *Really Wild Animals*.

THE INTERVIEW

"**D**UD-LEY! DUD-LEY!" squeal clusters of young women among the crowds lining the sidewalks of Fifth Avenue, as Dudley Moore's open, horse-drawn carriage makes its way down the center lane of the street. Looking comfortable and dignified in the coach, the British actor nods and smiles, reveling in the idea that he is both cynosure *and* sex symbol on Main Street in one of the world's great cities.

The urban idyll would make a fitting fantasy of conquest for the diminutive Moore, whose modest film career abruptly accelerated in 1981 with his portrayal of the rich, unreliable Arthur Bach in *Arthur*, a dark-horse comedy hit that earned Dudley a Golden Globe Award as Best Actor in a Comedy or Musical, plus an Oscar nomination. But no—this is still make-believe, a scene in the upcoming film *Six Weeks*, about a girl who is terminally ill. That tragic child (played by petite ballerina Katherine Healy) is snuggled against Moore in the crisp late-afternoon air. As the carriage continues on its way downtown, the throngs of bystanders suddenly realize that the attractive blonde sitting on the other side of 12–year-old Katherine is Mary Tyler Moore, Dudley's co-star in the film.

"Look how beautiful she is!" says one passerby, waving furiously as others follow suit. The fans catch Dudley's eye. He rises and makes an exaggerated bow toward mounting adulation obviously not meant for him.

"Mary and I were counting the number of *wild-eyed* fans along the street," says Dudley later with a smirk, "and we were deciding how many were waving at me for my beauty and how many may have been waving at her. We came out even."

Dudley Moore is currently one of the hottest leading men in Hollywood. He has also become a ubiquitous personality on the streets of the Big Apple in the last year, spending the better part of six months working first on *Six*

Weeks, which opens this week, and then on writer-director Marshall Brickman's *Lovesick*, with Elizabeth McGovern and Sir Alec Guinness.

"I *hate* shooting in New York," he says. "There's all this noise and honking, and everybody's a fascist, pushing, shoving, cursing. I'm the only one around here with manners!"

As a rule, do people usually recognize him on the street?

"They do—honestly!" he insists. "They actually do! It seems that everybody loved *Arthur*, from eight-year-olds to the elderly. One kid wrote to me saying that he'd seen it 28 times. Someone else told me that some people go to see it wearing top hats, and they've memorized every joke and talk back to the screen.

"Perhaps the fantasy of living Arthur's lavish New York life style is strongly appealing in these depressed times," he adds. "It certainly lifted my spirits—the amount of money I get for a film has tripled as a result!"

He shows the same impish smile he displayed as he hogged the limelight on Fifth Avenue.

But as it turns out, there's a lot less about Dudley Moore to laugh at than one might suppose.

Four-year-old Dudley spent a good portion of 1939 in the overcrowded Old Church Hospital in Rumford, England, undergoing surgery for his clubfoot. There was a war on, and he found himself the only child in a ward full of soldiers with missing parts. He was so terrorized by their shrieks of agony that he began to have vivid nightmares of his own deformity, grotesque dreams that would continue through his adulthood. He endured an extensive series of operations on his left leg from the time he was about two weeks old until the age of seven. When he was sufficiently ambulatory to attend school, he found himself incessantly bullied by his classmates, who regarded the bright young Moore as a "freak" and taunted him "like a wounded dog."

"With a clubfoot," he explains, "the foot itself is turned in. The leg is shorter, the calf is withered and the heel isn't properly formed, so you've got a large bump on the top of the foot. Both my legs are like that, but the right one righted itself. The greatest day of my life was when I finally wore long pants.

"My parents didn't know how to react to my condition. On the one hand, it didn't exist at all, and on the other hand I was crippled. There was a terrible polarity there. I didn't grow up so much as go on."

Born in Dagenham, England, Dudley is the only son (he has an older sister) of John and Ada Moore. "When I think of my mother's background, oh

God! Her father was a Christian Science faith healer and he also wrote books. My mother is very humorous and optimistic—and very anxious, which is something I think I've inherited."

Dudley's father was a withdrawn, taciturn man. When he did open his mouth, it was usually to rhapsodize about his work as an electrician for British Railways, particularly his skill with a contraption he called "the Super-sonic Machine," which detected flaws in railway axles.

"*Fascinating*. He was very proud of that," Dudley deadpans.

John Moore died some 10 years ago, and his son took it hard. "I wish we had talked more," he reflects somberly. "If he were alive today, I'd get him into a corner and find out who he was." He displays his father's watch ("We snatched it off him as he lay there on the slab") and reads the inscription on the back: B. R. EASTERN REGION, J. MOORE, 45 YEARS SERVICE. Dudley had it appraised and was told that the watch—the only memento he has from his father—was worth a "measly" two pounds.

"I saw my father as being tender; I felt it, but he didn't show it. He was sweet-natured without being very active about it. He and I never went anywhere together, meaning just the two of us. I never had a down-to-earth conversation with my dad. He was very hidden.

"Seeing him in the hospital was a chilling experience, to say the least. He was dying of cancer of the colon." There is a pause, and then Moore begins to laugh. "I *think* it was cancer of the colon; either that, or of the comma or the apostrophe."

If you never caught the satirical stage revue *Beyond the Fringe*, have no records by the Dudley Moore Trio, and were not in a movie theater when the lights went down for such films as *Bedazzled*; *Thirty Is a Dangerous Age, Cynthia*; *Monte Carlo or Bust*; *The Wrong Box*; *Those Darling Young Men in Their Jaunty Jalopies* or Paul Morrisey's recent remake of *The Hounds of the Baskervilles*, your first exposure to Dudley Moore may have been his anti-seductive striptease in desperate pursuit of Goldie Hawn's attentions in *Foul Play*. Or perhaps his desperate pursuit of Bo Derek in *10*. But almost certainly you've caught him in his starring role as the rich, drunken wastrel in *Arthur* who desperately pursues Liza Minnelli while being assiduously pursued himself by his moneyed airhead fiancée.

Prior to his film career, Moore was best known in the States as one-half of a comedy writing-performing team with fellow Englishman Peter Cook. Cook and Moore met in 1959, shortly after Dudley completed his studies at Magdalen College, Oxford. Friends connected with the Edinburgh Festival came up with the idea of making a comic Oxford-Cambridge revue an integral part of the proceedings, since such productions had long been an attraction on the fringes of the festival (hence the title *Beyond the Fringe*). The revue enjoyed a long run in London and New York.

The team also wrote and performed for British TV, co-authored films, appeared on Broadway in a second comedy review, released three "very obscene" comedy records, and then went their own separate ways for a few years. Dudley concentrated on such projects as a screenplay based on *The Joy of Sex*; his concept, which stiffed with the studio heads, was to write a scenario about a man in the throes of a mid-life sexual restlessness who begins to seek out fantasy women. He later wound up playing that role in *10*, which pleased him on several obvious levels.

"I don't ever plan to do a role that would tax me or that is a challenge; a role is difficult insofar as it's unnatural for me," says Moore, seated at the piano in his beachfront home in sunny Marina Del Rey, Calif.

He rises and ambles around the room, examining his own stride.

"I need an orthopedic doctor again," he says. "The way my boots are built now, I don't think there's enough support. I have to get measured up and make sure I'm terribly level, and then have some sort of plaster cast to make sure of the size of the lift, 'cause my foot's also about a half-inch shorter. I notice my left hip is down a little bit. I don't know if it's happened with age or what. It's not that noticeable, but the foot flicks in a bit when I walk. There's an operation where they break the knee and move it around.

"I don't think I would have done that now," he adds with a smirk. "It's a little late in the day for that, wouldn't you say?"

Asked to describe his long-time friend, agent Lou Pitt says, "Dudley tries to find new ways to fight old battles, and you cheer him on. Off camera, he's the same way." Pitt tells a story about Moore's reluctance one evening to order a large meal for himself from room service at New York's Sherry Netherland Hotel. So he didn't; he ordered dinner for two instead.

"When the waiter came," says Pitt, "it seemed obvious Dudley was alone, and they both felt rather awkward. Dudley got up and did what he apparently felt was best. He opened the bedroom door a bit and said, 'Honey! Dinner's on!' The waiter fell for it, laid the dinner all out happily, and left feeling comfortable, while Dudley had his feast. We could use more people like Dudley Moore. He rounds out the little rough spots."

The man Pitt's talking about is *47 years old*. He has had *18 years* of analysis and group therapy, and he constantly doles out honesty-is-the-only-policy homilies like: "A lot of people get very secretive and put a lot of trust in friends because they're afraid of what might be revealed; 'cause they're ashamed of who and what they are. But with feeling better about yourself, the desire for secrecy dwindles."

Clearly, it is no accident that most of Moore's characters are beggars at the banquet, so insecure that they usually only get out of bed in the morning to check that their pajamas aren't on backwards. People like this would long for an adversary relationship with the world if they could just wrangle an invitation to it. But it is not to be, so they eat alone and make feature films to get attention.

If you bust Moore on the great discrepancies between his advice and his own actions, he grows whiney. "Behind everything I feel is the fear of being abandoned, or being left behind. Of course, you can keep your secrets and *still* be left behind, so it really doesn't make any sense."

A lot of people love to tell war stories about time spent on a shrink's chaise lounge; big breakthroughs in self-realization, emotional moments of connection and renewal. When Dudley reveals his psychological foundations, the words sound solid; but think about them, and they turn into applesauce.

"Some say that therapy makes jerks humble," he says, "but the other end of feeling like a humble jerk is being a pompous jackass. Somewhere in the middle lies the truth of it. We're all perfect in the sense that we're products of our environment and our families. What we are and how we survive in the world is a perfect adaptation to our past and present situation. The big surprise for me in therapy is that you go in thinking you'll change and become something different, and you come out being more yourself."

In Moore's case, a musician. Indeed, he appears much more intrigued with his first love—music—than his acting, especially since he's reduced the latter to simple self-impersonation. He is an accomplished classical and jazz pianist, with numerous albums to his credit. He composes scores for the films in which he appears, and it is no coincidence that music figures prominently in the lives of most of his characters. Both George Weber in *10* and Arthur Bach were pianists who used the instrument as a sounding board and crying towel.

The Steinway Grand in the center of Dudley's living room is his catbird seat and sandbox—unquestionably the most important piece of furniture in the place. "There obviously was something more urgent about comedy than music, so one took precedence over the other," he says of his career's convolutions, staring down at the Steinway's bared teeth. "It was an act of survival. And then I became more acquainted on a daily basis with the techniques of getting someone to laugh."

As a result, he finds himself spending most of his life doing work which he never enjoyed in the first place.

"I never agonized over music," he explains. "I *did* with comedy; it always prompted so much soul-searching, it never came easy. I wanted to be loved and accepted by the world. I was melancholically disposed towards gaining love and friendship because I felt if I was myself, people would reject me because I was deformed. People assume that a comedian who's 5–foot-2 with a clubfoot has to be married to a sheep."

On the contrary. Moore has dated and/or married some of the most beautiful women in the world. Yet he seems bewildered and even disappointed that his height and his clubfoot have not hampered his love life. Just as his comments about his late father usually end in sour gibes, there is a bitter cast to his clipped jests about his romantic involvements.

Dudley purchased his beach house in Marina Del Rey several years ago with then-wife Tuesday Weld, from whom he is now divorced. "You'd have to be married to her to know what it's like," he says with a tight smirk. "Just wait your turn; there's plenty of time."

Before Weld, he was wedded to actress Susan Kendall. "That was in 1966," he says. "It lasted a couple of years. I got married to Tuesday in 1976 or '77, and we were separated about three years ago, so it seems that I can only take two years of marriage." He hopes to get considerably more mileage out of his relationship with Susan Anton (whom he has been seeing for two years) despite the fact that she is nine inches taller than he.

"Susan and I found it peculiar at first, but now it doesn't bother us at all," he demurs. "I enjoy the legginess of her and she enjoys the *squat runtedness* of me! She likes to put on my pants and see them halfway up her leg for a laugh, and then I'll put her bathrobe on. It's good; she always had to deal with her height too. I can't dip her on the dance floor; and I think she misses not having an arm 'round her shoulder, but what the hell, life isn't perfect."

Says Anton: "It aggravates the hell out of me that people emphasize the height thing in our relationship. I think people would be damned lucky to be in this position. I met Dudley on February 11, 1980, at the National Association of Theater Owners Awards; he was one of the hosts. I don't normally approach guys, but when he walked onstage, he made me laugh, and I hadn't had a hearty laugh in ages. I felt something and ran after him.

"He can meet you and get into you right away. He has great compassion, and that may be the benefit of all his years in therapy. We all go through things, and I've been able to get therapy through Dudley. Dudley taught me to confront things and accept my temper rather than accommodate other people. I used to think jealousness and possessiveness were bad things. I don't anymore."

The issue of jealousy is a sensitive one in the Moore-Anton household, just as it has been in Dudley's world for a good, long time. But for him it was initially precluded by a paralyzing shyness.

"Being a teenager was hell," he says. "I'm amazed I didn't have a heart attack during that period, wanting to approach a girl and not having the nerve. It was like that for all my school life—Oxford, too—and the idea of success attracted me because it was an introduction to people. They knew of you before you knew of them, and you could slip into an acquaintance more easily. I don't think I got through that crap till maybe three years ago, although it was obvious from the women I was with at the time that there was nothing wrong. I was getting to be with the women I really wanted."

Now that he's got them, however, he has to learn to function comfortably in their midst. Having spent decades poring through tomes on psychotherapy, philosophy and psychology, he was recently immersed in Gay Talese's *Thy Neighbor's Wife*, particularly the portion concerned with the "sexual commune," Sandstone.

"Er, Dudley," I venture, "I've gotta tell you that I was, well, almost embarrassed to find that your beachhouse is strikingly similar to the one in which your songwriting character in *10* did his composing. You and he have similar life styles, similar sexual anxieties. You once wrote and scored a British film called *Thirty Is a Dangerous Age, Cynthia*, about a lonely young man fearful of facing his 30s unattached. Shortly afterward, you, at 31, married for the first time. There appears to be a pattern in these congruities."

"Why, ahh, absolutely," Moore acknowledges with reluctance. "And I used myself very strongly in that character in *10*. I'm . . . *glad* you were embarrassed, because that tells me I've succeeded in the role."

But, I say, I wasn't embarrassed by the character, hapless as he was. "My embarrassment resulted from your resemblance to him."

"Well, I've brought my own fantasies into my life," he counters. "I feel, basically, that I can have what I want."

And what, in his wildest fantasies, does Dudley Moore desire?

"I'm not telling you," he says with a nervous laugh. I'm not a *complete* fool."

The next few months are likely to severely test Dudley Moore's knee-jerk self-deprecation. The critics are going to be watching very closely to see if the little guy can play straight man in a solemn tear-tugger like *Six Weeks*; his musical abilities will also come under scrutiny, since he composed the film score. And more strangers are sure to be traipsing through his living room asking him to play piano for them and explain who he really is.

So just exactly who—one last chance, fella—is he?

"I'm—"

There is a thunderous crash in the backyard, where a construction crew is unloading heavy equipment for use in renovation of the beachhouse next door.

"That's probably a good description of me," he says with a soft chuckle. "The sound of falling metal in the garden."

Dudley Moore may one day reminisce about that statement as the beginning of the big breakthrough.

Andy Kaufman's Bout with Broadway

"I did a good job as an evangelist in a movie called In God We Trust," said Andy Kaufman, reflecting on his win/loss tally in television and films as he walked around the red, white and blue boxing ring that was the centerpiece for the ill-fated Broadway show, Teaneck Tanzi, The Venus Flytrap. "Heartbeeps was terrible; I didn't do a good job and the movie was terrible!!"

Lapsing momentarily into his portrayal of The Referee in *Tanzi*, he bounds into the ring and begins testing the ropes for flexibility by throwing himself against them. "You want plenty of give," he exclaims, letting himself be flung slingshot-like onto the canvas, "and a mat that sounds hard as the body hits it but just has a firm bounce!"

Then Kaufman eased himself out of the ring, dusted off his blue flannel shirt, jeans, and hush puppies, and resumed his meek assessment of his feats and bad falls as an actor. "*Taxi*, it's hard for me to judge," he mused. "It's a good show but I did my best work with that Latka character five years before the show ever went on."

For the record, *Teaneck Tanzi* opened at the Nederlander Theater in New York City on April 20, 1983, and closed the same night. But then a similar fate often befell Kaufman's ultra-obnoxious Tony Clifton character—sometimes played by Kaufman in heavy makeup but also clandestinely assumed by comedy writer Bob Zmuda or Andy's brother Michael.

Few aspects of Kaufman's career could be taken at face value. While appearing at Carnegie Hall in 1979, Kaufman gave a seat on the stage ("the best seat in the house!") to his grandmother, and then revealed at the close of the two-hour program that "my grandma was played by Robin Williams"—who tore off his disguise as the crowd roared. Afterward, 2,800 members of the audience were escorted to waiting buses and taken down to the New York School of Printing to get milk and cookies—as promised—from Kaufman's real parents, Stanley and Janice Kaufman.

In December 1983, Andy's doctor told him he had lung cancer; it wasn't a put-on, although Kaufman may have believed, and others still believe, that it was. He died on May 16, 1984. If the man's own statements about his age could be believed (see the interview that follows), that would have made him 47, but more credible sources claim he was 35 when the end came. Then again, Kaufman could have gotten his nascency confused with that of Tony Clifton.

Kaufman's memory has been kept alive by fans like the band R.E.M., which composed the 1993 Top 30 hit "Man On The Moon" as a tribute to him, inserting footage of his Elvis impersonations in the music video for the song.

In addition, Kaufman's co-star on *Taxi*, Danny DeVito, announced he was developing a film biography of Andy through DeVito's Jersey Films production company, with Milos Forman said to be the likely director. Some fans hoped the picture's release might coincide with the denouement of an ominous vow by Kaufman to fake his own death and return on his birthday (January 17) in 1999.

THE INTERVIEW

LADIES AND GENTLEMEN! In this quiet corner of the Chelsea Tavern, ordering a weekday luncheon consisting of split pea soup, fettucini Alfredo, potatoes smothered in baked cheese, a double espresso with heavy cream on the side, a second order of split pea soup and extra croutons, and, "well, maybe something else in a minute, lemme think about it . . ." is Andy Kaufman pot-bellied, disheveled star of the new Broadway musical *Teaneck Tanzi, the Venus Flytrap* (billed as "a Comedy About Love and Wrestling"), and er, Intergender Wrestling Champion of the World!

"I've had 400 matches with women over a four- or five-year span, and I'm undefeated," Kaufman insists as he takes off his ratty brown overcoat and slumps down in his chair, addressing his assertions to the bemused waiter, the startled diners in the opposite corner of the crowded restaurant and, by extension, the immediate world. "After a few years of matches in professional arenas like the Chicago Amphitheater, doing regulation inter-gender wrestling on mats or in rings, I was awarded the world title by the Intergender Wrestling Commission and given a big championship belt!"

Whoa. Time out. The Intergender Wrestling Commission? Who's behind this organization? Where is it based?

"Oh, w-w-well I dunno," the abruptly meek Andy stammers, eyes as blank as buttons. "I don't know where they're based. All I know is that they gave me a belt and sanctioned the matches. I think they're based in Miami, Florida. You can phone them." (A later check showed no telephone listing for any such organization in Florida, or any other of a half-dozen states Kaufman also suggested.)

It's another typically obtruse/obtuse encounter with oddball "entertainer"— he prefers the term to that of "comedian"—Andy Kaufman, the addled Dadaist who broke into comedy in the early 1970s by lip-synching Mighty Mouse children's records and eating his supper on the stage of the Improvisation, the West Side comedy showcase. His peculiar performances led to guest shots on *Saturday Night Live*, imitating Elvis and reading aloud from *The Great Gatsby*, and eventually to the featured role of sex-starved, immigrant mechanic Latka Gravas in TV's *Taxi*. Though many find him funny, he correctly points out that he has never included a joke in any of his various acts. Indeed, his original audition for *SNL* consisted solely of an unrelentingly deadpan recital of the lyrics to "MacArthur Park"—twice.

Kaufman is presently unwelcome on the program. And while he still pops up on another NBC late-night staple, *The David Letterman Show*, crowd reactions have been muted since the evening he lumbered on with a convincingly cosmetic (it was Vaseline) runny nose to give a point-of-tears account of how his wife and kids had just left him, his career was in the dumps, and his spouse's lawyers were in hot pursuit as he scrounged for gigs at dinner theaters in the Midwest. He'd begun to panhandle in the Letterman audience when NBC security guards hastily escorted him out. "That was *planned*," he says as the first round of pea soup arrives. "I used to do that sob story routine at the Improv. If you examine what I do, you'll see not all of what I do is supposed to be funny. What I don't understand is why people say, 'What's so funny about this?' and get mad."

More recently, however, spectators have been wondering why Andy Kaufman supposedly pretends to get angry, and then expects them to find it amusing. The most celebrated incident was a 1981 episode of *Fridays*, ABC's fuzzy *SNL* replica, in which Kaufman declined, on-camera, to participate in the closing skit, cast and crew being goaded into a thoroughly authentic-looking donnybrook that saw producer Jack Burns taking a swing at the recalcitrant "entertainer."

When Andy isn't in the midst of a melee, he's usually deporting himself like an airhead ascetic, his appearance akin to an unmade flophouse mattress, his little-boy speech pattern so unnervingly modulated it registers like broken fingernails scraping a grammar school blackboard. And for someone who claims to be a three-hours-a-day devotee since 1968 of normally tranquilizing Transcendental Meditation, randy Andy has been growing increasingly contentious.

As a result, his landing of the role of the referee in *Teaneck Tanzi*, which opens April 14 at the Nederlander, probably couldn't have occurred at a more opportune moment. So what's the story behind his involvement in the production?

"Excuse me," he demurs contritely, after dispatching the waiter with a request for still more croutons."I think we should pause while I say a silent grace." He shuts his puffy eyes and bows his head for what seems an interminable TM trance—and may be yet another unctuous put-on. Even in repose, Kaufman arouses one's ire. He's an ideal choice for a wrestling referee, because you want to murder him.

"Andy had to audition for the role, just like everyone else," says Chris Bond, 37-year-old British director of *Teaneck Tanzi*, whose wife, Claire Luckham, wrote the script. "He did a script reading and then sent me videos of some of his wrestling matches. Although our so-called wrestling is rather carefully choreographed, I felt he was perfect for the referee because he has a natural rapport, so to speak, with the audience. And while there is a very detailed script, he still has opportunities for improvisation, as well."

Currently enjoying a successful run (as *Trafford Tanzi*) in London's West End, the play was created in the late 1970s. "Claire was intrigued by the dynamics of professional wrestling and had attended the matches," says Bond. "She felt that most women's roles in the British theater were generally a bit too passive, and she hit on the idea of a female superhero who also happened to be a wrestler."

First presented as *Tuebrook Tanzi, the Venus Flytrap*, in pubs and clubs in Liverpool in 1978, the play takes place entirely in the ring, the cast of characters singing, dancing and tusseling with each other as Tanzi settles a life-long litany of emotional scores. Her mother, father, boyfriend and others are each bounced off the ropes, slammed to the mat and pinned with a flurry of Irish Whips, Head Mares, Heel Picks and the fearsome Venus Flytrap. The cast of the American production features Caitlin Clarke and rock singer Deborah Harry alternating as Tanzi.

"We have alternates in the key roles because the play is extremely demanding physically," says Bond, talking in a dingy West Side rehearsal hall while cast members in sweat clothes rehearse a song ("Tanzi you're a peach/We were made for each other/Tanzi, Tanzi, you're so sweet . . .") in a red, white and blue platform ring. "We once tried in a London production to have one actress play Tanzi six times weekly, but it was too grueling. Deborah and Caitlin will each do it four times a week. It was a pleasant surprise when Debby tried out for Tanzi," Bond adds. "Turns out she's always been a big wrestling fan. We tossed her around a bit at the audition and she took her lumps well. All in all, we've got quite a nice team on our hands."

Back at the restaurant, Kaufman emerges from his prayer session. "So! It's been four weeks of rehearsal and I haven't been taking any baloney from my wrestlers," he says. "If anybody gets out of hand, I take a firm hand in settling things."

Providing it's part of the script?

"Maybe yes, maybe no!" he snaps as his main courses arrive. "I'm a champion, a wrestling great and I'm not like some little ref who can't handle the big feuds. . . ."

For those wishing to contest either the ring tactics of *Tanzi* cast members or the rulings of the ref, demonstrative audience participation reportedly will be encouraged. "I can handle 'em all," says Kaufman, who maintains that he was the brunt of unsportsmanlike conduct in April 1982, when 234–pound

Jerry Lawler subdued him in a Memphis exhibition match with a neck-crunching ploy called the Pile Driver. Andy wound up in the hospital and then spent several weeks in a neck brace. "Lawler used an illegal move, banned in Memphis," he says, "and I learned my lesson. Anyone who thinks wrestling is staged should have been in my position. I'm never going to wrestle a man again—*only* women."

The son of a retired costume jeweler from Great Neck, L.I., Kaufman grew up watching Bruno Sammartino, Skull Murphy and his hero, "Nature Boy" Buddy Rodgers, pummeling each other on the televised wrestling cards at Sunnyside Gardens. Andy likes to rapsodize about the high points in Rodgers' flamboyant career, and at such moments he seems most genuine, recalling a time before he himself had an image, however muddled, to protect.

Buddy Rogers, your boyhood hero, was the world wrestling champion until he lost his title to Bruno Sammartino in May 1963. I'm told Buddy's since become a personal pal of yours.

He's a good friend of mine. He managed me in one of my matches around December of 1979; it was a big match on *Saturday Night Live* that Buddy coached me for. I grew up in Great Neck, Long Island, and I used to watch wrestling from Sunnyside Gardens on TV and "Nature Boy" Buddy Rodgers was my favorite wrestler. "Handsome" Johnny Baron was also great because he was friends with Bobby Davis, who always dressed nicely in a tuxedo, was Buddy's manager and also managed the Graham Brothers.

I was at Madison Square Garden the night that Buddy lost the title to Bruno. He had beaten Bruno many times before that, but I think he was discouraged after that. The Bruno match only lasted 48 seconds, and it ended with a backbreaker. After that Buddy retired. Who knows, maybe he was injured. I never really talked to him much about it.

I started wrestling officially in April of 1978. My style is inspired and patterned as closely as I can after Buddy Rogers' style. His style was a scientific catch-fall approach. When he stopped wrestling I stopped watching it for about ten years.

There's a lot of people who have patterned themselves after him; many try to look like him, with his shiny blonde hair, and some even call themselves Nature Boy! But he was the first. A lot of them used his phrases: "I've got the brains," and "I am the greatest." I think we know a boxer who started using that second one. Muhammad Ali used Buddy Rogers' style, but he may not know it because he might have been borrowing from another borrower, like Georgeous George.

Also, Buddy Rogers was the man, I believe, who invented the Figure-Four Grape Vine, or Leg Vine, as he sometimes called it. Nobody could put it on faster. As a kid, I felt, "Any friend of Buddy's is a friend of mine. Any enemy of his is mine, too."

And Buddy fought everybody! He fought Killer Kowalski, whose big move was the Claw Hold—until they outlawed it. Kowalski also liked to try and break people's legs. The Figure-Four Grape Vine has broken some legs.

I've never hurt anyone and nobody's ever hurt me, except for the one time I wrestled that man down in Memphis. And that was when my neck was hurt with an illegal Pile Driver.

Speaking of your Intergender Wrestling Commission title and your undefeated status, I thought you were recently pinned in the mud by a woman during a West Coast match.

[*Aghast*] Never! What happened was I was a spectator at a mud-wrestling club in Los Angeles called Chippendales, and at the end of the night the audience drafted me to go into the mud. I was bluffing and I didn't want to get into the mud.

People think I'm involved in mud-wrestling and I'm not. I'm now strictly involved in intergender wrestling, which is straight wrestling on mats or in rings. I've done it professionally in professional arenas like the Memphis Coliseum and the Chicago Amphitheater.

The reason I'm associated with mud-wrestling is that I was drafted by the audience in that club and I bluffed and said, "The only way I will wrestle in mud is if all of the six ladies who wrestled tonight get into the mud with me, and I'll wrestle all six of them at once!" Meanwhile, they had all showered and dressed. But lo and behold, all six of them did change back into their suits and got into the mud with me. And I pinned ALL of them!

Now, the publicist for Chippendales was sitting there at ringside and what she did was encourage the photographers to take pictures of me, and the pictures they took were of me down, with the lady on top—which is bound to happen during a wrestling match. So what the club did was send the photos off to magazines and they published that I lost the match. That was completely a lie. I have never lost a match.

But I think that wrestling is the finest and oldest sport known to man. It's been around since the caveman, before the ball and the wheel were invented.

A lot of people perceive all wrestling as low-rent fakery.

I used to think that, but last year I wrestled a professional wrestler and I was in a hospital for three days after that. Anyone who thinks wrestling is staged should wrestle a professional.

The point in wrestling is to make the guy submit. My best hold is my headlock. I'm very proud of it, too. I defy anyone to get out of my headlock using a legal move. I had a cab driver the other night who said that no one could keep him in a headlock because he would use a cross-nose block. He stopped the cab, got out, and tried it on me, but it didn't work. I also defy anyone to put me in a headlock and keep me there.

What's your outlook on your character in Tanzi, The Referee?

The Ref is a guy who's been a loser for thirty years. He's been on the road promoting matches and now this is his big chance, the big time. He puts this show together on Broadway, but the only thing he knows how to do is promote wrestling matches so he puts on a wrestling show, because he doesn't know any better. He's a nice guy.

Everybody in the cast fights. The play is the story of a girl growing up to be a woman, and all her childhood tribulations, and it's told using the ring as a metaphor for her life. She wrestles with her father, her mother, her husband, her shrink, and settles emotional scores.

I'm an objective referee. I wanna make sure that if there's any wrestling to be done it will be done with an impartial guy in charge. It's a demanding role. Once in a while, when either the actors *or* the characters get out of hand, I will step in and I will not take any baloney from anybody.

It's hard to tell if this role is a departure from your career in comedy. Is it a step sideways, or a move forward?

[*Shrugs*] I'm not a comedian. I started out as a children's birthday party entertainer, and my act evolved from there. I never tried to be funny, though. But because people found things I did funny, they labeled me a comedian. But if you examine what I do, you'll see not all of what I do is supposed to be funny. People get mad sometimes and say, "What's so funny about this?" What they don't understand is that it's not supposed to be; it's supposed to be entertaining.

Since you originally intended to entertain children, what was your own child-hood like?

I was born January 17, 1937; I'm 46. My grandfather Paul used to buy me Elvis Presley records when I was about seven. Then in the summer of 1959 he bought me "Got The Feeling" by Fabian, "Mary Lou" by Ronnie Hawkins and "I Need Your Love Tonight" by Elvis Presley.

My hobbies besides wrestling were horror movies and rock and roll. Fabian was my favorite singer, and then Elvis. I chose Fabian over Elvis because he was the first guy I ever heard.

It's funny, if you hear a song—this is my theory—for the first time, it doesn't matter if it's the original or a copy, you're gonna think it's the best. See, when Elvis went into the Army, Fabian came on the scene, and that was when I really got into liking rock and roll. Fabian became my idol. I was very nervous and shy as a kid.

Immersed in memories from what was apparently a rather lonesome child-hood, Kaufman suddenly realizes he's late for rehearsal. He pulls his coat on as he vainly attempts to wolf down the rest of his food. Why did he order half the lunch menu?

"I don't get to eat again until 10 p.m. because I meditate on the dinner break," he moans. "The idea of going without food completely freaks me out."

Does Kaufman expect *Teaneck Tanzi* to spark new interest in his favorite sport?

"Uh-huh!"

Any other career plans for the future?

"When the play's through, I want to be in a good movie," he says, moving to go. "My last, *Heartbeeps*, wasn't. Also, I want to publish a novel I've been writing for 12 years about a guy named Huey who starts climbing a mountain at 19 and doesn't finish until he's very old. I've written a thousand pages and absolutely everything happens in it. It's the kind of book you see yourself in."

And how does Andy Kaufman ultimately see himself?

"Seriously?" he asks, pausing at the door. His brow wrinkles gravely. "Well, besides as a wrestler, I see myself as a possible successor to Buffalo Bob Smith, hosting a new version of *The Howdy Doody Show*. I know Buffalo Bob personally, and he says he thinks I could get the rights to the program. How do you think 'Buffalo Andy' would grab the kids?"

With a headlock, one assumes. But one hopes the new Clarabell would be able to rescue the poor tots with a flying Venus Flytrap.

"Listen," he counsels, sounding very protective of the mythic circus town of Doodyville. "Even kids in the Peanut Gallery know that if they were taught to wrestle there wouldn't be any more fighting. Wrestling is a gentle sport if you play by the rules. Whenever I've had an argument with somebody I've said, 'Let's wrestle it out!' No one gets hurt, and at the end we're both friends and everybody agrees, and it brings peace to the relationship."

Providing one's opponent, in or out of the Peanut Gallery, is willing to submit.

"Uh huh. The point in wrestling," he repeats, unsmiling, "is to make the guy *submit.*"

Julie Andrews:
The Sound of Musing

As far as Julie Andrews was concerned, her initial association with The Sound of Music was a joke—literally. A year
before she was cast as Maria in the screen edition of the Broadway
hit based on the life of Austrian postulant Maria Augusta von
Trapp, Andrews' 1962 TV special with friend Carol Burnett, Julie
and Carol at Carnegie Hall, featured a wicked parody of Music
titled "The Pratt Family of Switzerland." In the sketch, Julie performed a scathingly effective spoof of Mary Martin's starring role
in the stage show.

Across the half-century span of career, Andrews and her professional milieu have long been mistaken as breezy, anodyne and cloying, when it's actually been aggrieved, bumpy, and bittersweet. Wisely, she turned down the lead role of an ex-hooker in Richard Rogers and Oscar Hammerstein II's *Pipe Dream*, a stage adaptation of John Steinbeck's *Cannery Row* (which proved to be Rogers and Hammerstein's sole failure), opting instead to take the title spot in *Lady Liza*, the musical version of George Bernard Shaw's *Pygmalion*, which would gain fame under its final title, *My Fair Lady*.

Offered the lead in *The Sound of Music*, Andrews still feared the storyline was "awfully saccharine," but negotiators for 20th Century-Fox indicated they would reduce the level of "sugar" in her part. During the filming of *Music* in the Austrian Alps in June 1964, Andrews found the guitar-playing scenes in the mountaintop meadows to be so nerve-wracking that it took a belt of 100–proof schnapps from a farmer to steady her will. Local cow herders, angry with the pasture-disturbing artificial brooks and pseudo birch groves that Andrews traversed in the movie's opening, stabbed a pitchfork into the stream bed and drained it dry. Amid these difficulties, the real Maria von Trapp visited the cast on location, befriending Andrews (who later sang with her in several concerts) and even appearing as an extra during the fountain-in-the-city-square scene as Andrews sings "I Have Confidence."

A box office bonanza internationally when it was released in 1965, *The Sound of Music* bombed in Austria, where theater owners pulled it from circulation after three days, never to be seen again. Reasons cited included the absence of native songs, liberties taken with period costumes and locations and other stylized departures from two earlier German film productions, *Die Trapp Familie* and *Die Trapp Familie in Amerika*. But the central reason seemed to be its depictions of Nazi villainy in the country, fueling an outcry that spread to Germany, where headlines like "*Will Hollywood's Hate of Germany Never End?*" were widespread, prompting the Munich branch of 20th Century-Fox to excise the last third of the picture. (The offending German executive was fired and the footage was restored, but the unexpurgated version failed in Germany nonetheless.)

Andrews' decision in 1982 to star in the American film remake of *Viktor und Viktoria* (the 1933 picture conceived by Hans Hoemburg and written and directed by Reinhold Schünzel) seemed hazardous but it became the artistic return to form she'd sought for nearly two decades.

"There was a very petite lady who I met in my vaudeville days, she dressed up as a man, usually in tails," Andrews confided during the full day we spent together in Manhattan in '82. "I worked with her twice, and she was given to strutting, very proud, in a masculine voice. I first used that lady for a production number I did in *Star!* [1968], called 'Burlington Bertie from Bow,' and I dressed up as a man. Actually, *Star!* and *Victor/Victoria* were my toughest films, really.

"In all these departures from the norm, I do myself a lot of damage," she assured with a dark laugh, "but they're worth it."

MGM's *Victor/Victoria* gained Andrews a Golden Globe Award and an Oscar nomination as Best Actress, with six other Academy Award nominations. (But only Henry Mancini and Leslie Bricusse won, for Best Score.)

Presented with the customary pot as Woman of the Year by Harvard's Hasty Pudding Club, she wondered, "Is it all right if I throw up in it?"

After several films (*The Man Who Loved Women*, 1983; *That's Life!*, 1986; *Duet for One*, 1986; *A Fine Romance*, 1992), Andrews came back to Broadway during the 1995–96 season for a stage treatment of Victor/Victoria directed by husband Blake Edwards. It was a box office smash, lending excitement to an otherwise sleepy Broadway season. But when Andrews learned she was the only Tony Award nominee amongst the Victor/Victoria company, she calmed the crowd at the close of her 318th standing ovation in as many performances to announce, "Sadly, I cannot accept this nomination"—her third and likely last chance to ever earn theater's highest honor—"and prefer to stand instead with the egregiously overlooked . . . 75 other members of the Victor/Victoria family."

The show's cast and crew responded several days later by presenting her with a silver bowl from Tiffany's, and installing a five-foot mockup of the Tony medallion in her dressing room. In February 1997, Andrews was inducted into the Theater Hall of Fame.

After 722 performances, Andrews ended her Broadway run on Sunday, June 8, 1997, as all assembled, including the entire audience, serenaded her with "Edelweiss." Actor Christopher Plummer (appearing nearby in the play *Barrymore*), stepped in by surprise to lend his voice, much as he had during the filming of *The Sound of Music*'s "Edelweiss" scene in August 1964. Andrews burst into sobs.

THE INTERVIEW

THE CURTAINS OF THE 1930's Paris night club part, and there, on the stepped pedestal, is the sequined star of the show, a dazzlingly beautiful woman, aristocratic in bearing, but alluring as the pit band slithers into the opening production number, "Le Jazz Hot." The music is subtly suggestive, the elegant woman slowly succumbing, as a qualmish reserve is quietly stripped away. Her trim, athletic body is well-suited to the elastic tempos of the sinuous song-and-dance routine, and as the show mounts to a climax, the stirred audience applauds wildly.

The star steps to the apron of the stage, flashing a generous smile as the crowd thunders on. But then the smile fades, she lifts her hand to her hairline and curtly rips her female wig from her head to reveal that she, it seems, is a he. The fans are shocked, stumped, stunned into momentary silence by the gender ruse, and then they rise for a standing ovation.

Having completed the ritual that ends all female-impersonation acts, the star stiffens in the wake of the applause, his mouth a tight slit, his eyes glowering fiercely. If not for the sake of his dignity, his face would contort with pain and contempt for *her* admirers, those who were fooled and entertained by a shallow disguise. The game is up, but nobody really wins, because the star is loved not for who he is but for who he isn't. Yet "he" in this case *is* actually a she, actress Julie Andrews, taking the part of a singer who's down on her luck and who must pretend to be a man pretending to be a woman in order to survive.

It is a powerful scene in an intriguing movie, *Victor/Victoria*. This film, directed by the star's husband, veteran film sophisticate Blake Edwards, features make-believe within make-believe within make-believe, in a sequence almost too disorienting to describe. But its impact on the star was direct. Months after the movie was completed, Andrews recalls the moment when she had to reveal who she wasn't in order to get the most positive response from her public. Again, the eyes fill with a dark fire, the mouth turns into the same, tight slit.

"Yes, the scene," says Julie Andrews, her voice trembling ever-so-slightly, "brought out *strong* feelings in me."

Radiant in a shimmering white silk dress, waiting outside the Waldorf Towers in Manhattan for her limousine, Julie Andrews stands out in the steel-blue twilight like a swan in a coal cellar. Her squarish, unlined face is cold and rigid with expectancy, but as the car slips into view, she relaxes, sighs, and displays perfect teeth as she giggles nervously. Oblivious to the consternated passers-by as she enters the car, she talks about a five-hour photo session shot by Irving Penn the previous day for a fashion magazine layout—elegant promotion for *Victor/Victoria*.

"It flipped me out," she says, almost choking on her own laughter. "They had conducted all these elaborate fittings for the clothes I was to wear—both male and female duds, of course—and this $7,000 Galanos gown, an original that had been flown in especially for the session, was much too small for me. Irving Penn says, 'Aw, what the heck!' and wraps it around my neck as a scarf. Wait'll Mr. Galanos gets a load of his $7,000 muffler!"

The last remark gets a hearty laugh from Julie's entourage, consisting of her personal secretary; a hairdresser; her manager and his wife; a publicist; Julie's daughter, Emma Kate, a buxom, vivacious redhead in her twenties, wearing snug black leather pants and a tight sweater; and Emma's boyfriend, who's a dead ringer for Timothy Hutton. If the laughter lingers a little too long, it's because the limo's anxiety-ridden passengers are grateful for even the smallest opportunity to relieve the mounting tension.

Julie and company are en route to NBC studios in Rockefeller Center for her guest shot on *The David Letterman Show*, the standard breezy chatter-*cum*-film-clip plug that has become a numbing rite on late-night talk shows. The star is a little edgy this evening because of the high stakes rolled in *Victor/Victoria*, a good-natured but hardly guileless comedy in which Julie's ruse—to convince *tout le Paris* that she is really a young Polish count with a crystal-shattering voice—is inspired by an unemployed gay cabaret croon-er named Carole "Toddy" Todd (Robert Preston). Based on Reinhold Schünzel's 1933 German musical-comedy miniature, *Viktor und Viktoria*, the film is the latest effort by Edwards (who directed five of Julie's last six movies) to provide his script-starved spouse with what she admits may be her "last stab" at commercial acceptance for "quite a spell." On this late-winter night, *Victor/Victoria* is still two weeks away from release, and Andrews, of course, has no idea that it's on the verge of becoming her biggest commercial and critical hit since the distant days of *Mary Poppins* and *The Sound of Music*.

Julie's title role in *Victor/Victoria* comes in the wake of some skimpy recent credits: a two-line cameo as a frumpy maid in *The Return of the Pink Panther* that ended up being cut; strong but subordinate appearances in *10* and *S.O.B.* (the latter featured her infamous breast-baring scene); and the unfortunate 1980 remake of *Little Miss Marker*. In *Victor/Victoria*, Julie obviously identified, to great effect, with the unemployed Victoria Grant, who must compromise her sexual identity to display her talents.

"With true female impersonators, the surprise is always when all the fluffiness comes off—and you see that there is muscle, an Adam's apple, hair on the chest," she says evenly. "I was supposed to be a slight fine-boned young man in my deception, so the rather hard look I shot out at the crowd after I tore off my wig was the only way I could reveal myself as something else than a crowd-pleasing female. It showed a rage born of

'Fooled you, didn't I?' defiance, a kind of 'Do you love me *now*?' aggressiveness."

During her first golden era in the midsixties, Julie was a notoriously contrary interviewee who once let a London newspaperman sit in her Hollywood publicity office for three days before she finally granted him an interview. (Their talk lasted seven minutes) In those days, she had a $70,000 apartment on the Paramount lot, complete with a special den where the then-five-year-old Emma Kate could nap, but the lavish quarters came with a hitch: hit movies, thank you. They failed to materialize, however, and Ms. Andrews was eventually asked to vacate the premises. While she never fell as far as Victoria, careerwise, or became as compromised as Victor, she's now allowing her anger over the indignities accompanying her box-office decline to show: "Success is bankable, talent is disposable," she says.

One senses another quality in her present uncharacteristically *un*crisp deportment, a quality that's a good deal more appealing. It is a tentative humility and acceptance that she's known failure, and springing from that acknowledgment, a certain approachability. As we speed toward NBC studios, our haste is merely a manifestation of the chauffeur's zeal; for a brief interval that may not come soon again, Julie is in no hurry, and her legendary guard is down. Weeks later, while reading Vincent Canby's adoring review of *Victor/Victoria* in *The New York Times*, in which he urged moviegoers to "Get ready, get set, and go—immediately" to see the film, one thought back on the day spent with Julie Andrews and realized she exposed an aspect of her nature almost certain to be submerged again in the hoopla following her big comeback.

At Rockefeller Center, a modest but unruly contingent of Julie Andrews fans is clustered in a tight phalanx before the NBC studio elevators. Walking toward them, she grabs my arm firmly, commandeering me as a chaperone.

"A good man's hard to find," she whispers with mock-sternness, preparing herself for a dash through the demanding group. We make it up to the studios with just minutes to spare before air time. Julie takes her place before the camera and is introduced by the gangly, gap-toothed Letterman, who proceeds to announce that her performance in *Victor/Victoria* somehow reminds him of one of the Smothers Brothers. Unsteady, she rears back, regarding Letterman with confusion and concern as the show breaks for a commercial. He leans over and whispers in her ear. After two more commercials (and much more conversation about her "great teeth" and the family home in Gstaad, Switzerland, where she and Blake's natural offspring and two adopted Vietnamese children now reside), Julie and entourage are back in her dressing room, with everyone wondering what Letterman whispered to her regarding the puzzling Smothers Brothers remark.

"It was bizarre," she says. "He said that one of the Smothers Brothers—he couldn't remember which—was too pretty to be a man. I told him, 'Leave it alone! Don't say something like that when we come back on the air! With this damned film I've got out, people are confused enough about all this gender business already.'"

We get up to leave, Julie leading the way, and NBC staff and crew press in to shake her hand and offer respectful kisses on the cheek. Passing the makeup room, Mr. Rogers, a tweedy refugee from his kiddy *Mr. Rogers' Neighborhood* show, spies her and literally begs for a brief audience.

"You *dear thing*, you *lovely thing*," he coos, stroking her hand. "You've brought so much joy to so many."

Julie thanks him, the fixed grin on her face wilting rapidly before his unctuous praise. She exits and is almost free of all well-wishers, when who should step out of a doorway but button-eyed anticomic Andy Kaufman. In his uniform of ironed blue jeans, pressed white shirt, and billowy makeup tissues tucked into his collar, Andy looks like the court jester in a psycho ward. And some would wonder if the resemblance isn't more than accidental, considering his extremely convincing weekly portrayal of a timid, sex-crazed immigrant mechanic on ABC's sitcom *Taxi*, as well as his repeated challenges—sometimes accepted—on *Saturday Night Live* to wrestle any woman in the audience.

If indeed Andy Kaufman is as loosely wrapped as he seems, and if this walking time bomb explodes in the vicinity of poor Mary Poppins, the ensuing scenario could be too grotesque to contemplate.

Meekly, as if dumbstruck, Andy slowly extends his pudgy hand. "Nice to meet you," Julie responds, waiting patiently for some sort of reply.

Silence. Andy is speechless. NBC security people huddle in close, fearful.

Andy stands gaping, seemingly devouring Julie with his eyes. Maybe this is some form of a put-down. Then again, he could have just fallen asleep, eyes wide, and standing up.

"Hokay, I've got to be going now," Julie says eventually with friendly finality. She pulls away from Kaufman's catatonic grip.

Our party is in the elevator, murmuring pensively about what a blockbuster *Victor/Victoria* is "virtually preordained" to be, when Julie Andrews breaks in with a query.

"Tell me now, why do you suppose Andy didn't challenge me to wrestle?"

The group pauses, waiting for Julie to answer her own question.

"I'll tell you why," says the star, with a mischievous grin. "He looked me in the eyes, saw beyond the stereotype, and knew that at least one side of me, either Victor or Victoria, would enjoy it *faaar* too much."

Could be. But this admission raises more questions than it answers. Which side of her might actually revel in the experience, and which side would recoil from it? Subtle male and female shadings of personality aside, the world has been trying to figure out the hidden dimensions of this actress for some time now, and Julie's own attempts at showing us her inner self have been mighty inconclusive. For years she's tried to shed layers of her prim screen persona, only to reveal more flawless Limoges beneath. But at forty-six, Julie Andrews says she is one performer who intends to keep "going wrong," that is, striving to ignore her static, stale image as Maria Von Claptrapp, until she finally generates a more vivid, authentic persona.

"I'm still seen as wholesome and too saccharine," she tells me with controlled petulance as we sit in her suite at the Waldorf Towers. Julie is pouring herself a spot of tea from a small, plump porcelain pot. "Obviously, *Mary Poppins* and *The Sound of Music* haunt me to this day—but I feel that I was typecast because of the salability of that image, and not because of any estimation, for better or worse, of my range."

She adjusts her smart gray skirt and purple silk blouse and lightly clicks the spiked heels of her cream-colored boots together as she seats herself before the fireplace.

"My second film, *The Americanization of Emily* [filmed between *Poppins* and *Music*], was about a woman who slept around a lot and behaved like a tramp, so my so-called prissy image should have been shattered then," she says, sighing and sipping her tea. "But for some reason, it wasn't. My screen departures from sweetness and light didn't alter my public persona because they didn't make much money or find an audience.

"Meanwhile," she says, smirking with indignation, "I'm the same disreputable lady I've *always* been."

Julie is fond of making such cracks to disarm—or rattle—listeners. A roguish Richard Burton, her co-star on Broadway, in *Camelot*, once phoned her during the show's run to blurt: "I hear you said you were the only leading lady I hadn't slept with! I don't think you should say those awful things about me!"

"Richard," she came back sweetly, "do you think I'd want *that* sort of thing to get around?"

She's also fond of raunchy asides, such as the one she shared with the late socialite-writer Helen Lawrenson while the two women were on the set of *Star!* nibbling a box lunch under the baking Riviera sun.

"Oh, well," offered Andrews wryly, as she peeled a piece of fruit, "nothing like a hot banana—as the actress said to the bishop." She then apologized for the tacky sexual quip, explaining, "It just slipped out—*as* the actress said to the bishop."

Julie's not playing it for laughs, though, when I ask about *S.O.B.*, Edwards's brazen parody of his wife's professional predicament, in which she both flashed her breasts and exposed her rump. "It didn't faze me in the slightest," she says bluntly. Since it took her husband ten years to complete the film, she says she originally thought, "This probably isn't going to ever be made, so I'll consider the concept of being bare-breasted and bare-bottomed later."

Her lips says she wasn't bothered, but her steely gaze poses a pointed, "What of it?!" Julie is a stunner when she's shooting off sparks. The fiery eyes take on luminescent acuity; the sharply angled lineaments grow taut with a ferocious magnetism, and the torso, every bit as lean and shapely as that of an athletic coed (skeptics may reflect upon the bedroom scenes with Dudley Moore in *10*), tenses with a sinewy seductiveness. Clearly, times have changed, Julie with them. Assailed by journalists over the years for the "hollow air-hostess charm" undercutting her natural appeal, she has been called one of show business's "prime purveyors of delusory pap." Maybe so, she now concedes, but she worked "damn hard" to win the title.

In 1953, eighteen-year-old Julie was spotted in *Cinderella* at the London Palladium and awarded the role of Polly in the well-received Broadway production of *The Boy Friend*. While in New York, she did a TV musical with Bing Crosby and then accepted the mottled Cockney mantle of Eliza Doolittle opposite Rex Harrison's Henry Higgins in Broadway's *My Fair Lady*. Harrison was against this casting, insisting that Andrews certainly wasn't the actress he'd select as a co-star. She was much too wooden to play her part, he insisted, and this claim seemed justified when Julie began to stumble over the subtleties of Eliza's metamorphosis from gutter snipe to lady. "You're playing this like a girl guide," director Moss Hart would rant as opening night neared. And although Andrews went on to embody Eliza for three-and-a-half years on Broadway and in London, the star herself admits, "I never got that part under control." In the course of the run, she did, however, get her life together— Andrews found a cure for the "great, crushing loneliness" that came of living on the wrong side of the Atlantic by marrying British set and costume designer Tony Walton, whom she'd first met in England while she was a child star.

One fateful night, when Julie was starring in her next Broadway hit, *Camelot*, Walt Disney appeared backstage to ask if she'd consider playing P. L. Travers's

Mary Poppins, but she put Disney off, certain she'd be picked for the peach picture of the year: *My Fair Lady*. Instead, she lost out to an actress whose singing had to be dubbed, Audrey Hepburn. Thus jilted, Julie reluctantly consented to do *Mary Poppins*, and soon after this film became the hit of the decade, Twentieth Century-Fox offered her $1 million to play another, only slightly less exotic governess in *The Sound of Music*. Julie had her sweetest revenge when production difficulties and scheduling strategies conspired to force the release of *Lady*, *Poppins*, and *Music* at roughly the same time. *Lady* did extraordinarily well, but Julie's movies were box-office bonanzas, and she was suddenly, literally, the biggest star in the world (including Hong Kong, where *The Sound of Music* was renamed *Fairy Music Blow Fragrant Place, Place Hear*).

She won an Oscar for Best Actress for *Poppins* in 1965; her triumph completely eclipsed Hepburn in *My Fair Lady* ("My thanks to Jack L. Warner," she jeered in her acceptance speech, "for making all this possible"), and $1 million immediately became her rock-bottom fee. But she didn't relish the thought of going through her acting life as the world's wealthiest singing wet-nurse and pleaded for scripts that transcended Hollywood's rapidly narrowing vision of her scope.

The professional lift Andrews had every reason to expect and hope for did not, for mysterious reasons, occur. Blame it on haste, distress, or both, but her next six films, *Torn Curtain*, *Hawaii*, *Thoroughly Modern Millie*, *Star!*, *Darling Lili* and *The Tamarind Seed*, all seemed more like differently flavored confections than pithy possibilities for Andrews to show new dimensions. (The late Alfred Hitchcock had to defend his motives for casting her in *Torn Curtain*, a sexy spy drama, by saying, "But don't you see the attraction? She's a blonde, and blondes make the best victims. They're like virgin snow, which shows up the bloody footprints." Andrews herself advised friends to avoid the film altogether.)

It was while she was working on *Star!* that she and Tony Walton, fed up with their constant career-triggered estrangements, all but ended their seven-year marriage with a formal separation. At this point Julie began dating the notoriously cynical Edwards, who had once dismissed her as "so sweet, she probably has violets between her legs."

"The first time I saw him," she says, "I remember thinking, 'There's a *very* attractive man across the room,' but we were both married at the time. I got a phone call from his office one day, saying that he would like to talk to me about a project, *Darling Lili*. He came out to the house, explained his concept, and asked if I would be interested. Professionally and romantically, things kind of started from there."

In 1968, during the development of *Darling Lili*, Julie and Tony Walton divorced and she moved in with Edwards. "It was our kids who indicated that it would be easier on them if we married," says Julie. She and Emma Kate, her daughter by Walton, had been sharing Blake's Beverly Hills house with his two children from a previous marriage, Geoffrey and Jennifer, and the brood finally banded together to pronounce the arrangement nerve-racking and to petition for a wedding.

"We married with much fear and trepidation," says Julie.

"I never thought it would last, frankly. We took it one day at a time, and we've been doing that ever since—for twelve years."

As the newlyweds watched *Darling Lili* slide into the dumper, they realized that their nerves were also seriously frayed, and both embarked on five years of analysis. Julie dropped out of the movie business for four years, and apart from her work in the early seventies on the short-lived *Julie Andrews Hour* for ABC, she stopped singing. "I have never found singing easy or enjoyable," she says. "I think I resist finding pleasure in it, probably because I was plunged into a professional life at such a desperately early age."

Born Julia Elizabeth Wells on October 1, 1935, in the quaint London suburb of Walton-on-Thames, Andrews was four when her natural father and her mother, Barbara, were divorced. Ted Wells, a schoolteacher who taught subjects as diverse as ironworking and English, remained close to Julie and her younger brother, John, usually spending half of each summer vacationing with them." I didn't see as much of him as I would have liked," she recalls, "but what I got was quality time. He's responsible for the saner part of my nature. Everything that was real and good, *he* gave me."

When Julie's mother, a piano accompanist, remarried a Canadian-born tenor, Ted Andrews, he began giving his stepchild vocal lessons "in order to get close to me." She resisted, regarding him as "an overpowering man built like Burl Ives, whose very size frightened me." But Ted Andrews was astonished by her formidable voice and bullied the child into joining his and her mother's modest act in order to beef up the gate. Julie debuted at ten, standing on a beer crate to reach the microphone she shared with her parents.

"I missed the real heyday of the music hall," she says of the era that saw her earliest performances. "It was on its way out by the time I got involved. I used to love to watch all the acts from the wings, but to be honest, the scene was horribly seedy a good deal of the time and the digs were hell, terrible boardinghouse after terrible boardinghouse. I resented my stepfather for bringing me into the act he had with my mother. He made all the decisions; he sold me. But he made me hang on to my talent."

When the London blitz began, the Andrews family moved to Kent, Julie was given her stepfather's name ("But I still feel more Wells than Andrews"), and the family launched a public-relations campaign to get attention for their child star-to-be. "They said my voice was discovered in an air-raid shelter when I stood up and sang for the poor, lonely, frightened people, but that's just a load of bull."

Two years later, her appearance at the Hippodrome in London (engineered by the ambitious Ted) permanently destabilized Julie's childhood rearing. Her mother took her out of the tranquil Woodbrook Girls School in Beckenham so Julie could continue touring and nixed suggestions that she attend the Royal Academy of Dramatic Arts, opting instead for a tutor. These memories still awaken some resentment in Julie, who was made to work too hard, too soon.

Through the hotel windows, a bright copper sun sinks behind the jagged skyline. Julie leans forward on the couch in her suite and begins to talk intently about her years of analysis. "I've always had to fight like crazy with, and catch up to, the good things that have happened to me in my life. I felt, ultimately, that I must fish or cut bait, and to do that, to become more adult and admit I was responsible for myself, only came about through analysis. And I didn't embark on that until my early thirties—after, of course, my biggest successes.

"The central battle in life seems to be communication, between countries, between diplomats, between husbands and wives. It's very hard to be honest and to say how you feel all the time. I find it extremely difficult. Shall I be tactful or shall I hurt someone with my true thoughts? It is a question I . . . continually *wrestle* with."

Her voice wavers as she completes this frustration-filled monologue, and then she continues, her tone growing softer and still more introspective. "Analysis has been a form of religion for me—no, it's taken the place of religion for me. My decision to undertake it came about as a result of a tremendous emotional build-up; the events in my life were incredibly positive, but I was not enjoying any of them. There I was in the sixties, having enormous success, but I wasn't happy, didn't understand why, and felt I was in an awful mess. I desperately needed some answers, and analysis seemed to be the best way of providing some for myself.

"Self-love, to revise my earlier statement somewhat, *is* my religion. So much evil and pain seems to come from thwarted emotion, small-mindedness, not being able to open your head to things—which comes from fear, largely of yourself and how you'll react to new information and situations. Analysis chucks out a lot of garbage and helps you get down to essentials."

One of the essential facts that Julie found she had been concealing from herself was an anger stemming from many sources: The actress raged because she was coerced into show business and forced to undergo grueling tours while still a child; because she was torn even further from her scattered roots every time she reached a new professional plateau; and, finally, because she was acclaimed as the cinema's queen of squeaky-clean callowness, only to be ridiculed soon afterward as a fossil from a naive, fanciful past. Behind her back, a careless Christopher Plummer took to calling Julie's singing in their mutual box-office gold mine "the sound of mucus," and another co-star described working with this by-now justifiably defensive actress as "like being hit over the head every day with a Hallmark card."

The vulnerability Julie so carefully hides from her press and public did surface in a children's book the star originally wrote for Jennifer, Edwards's daughter. The story Julie penned was, not surprisingly, about an orphan. *Mandy*, which was published in 1971 to excellent reviews, ends with the following passage:

> Mandy experienced a great warm feeling. She realized that never again would she go through long nights of aching sadness. There would be no more depressions that she couldn't understand. At last she had a home and a family and people to love and be loved by. She had found what she had been looking for all her life.

"I wrote that book off the top of my head," Julie says somberly. "Just the first things that came to mind."

Julie and Blake later adopted two Vietnamese orphans after friends Andre Previn and Mia Farrow suggested an adoption agency in Saigon. "Blake and I weren't having any success having kids of our own together," Julie says, "and we wanted children very badly." Adds the actress's long-time friend, Carol Burnett: "As a woman, one of Julie's greatest acts of courage was to adopt those orphaned infants with Blake. She was so devoted to them you completely forgot she wasn't their natural mother . . . and she gave up years of her professional life to care for them."

Thanks to *Victor/Victoria*, Julie Andrews is back in public favor again, and we have some fresh images in our minds when we think of her. Now the talk is of what the actress is doing with her talent, instead of why she bothered at all. "Blake felt the film could make a statement about homosexual liberation and how people feel about their sexuality across the board," Julie says, "but also it says something about the liberation of the inner self. The hardest thing for me in the picture was figuring out who I was, when. To be one thing while conveying another was, I guess, a good exercise—no, an *important* exercise for me. Even if I did get very unglued about it from time to time."

Timing and proper self-imagery are problematic in show business, where one can pick up the newspaper the morning after *Victor/Victoria* opens and find *New York Times* critic Vincent Canby praising you for "suggesting a sort of fresh-air version of Marlene Dietrich."

And even when you try to calculate your recklessness, the best laid plans can go awry. To illustrate, Andrews recounts a prank she attempted in the early 1960s with the help of Carol Burnett, another "good woman gone wrong."

Lyndon Johnson had recently been inaugurated and Julie was in a Washington hotel room, waiting for Mike Nichols, her director, in a musical review to be performed that night at the White House. Waiting with Julie was co-star, Burnett. Bored as they lounged about in their bathrobes, the two women got a little giddy. Says Julie: "We decided to pull a stunt on Mike to blow his mind."

Eventually, Nichols phoned from the lobby, saying he was on his way up to their rooms. Still in their bathrobes, the two women rushed out to the elevator and decided, after some "frantic brainstorming," to position themselves in front of the doors in a passionate embrace.

At the crucial instant, the doors opened and out stepped Lady Bird Johnson, accompanied by a contingent of Secret Service men. The First Lady and her retinue hustled past the bizarre floor show as the elevator headed down to the lobby again.

"With little left to lose at that point," says Julie, "we made one more attempt, and sure enough, out stepped Mike Nichols, who stopped, looked blandly, said 'Oh, hi girls,' and then sauntered past us into the suite." ("Julie is much bawdier in her humor than people give her credit for," said Carol Burnett when I asked her about this incident. "What would seem vulgar coming from me is often elegant when she does it. But the kinky elevator spectacle was all *her* idea, just to set the record straight.")

Up to now, Julie's sense of fun has been largely private, but no longer—now she may be expected to compete with Lily Tomlin, Dyan Cannon, Sally Field, Bette Midler, Goldie Hawn, and former co-conspirator Carol Burnett as a strong comic actress. Eventually, though, Andrews will probably have to exercise these newly discovered gifts on her own, without the emotional protection offered by her husband's direction.

"My recent departures from 'type'—in *S.O.B.* and *Victor/Victoria*—were all provided by Blake," she admits. "He knows me better than anyone, and he *knows* I have an unrealized potential in me for less-than-pristine performances."

"It's a delicate position that Julie and Blake are in," adds Robert Preston. "Blake is going to be hard-pressed to go further with image-busting efforts on his wife's behalf after *Victor/Victoria*."

The obvious next step is for Julie to fly a little higher by herself. Says she: "One of the by-products of analysis is the realization that there's only one you, now and forever, so you should like yourself enough to be all you can be. I found myself caring a great deal about my character in *Victor/ Victoria*—the dilemmas, the depressions, and the good times the character achieved. And frankly, I find myself caring quite a bit more about myself these days.

"But then I have to. It's been an awfully long time since *Mary Poppins*, God help me."

Network Television

Marie Osmond:
Avé Marie

"**D**o you want to go to the store with me?" asked the svelte and doe-eyed Marie Osmond late in the spring of 1977. "We don't have my secret ingredient."

Osmond was a case study of a restive American girl in quest of cheese-cake, driving to her local supermarket to purchase cherry filling for the dessert she was personally preparing for her guest, while also bubbling about the current Top 40 pop fare by Linda Ronstadt and the sleek, image-altering dresses designer Bob Mackie had created for Marie to wear in the new season of her highly rated TV show.

"This is my time to listen to the radio!" she giggled conspiratorially as she stepped on the gas, turning up the volume on Ronstadt's "Someone To Lay Down Beside Me," and then asking "What do you think of my little car? It's cute, isn't it?"

The young woman behind the wheel was a picture of coquettish aban-don—until we returned home to find Marie's gray-haired father quietly fum-ing, phone in hand, telling us he just dialed the police and was considering giving them the license plate number of Marie's new car, advising them to put out an all-points bulletin to track it down.

"We were getting quite concerned," he explained coolly as we met him at the front door and then hurried past into the kitchen. "My daughter doesn't usually go off on her own." And yet, career-wise, Marie would eventually be compelled to do just that. The *Donny and Marie* variety show, hosted by the devoutly Mormon sister and brother team of Marie and Donny Osmond, aired on ABC-TV from January 23, 1976, to January 19, 1979. But the world would grow weary of the Osmond duo's careful wholesomeness, even as Marie was chomping at the bit of her family's religion-steeped conservatism. A change seemed all but ordained.

At the time of these interviews, conducted during a week-long stay with the Osmonds at their condominium complex in Provo, Utah, Donny and Marie were doing well with a hit single, their prim recasting of the Marvin Gaye and Tammi Terrell soul scorcher "Ain't Nothing Like the Real Thing." However, civil rights groups were growing increasingly impatient with the Mormon creed the Osmonds embraced, since it barred African-Americans from rising within the ecclesiastical ranks of the Church of Latter-Day Saints. Get real, raged many black activists, or else.

Luckily, the Lord according to Mormonism works in strange and conve-nient ways. In 1978, the same year Donny and Marie Osmond released the *Winning Combination* album [with its Top 40 hit, "(You're My) Soul and Inspiration"], as well as the soundtrack to their movie, *Goin' Coconuts* (which boasted tunes like "You Never Can Tell"), the Church of Latter-Day Saints announced a timely new "revelation" overturning its explicit policy forbidding black men from being appointed to even the most humble of offi-cial positions in the Church's hierarchy.

Besides making the wider non-Mormon world slightly more amenable to the blue-eyed R&B of the true-believing Osmonds, this move enabled their Church to mount a wave of missionary activity in Africa and Brazil. It also helped open the way for Marie Osmond to persevere in prime-time TV, embarking in December 1980 on her own one-hour *Marie* variety outlet (which would continue in various time slots until September 1981).

As for the Osmonds, the family act that had been the springboard for Donny and Marie's success formally disbanded in August 1980. But by 1982, four of the Osmond brothers had regrouped to record country music over the next four years for, in succession, Elektra, Warner Bros. and EMI Records, while Donny inhabited the title role of a revival of George M. Cohan's *Little Johnny Jones* on Broadway, the show closing after one performance at the Alvin Theater. Donny and Marie appeared in Hawaiian Punch TV commercials. Jimmy Osmond, meantime, became a successful concert promoter, involved in major international tours by Prince and Michael Jackson.

Marie co-hosted TV's *Ripley's Believe It or Not* series with Jack Palance for the 1985–86 season and issued four country albums on Capitol/Curb between 1985 and 1989 (*There's No Stopping Your Heart*, *I Only Wanted You*, *All in Love*, *Steppin' Stone*), while notching No. 1 country singles with "Meet Me In Montana" (with Dan Seals), "There's No Stopping Your Heart" and "You're Still New To Me" (with Paul Davis).

Donny signed with Capitol Records and achieved a No. 2 pop hit from his *Donny Osmond* album in 1989 with "Soldier of Love," plus a No. 13 chart success with "Sacred Emotion." His subsequent *Eyes Don't Lie* record resulted in the No. 21 single, "My Love Is a Fire." In 1997 came his *Christmas at Home* album and the bonus *Four EP* with its single "The Echo of Your Whisper."

Jimmy rejoined the Osmond Brothers, now headquartered at the Osmond Family Theater in Branson, Missouri. Donny, a father of four, returned to the stage in the '90s, touring successfully in *Joseph and the Amazing Technicolor Dreamcoat*, Andrew Lloyd Webber's interpretation of the tale of Joseph of Egypt. Marie, a twice-married mother of six, starred on Broadway in 1997–98 as Anna in *The King and I*.

In August 1997, Columbia Tristar Television Distribution announced Donny and Marie Osmond would co-host a daytime talk and variety show for the 1998–99 season.

Twenty years prior, in 1977, Marie recalled the inception of the original *Donny and Marie* program. "Fred Silverman [then ABC-TV's programming chief], he saw us on *The Mike Douglas Show*," she said. "We were co-hosting, the two of us, and he said, 'Get me those kids.' ABC had approached us quite a few times before about an Osmonds show but we just didn't feel the time was right yet. I think people can identify with two people better than eight."

As for the quality of the talk on shows such as *Mike Douglas* or *Donny and Marie,* she added, "I try to know as much as I can but I think opinions should be left as opinions. We're entertainers, not politicians."

THE INTERVIEW

HERE COMES THE NIGHT. As if loosed from a tabernacle high in the 12,000–foot Mount Timpanogos, it overruns the Jordan River and the phlegm-gray Utah State Prison compound, where four bullets made a pudding of Gary Gilmore's fast-beating heart last January in blood atonement for his murder of two young Mormon men. In minutes, this great plain is dry and black as charcoal, and a raw wind rises up, scattering turds of tumbleweed along Interstate 15 as the darkness advances on a city of Zion.

By day, Provo, Utah, is a spectacularly beautiful hideaway where the sun—according to the Chamber of Commerce—"shines over 72 per cent of the time," most principally upon scions of the much-persecuted pioneer disciples of the Church of Jesus Christ of Latter-day Saints, who fled here via Salt Lake City in the spring of 1849. Nightfall, when it descends upon this wilderness, is swift and odious, a harbinger of Hell on earth awaiting all modern Lamanites, Jaredites and Nephites who dare spurn the witness of the Book of Mormon in these sinful Last Days.

The fingers of his left hand form a loaded pistol which he tilts to his temple—and fires.

"*Plunk!* That's it," says Donny Osmond with a smirk. "Nothing to it. You don't really feel a thing when you're shot in the head."

"Gilmore was shot in the *chest* by the firing squad," reminds Ron Clark, wiry public relations officer for both the Mormon Church and its foremost goodwill ambassadors, the Osmonds, as he pulls his chair up to the long table in the back dining room of The Plank, a Provo-area family restaurant.

"You know, there's no nerves in your brain," offers the cherubic teenage brunette seated across from Clark. "Brain surgeons don't need anesthesia for patients when they're operated on. There's no feeling there."

"Speak for yourself, Marie," chides brother Donny. "Just 'cause there's none in *your* head!"

As if on cue, the eight-odd Osmonds and friends bent over soup explode in boisterous appreciation of the vitriolic, television-honed teasings of

Donny and Marie; only this time the pundit/patsy roles are reversed, and the subject is not foolish pride or paper roses.

"A spectator at the execution says Gilmore was slammed backward by the force of those rifle shots," Clark continues with relish. "That's a lot of fire-power to have coming at you, boy! His hands gripped the seat he was strapped into"—Ron stiffens, wide-eyed, and white-knuckles his own arm-chair in illustration—"and then, after a moment or two, he just slumped for-ward, a dead man."

There ensues a brief, grave silence. Then, as a slightly flustered waitress dispenses the entrees, Donny tackles the knotty Bullet-in-the-Head question with his older brother, Wayne.

"I mean, what kinda sound does one make when it's entering your skull?" he wonders with a giggle.

"Oh, my gosh. I don't know," Wayne replies, greatly amused. "Now, let's see . . . it can't be *that* much of a thing, probably not too loud. . . ."

Donny begins exploring the possibilities, clucking and popping and send-ing his abettor into hysterics.

"A-*hoo, hoo!*" Wayne exults. "Ooh, Donny, come on! It doesn't . . . it can't be like *that!*"

Both share an extended convulsion and then settle down to their dinner. "But *say*," Donny declares at length, using a broiled shrimp as an exclama-tion point. "How fast would you think a bullet from the rifle would be trav-eling when it made its impact?"

"Umm, now that's interesting, isn't it?" his brother concedes.

Donny borrows a pen and sets to work multiplying numbers on the back of a place card as Wayne leans over his shoulder. The Osmond brothers' inquiry into the nuts and bolts of bloodshed captures the imaginations of others at the table, particularly Ron Clark, who embarks on a long, wistful recollection of mutilation and mayhem at the hands of "Charlie" in Vietnam.

"Getting shot is bad enough," he rules. "I've seen it. But you should've seen some of the other horrible things they'd do over in Nam. . . . I tell ya, right in the city, ol' Charlie used to carry these long knives with this curved double-edged blade, sharpened like a razor. . . ."

Marie Osmond makes a face like she's gulping down a grenade. Trying for the last 10 minutes to ignore the gruesome chitchat, she finally starts cutting in to direct bubbly observations on fashion, hairdos and Barry Manilow ("Don't you love 'Weekend in New England'—it's so pretty!") at a comely blonde girlfriend on her left. Unfortunately, the blonde lacks either the con-versational flair or the showbiz street smarts to sustain the obstructive banter. So the sick-shit table talk prevails. And Marie's gummy Studebaker grille of a smile dissolves into the barest taut slit.

"Well now, did you know that I saw a copy of the original Bowie knife the other day?" Wayne confides in an august whisper. "And my goodness— it was huge; really long and big, almost like a sword! And gosh, I'd hate to be caught by that, be slashed or sliced up or something!

"A bullet just goes in quickly and you never even know what hit you! You don't even hear the gun go off! Quick as a wink, it's over! But a Bowie knife; can you *imagine*. Why. . . ."

"—Be *gross*, why don't you!!!" Marie finally shouts with fitful vehemence. "Can't you guys see that I am eating?!"

Startled, Clark quiets down, while the Osmond boys sputter in distracted confusion.

"Ho! Well, it's okay folks," a red-faced Donny Osmond says. "That's enough of that stuff I guess, so let's, ah—tell some jokes! That's it! Now, I'm gonna tell you all a great one, my favorite Polish joke! See, there's this ventriloquist in a nightclub with a Jerry Mahoney-type dummy, telling Po—"

He stops dead, his pale features turning positively ashen.

"Er, excuse me," he begs the stranger at the table. "But you aren't . . . Polish, are you . . . ?"

"We want *The Donny and Marie Show* to have something in it for everybody, everywhere," gushes the 23-year-old Jay Osmond as brother Donny, 19, rewinds a color video cassette in the den of the family's Provo condominium. "We don't want to leave anyone out of the fun!"

"You bet!" says Donny as he steps back from the TV, brushing some nonexistent lint from the wide lapels of his tuxedo. The Provo High Senior Prom is mere hours away and both Donny and Marie are going, although not with each other. Marie—or "Sissy," as she is affectionately called—has only recently begun dating, while her lookalike brother is an old pro with some two years under his belt—figuratively speaking, that is.

"I've never been to a prom and I'm sure sorry about that," Jay allows as he surveys the bustle of activity in this room and the adjacent kitchen. In the far corner, by the stove, a cheerfully plump Mother Olive samples a supper goulash being concocted by the cook, as Donny stalks about, suspenders dangling, nervously adjusting his bowtie. Jimmy Osmond, 15, the tap-dancing butterball who has charmed half the planet's pre-teens (and their sexagenarian babysitters) with such showstoppers as "Give Me a Good Old Mammy Song," is drumming his fat fingers on the counter in anticipation of the biscuits browning in the oven. Father George Osmond, white-haired and bespectacled, is enthroned in a rocker in the center of the buzz, having a tranquil conference with his sad-eyed, 26–year-old son, Wayne.

Without warning, the large TV springs to life with a tape of the final *Donny and Marie* installment of the 1976–77 season. It's an ideal moment for Sissy to make her entrance, and she's dressed in a deceptively non-diaphanous pink chiffon gown—you *think* you're seeing something, but you're not. Like all her costumes, it is styled to add 10 matronly years to her appearance.

The flashing TV immediately captures her attention and she halts, staring, in the doorway, where she is soon joined by her co-host. As they grin, guffaw and even stomp with glee at the playback of their opening monologue, the room is transformed into a split-screen time warp in which art and life imitate each other to unnerving effect.

In a tight closeup, Marie rewards herself with a hearty laugh for a deft dig at her clumsy brother, while her mirror image fills the air with a live overdub of the same ebullience, complete with an identically gleaming set of Pepsodent-perfect teeth. Ditto for Donny, whose off-camera complexion remains the sort seen only on Ken dolls. In this house, the unreal *is* real.

After a blackout intermission where the commercial would normally be, the show resumes with its handsome host confiding that this is his favorite part of the program, since he can now take the time to do a serious song. Donny croons: *"When the deep purple falls. . ."* and is showered with purple socks, a scene which elicits a squeal of delight from Marie-in-the-flesh.

"He's worn purple socks forever," she later explains. "Actually, I started it for a joke present because his favorite color is purple. For Christmas about six years ago I gave him 30 pairs, and he's worn them every day since! Now he has hundreds. We buy white ones and dye them purple 'cause they're hard to find. He could be wearing aqua and he'll still put on purple socks! I was being funny and the *turkey* takes it seriously!" Sure enough, when Donny lifts his foot to buff his black patent slip-ons he reveals a bright purple ankle.

Since the originally four-, now six-member Osmond Brothers broke out of their Ogden, Utah, barbershop routine in 1962 to make their network TV debut on *The Andy Williams Show* (Andy introduced them as the "Ogden Brothers from Osmond, Utah") they've been a heavyweight Middle of the Roadcrew. After establishing themselves through regular spots on Williams' shows, guest shots on similar straight-laced variety hours and devoted attention to the state fair circuit, they attacked the recording industry. "One Bad

Apple" became a hit single in 1971, providing the heartland with an alabaster alternative to the Jackson Five. Since that time, the family has amassed 25 gold records, selling over 75 million lps and singles. Steady international touring has made the brood a global phenomenon.

Olive Osmond loves to tell the story about the time she and Jimmy were in the Louvre and a middle-aged Japanese man ignored the Mona Lisa in favor of her son: "He tapped him on the shoulder and wanted to know if he was 'Jimmy Boy.' In the Far East, Jimmy is so popular, the group is billed as 'Jimmy Boy and the Osmonds.' When we told the man it was Jimmy, he was so excited he could barely contain himself."

Elsewhere in the world, it is skinny, lantern-jawed Donny who is the focal point and reigning heartthrob, wooing armies of jailbait with recycled saccharin: "Puppy Love," "Go Away, Little Girl," "The Twelfth of Never," etc. The real mover in the Osmonds these days, however, is precious Marie, who simultaneously shed her baby fat and notched a big hit at age 13 with a Nashville rendering of "Paper Roses."

But it was not until the advent of ABC's *The Donny and Marie Show* in 1976 that she began burning her wholesome vivacity into the minds of legions of Middle American TV toadies. Playing Cher to Donny's Sonny in the show's utterly larcenous duologue format, she forged a boldly *square* form of bitchiness and introduced a uniquely prudish standard of dress and beauty. Across the nation, Cher's slinky, Armenian Morticia Addams look is being replaced by a baby doll approach whose sexual allure is tied more to the perverse thrill of backseat "Bobby, I just *can't*" protestations than any belly-button bravado. Each Friday night, more than 40 million people tune in to watch Donny and Marie's squeaky-clean cavorting—especially impressive when one considers that only five million more spent a slow weeknight viewing Richard Nixon's massively hyped Grandpa Walton apology for Watergate. Amazingly, the pair offer nothing more sensational than song-and-dance on ice skates and the pointless patter of Paul Lynde. Why, with all that flounce and gauze around her, no one even knows what Marie Osmond is *shaped* like! Nonetheless she is a powerful role model *and* sex symbol.

"A lot of girls who like Donny and stuff, they watch me to see what kind of clothes I'm wearing, how I'm doing my makeup, how I'm doing my hair, what kind of goals I've set—you name it," she says with bewilderment. "It's so scary sometimes."

Cultural clout of this magnitude does not come easy. Regardless of what one might think of the Osmonds' mode of entertainment, they cannot be accused of being anything less than hard-working professionals, constantly driving themselves to exhaustion with a fanatical work ethic that has its roots in their Mormon religion.

Marie logs a 14–hour day while the 22 weeks of the *D&M Show* are being taped in Los Angeles. She often squeezes a recording session in at recess. When the season ends, the family starts rehearsals for their annual Las Vegas stint, and then it tours, finishing up just in time to do it all over again.

It's a grueling regimen, but one which is lent a substantial nobility in the context of Latter-Day Sainthood, a faith which insists on thrift, industry and an apocalyptic self-sufficiency that requires each household to maintain a two-year reserve supply of food. Poverty is the badge of the shiftless backslider: The Lord rewards those who excel. Meantime, the Church Elders ask each member in good standing to contribute a tithe—10% of his yearly income. The Federal welfare system is off-limits: Mormons have their own relief program, in which the Church extends mostly non-monetary assistance to the downtrodden (food, shelter, motivation), but only if their families cannot afford to do so.

Each and every Mormon is on this earth to accrue Eternal brownie points; it's no secret that those who keep their shoulder to the wheel will be the recipients of a divine payoff. "The Lord teaches that 'As man is, God once was,'" says Father Osmond. "'And as God is, man shall become.' After all, we're all God's offspring and I like to think he wants us to grow up, same as I do my kids."

Realizing goals as great as these is no picnic, so the Lord has provided the family unit as a vehicle for instruction, solace and reinforcement. The Osmonds, not coincidentally, are as thick as thieves: so close, in fact, that they intend someday to build their own private community (the working title is "Osmond Acres") on a choice parcel of land above Provo.

George Osmond, land baron, cattle rancher, millionaire entrepreneur and stern-but-gentle patriarch of the Osmond empire has come a long way from his beginnings as a threadbare railroad brakeman. Although he has proved a shrewd, forthright straw boss, it should be remembered that neither he nor Mrs. Osmond was a stagedoor megalomaniac who shoved their sons and daughter into the spotlight. Rather, the whole affair was his boys' idea, growing out of the weekly, Mormon-recommended "Family Nights," where prayer and upright play are interspersed to foster a warm Christian hearth.

Coupled with the Church's emphasis on members sticking with their own kind in marriage and other forms of social communion, and a strict moral code that forbids everything from premarital sex to the ingestion of alcohol, coffee, tea and other stimulants, the Family Way can make for a peculiar brand of isolation.

"I've never drunk Coca-Cola," Marie states flatly, the beverage being an optional taboo because of its caffeine content. "I don't know what it tastes like but I'm sure I'm not missing anything."

Probably not. Still, the idea of a child growing up in America without a swallow of the Real Thing is oddly unsettling.

"It's really no good for you," she argues. "If you put a piece of meat in a glass of Coke overnight, the next day all that's left is just tough, undigested muscle fiber."

Junk food is tough to defend, but a debate on soda pop temperance misses the point. In the back of your mind, what you're hoping to find in most Coca-Cola settings is not tooth decay or muscle debilitation but a little flat-out, non-homogenized fun: sock hops, basketball games, beach parties, heavy petting. . . .

Watching Marie as she breaks away from the magnet of her own electronic image to rush around, puzzling over the pinning of her corsage ("Is it upside down, Mother? Should I put it on the right shoulder or the left?") one sees that no matter how mature her video persona, she's still a 17–year-old girl with a healthy capacity for adolescent anxiety.

"My parents always tried to make sure we got a very well-rounded childhood," she maintains. "But I feel like maybe I did grow up fast. I went through every stage but I went through them faster than normal. I guess growing up and associating with older people more so than kids my age, and always being in a private school where I was the only one in the class, was just more concentrated *work* and hardly any social life.

"I always say to myself, 'You can't have everything.' If I lived here as a regular person, I'd be going to Provo High and saying, 'I wish I could travel around the world.' Instead, I've been around the world *five* times. You can't have everything, but I'm trying. I *want* everything."

The clock says it's time to hurry. Marie's prom escort is a guy named Brett who attends Provo High. For him, tonight is one part of a time-honored teen rite he's living through. For his date, whose poise and astute beautycraft will make her a knockout amongst amateurs, it is a chance to touch another base in her accelerated growth.

There's a horn honking out in the cool night and she's heading for the door in a swirl of pink chiffon, flushed and laughing, her brown eyes alive with a girlish titillation that is absent when she cake-walks with Bob Hope or lip-synchs "I'm a little bit country" on Friday nights from the KTLA-TV studios.

Seconds after Marie exits, Jay is asking no one in particular: "Hey!! What time is she gonna be home?!" Getting no answer, he repeats himself; and then with a strange, awkward haste, disappears down the hallway, the question loud on his lips. Many a maiden has surrendered her innocence under the post-prom moonlight; does Marie's brother fear for her safety, or envy her sweet confusion?

With dinner still a few minutes away, I sit down with George Osmond and Wayne, listening for the first time to a long talk they've been having about recent activities on their ranch, situated some 130 miles to the north.

"We lost a pretty nice calf up there the other day," George recounts soberly. "It was really too bad."

"How did it happen, father?" his son asks.

"Wayne, you can't always foresee or figure these things. We had problems we didn't expect and it was a dry birth. We did our best, but we just took too long and pulled too hard."

"Uh-huh. . . ."

"And without meaning to, of course, well, we accidentally broke the poor thing's neck."

"Last night, Marie went up to the Provo temple and did 30 baptisms for the dead," says Olive Osmond.

With the dinner dishes cleared away, Mr. and Mrs. Osmond and I have retired to the front living room for a discussion of miscellaneous aspects of the Mormon creed. The rest of the house is quiet except for the distant murmur of the late movie Jay is watching in pajama comfort, and Jimmy's trumpet practice—he's butchering the melody line to Stevie Wonder's "Isn't She Lovely."

"Baptisms for the dead are part of the sacred ordinances performed by worthy members," Olive continues. "Not all Mormons are permitted to enter the temples for this work. They must earn a 'recommend' by showing the Church leaders that they are pure and living righteously. In the temple, you receive instruction and do these ordinances for your ancestors. We Mormons are very concerned with genealogies and all are required to know their family tree at least four generations back, so that if a relative has not been baptized through immersion by a proper [Mormon] priest, the Lord allows it to be done vicariously."

The Lord also allows Man to achieve his own omnipotent status. At this earthly stage there are at present two "historically valid" guidebooks to assist in this difficult process: the Bible (King James edition preferred) and the Book of Mormon, the latter being an account of God's activities in the Americas beginning around 600 B.C. and concluding around 421 A.D. The tale boasts a cast of characters supposedly descended from the Israelites, with names like Laman—who, incidentally, was evil. To separate the followers of Laman from the righteous portion of the population, the Lord marked them with the stigma of a bronze skin. The descendants of those bronze-skinned sinners are allegedly the Indians of North, Central and South America.

The Mormons have long been objects of suspicion and rough rumor because of their arcane temple rituals and practices among adult members such as wearing sheer torso stockings called "garments" or "shields"— sacred apparel, covered with secret symbols, which is seldom removed except, for instance, when bathing.

These minor eccentricities can't hold a votive candle, however, to the queer business surrounding the Church's priesthood, a multi-leveled order open to all pious males from the age of 12 on—providing they are not of the black race. When I asked Olive Osmond why this privilege was not extended to blacks, she stammered on about the Negro bearing the mark of Cain ("We believe they are descendants of Cain. When Cain killed Abel he denied his brother of posterity"), then retracted that statement, offering nothing more concrete in its place.

Intrigued, I sought and was granted an interview with F. Charles Graves, a High Priest and Director of Public Communications for the Mormon Church. Graves' explanation:

"Blacks can have full membership in the Church but are not permitted to have the priesthood at the present time. That change would come through the Prophet [roughly, the Mormon equivalent of Pope], through Revelation. And I can tell you that every Prophet we've had [twelve in all, from founder Joseph Smith in 1827, through Brigham Young to today's 84–year-old Spencer W. Kimball] has given very careful prayer and consideration to that policy and has asked the Lord about it. Since we've not had a change, the Prophet and we assume that the Lord wishes it to remain that way for the time being."

This policy seems to lack documentation, I tell him. What's the reasoning behind it?

"We don't know exactly, except that the Lord said so. There are a number of people who were not given the full priesthood. At the time of Moses and Aaron, the right to officiate at the temple was given to one tribe—Levi. Now, why? Well, the Lord didn't say why. You may recall on one occasion in the Old Testament, the Ark of Covenant being steadied by someone who didn't have the right of priesthood to touch it—and he was stricken dead. All I'm saying is that, historically, the Lord has told his Prophets to do certain things. He did not always tell them *why*."

While the Osmond parents will not be pressed on this matter (Marie later says she "admires blacks who become Mormons for their special faith"), Olive eventually concedes with a fearful quaver that "We have had some problems, some threats over the years concerning this question."

Threats against the Church or the family?

"They were . . . personal . . . threats."

I am surprised to discover that the Osmonds' publicly known Provo Canyon Road address is so accessible. Located across from the Brigham Young University campus in the heart of a business district, the two-story brick building is fair prey for the dozens of young girls who wait daily on the patio of the adjacent Roy Rogers fast-food outlet for a glimpse of Jimmy, Marie, Donny, Jay, Wayne, Merrill or Alan Osmond. They are anything but disappointed, as the normal comings and goings of the clan continue, unabated, right before their eyes.

Deciding that the living room is getting stuffy, George and Olive lead me downstairs—past the private office where Olive stores her genealogies, answers fan mail, and rejects any promo photos of Donny which disclose chest hair or a bulge in his crotch—and into their Kolob Recording Studio. "The word *Kolob*," Mrs. Osmond explains, "signifies the first creation, nearest to the Celestial, of the residence of God. It's also the name of our record label."

The three of us stretch out before the magnificent 24–track board that the electronically adept Donny installed himself. Long shadows play on the parents' faces, outlining the contours of their pleasant but rather plain features. Yet one can see clearly how Olive's sharp, delicate angularity merged with George's broad, rounded lineaments to produce a classic Campbell soup-kid countenance which reached its All-American apex in Donny and Marie.

"I want to make sure you know how we Osmonds all contribute to make this whole thing work," George asserts. "Let's take it from the top:

"Virl is 32 and married and he handles the fan club and magazine, while Tom, who's 29 and also married, has a print shop—but he's back in college now. Both boys have had serious hearing problems since childhood so they don't appear with the Osmonds. Of the rest of the boys, only Donny, Jay and little Jimmy are still single. Allan [29] does the finance and investments; Wayne supervises the records; Merrill [25] coordinates the TV work and Jay does the choreography. Donny, Marie and Jimmy push their talent, so we don't give them things to worry them. Mother here does the music publishing and mans the phones, and I'm the troubleshooter."

"And trouble-maker," adds Olive with a grin.

Is there much trouble with the fans?

"Whatzat?" says George. "Our fans? Well, we have a lot of nice people for fans. We don't perform in Utah, though, so that it's more of a home base where, say, Marie can do things like audit courses at BYU.

"Still, we must change our unlisted phone number every 60 to 90 days. It's amazing how they always find it out. One girl from the West Coast raised a fuss outside the door one day, saying her friends had just dropped her there and left. Jay let her come in and call home collect. Seems when she got the phone bill she saw our number on it and gave it out everywhere.

"The gang over at Roy Rogers is all right, they don't hurt anything. But sometimes we get these folks, kids *and* families, who come from all over and sit outside in their cars all day, looking at the house. So now we have a cop at night.

"I shouldn't be saying this, I guess, but the world certainly has some strange people in it. There, was this one man who used to stand out there all the time, nighttime too, looking up at the windows. I had to go and tell him to move along. You must do it sometimes, or they'll just hang around at night, watching, watching, always watching. . . ."

Marie rarely goes anywhere unchaperoned; usually she is in the company of one or more brothers. This morning, standing in the BYU cafeteria for a quick breakfast after her typing class, Marie briefs me conspiratorially. "Watch Jay around here," she says as we select a table. "He's majoring in meeting girls."

The rest of the immediate populace seems to be majoring in meeting Marie. As Jay roves, she is left vulnerable to any assailant. No one here, male or female—but especially male—can pass the table without saying an extended hello, many requesting her signature on a scrap of paper, or even a bit of her time. No boorish advances, you understand; the Osmonds shine brightest in the Mormon constellation, so everyone wants them at their dinner party or in their Bible study group. And Marie, obviously, is the prettiest centerpiece in Provo.

Upon our arrival home, I ask Marie how things went at the prom. She doesn't answer at first, and the question lingers in mid-air until she murmurs, "I guess I was disappointed a bit."

Why ?

"I didn't know what to expect," she continues, the slightest catch in her voice. "Because I, I had never even *been* to a dance. I think that was my second time into Provo High. The prom was in a gym, and it was decorated really nice . . . they had a waterfall and crepe paper . . . but it was just a . . . dance." She falls quiet and starts puttering in the kitchen. I notice her eyes have become filmy, a fine streak of mascara edging toward her right cheek. She wipes her eye, clears her throat and summarizes with forced animation. "So it was just, like, you could go to a dance but everybody was just dressed up. And I guess I expected something different—not knowing proms and high school too well."

Turning away, she disappears into her bedroom for a few minutes. When she emerges she is smiling once more. Marie decides she's gonna bake me a cheesecake. "It'll be a lemon cheesecake with a graham cracker crust and strawberries! I've *got* to make it for you—if you want it. *You do*?! Okay then, but I've never made it before . . . yesterday. That was my first time, in case it's average."

As we hunker at the kitchen table, crushing graham crackers with the bases of waterglasses, she talks about herself.

"I think the first time I was on television I was four or five. It was *The Andy Williams Show*. I danced with Andy and sang a real quick song. Then I worked mostly overseas on our tours, and I did a couple of commercials. I was kind of a chubby little girl—I don't think they wanted me on television much then. [*Nervous laughter.*] I decided when I was 11 that I wanted to sing. My little brother had gold records galore and I'm going, 'Am I gonna let him do this to me?!' And so I decided to do it . . . and lost some weight.

"I'm a very basic person," she continues, smiling as she pulverizes a second stack of crackers. "To me, show business is a business, it's not my entire life. I have other interests. My goals aren't: 'Oooh! I wanna become the biggest singer in this world!' I want to have a family. I guess that's the kind of upbringing I've had. I believe strongly that, sure, it's good to make a specific thing your field, but that's no reason why you can't do other things."

For instance?

"I enjoy accounting, bookkeeping, so I'm not going to deprive myself of that. It's very important for any girl to know how to run books and take care of the money and be useful. One of the main problems in marriage is that they can't keep the checkbook balanced—they fight about the money.

"See? I'm a normal person! It's a compliment that people think of you as special but I love to talk to people to let them know I'm *me*. That person they see is—I wouldn't say another person—but you have to do certain *things*. Like, I knock Donny a lot on the show. Sure we tease, but people come up to me and say, 'Are you always that *rude*?' And I have to say [firmly]: 'No. I'm not. I hate to disappoint you.'

"Donny is *not* a klutz—okay?! And on the show, he always does dumb things. But he doesn't really—I mean, he does *sometimes*, but you have a certain TV image there."

Wayne Osmond strolls in and, speaking of images, asks me, "Have you seen the cover of Marie's latest album [*This Is the Way That I Feel*]? She's dressed up and sophisticated, you know? I mean, now she's a young woman! But what I think is kinda neat, to tell you one funny report, is there's this guy down in this ABC affiliate station in Atlanta, and he had this picture of this nude girl on his wall . . ."

"Hmmm," Marie pouts, "I haven't heard this one. . . ."

". . . And he tore it down," Wayne trumpets, "and put Marie's album picture up!"

"Have you heard about this DJ up in San Francisco?" Marie giggles excitedly.

"Naw! What'd he do?"

"He dedicated this unbelievable song to me! It was called 'You Sexy Thing' or something like that, and he goes: 'Donny Osmond, close your ears, 'cause I'm dedicating this song TO YOUR SISTER!!!'"

They howl uncontrollably.

Blame it on the cheesecake: we're late for Marie's afternoon New Testament course at BYU, taught by Brother Rodney Turner. All the desks in the tiered lecture hall are taken, so she and I must sit alone on the wooden steps. Marie doesn't appear to mind as she unzips her Bible, opening it—as the short, graying Turner orders the entire class—to I Timothy. The book is given to me to hold, and as we huddle close together, poring over the first Epistle of Paul the Apostle to my namesake, I realize with a single wandering glance that I am the envy of every male in the room—excepting, of course, Jay Osmond, who's sitting in the front row—and probably multitudes of puppy-lovers the world over, as well. Marie's perfume is faint but fills my head; she looks as comfortable as I feel and her beatific expression betrays . . . nothing.

Outside, a bevy of coeds strides past the hall's open door—and stumbles back, pointing at us, whispering vital observations and joshing each other. They will linger there for the duration of the class.

"Now listen to this, Jay," directs Turner semi-sternly when he reaches Chapter 6:9–10, reading it aloud:

"But they that will be rich fall into temptation and a snare, and into many foolish and hurting lusts, which drown men in destruction and perdition! For the love of money is the root of all evil."

Thus admonished, Jay and the rest of us are told to move along to Titus, Chapter 2, "where you all can find some advice concerning conduct; but particularly you young women.

"He says young women should love their husbands and children, be chaste, discreet, be good homekeepers, obedient and so forth," Turner summarizes, adding: "There's certainly a message here for advocates of women's lib. The women are also to dress modestly, not to wear expensive jewelry, a lot of make-up, big hairdos, what-have-you, but rather to be dressed in *virtue*. They are also not to talk in church—Remember I Corinthians, Chapter 14, Verse 35:

"And if they will learn any thing, let them ask their husbands at home: for it is a shame for women to speak in church.

"There the Lord is saying, 'I don't permit women to teach or usurp authority in church, because Eve was fallen first, then Adam. Man has preeminence and therefore she ought to keep quiet—she got us into that trouble, so she ought to keep quiet and not get us into any more. [*Polite laughter.*] But women shall be saved in child-bearing!

"It is interesting in Scripture," Turner mulls, "that when you really read it closely, you see that the stress is on the men rather than the women. The women will be saved if they'll just accept their womanhood, fulfill their roles as women, live the Gospel, learn in silence. That's all that's necessary."

I look up at Marie. Does she accept this catechism? She is smiling slightly, her gaze fixed on Brother Turner, and she keeps her silence.

After class, he asks for her autograph.

In less than two hours, night will again be upon this mountainous land of teen angels and apprentice Christs. Sitting alone, together, on the huge couch in her living room, Marie plots her future for me with all the care that Prophet Joseph Smith must have given to deciphering the sacred Plates he was entrusted with as a young man. "It's a big responsibility," she says, "when the world's watching.

"I've been approached to do movies but either the time wasn't right or the part wasn't right. There are certain things I wouldn't play."

What kind of roles would she prefer?

"I don't know. I don't know what kinds of movies are really going big nowadays. It's hard to tell. Certain parts would go against my beliefs and my standards—I just wouldn't do 'em. I'm sure you know what I mean.

"Are you kidding?!" she retorts rhetorically. (I never asked, I swear.) "I would never play *that* kind of lady!"

When it comes time for the Osmonds to construct their exclusive Land of Os, will Marie reside there with her parents and brothers?

"I don't know about *me*," she says with trepidation. "I'm gonna have to go with whomever I marry, right? But as far as all my brothers, yeah, they will. Everybody says, 'Gee! Are you people for *real*?' Yeah, we're for real! We have a saying in our family: No matter what decision you make, no matter what you do, it's always family first, religion second, and business third."

One might have supposed her religion would come first.

"As a Mormon," she counsels, "if you have your family first, you usually *do* have your religion first.

"My family, we're very blessed people I think. We've had times when things happened to us that have been very great tests. My brother Donny almost lost his life. He was about 12 and he kept having these attacks, and went on for about five years without knowing what it was. They were stomach attacks: he'd curl up in *pain*. He'd been to doctors throughout this world who didn't find anything. We thought maybe it was from eating some wrong kind of food.

"Finally, when he was about 14, we went with him to the emergency room in the hospital. He was getting worse and his white corpuscle count was going up and up. They said if we didn't do something, he was not gonna be here much longer.

"They opened him up and it was his appendix—it was going underneath his liver—swollen to five times its normal size! Turns out he had first gotten the problem when he was nine! But whenever he'd get these attacks, my father and mother would lay on hands and give him a blessing and he'd get better." Clearly, Donny Osmond could have died five years ago.

"The doctor, when he took [Donny's appendix] out, he said, 'It's really interesting; the appendix had scar tissue on it. I don't understand it! Appendixes don't get scar tissue! [Medically, a shaky statement, at best.]'

"You see?! The Lord had been watching over us! I was in a car accident in L.A., driving back from the TV show about a year ago with my mother in the car. I was tired and didn't realize it. And I ran *into my father's car* while we were going about 50 miles per hour. I smashed my face—my mouth and eye—and my mother broke ribs and bruised her heart.

"You've gotta trust in the Lord," she insists fervently. "There were so many ifs involved in the accident. If my mother hadn't been lying down—and my mother *never* does that—she would have gone headfirst through the windshield. And if I had not been wearing my seatbelt, I would have been all over this world in *pieces*. If I had hit my head a little further down I would have lost my eye and smashed my teeth! Instead, I bit through my mouth and also tore the skin around my eye. I still have a little bump there," she says, touching her upper lip.

"I had my mouth operated on to have some of the scar tissue removed. You'll notice on last season's shows, I didn't have it done yet and this big thing is hanging there and I hated it! It's so gross. I ripped through all my muscles in my mouth, clear back. Afterwards, the muscle in front was very weak and there was a piece of skin hanging there. It sounds so gross—I mean it wasn't *obvious* gross, it was just a little extra piece of fat. Ugh! Gross! This sounds really awful!

"But anyway, the point is, these were tests for us."

The day after tomorrow, Marie Osmond is to begin the intensive rehearsal for her family's Las Vegas extravaganza, pausing only to spend a morning at the ground-breaking ceremony in nearby Orem for a multi-million-dollar Osmond TV and film studio in which *The Donny and Marie Show*, starting with the Christmas program, will henceforth be taped. Sandwiched between Vegas and TV is more touring, and there's another solo album to be considered. As her workday lengthens and her environment grows more insular, the last question seems the simplest, and the hardest. Is she satisfied with her lot in life?

"I believe I am," she says, baring her inimitable smile. "You know that 'perilous' skit you saw yesterday on the tape of our TV show? Where I was up on the mountainside, hanging from that tree? I enjoy doing things like that, where you can just let go and scream—they feel good. Who gets to do things like that, 'n' be insane? I mean, I don't know if I would do that here in Provo, Utah.

"Like when I did a 'Marie Heartburn' thing based on *Mary Hartman*. It was interesting because I had never seen her show. What's the name of the lady who plays Mary? Louise Lasser; yeah. I did a number on her, where I was just spacy. They told me what she was like and I did this thing where *nothing* fazed me.

"In a funny way though, it was depressing. That's one thing I could never do: watch a soap opera. My sister-in-law, the one married to my brother, Tommy, she was hooked on *General Hospital* 'n all of 'em, and decided she had to quit. If it was me, I would be going: 'Why am I wasting my life on this when I could be reading or learning, instead of sitting here spending an hour watching some poor person trying to work out her problems?' How boring!

"Although," she confides sheepishly, "I *did* get caught up in one soap opera for about two weeks.

"I was sick for a couple of days a while back and so I turned on the television and I got into this show something bad. Pretty soon, I found myself having to *come home* during the day to watch this stupid show! And I don't even have any time to watch TV! I mean, I'm so busy I don't have time for anything! And I started thinking, 'Why?! What are you *doing*? You don't need this! It's stupid! Forget this show!'

"So right there, I stopped watching it. And I haven't gone back. Honest."

What was the name of the show?

She blushes deeply.

"It was called . . . *The Young and the Restless*."

The Johnny Carson
Interview

Johnny Carson marked his 50th year in broadcast entertainment in 1997, having debuted in Lincoln, Nebraska, in
1947 on KFAB radio's Eddie Sosby and the Radio Rangers comedy series with the first script he'd ever written. Long before
either The National Lampoon Radio Hour or the Saturday Night
Live programs, Carson (who also played the parent of actor Ed
Moore's imbecilic Sosby character) was forging an offhand style
of wit that bore a strong resemblance to what would come:

"Today, the KFAB If-You-Don't-Like-Us-Turn-Off-Your-Radio Players bring you another stirring drama of the life of Eddie Sosby, or *Into Every Life a Little Drip Must Fall.*"

In between a hospital birth tableau in which the physician can't determine Sosby's sex, and a closing sequence in which Eddie has become a guitar-plunking singing idol, Carson wrote a series of blackouts in which the boy flunked kindergarten sandbox, flubbed his music lessons, took his first interest in girls ("Hiya babe, Ya wanta wrestle?"), graduated "Magna Cum Lousy" from high school and ran the wrong way for a touchdown at Meatball Tech. At the show's conclusion, Sosby's mom coos that her boy is now "a big radio star."

"Yes sir," agrees Sosby Sr./Carson, "he's done purty well for himself. You know, I think it was purty smart of him to change his name to Sammy Kaye."

Kaye, of course, was the popular Midwestern dance band leader whose "Swing and Sway with Sammy Kaye" slogan heralded a host of No. 1 hits between 1935 and 1965, including "Rosalie," "Love Walked In," "Dream Valley," "Chichery Chick," "The Old Lamp-Lighter," "Harbor Lights" and the theme from the film *Charade.*

As an amateur musician, Carson would have viewed Kaye as part of the regional musical establishment, while the Eddie Sosby character represented the talentless misfit who often failed upward in the popular music industry. Thus Carson, the comedy writer/performer, was taking no sides or prisoners in his inaugural radio skit, preferring the puckish lone dissenter role he would always handle so well.

And yet throughout his long career, Carson would remain uncommonly attuned to the feelings and sensitivities of his vast *Tonight Show* audience. "You try to edit yourself, and I have a pretty good track record," he mused in his Bel Air, California, home during the first of a series of interviews—the lengthiest and most comprehensive of his entire career—that took place during 1978 in Bel Air, backstage at NBC-TV Studios in Burbank, California, and at the Sherry Netherland Hotel on Fifth Avenue in New York City. "Tragedy affects almost everybody the same way, but comedy, you never know," Carson continued. "If you put on a dramatic show, for example, you can have a scene that will universally get the same reaction. A child gets run over—that hits everybody the same way; it's sad, it's a terrible thing, there's a common denominator there.

"Not so in comedy. You can do a joke or you can do a line and it will only get a reaction from people depending on their point of view. We're talking about a craft, and all of a sudden it gets very, very heavy when you start to analyze it."

The same is true of Johnny Carson himself, a modern American master of television as an instrument of communion; and yet on a personal level he remains one of the most remote figures in the history of the medium.

In the years after this interview, Carson suggested this reporter return to the set of *The Tonight Show* from time to time and watch the tapings, an intriguing offer accepted on several occasions. Carson was genial in his subsequent greetings, striding off the set before airtime to shake hands and chat briefly, sustaining an assured and attentive public presence even as his personal life endured an escalating level of sadness and upheaval.

On November 7, 1982, Carson and his third wife, Joanna, were formally separated. On April 8, 1983, Carson flew from Los Angeles to Arizona to be at the bedside of his father, Kit, who died the following night. His mother Ruth passed away in 1985.

In August 1985, Johnny and Joanna Carson reached a financial settlement in their divorce, his ex-wife receiving a package of securities and assets worth over $21 million, or roughly $2 million more than Carson's yearly salary as host of *The Tonight Show*.

In the afternoon of June 20, 1987, in Malibu, California, Carson wed his fourth wife, the former Alex Mass of North Hills, Pennsylvania. She wore a white gown and held a bouquet of pink roses. He wore a blue suit. Carson's brother, television director Dick Carson, was the sole guest and witness.

On June 21, 1991, thirty-nine-year-old Richard "Rick" Carson, Johnny's second of three sons by his first marriage, was killed when his four-wheel Nissan Pathfinder went over a 124-foot embankment on a service road off Highway 1 in Cayucos, California, 1,180 miles northwest of Los Angeles. Police said that Rick, a photographer, was apparently distracted by the view when his car tipped off the roadway. A private funeral was held that Sunday in Los Angeles.

On July 17, 1991, Carson ended the evening's *Tonight Show* by eulogizing his son, calling him "an exuberant young man, fun to be around. . . . He tried too darn hard to please." He showed a portrait shot of Rick, and then introduced a sequence of his landscape photographs. It was a moment of unprecedented on-camera intimacy from a man who proved television was a uniquely potent context for such gestures.

On May 22, 1992, Carson hosted his last broadcast of *The Tonight Show*, Bette Midler singing "One for My Baby" to him and then dueting with Johnny on his favorite song, "Here's That Rainy Day."

In 1993, he received a Kennedy Center Honor for achievement in the performing arts, confiding a few days before the ceremony that, "After Ricky died there was a period there where it was very difficult for me to get on track, because it makes you very conscious of what's important when you lose a child."

Despite his semi-retirement from the entertainment industry, Carson still commutes between his Malibu home (where his art collection includes his late son's photographs) and his Santa Monica office to oversee his business interests. He and wife Alex vacation at a home near Aspen, or travel to Russia, England and Africa.

In 1996, Buena Vista Home Video began issuing a series of *Tonight Show* highlights, including a critically and commercially popular digest of stand-up debuts from such comics as Jerry Seinfeld, titled *The Comedians: Good Stuff!*

Despite the music frequently featured on *The Tonight Show*, the emphasis on comedy in the Buena Vista series reflected an outlook of Carson's that harkened back to his days writing *Eddie Sosby's Radio Rangers*. As he explained in Bel Air in 1978, "A good singer can sing any song and the audience goes 'Ooh!' A comedian's got to go out and do *new* material that is humorous. That is a far more difficult task in life."

THE INTERVIEW

He sits behind his microphone
He speaks in such a manly tone . . .
Don't you think he's such a natural guy?
The way he's kept it up could make you cry.

The Beach Boys, "Johnny Carson"*

Back in the late fifties when ABC-TV's *Who Do You Trust?* daytime quiz show was headquartered in New York's Little Theatre, host Johnny Carson and sidekick Ed McMahon were frequent patrons of nearby Sardi's bar. On at least one occasion, the pair enjoyed an overlong recess with their favorite publican and returned to the studio fairly pie-eyed. During the afternoon taping, Carson sought to engage the show's guests in his usual wry repartee, but his liquid lunch had all but derailed his train of thought, causing him to repeatedly ask the contestants if they were married, where they hailed from, etc. Realizing his own limitations, Carson managed to turn the dangerously muddled situation into an uproarious circular conversation

*By Brian Wilson, 1977, Brother Publishing.

that delighted the studio audience and compelled ABC to let the questionable program run. To this day, Carson says that it was one of his favorite moments before the camera; he had fashioned another victory from near failure and offended no one in the process—because he let everyone in on his predicament.

Whether he is dispensing sly double-entendres or topical barbs, Johnny disarms us with his personable delivery, as if each hit-or-miss crack were a parlor trick between mutually pleased friends. His true close friends are extremely few in number, however, and as guarded in their comments about him as he is about every aspect of his personal life and private self.

For seventeen years, he has been a mighty distraction in the nation's bedrooms, keeping 15.5 million of us awake with his well-ordered antics. A true show-business legend, he has demonstrated unparalleled staying power in a medium characterized by shooting stars and swift burnouts. Yet few figures so famous in their own time have remained so elusive.

The fifty-three-year-old Carson has long since given up the jovial nightclub binges of the sort that once prompted an indignant Jacqueline Susann to dash a Black Russian in his face. He and his statuesque third wife, Joanna, now usually confine their socializing to small gatherings with such friends as Henry Bushkin, Johnny's lawyer and trusted confidant. When not working on *The Tonight Show* or paying his annual visit to the Las Vegas stage, Carson is usually at home reading, watching TV (sparingly), playing tennis on his own court, working out in his gym, pounding skillfully on the set of white pearl drums that sit across from his gleaming weight-lifting apparatus, or practicing other enduring hobbies like magic and astronomy. When it comes to personal deportment and late-night comedy, the venerable host of *The Tonight Show* trades the capital sin of excess for the cardinal rule of *control*.

As a result, he is a virtual nonentity to the gossip columnists that haunt the lavish premieres, gaudy receptions and chic bistros that are the stomping grounds of the star community—a fact that pleases him greatly. And he has hardly made himself available to other members of the press; this is his first in-depth interview in eleven years.

John William Carson was born in Corning, Iowa, on October 23, 1925, the son of Homer Lloyd and Ruth Hook Carson. The elder Carson was an itinerant lineman for an electric company, and the family (including daughter Catherine and son Richard) moved during the first eight years of John's life to numerous other small towns in the state (like Shenandoah, Clarinda and Avoca) before settling in a large, frame house in Norfolk, Nebraska. By all accounts it was a secure childhood. Homer Carson landed a supervisory post with the Norfolk power and light company and the Carsons spent their summer vacations on a lake in Minnesota.

A shy child, Johnny nevertheless mustered the courage to make his acting debut as a bumblebee in a grammar-school skit. Roles in other school productions followed, and he simultaneously honed his household flair for mimicry, most notably a creditable impersonation of Popeye. At twelve, he came upon an inspirational text called *Hoffman's Book of Magic* and quickly became immersed in the art of illusion. He sent away to various Chicago mail-order houses for additional manuals and tricks, and shortly thereafter received a black, velvet-covered magician's table from his parents for Christmas.

Armed with these tools, "the Great Carsoni" first appeared at the age of fourteen before the local Rotary Club, his prodigious feats of prestidigitation rewarded with a purse of three dollars. His interest in dramatics and magic grew as he entered high school, and he shunned sports in favor of school plays and presentations of magic for Norfolk 4–H picnics. To earn additional money, he worked part time as a movie usher in the Granada Theater and sold *Saturday Evening Post* subscriptions door-to-door. A good student, he also wrote a humor column for the Norfolk High newspaper and contributed random notes of levity to the high school yearbook:

> Football season opened this [September] and I went out to make the team. I would have too if they hadn't found where I hid my brass knuckles. . . . November was the month of blackouts, which the students enjoyed very much. December ended with Bob Jesson waiting at his fireplace for Santa Claus and bag. Bob was interested in the bag, I believe. . . .

After graduating from high school in 1943, Carson toyed with the idea of becoming a psychiatrist or a journalist but shelved both notions when he was accepted in the navy's V-12 training program. He later attended the midshipmen's school at Columbia University and ultimately was assigned to the battleship *Pennsylvania*, bringing a footlocker of card tricks along for comic relief. Between entertaining his fellow swabbies and fighting in the Pacific, Johnny once found time to amuse Secretary of the Navy James Forrestal for several hours with his best sleight of hand.

Carson entered the University of Nebraska after his discharge in 1946, majoring in journalism with the intention of pursuing a career as a comedy writer. Boredom set in and he switched to radio and speech, a move that led to a ten-dollar-a-week writing job on Lincoln's KFAB radio station in a comedy western entitled *Eddie Sosby and the Radio Rangers*. Carson eventually wrote a senior college thesis, "How to Write Comedy Jokes," that was fleshed out with taped excerpts from the popular *Fibber McGee and Molly* program and the shows of Fred Allen and Jack Benny. The effort earned him an A.B. degree in 1949 and he settled in Omaha with his new wife, a fellow graduate and former magic assistant named Jody Wolcott.

In time, Johnny got his own show, *The Squirrel's Nest*, on Omaha's WOW-TV. He also served as a disc jockey on WOW radio, often butchering the commercials of such local advertisers as the Friendly Savings Bank. ("Drop in any time. At two or three in the morning is fine. Help yourself. Just leave a note.") With the help of a cameraman, Carson put together a half-hour audition film of his best routines and spent his vacation peddling it, to no avail, in San Francisco and Los Angeles. At length, a family friend intervened and recommended Johnny for a staff announcer job at KNXT-TV in L.A. This opportunity was parlayed into a Sunday afternoon broadcast, budgeted at twenty-five dollars per show, called *Carson's Cellar*. Among the *Cellar*'s avid fans was a fellow named Red Skelton, who hired the witty young man as a writer and supporting player on his CBS-TV program. One night during rehearsal, Skelton was knocked cold by a breakaway door that failed to fulfill its function and Carson was called in to substitute for the unconscious clown prince of television.

This stroke of luck led to the fateful creation by CBS of *The Johnny Carson Show*, a thirty-nine week clunker that was canceled in the spring of 1956. His burgeoning career suddenly deflated, the semistar found himself playing a club in remote Bakersfield, California, to half-interested houses.

Borrowing money from his father and a bank, Carson and family left for New York, where he joined the Friars Club and gradually repaired a shattered reputation with his deft roasting of such sharp-tongued colleagues as Jack E. Leonard. Hired by ABC to handle *Who Do You Trust?*, he built the whimsical quiz show into the network's biggest daytime attraction. During the evening, he occasionally filled in for Jack Paar, who was then hosting *The Tonight Show*, over at NBC. Admiring his quick, off-handed approach to comedy, the networks offered Carson starring roles in various sitcoms, but he always declined and held on to his "secure" position with *Who Do You Trust?* But as Paar began to publicly reaffirm his intentions to leave *The Tonight Show*—and mentioned Johnny on the air as a possible successor—NBC redoubled its efforts to lure Carson away from ABC. He finally gave in to their entreaties and signed on with a first-year salary of approximately $100,000. On October, 1, 1962, at 11:15 p.m., Groucho Marx introduced

Johnny Carson as the moderator of *The Tonight Show*, and a new era in television, and comedy, was born.

Johnny's guests that inaugural evening were Joan Crawford, Tony Bennett, Mel Brooks and Rudy Vallee, and the band was under the direction of Skitch Henderson, with Doc Severinsen on trumpet. Ed McMahon, of course, was the announcer and resident straight man, duplicating his earlier duties on *Who Do You Trust?*

The New York Times bestowed a favorable review, the writer noting that, "at the onset he [Carson] said he was not going to describe every guest as an old and dear friend, an indication of a refreshing attitude against prevalent show business hokum." In summation, the *Times* ruled that his "healthy independence" could "wear very well."

The same could not be said for Carson's marriages. His first had produced three sons—Chris, Ricky and Cory—but little lasting happiness. As his star ascended, a year-long separation from Jody sank into eventual divorce in 1963. In August of that year, Johnny was remarried to Joanne Copeland, 30, a vivacious, dark-haired actress that he had met briefly years earlier. A former airline stewardess, she was currently appearing on a daytime TV program called *Video Village*. The couple separated seven years later, and was divorced in June 1972. That August, Carson made the surprise announcement during the tenth anniversary party for *The Tonight Show* that he had secretly wed divorced ex-model Joanna Holland that afternoon. The celebration took place in Los Angeles, and the New York-based *Tonight Show*, after having made regular "trips" to the West Coast during the latter part of the decade, soon after relocated permanently in California.

The ever-faithful Ed McMahon left his wife of twenty-seven years and four children to follow the show to L.A., and in short order his marriage was dissolved. He has since remarried.

Professionally, the years since have been relatively peaceful and prosperous ones (insiders estimate that Carson now banks as much as $4 million per annum for his services), although there have been occasional storms, such as Johnny's ire at being preempted by night football games; or his suit against a toilet manufacturer to prevent the production of a portable "Here's Johnny!" commode; or his lingering threats to leave *The Tonight Show*, first expressed in 1967 after NBC allegedly violated his contract by showing reruns of the program during an AFTRA strike.

Carson himself has become a kingpin of our popular culture, and *The Tonight Show* is a kinetic icon for adults of all ages. His conversational comedic style, which he acknowledges as having been shaped by such early heroes as Jack Benny, Bob Hope and George Burns, has become the very paradigm of nonchalant patter for every aspiring young stand-up or sit-down wit.

As a fashion plate, he has easily eclipsed such seminal Tinsel Town trend setters as Fred Astaire, Adolphe Menjou and Cesar Romero with his smart, ungarish taste in sportswear. When he adopted the turtle-neck sweater as a respectable alternative to a shirt and tie, millions of American men responded in kind. His Johnny Carson Apparel, Inc., formed in 1970 in conjunction with the Hart, Schaffner & Marx Company, continues to thrive. Likewise, since wife Joanna convinced him to stop tinting his hair and let the silver shine through, the look has been universally embraced as the hallmark of seasoned suavity.

But behind his affecting raiment and distinguished visage, the private Johnny Carson retains the same intensely reticent disposition he has carried all his life. So when his puckish off-camera side does surface, it sometimes catches even his oldest associates completely off-guard.

"I'm always impressed with how funny he can be off-camera," admits veteran *Tonight Show* writer Pat McCormick. "One time I went into the Polo Lounge [in the Beverly Hills Hotel] with him, and the guy at the door insisted that he wear a tie before he could enter. So he went off to his room and put on a tie, but took off his shoes and socks. I was amazed. And there was no rule in the place about shoes and socks, so he just walked in, sat down and put his bare feet up on the table. The guy at the door was stunned. It was a hilarious night."

A few practical jokes notwithstanding, Carson is a man profoundly uncomfortable with his own emotions, and unable to express his pain, insecurity and deep caring without considerable difficulty. A frequent giver of generous, thoughtful gifts, his magnanimity is one manifestation of his submerged sensitivity, but sometimes such distanced overtures to others simply do not suffice.

"They were changing the sign on the Shubert Theater across the street and we spent most of the time looking out the window at that and commenting about it," says Ed McMahon, recalling the day in 1957 when Carson interviewed him for the announcer's job on *Who Do You Trust?* "We spent five minutes together, and then he said, 'Well, thanks a lot, Ed, for coming up. I appreciate it.'

"I walked out and I was convinced I had blown the job. I figured he didn't like me; I'm not the type he wants. A couple of weeks later a guy calls me on the phone and says, 'When you start Monday. . . .' And I said, '*What?*' Everybody assumed I knew I had been hired!

"Johnny has a very strong shyness," McMahon explains. "I think he would love to have hired me without meeting me, because that meant getting out of his shy character and into being Johnny Carson, and that's something that he has to turn on."

Usually, Carson hides behind a precise, dispassionate regimen, and expects others to understand.

"When you never hear anything from him, you're doing a great job," says McMahon, "because he doesn't constantly send you laudatory phrases or gestures. It's just assumed you're doing a good job, or you wouldn't be there. And we have the kind of friendship where we don't have to keep saying to each other, 'I'm your friend.'

"On the show he likes efficiency. It's all done in a pattern. I mean, I psych myself up at a quarter after five every night and I walk into his office to see him. Everything is geared so that he and I will see each other and chat for five to seven minutes each day beforehand. And we'll just kind of ramble— we never talk about the show; I never hear the monologue—until I leave him at twenty-three after five to go down and do a five-minute warmup with the audience. And I usually leave his office laughing.

"He has great difficulty in getting his emotions of love and warmth out," McMahon confides. "I'll tell you a story I don't think I've ever told anyone before, that explains a lot about the man and our relationship.

"One night after the show about ten years ago, he was so nervous he was chain-smoking cigarettes, and he said, 'C'mon, I want to talk with you,' which was *very* unusual. It was the last night of our performance in Hollywood, back when we were based in New York and used to come out a few times a year. So I said to myself, 'What the hell is *this*?'

"He said, 'Let's go outside.' So we went outside the studio to a quiet room. And then we went into *another* room, and he lit another cigarette. And he said, 'I have something I want to tell you.' I thought, 'Jeeze, this is it. I'm getting the ax. He couldn't bring himself to tell me before.'

"And finally he says, 'I just want to tell you that I know what you're doing; I *know* what you're doing. I know you're helping me out there. I know what a supportive person you are. I know that you are. . . .'

"He was trying to pay me a compliment but he was having the greatest agony in doing it. I couldn't handle it. I was in tears, and I left the room and I started running down the hallway at NBC. He came out after me and over my shoulder I could hear him yelling, and I looked and saw that he was crying too. And his final words to me were: '*You see, goddamnit. You can't take a compliment any better than I can!*'"

It is sunny but cool on the November morning that I arrive at Carson's Bel Air mansion. Before admitting me, a beefy guard at the front gate punches the button on the outdoor intercom and confirms my appointment. The expansive compound consists of a large, modern-art-filled ranch house and a smaller two-story building that contains Johnny's private study and gym, the two adjacent structures flanked by a kidney-shaped swimming pool, tennis courts and lush, manicured grounds. Barefooted and dressed in tennis whites, Johnny greets me at the front door of his study with an iron grip of my hand and then sits me down inside on a long couch amid his many mementos, among them a prominently displayed photo of himself with Hubert Humphrey.

"It's about time we spoke in person," he says with a businesslike smile, alluding to the months of phone conversations that preceded our meeting. Up close, his strong, flinty features are lined and accented with a salt-and-pepper stubble. The eyes are blue-green and piercing, and his frame is trim, muscular and agile. Obviously tense, he drums his fingers, taps his feet and rises from his chair opposite me at measured intervals to pace in a tight circle and light another Pall Mall—but his steely eyes remain fixed on mine with nary a dart or a flutter. During our initial head-to-head exchange (and a followup session a week later at The Pierre in Manhattan), his manner is affable but resolute. Clearly, he sees our talk essentially as a task, but one to which he is determined to lend a cordial, relaxed air. (After the first interview he is markedly becalmed and gregarious, as if a burden has been lifted from him.)

That night, I stand on the sidelines in Studio I on NBC's sprawling Burbank lot as bespectacled executive producer Freddie de Cordova warms up the audience for a Wednesday installment of *The Tonight Show* that features guests F. Lee Bailey and Andy Williams. De Cordova baits the anxious crowd, toying with their dismay at the prospect of an absentee Carson, and then proclaims, to elated cheers, that Johnny will indeed be hosting tonight: ". . . and we're just as surprised as you are!"

Big Ed McMahon hurries out to detail the ground rules of audience participation, consisting mainly of repeated pleas for wild applause for whatever may ensue. A gaudily attired Doc Severinsen cranks up the brassy theme song as McMahon barks his intro, and then Ed intones the prayerlike "*Heeeerrrrrrre's JOHNNY!*"

The white-suited star strolls out through the parted curtains that hang between his tiny desk and the bandstand, flashing a winning grin and clicking into his time-honored repertoire of nervous ticks: the craning of the neck, the smoothing of the tie, etc.

Carson's in high spirits and his monologue flows out briskly to an enthu-siastic reception; he winks to the cameramen and jokes easily with the tiered throng before him. It's another round of *The Tonight Show*, the sight all too familiar, yet still strangely fascinating, and every mechanism in this curious little universe is in its place and operating like clockwork.

Johnny utters his last opening quip with habitual panache, and the wholesome, fresh-faced audience settles back as if in church for a live dose of the safe, comfortable ritual. He signals to the band and winds up his golf swing as the booming music segues into a commercial break, but tonight Johnny draws out the gesture just a few seconds longer than usual, careful-ly watching his monitor for the station break as he delivers a loud, robust "Ahhhhhhhhhhh—*shit!*"

———————————————

[*Smiling*] I gotta tell you from the start, I don't know anything about comedy.

[Laughing] *Oh? Well, I don't know about that.*

I don't know many people who do, strangely enough.

A lot of comedians, comics and humorists prefer to be funny than to talk about being funny.

Yeah, because you always end up being pedantic or really unctuous. If you try to analyze a joke and dissect it, take it apart—it's no longer funny. Unfortunately, when you talk about humor, comedy, it's so relative. That's the big problem. The worst thing you can say about anybody is that he has no sense of humor. That's the crusher of all things; the girl says to the guy, "*You have no sense of humor.*"

But everyone *has* a sense of humor. A lot of things that some people find funny, other people just don't find funny, so that is the problem for come-dians or people who do comedy—just trying to find some kind of a common denominator if there is such a thing, or just reach as many people as you can. But it's a very hairy problem. That's why you have somebody who will say, "Gee, I think Laurel and Hardy are wonderful," and somebody else will say, "They stink, I don't understand them."

They might be put off, for instance, by the pratfalls, the buffoonery, one shov-ing the other.

That's the big problem when you start discussing comedy. When you say,

"What is funny?" I don't know. It sounds like a copout, but I don't really know until I go out and do it—and I just hear the laughter. I like Laurel and Hardy, but I don't see them just as pratfall comedians. If you study Laurel and Hardy, it's a very, very special relationship. Books have been written on it. At times they are very polite, they are very protective of each other. Whenever Ollie introduces Stan, he says [*doing an effective Oliver Hardy imitation*], "*This is my good friend, Mr. Laurel.*"

He'll be very courtly.

[*Nodding*] Very courtly manners. But . . . and then when they go at each other, it's "Stanley!" and so forth. There's a wonderful relationship between the two of them. I think a lot of their humor is very good satire, a lot of it's slapstick, but . . . I keep looking at that pillow over there [*indicating an embroidered pillow on a nearby couch*].

[Reading the pillow's needlepoint axiom] *It's all in the timing.*

Yes, it's all in the timing, as far as I'm concerned. Humor is so much timing, and that's why, as we talk here for reproduction in print, I know that you can never make that transference from the audio sound of a joke or delivery, with all the nuances, to paper. That's why some funny people who can write very well—for example, S. J. Perelman's a good writer; H. Allen Smith had a brief flurry where he was funny—never fared too well when they tried to do it in person.

I think there is a noticeable shift in the comedic climate from time to time in this country.

When you were writing that humor column back in Norfolk High School, what was the climate?

I emulated a lot of people when I first started. I think everybody, when they first find out they can get laughs as a kid, they steal deliveries, steal the jokes that are kind of current at that time. I was an admirer of Fred Allen, Jack Benny, all the radio comedians in that day, and your humor takes on their realities because you haven't developed your own style yet.

I was writing jokes more or less in the style of a Bob Hope. Picture jokes of that style, because I'd listen to him. And then sometimes I would copy Fred Allen. I loved Fred Allen because he was one of the true natural wits, a man who could sit around and say amusing things and not make jokes.

There are a lot of good deliverers and there are a lot of good stylists, but the genuine wits are few. There's that old cliché that you hear over and over again: that a comic says funny things and a comedian says things funny.

But Fred Allen, to take a specific example, was a man who wrote very funny. I remember I used to have a few letters from him, and in his letters he would really take time—he was a laborious kind of writer—to write amusing things.

Well, Fred Allen was one of the great wits, but he was very critical of TV throughout his career, even when he was on TV.

I think television, when Fred was alive, was so basically new that maybe he didn't even really see the possibilities in it. And Fred was not a particularly attractive man, in that he was kind of dour-faced. His sense of humor had more appeal than his appearance, and he sensed that. I think Fred would be much more acceptable nowadays, especially his cynical observations of what the hell is going on. He was ahead of his time in a lot of things he did.

He did a lot of satire, a lot of social commentary, and it was interesting, because he and Milton Berle coexisted on TV, around the same time that TVs were owned mostly by well-to-do people and not the broad-based radio audiences they'd both previously known. Berle was very big on using TV in a very flamboyant way with relatively big productions and outlandish pratfalls, but Allen remained a true wit in a simple setting.

Sure. Fred Allen's a verbal comedian and Milton is a physical comedian. I can tell you a joke that Fred Allen did about Milton Berle when Berle, at the time, was on television on Tuesday nights; that was the big night, and people would stop in at bars to watch *The Milton Berle Show.* Fred was still on the radio at the time, and I remember a bit where Fred's wife, Portland, came on and said to Fred that Milton had missed his television show on Tuesday night because he had the flu. Fred said something like [*mimicking Allen's dry, nasal delivery*], "I don't know how Milton could get sick. He's got enough mold on his jokes to make his own penicillin." That's a witty joke.

Well, it's very much to the point, too. Whereas with Allen's satire and social commentary, there was always an immediacy to what he was saying, Berle was immersed in a tradition of gag lines and vaudeville immersed in slapstick.

[*Smiling*] But of course, Fred was a juggler, you know, in vaudeville. He worked first as Freddie James, World's Worst Juggler. He later became a writer and a wit. He wrote a good deal of the shows himself; I think Fred Allen would have a resurgence if he were still around.

Speaking of Fred Allen and his work as a juggler, you worked a Midwestern circuit as a magician when you were a young man. Did you ever read and employ comic tools in your act, like a Bob Orben-type book of patter?

Oh, sure, sure. And Orben's still in business, writing funny stuff for magicians. I think when you're a kid, you look at all that stuff. I remember buying some Fun Master gag files at one time. Then you realize very quickly that most of it is stock type of humor. But until you learn to write what you can do and what works for you, you grab a little of this and a little of that.

My magic really became comedy. I played it more for laughs. I did all the sucker type of tricks with the audience, doing jokes along with them.

Humor also serves as a convenient form of distraction to help carry the magic off.

[*Grinning*] Oh God, you're taking me back. Yeah, the trick would go wrong, or it wouldn't function right. The use of humor as a counterbalance or a saving device became a matter of experimentation.

You've always been good at working with situations where things don't go right, and that's more advantageous to you than if they did go right.

I do a lot of reaction type of comedy I guess. You react to the situation. You play off what is happening, trying to make something out of a disaster. People love to see if you're going to get out of it.

I think that one of the things that is the most innovative about The Tonight Show *is the way that you work with the camera. The camera and, as a result, the audience become accomplices or conspirators with you. I think about George Burns and Jack Benny referring to the camera and using the camera as sort of a confidant, but that was always in a scripted context. You've been very successful with instilling a kind of vitality in the camera as a presence, to where we feel a sense of intimacy.*

Well, television is an intimate medium. I'm not conscious when I use the camera. I know it's there. I use it like another person and do a reaction at it—lift an eyebrow or shrug or whatever. I'm conscious of it, but I'm not conscious of it.

There is a real sense of . . . naturalness in the way you work with the camera that makes the air of intimacy so convincing.

And I think the director, Bobby Quinn, who's worked with us for many years, can almost read if I'm going to do a reaction to what is happening. So I will know that maybe this camera is going to be up and I can react to the situation and do a "look" and then go back to what I was doing.

The Tonight Show *is one of the few places on television where one can see stars, prominent people, and you'll get a glimpse behind their public personas.*

Sometimes you cannot penetrate them. You know they will do what *they* want to do. You try to break through and get them maybe a little off-guard and have some fun, because otherwise it becomes [*stiffly*], "Tell us about your latest movie," and all of those obligatory questions you have to ask occasionally.

It's easy to be socially relevant. I could go in at five tonight and say, "Give me four guests, give me the heads of the prisons of California and give me a politician and give me some psychiatrists and we'll just discuss what happened in Guyana." And you can sit there and discuss people in cults and get very heavy, and everybody will say, "Oh, that's very socially relevant."

That's a talk show, but that's not what I do. I'm an entertainer, and I *always* look at myself as an entertainer. So it has bothered me for a while when we would get a little flak from the critics saying we're not doing anything "deep." *That's not the idea.*

Yet, there is a topicality to your show. You'll come up with witty jokes—not gags—about Watergate, Camp David, drugs, changing sexual mores. . . .

I think some of the material we've done on political things is some of the best material on the air. And it does get a strong reaction—especially in the political arena. We sense the mood of the country very quickly.

For example, I remember when Agnew was first selected as vice-president, it was easy to do jokes about him; nobody knew who he was, and he was good fodder for material. Then, when Agnew became the voice of so-called Middle America, all of a sudden the jokes were not particularly funny.

When he fell into disfavor, then again you found out that the people would buy the caustic material. Same thing with Nixon.

To take another example: when Wilbur Mills was in trouble with the infamous Fanne Foxe and the Tidal Basin thing, it was funny until people found out he was an alcoholic. And then you knew immediately to stay away from it, because you were taking advantage of someone after the man came out and admitted it.

Has there ever been a joke you felt uncomfortable doing, either at the time or in retrospect?

NBC used to come to me years ago. They wanted to see the monologue before the show, and I said, "No, I can't do that." I can't have somebody sitting up in an office and making capricious judgments on what he thinks is funny or not funny. I said, "You're going to have to trust my judgment," and they have. And nobody sees the monologue outside of the writers and myself; they give me the stuff, and I add to it or edit it, and put it together. *Nobody* sees it until it's done. And I don't think in seventeen years there have been more than one or two instances where something might have been cut.

Have there ever been any specific skits that you wanted to get on the air, but which you later thought better of?

We had a thing we wanted to do once on Siamese twins, and it bordered on the uncomfortable, because we figured people would say, well, it's a physical handicap. Although the material was funny, we might have offended somebody. Yet, it's *impossible* to do humor without offending somebody.

If I do a joke about President Carter, people are going to get angry. If I do a joke about Amy Carter, or if I do a joke about Nixon, or if I do say something about Bert Lance, like when he was in trouble, certain people are going to get angry. But otherwise, you keep saying, "It's so hot that . . ." or, "My wife is so fat that . . ." and you can't really do that if you're going to say anything and make some point.

You've always had a kind of iconoclastic flair in your humor, even going back to when you were working on the radio in Omaha. In Kenneth Tynan's [1978] piece in the New Yorker, *he wrote about these formatted, prerecorded interviews you would receive at the station and then mischievously distort.*

I know what you're talking about, and I loved that. In the old radio days, the record companies would send out these prepared interviews, and they would send you a script so you could interview the recording artist. You'd play the Patti Page tape and say, "Gee, it's nice to have you here today, Patti," and she'd say, "Thank you for inviting me tonight; it's nice to be here." Then the next question would be, "When did you first start singing?" And the taped reply would be, "Well, I think I was about ten years old, and I was in a church play or something."

So I just wrote my own questions, and I'd say, "I understand that you hit the juice pretty good and you've been known to really get drunk pretty often. When did that start?" Then they'd play the cut, and she'd say, "Well, I think I was about ten years old, and I was in a church play . . ." and it was wonderful. Just these insane, wild, provocative questions, and then the engineer would play this innocent track with the prerecorded reply. They quit sending them to us very soon. I've always liked irreverence.

I recall watching Who Do You Trust? *when I was a young kid, and there was always a sharp wit there, in the same way there was on Groucho Marx' show. You've always tried to expand the boundaries of whatever format you were in.*

I think I have to. *Who Do You Trust?* wasn't really a quiz show. The quiz at the end was just a device to bring people on and have some fun. It was à la Groucho. I've always liked that kind of humor.

You also did a television show called Earn Your Vacation *in 1954.*

God, that goes back, originally, to radio in the Fifties. People came on the show to win a trip. The people came on, and I'd do the comedy interview and then play the game. That was more a game show because there was a big prize involved. *Who Do You Trust?* was really [*laughter*] . . . I don't even know what the hell the point of the game was.

What single person do you admire most or emulate to some extent? A lot of people say that you were very close to Jack Benny and that he was instrumental in helping you get going on TV.

We were good friends. Jack, yes, I admired very much. Fred Allen was another one. Jack was really one hell of an actor in playing a role, which I admired. If you had followed that show at all and you could write, you could almost write it yourself. The characters were so well identified and well established that it was wonderful and unique.

He was always the target of the humor, and then in reaction he would build up sort of a vocabulary of facial quips in the same way that you have a familiar wink or a look of exasperation.

Yes, that image of put-upon frustration. Jack was very smart. He played off of his cast; they would put him down, and he would react. He was basically a reacting type of comedy character and it wasn't important to him who got the laughs on the show. The *show* was the thing. It was never the *Don Wilson Show* or the *Dennis Day Show* even though they might get tremendous laughs. It was always *The Jack Benny Show*. That's important, because if the show is working, it's yours.

You should try to help the guests be as good as they can be, because the better the guest is, the better I'll be. I've got Buck Henry on tonight. I always look forward to having Buck on because I know we'll start throwing things around, and we don't really know where it's going, and all of a sudden we're into something and it's good. Somebody like Buck Henry, who thinks funny and has got a rather bizarre sense of humor, brings out the craziness in me. Some of the best moments are times like that.

Who else is a favorite of yours?

Well, the problem is, if I started naming favorites, guys are going to call me tomorrow and say, "How come you didn't mention my name?" There are a lot of people that work in different ways. I like to have [Buddy] Hackett on. Hackett is a self-starter. [Bob] Newhart, to me, can be very funny. Carl Reiner is fun to sit and verbalize with, because things sometimes will just take off. When Mel Brooks is on I sometimes start doing things I wouldn't otherwise even think of doing.

The outrageous moments on the show are the most memorable.

Many of them are wonderful low humor. I mean, there's nothing wrong with low humor if you do it well. Low humor can be very effective. I can sit and talk with a Buck Henry and it can be intelligent and funny. Then I can still get up—if I want to—and do a sketch that is a complete knockabout type of thing—whether it's Art Fern doing the Tea Time Movie—and get away with playing both ends of that spectrum. The audience will buy it. In other words, you can do a complete burlesque thing, low burlesque comedy, which you don't see much anymore, and then turn around and still do a stand-up routine or a sit-down exchange that has a certain air of sophistication.

I think we really stole the name of the Mighty Carson Art Players, by the way, from Fred Allen. Fred Allen used to do the Mighty Allen Art Players.

Whatever you're doing, belief is never suspended. Whether it's skits or banter or characterizations, everything retains an impromptu quality.

And yet some of these things I started putting together years ago. The old lady, the Aunt Blabby character, I had done years ago in Omaha. I did her on local television back there, and she just evolved over a period of time. Art Fern, the Tea Time Movie host, grew out of a local slickster salesman on TV; he had a little pencil mustache and a very bad toupee that looked like it had been painted on his head. It's just a takeoff on the guys out here in California who do their own selling, whether they're selling the "Miracle Vegetable Cutter" or whatever, and he just became a good running character.

The character I've been doing lately, Floyd Turbo—he's the epitome of the redneck ignoramus, and he always takes the "prohunting" or "pro-Concorde" stance. I'm still working with Turbo. I find things each week when I go out to do it that I throw in: his gestures at the wrong time, his not knowing where he's supposed to be, his feeble attempts at humor, his talks about things he doesn't quite understand. But usually it starts out as a one-time shot.

When we have a sketch, we get, like, one run-through and that's it. And I like it better that way because it's Parkinson's Law that if you've got a week to get ready, it takes you a week, and if you've got a day to get ready, it takes a day.

In the early days, in that small-screen format, TV was trying to evince a flamboyance that would rival what was being done on the wide screen. Yet The Tonight Show, in its unique comedy context, is very simple, completely unadorned, not at all like a conventional variety show.

The gingerbread doesn't help you much. When NBC put on *NBC Follies* years ago, they spent a lot of money building a proscenium stage, and they had these girls coming down in Ziegfeld-like costumes, and it didn't work because that essentially is Broadway and Hollywood—and TV is still an intimate type of thing, basically.

Take the obligatory dance numbers they have in Broadway or variety stage shows. You see twenty dancers come out with a huge production number. It's really a filler to get ready for the next sketch or whatever. TV doesn't need that.

Ed Wynn told me years ago about girls on television; he said [*imitating Wynn*], "What's sexy about a three-inch girl?" The point he was making was that when you see them on Broadway and they come down on-stage and they're bigger than life, that's one thing. When you see them on television, it's often pointless and unimaginative.

You've talked to me in the past about "pure television." What is pure television?

To me, it's still the *performance* on TV that is most important. The personality is more important than all of the dance numbers and the big production things. I always thought those things have been kind of lost on television, because they ignore the automatic focus that TV provides.

But I got the feeling, even if you take all that glitter away, and pare it down to a spare sitcom or variety format, it's still not the kind of pure television that you were talking about.

Well, pure television to me is also immediacy. That's why I don't like to do *The Tonight Show* a week or two in advance, like a lot of shows do. I like to be able to go out tonight and talk about what's happening *today*. So the immediacy of doing this kind of show, I think, has a certain value in it. People *know* it's happening right now.

Sure, we're delayed on tape, but we don't edit the show; we don't shoot two hours and edit it down. When *Saturday Night Live* says, "Live, from New York!" it's live in the East but it's not live out here. Doing it the same day on tape is exactly the same thing as doing it live.

In both programs there's also the element of risk.

And I think that's a part of pure television. We don't know on any given night how it's going to go. You get an immediate feedback from the audience on what you've done, and if it all falls together, it's a great feeling. If you've had troubles, you say, "Okay, there's tomorrow night." Every night cannot be a winner. Although I don't do it five nights a week anymore—I'm doing it four this week—there's no way you can go out and have everything be of high quality.

You don't stop the tape even when people are being off-color or whatever. You might bleep it out, but people can see that things were getting out of hand.

Yeah, I think there's that aura of "What's going to happen? How are they going to get out of this? This is not going well." That, to me, is what television started out to be. Now, mainly, it's a device for screening movies or situation comedies with canned laughter. And *The Tonight Show*, or shows like it, I think—if they all went off the air, it would be too bad for television.

Obviously you don't care for canned laughter.

I never liked . . . excuse me, I'm going to sneeze here. *Aha-choo!* Sorry, I wish that sneeze could've been funnier, but then it probably would have been prerehearsed and on videotape.

But I never really liked canned laughter, although there are places for it. But you really have to know how to use it. There is a truth that laughter begets laughter to a certain extent, but most shows use it so horrendously. Pretty soon there's no distinction between what really deserves a laugh and what doesn't.

But it can help a show, I think, if it's done well. Jack Benny used to use it so well that people didn't even know he used it. I once saw Jack go out and do a monologue to a set of empty seats; there was nobody there except a couple of stagehands. It was a filmed show. And Jack walked out and said "Good evening" and looked at the audience—there's no audience there— and he does his joke, and he paused because he knew exactly when he should.

Are there any sitcoms that you enjoy?

Oh, I think the writing in *All in the Family* and the old *Mary Tyler Moore* and *Maude* shows was some of the best writing that was ever done on television. I think there are more laughs in an *All in the Family* show than there are in an evening on Broadway.

People forget that. You go to see a Broadway play that was supposed to be a comedy and you come out and you say, "What are they talking about? It wasn't that funny." Then you sit down and watch an *All in the Family* episode or *Mary Tyler Moore* and it's wonderful humor. Some of the stuff was superb.

First of all, I think that people have to like the people that make them laugh. I think it's so important. They have to like or identify with the characters. The thing that made *All in the Family* good was that you had wonderful people doing it. You had Carroll O'Connor, Jean Stapleton, Rob Reiner and Sally Struthers. The rapport that they all had together was strong and they fleshed out the characters so well—as they did on the *Mary Tyler Moore* show. They all had this wonderful interplay, they all had *their* moments, and they all flattered each other, complemented each other. You don't get that on most of the shows. Those are few and far between.

These days, comic actors compete with each other too much I think.

Yeah, everybody does. In some of the stuff I see, the kids are funny, the housekeeper is funny, the garbage man comes on and *he's* funny. Everybody is throwing funny things around, but there are no convincing relationships between the characters.

Well, in the first place, you don't really give a shit. You don't *know* these people, so you don't care. Writers have just written jokes for them.

Sometimes people say that there's a hot-seat quality to sitting next to you on The Tonight Show. *How do you feel about that?*

I don't know. A lot of people have never been on before. They've been watching the show for years, and now they find themselves sitting there in a position that they've always been *watching*. I can understand why that would make you feel uncomfortable. Hell, if I went on somebody else's show and sat there, I could be uncomfortable, because, in a way, the guy behind the microphone has got the bat. He's in charge.

I don't think I've been guilty of making people feel awkward. If they feel uncomfortable, I don't think it's because of the way I've handled them; I certainly don't want them to be, because it doesn't work for me.

Weren't you on The Dick Cavett Show?

I did a show with Dick Cavett, and I did ninety minutes with David Frost once, and I felt a little awkward. I was not completely in control. I was not in charge there. When somebody else steps out of that role and into another role, they are not in command, and the guy usually behind the desk is supposed to be in command of the situation. So I think that makes for a little awkwardness.

When I see you helping guests through the show who are very nervous or even drunk, and then, in some cases, you'll go to a commercial, and then the guest will discreetly take his leave, it reminds me of one of your big breaks—when you had to fill in on the old Red Skelton Show *after he had an accident. He is one comedian that I can think of whose comedy has always had a consis-*

tently life-affirming tone. And very kindly, especially in his pantomimes when he's depicting old people, like his famous sketch of the old man watching the parade.

I like to work with elderly people and children. I don't know why. I respect older people. I like working with kids. Maybe it's the vulnerability of them. There's a charm about older people that sometimes is childlike, and I enjoy them because, first of all, they can say anything they want to, which is just great. Age gives you a leg up on what you can say, because you don't have to account to anybody. You've lived your life and earned the right to sound off.

They'll just say, "Oh, well screw that, I don't like that, that's a lot of shit." And they lay it right out.

Critics, at the same time, have said that you have a schoolboy quality, a puckishness that isn't seen too often on TV.

[*Intrigued*] I suppose that's only because of the face. I've never had a particularly old-looking face. Even when I was thirty or thirty-five, I looked like I was twenty-five. That may be changing rapidly now. But if I looked different, you probably wouldn't have that attitude. Or maybe it's because I was born in the Midwest; you know, Mel Brooks calls me "Supergentile," "Super-WASP," and maybe it's that particular look, but that's just what I am.

Well, what was your first exposure to something funny while growing up?

[*Very pensive*] Gee, that's tough, I've never really thought about that. I was always involved, even in grade school, in school plays or just screwing up or being silly in front of an audience. Maybe it was a self-defense type of thing, but I can remember doing that clear into high school.

I remember once in grade school—this won't sound funny now, but I thought it was very funny then—we had to do a fifty-word speech or a hundred-word speech on dogs. I can still remember it, and I got up and just recited names of dogs. It's not funny now, but at that time it was successfully silly. I was in all the school plays in junior high school, wrote a column for the school paper in high school, called "Carson's Corn." [*Laughing*] Do you believe that? Yeah, I did all the stuff for the high school annual.

Did you have any exposure to vaudeville?

Not vaudeville in terms of the Keith circuit or anything like that. I would go down to Omaha and see all the stage shows. I can remember touring shows coming through the Midwest, what they called tent shows, and I was *fascinated*. It would be the repertory company that would come around, maybe they'd call it chautauqua in those days. I remember going down to Omaha and sitting on wooden benches for a dime, and they would do a comedy; next night it would be a drama with a cornball villain and so forth.

Was there anyone in particular that impressed you? Stuck in your mind?

There were no stars or names as such; they were just touring groups of actors making ten bucks a week or something. But to me, the fascination of getting up and putting on a costume or makeup, even in high school, to be in a play where you're actually putting makeup on your face—it made you different. I mean the kids knew, hey, you were a professional, *you're putting makeup on*. You were *different* from other people. You were up on the stage and they were sitting down here, and there's a certain, I don't know if you want to call it . . . power, but it makes you different. That's why a lot of performers sometimes are good in front of an audience and not particularly good on a one-to-one relationship.

I always felt that when you succeeded Steve Allen and Jack Paar as The Tonight Show *host, you altered the show to suit your personality. It had to be as different as it made you feel.*

[*Solemn*] I remember when Paar was on there, people said, "Nobody will ever replace Paar." Well, that's true; Paar was Paar. I didn't go in to replace Paar. And I originally turned *The Tonight Show* down when they offered it to me, when I was doing that daytime show and I was getting pretty good money for it. It was comfortable and it was easy. I said [*fearfully*], "I've got to follow this emotional, crazy man—who had his own appeal to people because of his vulnerability and his outbursts?" It worked great for him. I realized that *I* had to go in and do what I did, whatever it was, and the audience would either accept me or they wouldn't. And when I give this thing up, somebody will come along and do it. They'll discover somebody else.

Friends of yours have said that you'll still be there in 1985.

I doubt that. I don't think so. We're going on seventeen years. I don't want to sit there when I'm an old man. I'm fifty-three now; I don't feel anywhere near fifty-three, but I don't envision sitting there in my sixties. I think that would be wrong.

You have become—and this is just a fact—so much a part of this culture. If you weren't there, I suspect there would be a real gap. This sounds very sentimental, but, if there's nothing going on on a weeknight, you're home and there's very little to look forward to, you can always turn on The Tonight Show *and see you.*

[*Long pause*] That's flattering. I think one of the things is that we're about the only show that does day-to-day humor. There's no other show that does it. *Saturday Night Live* is on three times a month; they do sketches. The monologue, for example, to me is a very integral part of the show. Being out there every night, it's the only show that I know of on television where anybody is commenting on what's going on in the country every single day.

But why do you think people feel so comfortable with you?

I can't analyze that. I really can't. I just do what I do. People ask me, "How do you analyze that you've stayed on seventeen years and the competition has dropped off?" See, either way you answer that, you end up sounding like a schmuck.

If you say, "Well, obviously I do a much better job than they do," or say, "I'm more talented," then people say, "You egotistical bastard!"

If, on the other hand, you play Harry Humble and say, "Gee, I don't know," then that sounds idiotic, too. So no matter what you say people say, "Aw, come on now."

I don't try to shoot for an average audience. I do the things I like to do, and I think I've learned what people will accept from me. That's just an intuitive thing.

In the past you've made remarks that seemed critical of Dick Cavett.

Yeah, I didn't mean that. It sounded, when it came out, as a put-down, and I didn't mean it to be. I'm fond of Dick and I know him well, and I think he's a bright, amusing guy, but I've often wondered if Dick wants to be an entertainer or a talk show host.

People say, "What's the difference between you and Mike Douglas and, say, a Merv Griffin and so forth—you're all doing the same show." And I'll say, "Well, there's one difference," and this again is not being patronizing, but I go out on concerts, have for fifteen years, I play Las Vegas every year. I do a stand-up act. The other people don't. I'm basically a professional comedian and it doesn't bother me to say that.

I always had the feeling that it bothered Cavett to say he's a professional comedian. I don't know why. There's nothing wrong with being a comedian. But that word comic or comedian bothered him. Like he'd rather be known as a wit or as a humorist.

Some people see being a comedian as lowbrow.

[*Riled*] Baloney. Jack Benny was a comedian. Jimmy Durante, Fred Allen and Skelton—all comedians. What's wrong with being a comedian? It's *not* lowbrow.

The Tonight Show *has always been a major vehicle for new comedians. In that respect, there's nothing else like it on the air.*

Because I realize that is the hardest type of entertaining to do—to stand by yourself and make people laugh. And anybody who says anything different is crazy. You can ask George Burns, you can ask any of the people who "stand." That's a lonely type of existence to get out there, one on one, and you don't have any instrument, and you're not dancing, and you're not singing the latest hits. That is a tough way to make a dollar. It's lonely; you've only got yourself.

Why do you think that you're such a staunch supporter of these new comedians and no one else really does it?

They have 'em on their shows. . . .

Not to the extent that you do.

Well, because it's a hard commodity to find, first of all. There's thousands of singers who can come out and sing a song. There are, however, not many young comedians who can come out and do six, seven, eight minutes. And it's fun to see it when they do come on and hit and go on to other things.

Joan Rivers, Flip Wilson and a lot of them are working now. Freddie Prinze, before he shot himself; and Johnny Yune is a new young comedian who's come on who I think is going to be good. It's fun to watch that happen.

Do you offer advice or counsel to these people before or afterward?

If they ask. If I feel they will take it well, because I don't want to be patronizing. But most of them know. They appreciate it. I mean, if somebody came to me when I was starting and said, "Hey, this would work for you," I'd appreciate it.

Freddie Prinze was so young when he came on the show and, prior to his appearances, he hadn't had a tremendous impact. Did you offer him any advice before or afterward?

Only once did I offer him some advice, and he asked me. He was going to do a joke where he was going to say "fuck," and he said, "What do you think?"

I said,"You're too young to get away with it. Jack Benny could come on, even though it was a mixed adult group, and do it, and the shock value would be funny. If you do it, they're going to resent it."

Did he do it?

No, he didn't do it.

Do you have any other perceptions about Freddie and the way he was?

I didn't know him well. I would guess it was too much, too fast, too soon. He came out of a minority background—from nothing—and being Puerto Rican and in the minority, and then all of a sudden having this tremendous surge of popularity, it's tough to handle. The money is there, the girls are there, the hangers-on are there. You fall into the drug thing. Liquor, pills; it's too bad.

I think he was simply unable to handle all of the shit that came down on him. He was twenty years old! And that's not the first time that's happened in our culture, as with rock stars that have not been able to handle fame and money thrown at them.

They mistake the recognition for importance. They have the fame, the recognition, but they ain't important. They're demanding this, they're demanding that because they've heard that's the way you do it. And your major stars, who are really secure and comfortable, they never have that problem. They walk in and say, "Where do you want me to stand?" *Boom.* And they just do it.

You usually don't have any rock & roll or hard rock on the show.

No, and I'll tell you why. Because it's too much of a problem for us every day to set them up. I had a group on once—I can't remember the name of the group [Youngbloods]; I don't think they're in the business anymore—but they were really hot and they didn't like the platform, they didn't like the risers, they didn't like the lights; they were talking to my director—who had only been directing for twenty-some years. So I went in and told them to pack up and get the hell out of the building.

I went on the air that night and I said, "We had booked, tonight, the so-and-so group. They didn't like the lights, they didn't like the directing, they didn't like so forth; and so I told them to go home, blow their noses and when they grew up they could come back and be on the show." And the audience applauded, because they had had it with that kind of behavior.

Is there anybody in rock you enjoy?

Oh sure. The Stones, and I think that Chicago and a lot of the groups are sensational. The Beatles were most talented; they could really write music. But some of the stuff I see nowadays . . . it's like what Artur Rubinstein once said when I asked him to comment. He said: "I cannot comment on something I don't understand."

It's a howl, it's noise, it's a happening. Sometimes I cannot separate the musical talent from what is going on onstage. I cannot really separate it. The kids are screaming and you can't really hear anything. I can't understand, for example, how 100,000 kids can go to a speedway and be a mile from something going on onstage there. But it's the being there, being with your peers; it's the culture. I'm there, I was there, but, as far as the music, I think it's sold an awful lot of junk under the guise of talent. But kids, you see, are very fickle and there'll be another band along next week. If that one falls out of favor there's somebody else. We can go back to David Cassidy, you know. First, David Cassidy, next week there's another hero, somebody to identify with.

Unlike some rock stars, virtually all comedians make themselves vulnerable to the audiences.

We go out naked.

Also, there's an axiom that most comedians—a variation on the sad clown thing—are very intense and self-absorbed.

There's a certain amount of truth in that. A lot of comedians are introspective, not the "sad clown" syndrome exactly; it's more like the myth "to be funny, you must have suffered." You must have been raised on the Lower East Side, and you must have fought your way out of this deprivation to be funny. That's not really true. Do you have to starve, be deprived, to be a great writer?

But I think there's a certain thing in creative people—and I'm not a psychiatrist—but I have found that people who are in the creative end of entertainment are not normal by most standards, whatever "normal" means. That is, as Margaret Sullavan said, "It's not normal to walk out and bare your soul to a bunch of strangers, that's not a normal thing for someone to do." Most people find that very awkward, and entertainers do it. I find that most comedians are a little cynical, as well they should be.

And I *am* cynical about certain things. And people sometimes mistake the cynicism for being abrupt or cold. I think it's just the way you perceive things around you. You've seen the silliness, the absurdity, the craziness that goes on in the world and you jump on that and expand it. You look at things in a different light. That's what makes comedy.

Comedians are highly competitive, many of them. I think it was Lenny Bruce who said, "Comedians hate to see other comedians get laughs." There are certain guys who really suffer when they see other comedians really scoring. I don't. But I know a lot of guys where the competition among them is just ferocious. They talk about friendship and so forth, but a lot of them would kill each other. There's something bizarre about guys who do comedy.

I find an intensity there.

[*Nodding*] And a certain amount of hostility.

I think Richard Pryor, for instance, is very aware of it himself.

Certainly. Of course, and he is. And he can be a very funny man. I'd like to see him not be so dirty, 'cause I don't think he needs it. But I think that's part of the hostility, and he comes out of the street, and it's street language. And you either buy it or you don't buy it.

Redd Foxx is a terribly angry man, and I think he knows it. He's very hostile. And I don't think it's healthy. I think it's hurting him a little bit. It's just a big game, it's a fuckin' game when you come right down to it. It's ridiculous, the competition, the drive and all of that. And people running around trying to be happy, not even knowing what the hell it is. I think *that's* a common denominator.

Another question I want to ask. A comedian who does very well on the show seems to get invited back to the couch. Is that a deliberate gesture?

We try to figure out, first of all, if a guy has had six or seven good minutes. If he comes to the couch and he doesn't do well, if you don't know him well enough yet, that does not help him. He comes out as a klutz. Once a guy's established and the audience knows him, he can come to the couch, you don't have to have him do a stand-up first because you know he's bright enough or can deliver a stand-up sitting down.

How do they know when to come over after they've done a well-received stand-up routine?

That's usually done before the show. Some people resent it, especially agents. Agents resent it more than the talent. That's a certain "goodie." A sign, I guess, that you have arrived when you've come to sit in the chair. But if you are dismissed, it's not being cruel. It's what works for the show. *The show's the point.* Sometimes you have to do it that way.

I've booked guests at times that did not get on. Some other guest may have an ulcer or makes leather belts and is going to come out and talk about it, but if a comedian is working well, it's silly for me to say, "Well now we've got to stop this and bring out so-and-so, who's going to tell us how to make leather belts." I don't give a shit at that time. I don't want to wreck the pacing of the show. [*Adamant*] *We create the show while it's on the air.*

People have said that Ed McMahon has one of the most engaging laughs in show business, while others have been very critical of him.

[*Irritated*] He's not sitting there going "ha, ha, ha" at everything I say. It's just the nature of the man. He can't be all things to all people. Somebody might say, "Ed's got to laugh at everything Johnny says. . . ." We just fall into funny things together, and some of them do become rituals of a sort that we do too much, but we enjoy each other. We've been good friends for a long, long time.

Who directs the writers?

Well, I talked with them this morning. If I get an idea, I'll call the guys and say, "Let's do this." I used to write for Skelton, and I write a lot of my nightclub material, and I contribute a certain amount to the show. The job of a comedian is to be a good editor and say, "That's good" or "I don't like it."

You don't have to give any reasons. It's a very tough show to write.

Ernie Kovacs was a real innovator and recognized the possibilities of that form of pure television where the camera is a partner in what's going on. Were you an admirer of his?

Well, here's where I may get in trouble, if you want me to be honest. Kovacs was an innovator. I didn't know him, I had only met him. So I don't know whether he was really a funny guy. I know he did bizarre things, but most of the stuff, if you look at it in retrospect, does not hold up very well. Because he fell into certain devices, using camera tricks, sound effects, as kind of shock things. And I didn't find them that funny.

I thought he was trying to make a point about the surrealistic qualities of humor, and he sought to explore these notions—funny or not.

I think he had a point of view, and I guess I just wasn't a Kovacs fan. And that's taking nothing away from him. A lot of people think Chaplin was the greatest of all times. I don't hold with that. That's almost sacrilegious to say if you are in comedy. Chaplin was a superb artist but I don't think that everything he did was all that great. I think that some of the stuff that Buster Keaton did was as good as Chaplin's. He just didn't touch people like Chaplin did. Chaplin seemed to be able to touch both bases—pathos *and* comedy—better than Keaton. But I think that Keaton was a better physical comedian.

Polite drawing-room humor is a dying art. Comedy is more aggressive these days. Looking back, actors like W. C. Fields kicked the ball in that direction.

Fans today, they would love Fields, you know. Because he was against *every-thing.* Kick a dog in the ass, rail against every social convention. There was a black humor, a hostility there. He had a terrible childhood, you know, ter-rible childhood.

What do you think of the kind of black humor you see on Saturday Night Live?

I've often thought being bizarre just to be bizarre is no good. I've seen *Animal House,* and the kids will probably hate me for saying that I don't think *Animal House* is very funny. Again, it's my own personal point of view. I don't think it's very clever. To me, a food fight is sophomoric.

Those sophomoric qualities are also in the slapstick tradition.

Don't misunderstand me, I like slapstick. Laurel and Hardy did a lot of slapstick, but there was a certain timing and cleverness about it, a certain reaction, an interplay. All I saw here were a bunch of people doing crazy things.

It's a distillation of the college humor. . . .

[*Arguing*] It's outrageous to be outrageous. Woody Allen's *Annie Hall*, to me, was a far better, more clever picture. It was funny, he said funny things. But he made social points along the way. It was a tender relationship between people.

Chevy Chase said recently that he felt it was very gratifying for all comedians that Woody Allen won the Oscars for Annie Hall. *He said it was a sign that a comedian was finally being taken seriously. Did you feel that Allen's awards represented a significant breakthrough?*

Yes, in a way it was, because it was the first time in my lifetime, I think, that comedy has really been honored. Comedy has always been thought of as frivolous and not too important and doesn't have the social meaning, you know, as a "deep" picture, when in fact it does. I mean, what if you didn't have the comedians? What if you didn't have any funny people?

Making people laugh is so damn hard. If you talk with Steve Martin, I think you'll find Steve a very introspective man, and very quiet and bizarre in many ways, but I don't think you'd find him, if you sat around in a room with him, hysterically funny. I think you'll find Mel Brooks more that way, because he has to be silly all of the time. He'd be sitting there saying,"Well, I'll-tell-you-this—" and he'd be doing a shtick, and that's Mel.

Still, I think they all spend a lot of time thinking about the human condition. Would you describe yourself as intense or introspective?

I suppose. I'm an extrovert when I work. I'm an introvert when I don't. But if I'm with a group of friends and things start to cook, I'll get in and be very funny, start to function.

Are you a big reader of humorists?

Yeah, I've read a lot over the years. You know, Stephen Leacock, Benchley and Mark Twain. I think the first book I ever read on humor was by Max

Eastman, when I was in high school. He was explaining jokes, why people laugh.

George Burns put it as well as anybody. He says, "If you laugh, it's funny."

Are you conscious of the enormous influence The Tonight Show *has?*

Only when I get out in the country when I go play concerts. It's amazing to me, the reaction. I get so close to it that I really don't realize sometimes the power or the exposure of that show.

You are, in my mind, a great believer in television and its possibilities to influence people and inform them.

Basically. I can go do a concert in middle Iowa somewhere, and those people are aware. You can go out and do humor about what's going on, politically or otherwise anywhere in this country, and they know what's going on—because of television.

Look what the kids are exposed to by the time they are six. Forgetting the commercials, just look at what they are exposed to. It's incredible when you start to think about it. Thanks to TV, you see men walk on the moon. They can see almost anything at all. And it's great if parents are really selective—of course, parents don't want to do that, because that's a responsibility they don't want to take. And I get so mad at the critical put-down of television all the time, that a child may see 25,000 murders and that you can't be with a child all the time to see what he's seeing.

Also though, especially in young minds, you have the notion of TV keeping one company. Problem is, people see lives on television and they don't compare favorably with their own life in any way, shape or form. Their frustrations are fired.

That's true; I did a special [in 1969] for Monsanto, which they hated. But I liked it. They missed some of the points I was making. For example, in the special, I opened up on a television set, a close-up, it was a toy commercial: "Hey kids! Be the first in your neighborhood to have this wonderful whatever-it-was for $29.95." And we pulled the camera back slowly, and it was a tenement flat. There were three little black kids, whom I hired from Harlem, sitting in a one-room flat watching the TV. A poor black lady and her kids were lying on a bed, just looking at this commercial. And I felt it was making a very poignant point. They were exposed to this, but it was completely out of their realm of reality, and the announcer was saying, "Run out and tell dad, be the first in your neighborhood, etc." and these kids, who had no dad, were just watching it.

For them, at that moment, it would be easier to go to the moon.

That's right. That was the point we were making. One of the critics said he didn't understand why, in the middle of the show, we had this toy commercial.

Still, you believe that TV has been a great informer.

It *can* be a great informer. I don't know whether it is. You see, I've always felt, when they say the job of television is to educate—I don't think that is the job of television at all. That's the schools' job and the parents' job. People who think you can put a kid in front of a television set and he is going to learn are crazy. You still need that relationship, I think, with the teacher and other students. With education you've got to participate. The only reason I ever learned anything is that I had teachers along the way that I enjoyed, that got me interested. The television set was going to be the great boon of civilization. It doesn't seem to have worked out that way.

On the show sometimes, people have to be informed to get the joke. You assume they are.

Absolutely. It is assumed that the people have read the paper, but as you know, most people don't. They get most of their news from the six o'clock or the eleven o'clock news. That's usually adequate for my purposes, but it's not the same thing. There was a joke I did one night mentioning Alexander Haig, and the audience hadn't the slightest idea who Alexander Haig was. They simply didn't know. Sometimes it bothers me a little bit that they might not know what I am talking about. I read a survey last week, and it said that a large percentage of the American public had not read a book since they got out of high school. They read magazines, periodicals, but not a book.

To read about what Bianca Jagger is doing is not high on my list of priorities. I could not give a shit what Bianca Jagger is doing, or what Jackie O. is doing, but those are the people you constantly read about. I guess it takes folks out of their ordinary humdrum lives when they read about Suzanne Somers. Nobody's life is humdrum, but they all crave information on instant celebrities. They have this voracious appetite for making new stars. Whatever happened to Henry Winkler? The Fonz? I mean, is that interesting?

Do you feel that it is incumbent upon you to have these celebrities on the show?

Yeah, but without going into their names, some of them don't have anything except their manufactured celebrity status. Yet we would be foolish if we didn't put people on who are in the public eye. You can't just have the people you want. You'll have a show booked sometimes with "names" and it doesn't work. And the next night, you'll have a show where nobody is particularly big-name, and it's magic.

Do you watch the show when other people are hosting?

Very seldom.

Any particular reason for that?

No.

How about watching yourself?

Joanna will watch my monologue. I won't because I've done it. And sometimes I don't like to look at it because maybe I'll think of other things. If we're doing a new character, a new sketch, or something has happened on the show that went crazy, I might look at that. I don't particularly like to watch myself unless I'm doing something really good.

How do guest hosts get chosen?

We just have a number of people and we just submit them or Freddie [de Cordova] handles it, 'cause that's a problem, to find people who can sustain it for any length of time. It's not so difficult to do one, two or three nights. The trick is to do it for a week or two.

What's the story on the controversy with Chevy Chase and whether someday he'll take over the show?

You know something? I don't know how that started. I really don't. I didn't know Chevy Chase outside of seeing him on *Saturday Night*. I started seeing these things in magazines, about Chevy Chase making remarks about

The Tonight Show. Some of them were little zingers. From the way I saw it, I got the impression that somebody was doing some publicity for somebody and was planting it.

I don't have a publicity agent. Haven't had anybody for years. I have a lawyer, that's all. I don't have any press people or anything. So I'd read these things and some of them are little zingers. Chevy saying, "Well I can't see myself sitting there talking with some dumb starlet for ten minutes."

Well, I might reply, "Who's ever asked you? Who thought you could do it in the first place?" As if that's all there is to it. I did throw a line against Chevy Chase once. Somebody talked about ad-libbing, and I said that I didn't think Chevy Chase could ad-lib a fart after a baked-bean dinner. I think he took umbrage at that a little bit.

But people love to read this shit. That makes a story. I remember once Streisand, she was booked on the show and we had a call that afternoon saying she wasn't going to come; I don't know why. But we billboarded her for two days.

I went out and said that Barbra Streisand was supposed to be here, she hasn't been here for twelve years, but I think it will probably be another twelve years before she is asked back. It was just a little joke, nothing vicious. [*Smirking*] So the next night, I get Madlyn Rhue, and we dressed her up in a Streisand get-up and she started to do "People." For a moment you couldn't tell if it was Streisand or not because she was lip-synching. I walked over and said, "Thank you, but we don't need you." And she walked back to the curtain and it was wonderful. I was just taking advantage of what was going on. And of course the papers picked that up and they made a big thing about Streisand and I having a quarrel.

Speaking of this, I remember the time that Dick Shawn was hosting the show and he turned the set completely upside down, knocked over your desk and used it as a boat for an ad-libbed routine.

[*Sternly*] He had no right to do that.

To a great extent that little living room seems like your living room.

Yes, and when I heard about Shawn doing that, I didn't like it, to be honest with you. I didn't see the show, but when somebody told me that he tipped over the desk and did all this, I just didn't like the idea of him taking it and then dumping the thing all over. It just wasn't his prerogative to do that. You'll notice that Shawn hasn't been on the show since then. I think he probably did it out of desperation. When you get to a point when nothing's working, you think, "What can I do to get their attention?" You drop your pants or you tip over a desk. If I got up and set fire to my desk, I'd have a right to do that. It's *mine.*

Later on, there was a show one night where your desk was a breakaway desk and you destroyed it.

Right. It had big shock value. We pulled in a breakaway desk one night. Just to break the pattern. See, the trick is you try to keep from being boring, which is the worst thing in the world. You don't want to go out and bore people. If there's any format on the show, that's the format.

Television does great things with news. They do great things on sports. They cover political things well—I think the coverage of the Middle East thing—it's been fantastic coverage.

They went to the moon and sent it back here and you see it, but people forget those things. They see *Three's Company* and they're all worried about tits and asses, the "jiggle syndrome." You know, girls running around with their boobs jumping up and down a little bit and that's a big crisis in the country. It's not going to get any easier to present quality.

We did a couple of jokes on Carter's son getting divorced, and you have to be kind of careful that you don't get too personal. *Saturday Night Live,* on the other hand, will go after anybody. They've done some outrageous things, and I don't always agree with them. I think the thing they did on Claudine Longet, while it was funny, was unfair, and I think some of the stuff they did on Patty Hearst at the time was really unfair. No matter what position you take, the girl was really in serious trouble. And Claudine Longet was up for manslaughter, and they were doing a thing, a skiing thing, where shots were ringing out and everybody was falling down dead. For some people it was very funny, but other people thought it was very unfair. But that's a judgment. And what one person sees is not what I'll see.

How about something that pertains to the political climate, to CIA meanderings.

We've really whacked away at some of those things, like the FBI when the Watergate thing was on.

I got the impression you felt very strongly about Watergate.

I did. I guess, like a lot of people, I felt let down. I resented people like Nixon and Agnew moralizing from the tops of their voices about morality and putting down the kids who didn't want to fight in Vietnam and talking about high moral principles when they were deceiving everybody. If they weren't so damn highly moral about it, it would be one thing, but I don't know how many people even know how much they were screwing the political process and using it for their own benefit. I think politicians in those positions have to have better standards. If they ask for those jobs, then they better have better standards than the rest of us. I'm not saying my morals were any better, but I wasn't the president. And I think when you're in those kinds of jobs and you have the public trust, then you should play it by the book.

Maybe that's tough for people to do, but you can't go on moralizing about how people should behave and what they should do when you're not doing it yourself. It's like the religious leaders around, you know, all getting rich on the world's guilt.

Are there any people you'd love to have on the show but have never corralled?

I keep kidding Cary Grant every time I see him. It's become a running joke now, 'cause he just won't do it. He just feels uncomfortable, and I understand that. Bill Boyd was another one—Hopalong Cassidy. I wanted to get Bill Boyd on the show, and he was a big fan of the show. I remember sitting with him in Danny's Hide-a-Way in New York, and he said, "Johnny, I love the show, but I don't want to hurt the image." He just felt uncomfortable. I liked him so much 'cause he was an interesting character. He was married five times, you know. He was a Hollywood leading man in the silent days that most people have no knowledge of. Handsome guy, one of the most handsome men I've ever seen in my life. White hair. But he wouldn't come on. Wanted to get him on with Gabby Hayes. Couldn't get him on.

Anyone else in public life?

I don't have politicians on very often for one simple reason: I find that most of them are not very entertaining. They'll tell you what they want to tell you and no more. They always have an image or set point of view, and you get into equal-time provisions as soon as you do it.

There are other shows that can do it better. *Meet the Press* does it better. *Face the Nation*, that's their thing. They can do it much better than I can do it. I don't want to be in the role of inquisitor. I don't think people want to watch that at 11:30 'til one at night. I never have thought that. Not for me anyway. I don't want Yasir Arafat on the show. I don't want to sit and talk to Menachem Begin. Not that it wouldn't be interesting, but I don't think that in the format of our show that's what I want to be.

I recall a time when you had Nixon on when he wasn't running for office, after he lost the California gubernatorial race.

Sure, that was fun, that was different, 'cause he wasn't running at that time and he was a national figure. I had John Lindsay on in New York, and that was fun. I only had John on because we were friends and he was kind of a charmer and almost a professional himself. And I had Agnew on, and he bored the shit out of everybody and moralized. I liked Hubert Humphrey very much. I found Hubert Humphrey a nice man.

Bobby Kennedy I had on, because he's a Kennedy, but there, you see, you're dealing with somebody bigger than life when you have a Robert Kennedy on. You're not dealing with a William Proxmire or Wally Hickel or somebody like that, and I had Johnson on once. But in the long run, it doesn't really go anywhere, 'cause then you fall into the equal-time thing. And I don't want the show to become a political forum. Most politicians are so politically oriented, self-oriented.

Ronnie Reagan, I know well, and I had Ronnie on two days before he announced he was gonna run [for president], but he wouldn't tell me on the show, right? I would say, "Ron, is there anything you want to tell me tonight?" And the audience would giggle, and I would say, "Now come on, Ron." Well, he knew he'd decided, but he's not gonna tell me. So I don't really get an honest interview. Politicians are only gonna tell you what's gonna make them look good, and you're not gonna get much deeper than that.

Why did the show move from New York to Los Angeles? I've heard a lot of reasons.

We found it was much easier to work out here. Facilities are better. Studios are better. It's all in one building. If we want to do a sketch, all I have to do is call and say, "I need a bathtub that comes through a wall," and I've got it tomorrow.

The facilities in New York are terrible. All the shows moved out. Where you used to have the Sullivan show and lots of variety shows, they all disappeared. There's nothing coming out of New York now except news and a few game shows. That's it. And at this point in my life, I enjoy playing tennis, enjoy going to the beach. I lived in New York seventeen years; I like the idea, as corny as it sounds, of a yard and a house. Maybe that's the old Midwestern values, but I like being able to walk outside in the morning and sit around; you can't do that in New York. That's the only reason.

People remain nostalgic about those old days when The Tonight Show *gang hung out in John Hurley's bar on Sixth Avenue, for instance, with Mitch Miller and everybody.*

Yeah, that's true. And I can remember the early days in California nostalgia, but all those places are gone now. You'd say, "Hey, let's go to Ciro's. Let's go to Mocambo," and the Sunset Strip had what was supposed to be glamour. There was a certain style to it, but that's gone. Those days are gone. And it's like the Oscars. You know, I'm going to host the Oscars this year, and somebody said, "Why don't we make it like the old days and the glamour?" I said you can't. Don't they understand? Gable's *dead*. Jimmy Cagney's sitting on a farm; Bogart is dead; all of those bigger-than-life people. I said you're talking about something that was in the Thirties and early Forties and is gone. People keep saying, "What happened to the glamour days in Hollywood?" It's a new era.

When you mention hosting the Oscars, I recall a number of times you were offered nice movie roles and you always turned them down.

I haven't seen anything I really liked, to be very honest with you. They were just movies, and any idiot could make a movie.

Blazing Saddles *was one film offered to you.*

Yeah, and I'm only off three weeks at the most at any time. You can't make a picture in three weeks. And at my age now, being a movie star doesn't excite me that much. The only thing that would be nice, I suppose, would be to have international recognition. They would know you in other countries if you made a picture. Maybe I will sometime, I don't know. I might sit down with somebody and write it.

I know that you worked briefly on the stage; did you ever have any inclination to do something like that again?

I don't have that drive. I don't know why. Some people think you have not lived or satisfied your psyche unless you appear on the boards on Broadway. I have great respect for Broadway actors because I know the discipline that is entailed in doing something night after night, the same lines. I found that I only did *Tunnel of Love* for three months; I thought it very boring after a while, but that's the challenge of a good actor, just to make it fresh every night. I enjoy the feedback you get from it. Especially *The Tonight Show*. I don't think I'd be happy doing a situation comedy anymore. Sure, I never have, but I can't see myself going and playing a role as a private detective in a situation comedy because I think it'd probably be pretty dull. And I have no desire to do specials, because on *The Tonight Show* there's almost anything I'd want to do on a special. We do sketches, we do blackouts, do the characters, et cetera.

I only did one special for Monsanto. But nowadays you see . . . suppose I put a special together. Somebody says, "Okay, Carson, we want to go on at eight at night." Then you find out that ABC has bought a two-hour movie, *Poseidon Adventure* or *Animal House*, and they throw it on opposite you. You're going to get killed. Television is the only industry that eats its young.

I wondered if you think TV, across the board, reflects the prevailing tastes and interests of America.

That has always been a subject of great discussion. When critics complain, the usual reaction from the networks is that we're giving the people what they want. But that also applies to car manufacturers, when you think about it. They always say, "Well the people want big cars; they want lots of chrome." I'm not sure they *are* giving the people what they want. If they've never given them anything else in quantity to sample, how would you know what they really want?

If you went out on the street and asked a hundred people what was wrong with television, many of them would probably say, "Well, there's not enough fine drama, not enough documentaries," et cetera. They would try to be eclectic in their answers because they don't want to look like dummies. They would all say there's not enough news, there's not enough social relevance in television. And yet, when you put it on, the people en masse don't seem to watch it. If 20 million people watch something in this country, that's not enough of an audience, which is kind of sad in itself.

It's my opinion that TV usually caters to the lowest common denominator, especially, in terms of humor.

I suppose. I think it was George S. Kaufman who said, "Satire closes Saturday night." I suppose if you tried to do what you would call an esoteric—I hate that word—satirical type of comedy review, you'd have an audience for it, but you wouldn't have a *mass* audience for it. I think they probably go for a more general audience type of comedy that people can easily relate to—where they don't have to think too much.

Then you come down to the question: What is television's job? What is its role? As long as television exists to sell products—and that's what it is in the long run, a medium to sell beer, soap, cigarettes, deodorants, breakfast cereals—there'll be problems with overall quality. As an advertiser, for example, I can see very well why a soap-manufacturing company would buy *Laverne & Shirley* versus *Monty Python's Flying Circus*. It comes down to the numbers again.

The Tonight Show *evinces a liberal attitude. But I sometimes wonder how much of the audience objects, from point to point, when a lot of things are bleeped out.*

We get letters like that from liberal people. It's a little ridiculous to bleep a dirty word, whatever it means. Even "damn" and "hell," for years, were not used in motion pictures, which always intrigued me, especially when you see a war picture.

I was watching *Patton* the other night, and it was remarkable that they let "bastard" go through. They wouldn't let "shit" go through, you see. They had to draw the line there, because that was apparently corruptive and too much for people to take. They substituted "dung." And you'd see Patton say "horsedung." And I thought that was hysterical. Somebody sat in an editing room and said,"We have to edit this. What can we have him say instead of 'horseshit'?"

Probably the most commonly used phrase, by men, women and children at any time during the day, is "Oh, shit." You step on your friend's toe and you say,"Oh, shit." George Carlin does a whole thing on it. But you see, they still had to draw the line on that for mass consumption on television. For some reason, Patton saying "horseshit" was going to have some effect; I don't know what effect it would have, but that's worthy of sitting down and having a psychologist, a sociologist discuss that. What would that have done to people? Would children be corrupted? I doubt it, since every four-year-old is saying that word, whether he knows what it means or not.

Back to the monologue—the other night when you were going into a com- mercial, you closed with "shit!" And the audience was stunned.

Shock value. Nothing but pure shock value. I did it one night inadvertently.

A joke had died or something, and I had said, "Ahh, shit." Again, it's the way you say it, it's how you say it, it's the *attitude* when you say it. You can say that word, and it can be so inoffensive and you can say it and make it offensive.

Did you ever hear the Beach Boys' "Johnny Carson" song?

Sure I heard it. Someone sent it over to the office. I don't think it was a big seller. I think they just did it for the fun of it. It was *not* a work of art.

How do you unwind from the tension of a life of television? I know you play a lot of tennis, also, you've done some sky diving.

Many of my outside interests started, basically, for the show, my own amusement, the Walter Mitty syndrome. Plimpton has done it. Everybody's done it. It was just a thing of getting involved in kind of hairy experiences. It was good for the show. I think the first one I did was pitching to Mickey Mantle and Roger Maris at Yankee Stadium. Then I drove the Indy car, I flew with the Thunderbirds in their air show, did some sky diving, quarterbacked the New York Jets for a series of plays. Those kinds of things. It was fun. It was good for the show, it was fun to do. The network didn't even know I was going to do it [*laughter*]. But you reach a point where there aren't that many things that are really hairy or exciting enough. Once you've done the free-fall parachute stuff and flown with the Thunderbirds, where do you go? What's left?

Pat McCormick told me a very funny story about one time when you were going into the Polo Lounge, and you didn't have a tie. So you put on a tie, but you took off your shoes and socks.

[*Laughing slyly*] I stayed there almost the whole night. I remember we went out somewhere else later, with me still not wearing shoes or socks, and nobody said a thing. Maybe 'cause I had a tie on. It wasn't in the rule book I guess.

Do you enjoy practical jokes like that?

[*Laughing*] Yeah, but you don't find any good practical jokes anymore. The old days of practical jokes . . . somebody did a whole book on them, H. Allen Smith's *The Complete Practical Joker*. Practical jokes are funny as long as they don't hurt anybody.

Another example?

Oh, when Freddie de Cordova came back recently from Africa—he was over there with Irving Lazar—I got our set designer to come down with all of the staff, and we redid Freddie's whole office. We tore out all his furniture and redid it like an African hut in the bush. And I hired two black guys with drums to come in, and all the staff showed up. I had a pith helmet, boots, shorts and his whole office was palm fronds and stumps. And when he walked in that morning, we had sound effects with the jungle noises, like an African village. That was funny! Just for the reaction. He couldn't get over it. That was a fun joke but it's just hard to do. For the whole day he had to keep it that way. He could hardly find his desk.

I recall seeing Rodney Dangerfield for the first time on your show.

I knew Rodney when he worked under another name, Jack Roy. Fifteen or twenty years ago. He worked the mountains, the clubs, then he stepped out of the business for a while. I think one of his lines—goes to show you how successful he was—was that when he retired he was the only one who knew he had retired. And I asked him one night, "Do you know where you got the name Rodney Dangerfield?" He says,"No, I don't." And I told him where the name came from.

I remembered a sketch that Jack Benny did some twenty years ago on his show, and here, I said, is the way the name Rodney Dangerfield came about. Jack and Mary Benny were holding a party. And Jack came into the room and said: "Mary, who's coming to the party tonight?" They had a big guest list. And Mary said, "Well, Jack, the Gary Coopers can't make it, Gary is making a picture." And Jack said, "Aww, they can't make it?!" And then she said, "The Ronald Colmans are busy, Ronnie was busy tonight." And Jack would go, "Ohhh, they can't make it?!" Then she said, "Jack, the Jimmy Stewarts also are not able to come tonight." "Well, who *has* accepted?" he asked. Mary said, "So far, we have Rodney Dangerfield." And there was a scream. The audience loved it.

Rodney's a funny man; he's got the physical appearance and the voice to do those put-down lines. Unfortunately, he's trapped a little bit in that character. But what he does he does very well.

I saw Andy Kaufman opening for Dangerfield at The Comedy Store in L.A. He was working in his persona as Tony Clifton, a potbellied Borsch Belt comic who's so obnoxious he compels the crowd to boo him offstage.

Kaufman will take a chance and say: "How far can you go with something? How far can I stick with this before the audience will either buy it or get outraged?" He's a funny cat, takes a chance. He comes out and he experiments with an audience and will stand up there and will face them down. Sometimes you hit, sometimes you don't, but that's the only way; you have to take a few chances and do something to see what kind of reaction you're going to get, otherwise you don't find anything new to do.

If you look around, you see right now with Steve Martin, with an Andy Kaufman, with Robin Williams, this kind of out-of-the-wall, bizarre comedy. *Animal House* certainly brings this out.

Does this brand of humor reflect something more than the desire to break new ground?

I don't know. I just see that trend, with Steve and Andy and Robin Williams coming to mind as exponents.

Some observers feel that the Second City improvisational theater, the National Lampoon, Saturday Night Live *and performers like Steve Martin have helped spawn a unique strain of humor. It's iconoclastic, very personal, and sometimes rather black humor. I've heard it called the New Humor.*

Well, humor has changed somewhat; it has expanded. Especially on TV. A lot of restrictions and taboos are gone from TV in terms of what you can talk about. It's a lot freer. I can remember that ten to fifteen years ago I couldn't tell a joke about pot on the air; couldn't even mention it.

I think the *National Lampoon* is good at what it does. It's got an effective parody style, one that can be accurate. What they do is often blunt and cutting and it's important to have that voice. I've just seen their Sunday newspaper parody and it is very funny. It's really right on. I think it's one of the best things they've done.

As for Steve Martin, he has a likable comedic style when he works within the framework of the white-suit-and-banjo character he's created; in his act, you see, he's a schlemiel pretending he's not. It's well done, but it can be limiting. He's been doing it for a while, so I'll be interested to see where he goes with it, where he takes it in the future.

Saturday Night Live's cast takes a lot of chances, a lot of real risks in the kinds of things they do, and I've liked a good many of them. The fact that they're live and the element of risk involved has a lot to do with their humor and its impact. [*Coyly*] And if they don't always turn out funny, well, they don't seem to get terribly upset about that.

All good comedy has a dimension of risk, and on your show you seem to accept and enjoy that fact.

The charm of *The Tonight Show* is greatest when things are not going well. That's the challenge. When the elements are right and everybody's free-wheeling, it stimulates both comedians and other guest performers and it becomes a stream-of-consciousness thing. On other nights, the trick is to make something out of what *isn't* happening. [*Laughter*] But every night, it's like walking along the edge of the Grand Canyon—at any time, somebody might push you off.

Is it especially hard for a woman to be a comedian?

Very difficult. It's because of the old role models that are assigned. A woman is feminine, a woman is not abrasive, a woman is not a hustler. So when you see a gal who does "stand-up" one-liners, she has to overcome that built-in identification as a retiring, meek woman. I mean, if a woman comes out and starts firing one-liners, those little abrasive things, you can take that from a man. The only one who really does it is Joanie Rivers, who's had, I think, great success with being a stand-up *comedian*. The other gals, like Lucille Ball, who was obviously a great comedy actress, and Carol Burnett—it's a different role that they play than standing onstage and doing jokes. I think it's much tougher for women. You don't see many of them around. And the ones that try, sometimes are a little aggressive for my taste. I'll take it from a guy, but from women, sometimes, it just doesn't fit too well.

Have you thought about the limitations and frustrations of comedy?

The philosophic questions about laughter leave me cold. I know what I can do and what I think is funny and what makes me laugh. And what I can do that makes people laugh. I prefer to concentrate on what I know.

So many people would like to get to know you better; what's the most frequent reaction that people have when they run into you, meet you?

I've been so visible for so many years. Somebody once said that I was one of the most recognizable people, at least in the United States, which is only because I'm going on seventeen years on *The Tonight Show*. Plus doing five years on the daytime show. Somebody almost has to go out of their way not to see you, if you're there. But that applies to anybody in the public eye.

The standard reaction or remark, really, used to be: "I go to bed with you every night." After a while that loses a bit of its pungency. The show has been on so long; you know I've had kids come up to me who weren't even born when I started the show. You have a whole new audience of young kids, maybe thirteen, fourteen, fifteen years old, who are discovering the show, and it started before they were even around. That's intriguing.

What always amazes me about *The Tonight Show* is the age span of the audience. It goes from twelve-year-olds on up. They'll see it on Friday night. I get fan mail from seventy-five-year-old people. Mail from college kids, the so-called sophisticated or hip crowd.

How did that Casablanca record come about? The two-record set of highlights of the show?

It wasn't my idea. It didn't do very well, strangely enough. I wasn't particularly enthralled with the idea because I think a lot of things we do don't transfer from video to audio very well.

This obviously is a completely hypothetical question: Do you think that you and your kind of humor could have worked out in England?

Let me put it this way. They've wanted to do *The Tonight Show* from England. I saw Paar do it. He had *The Tonight Show* over there and it didn't work very well. And Cavett went over there and it didn't work very well. I said, "I would be happy to go to England and do *The Tonight Show* if you will get English television to carry the show for about six weeks before we go over there." To walk in cold where they don't know who the hell I am or what I do is a difficult thing to do.

People always have the idea that the English love sophisticated comedy, dry wit and so forth. Not true. If you go and look at English television and the comedians, a good percentage of it is low comedy. They go in for a lot of music-hall bandy, dropping of pants, toilet jokes, it is incredible. When I first saw it, I was expecting Noel Coward; I was thinking of the witty, dry British sense of humor, and I saw these guys out there doing wee-wee jokes. Also, they love guys in drag, and infantile humor.

It's interesting that no British comedian that I know of has ever been a hit in this country. I don't mean Terry Thomas, Peter Sellers and those kinds of folks—they're actors. And yet our comedians can go over and play the Paladium and be big successes.

Rock music doesn't go over well in prime time. It's another unsuccessful transplant.

Television is not a good medium for music generally, because people have a $600 television set and the speaker is a little two-inch thing in the set. That's not a good way to listen to music.

Tommy, I guess, was the first big thing where they tried to carry rock into a different medium, an opera, and it had a modicum of success. But I don't think it was a big hit. And *The Rocky Horror Picture Show* . . . it's almost become a cult. *Sgt. Pepper* of course was a monumental bust. *Grease*, from what I read, is apparently not very good.

I've seen the members of Kiss interviewed. It was like interviewing four children. They really didn't have anything to say. They were all caught up in what they're doing, and [*bitchy*], "Man, we put the makeup on, I'm not going to be seen in public without the makeup. . . ." I find it all superficial.

The one I talked with that I liked is Alice Cooper. I found him a very charming, interesting guy. So I take it back. And I do like him. 'Cause I think he's got a little more perspective on what he's doing. I've met him socially and I've had him on the show. When I see a guy named Alice Cooper and I look at his shows, I have already prejudged him, which you shouldn't do.

I can't put rock & roll down because anything that's lasted as long as rock & roll has, you can't dismiss. You can't say it's a fad. It *ain't* a fad.

Ever been to a Rolling Stones concert?

I saw one in New York once. It was crazy. Absolutely crazy. I went with some people from the station, just so I knew what I was talking about. It's just mass hysteria.

Was that in 1975 at Madison Square Garden?

No, it was earlier than that, but it was like mass hysteria. It was like when the Beatles first came here, it was just mass hysteria. Pubescent hysteria.

Are you sorry you didn't have the Beatles on the show?

You know, it was funny, they were fans of the show, because I remember when they were first on the Sullivan show, when they first came here, and

Ed Sullivan told me [*imitating Sullivan*], "These youngsters are really, really fans of the Johnny Carson *Tonight Shoe.*" I guess it's one of the shows they'd seen when they first visited the States and were checking out our culture.

You know [*sadly*], if I gave you a list of the people who had been on the show that are dead, it would stagger you. When I start going down the list of the people that have been on the show from the opening show—Joan Crawford, Groucho Marx, Charles Laughton to Peter Lorre; you know, big, big names like Sophie Tucker, Ted Lewis, Jayne Mansfield and, recently, Freddie Prinze, Jack Cassidy. Hundreds and hundreds of people have passed away in the last seventeen years that were all on the show. It gives you a strange feeling sometimes.

Is there anybody in history that you would've liked to have on the show?

[*Smirking*] Attila the Hun.

I think you two would've done some pretty wild slapstick routines together.

[*Laughing*] That's an interesting question, really. Da Vinci probably; he could've been a hell of an interview. Or Isaac Newton, because my hobby is astronomy. I'm fascinated with astronomy. I was up at five the other morning. I woke up—I think the dog was barking—I came outside and got the telescope out and was sitting there at five in the morning. It's a real mind bender. Gorgeous. Yeah, somebody like Newton, Keppler, Copernicus.

In a book called The Human Comedy *by William Saroyan, he writes about how people make transitions in their lives: you just presume everything is there and will take care of itself, and then there's that transitional period in everyone's life when they realize if they are going to be happy for the rest of their lives, if they're going to enjoy life and fight off the boredom that's probably the big enemy of life, they are going to have to make a conscious effort to make themselves happy. I've wondered if there was a certain point in your life, a certain moment of self-esteem and self-worth upon which you built every other experience.*

I know what Saroyan's saying. There comes a time or a moment, I don't know whether you can say it precisely, when you know in which direction you're going to go. Even when you're young. But you don't know *why* exactly. I know it happened to me when I was quite young.

You go through those phases—"I'll be a doctor or I'll be . . ."—the standard things. But I think it's when you find out, at least for me, that you can get in front of an audience and be in control. I think that probably happened in grade school, fifth or sixth grade, where I could get attention by being different, by getting up in front of an audience or even a group of kids and calling the attention to myself by what I did or said or how I acted. And I said, "Hey, I like that feeling."

When I was a kid, I was shy. And I think I did that because it was a device to get attention. And to get that reaction is a strange feeling, it is a high that I don't think you can get from drugs. I don't think you could get it from anything else. The mind starts to do things that you didn't even realize it could do. It's hard to explain.

And you walk off and you're just, everything is such a high, and it's a great feeling, and that's why many performers have very big highs and very big lows. Most of them that I know. I know I do.

People don't understand that. They put you down as being standoffish or cool or so forth. It's not *that*.

I suppose it's the manipulation, I suppose it's the sense of power, the center of attention and the me-ism. And performers have to have that. You see, that's one of the things that goes against the grain of being brought up; you should be modest, you should be humble, you shouldn't draw attention to yourself. Well, to be an entertainer you *must*.

You gotta be a little gutsy, a little egotistical, so you have to pull back sometimes when people say, "Well, he's stuck-up." Stuck-up is only another word for self-conscious. You aren't stuck-up. You are aloof, because you aren't very comfortable so you put up this barrier.

Do you recall the specific moment—a spelling bee or a class recitation or a play or something—when you crossed over that barrier?

I think it was in a play. A Christmas play, as a matter of fact—Dickens' *A Christmas Carol*. My classmate Dorothy Ward played the Ghost of Christmas Present. I played the little boy who went to fetch the turkey, and this man, Scrooge, gave me a shilling to do it. And I realized that I was the center of attention. I realized that people were saying, "Hey, look, he's in a play." That makes you different right off, you see. You're stepping out of *here*, and you're stepping into a make-believe world, and all of a sudden people are looking at you. You like that, but at the same time, you find that you have an ambivalent feeling.

So you had a shyness and an awkwardness that you had to conquer?

[*Sheepish*] Yeah, oh yeah. I just felt uncomfortable. I still feel uncomfortable in large groups of people. Not audiences, mind you. With audiences, I'm fine. I can go out in front of 20,000 people because I'm in charge. See, most entertainers feel that way. When you walk into a large group of people, you're not in charge, and all of a sudden I sometimes feel uncomfortable.

It's hard to find a focus.

That's right. You see, when you're on the stage all the focus comes *here*. They're watching you and you're in control. Now you walk into a reception or a cocktail party full of 200 people, I find that unsettling. I know a lot of people who are entertainers, they, you know, get up against the wall at these times or sit in a corner. If they're up in front, they're fine. So there are two ambivalent things at work there. David Susskind's favorite word, dichotomy, which he loves to use—there is that in performers.

I think people who are creative, in the arts, also seem to have larger appetites for life than most people, to excess usually. Whether it be drinking, whether it be sex, whether it be anything, the appetites seem to be larger. I don't know why, but they seem to be that way. And with writers too—most of them don't seem to be terribly happy people, whatever that means. Because I guess you are always in a way trying to prove yourself, and as an entertainer, you're always in front of an audience. People say you're only as good as your last performance.

Has there been a firm resolve in your life to maintain a sense of moderation in things?

Yes. As you get a little older and you get a little more mature, you should get a little wiser. You shouldn't be as dumb as you were at twenty. I don't have maybe the insecurity I did. I'm quite secure in what I do now and I know that what I do, I do well. And God knows I've got, materially, anything that anybody could ever want. So I don't have that worry. Now to most people that would be serendipity, to be financially independent, but that doesn't mean a thing, really, in the long run. Having not had it and then having had it all, I can say that I *know* the difference, and all that money gives you is the state of not having to worry about money. That's *all* it gives you. Nothing else.

And along with money comes responsibility, you know, and how you handle it and what you do with it and what you make out of it. It doesn't give you much else. It means that you have, as performers will call it [*grinning shyly*], "fuck you" money.

Now what does that mean? All that means is that I don't have to do what I don't want to do. Someone says, "We want you to go out and do the show" and you say [*laughing*], "Fuck you! I don't have to do it." And that's very important for an entertainer because when you're scrambling, you do *everything*. You take this, you do this show, just to pick up a few bucks. You need the exposure, you gotta go here, and you should show up at this party and you must do that.

Your self-esteem takes some hard knocks.

I think so—until you get to the point where you can say, "I don't have to do that," and so you can be selective in what you want to do. But you know, I've been very fortunate in this business. Whether I'm basically a lot happier now than I was then, I'm not sure. I'm not sure.

Being happy is always a process.

If you ask people what they want, they'll always say they want happiness, but that's not something you go out looking for. That comes to you as a result of what you're doing. That should be the result of your family, your work and your accomplishments. If everything goes well, you should be reasonably happy. But you can't go out and *look* for it.

So, all things considered, you're happy with the way everything has turned out.

Yes, but well, you know, it depends. Do you have a capacity for happiness? A lot of people don't have a capacity. I don't know how big my capacity is. It's not as big as a lot of people's, but I'm getting better at it all the time. I think you should. I think as you get older you ought to get better at those things and get your priorities together to find out what really is important to you. To me, my work is important. And I think for a man generally, that's probably true. You know they say for a woman, her marriage and the family life is more important, but I think that's changing too. Women are now finding that what they do as a person is more important, but to a man, it's always been his work. When I say work, I don't mean *career* exclusively, but being up there is more important to me. The family is an important part of it, but it can't be everything.

But you envision a time when there may be a radical change and you won't be working on The Tonight Show *anymore.*

[*Wistful*] I want to be able to say that, and I don't know whether I'll be able to handle that. I say to myself, "Can I step away from *The Tonight Show* or entertainment and do something else and be happy?" Probably not, because I think once you've been exposed to something like this or you enjoy it, you can't turn around and become an architect, you know, or say well, I'm going to just completely put that aside and try another career. I am involved in other things, other interests, businesswise, that I find fascinating. But I think I would always like to entertain. You know, it may not be *The Tonight Show*, but, my God, nothing lasts forever. It could've been a lot worse. But I can always have the concerts and do guest shots on other shows or do occasional shows myself, or maybe even a picture. [*Laughter*] Who knows?

All in all, it ain't been a bad trip.

Alan Alda:
All Nice Men Have Their Limits

M*A*S*H, *otherwise known as the 4077th Mobile Army Surgical Hospital unit, decamped from its fictional base just a few miles behind the front lines of war-torn Korea on February 28, 1983. It was 30 years after the United States and China parleyed a ceasefire in the conflict. M*A*S*H, the highly rated CBS-TV comedy/drama series, endured for 11 years; the Korean War ended after only three.*

Writer-producer Larry Gelbart and colleague Gene Reynolds gave the *M*A*S*H* TV program its sense of offbeat breadth and possibility; actor Alan Alda embodied its warm humanity.

One of the best, and best-loved, programs in the annals of television, its critical eminence and surpassing appeal were also due in no small part to the talents of Alda, who starred as Captain Franklin "Hawkeye" Pierce, a sarcastic but soft-hearted surgeon from Crabapple Cove, Maine.

Alda's father, actor Robert Alda, a sizable influence on his son, suffered a stroke in 1984 and never recovered, dying in 1986 at the age of 72. The parent never had the career he wanted, early on bequeathing his boy with a kindly if sometimes disconcerting longing for control.

Amiable but driven, Alan Alda would attain the singular career distinction of winning Emmys for acting, writing and directing. His frequent added role in numerous *M*A*S*H* episodes as a writer ("The Longjohn Flap," "Comrade In Arms, Part I," etc.) or director ("Mail Call," "Dear Mildred," "The Late Captain Pierce," "Bulletin Board," "Dear Ma," "The Kids," "Margaret's Engagement," "Exorcism"), or both ("Dear Sigmund," "Hepatitis," "Fallen Idol," "Comrade In Arms, Part II," "Inga," etc.) lent immeasurable quality to the ongoing effort.

Dr. H. Richard Hornberger *aka* Richard Hooker wrote the original novel (derived from his experiences with the 8055th MASH unit in Korea), director Robert Altman took it to the movies in 1970, its TV debut came in 1972 and Alda co-wrote and directed the final two-and-a-half-hour TV episode, "Goodbye, Farewell and Amen," which became the most widely watched television program of all time, drawing a 60.3 rating and a 77 percent share of those viewing the tube that Monday evening in 1983.

After *M*A*S*H*, Alda wrote and directed a host of engaging movies, among them *Sweet Liberty* (1986), *A New Life* (1988) and *Betsy's Wedding* (1990), besides excelling as an actor in *Crimes and Misdemeanors* (1989), *Whispers in the Dark* (1992), *Manhattan Murder Mystery* (1993) and *Everyone Says I Love You* (1996). He also hosts the *Scientific American Frontiers* series on PBS, and appeared on Broadway in the 1998 play, *"Art."*

Contemplating life as it's acted versus life as it's lived, Alan sat in "The Swamp," Hawkeye's tent on the Los Angeles set of *M*A*S*H,* in 1981 and offered a philosophical overview: "I find that there are many moments from which many things flow. That's why I don't believe in movies in which cataclysmic things happen to people and their behavior is forever changed. I think there are a lot of small changes, understandings. I like comedy that lets you know there's pain going on underneath. You have to accept people and their imperfections, and work with who you've got."

Like Hawkeye as Alda envisions him, and like most of us, Alan would prefer to be liked, understood, and left to his own sense of purpose. This becomes
plain in the story that follows. But such things aren't always possible.

Dr. Hornberger, a staunchly conservative Republican, adored the Altman
film made from his (asterisk-free) *MASH* book, but never warmed up to
Hawkeye as scripted and portrayed by Alda.

"My characters weren't so liberal," Hornberger once complained. Fair
enough, but Alda's character was wittier, more complex, and more compassionate.

THE INTERVIEW

STROLLING OUT of the harsh glare of the klieg lights on the set of television's *M*A*S*H* and into the warm Los Angeles sunshine, Alan Alda
waves cheerfully to a friend who happens to be passing by and then responds,
blank-faced, to the question posed by the reporter walking at his side.

"Do I have any hobbies?" he murmurs. "Well, I play tennis most mornings at six-thirty with this buddy of mine."

Who's his partner?

"I don't want to get into that," he replies.

I stop walking. How, I say, does he expect anyone to ever write a decent
profile of him if he won't even divulge the identity of his tennis partner?

He stops walking. Scratches his stubble.

"I guess you're right," he says, a grin growing on his lips. "Boy, you're
stuck with a real ass, eh?"

Alda, comfortable in a suit of army fatigues that must have been tailored
for a scarecrow, walks past the Twentieth Century-Fox lot where *M*A*S*H*
is filmed, and guides me into the studio commissary. He orders and sits in
silence until the food arrives. Shoveling forkfuls of ratatouille into his
mouth, he admits amusement with our gently escalating confrontation.
We've been talking since mid-morning during the shooting for the last
M*A*S*H episode of the season, and he's beginning to realize that he's
stuck with a writer who is going to make an issue of his legendary reluctance to tell interviewers anything of consequence about himself.

So how would *he* approach the writer's assignment?

"I would spend time with him—meaning me—and watch him work. I
would sit with him and eat with him and drink with him and shoot the
breeze and try to make real contact underneath the assignment. And I would
also not betray him and I would let him know that I would not. And then I

would withhold stuff that I thought would hurt him." Pause. Booming laugh. "Unless I had to get *even* with him for something."

After spending months shadowing Alan Alda, the best-loved television actor in America according to the 1980 People's Choice awards, the only thing a reporter might want to get even with him for is his maddeningly genial penchant for noncooperation.

Up close, the boyish good looks are surprisingly angular and craggy, the worry lines on his brow boldly accented, and the creases that frame his mouth a deep parenthesis. His thick salt-and-pepper hair is combed and flattened like a schoolboy's. He talks like he moves, sprightly but with a hesitant lope, as if he might turn back in the next moment to retrieve something he left behind. His eyes are kindly and unwavering, but he looks *through* you out of a curious sort of courtesy, as if looking directly *at* you would be an intrusion.

Alan Alda (born Alphonso d'Abruzzo) comes from a show business family, father Robert Alda (also Alphonso d'Abruzzo) having risen through the vaudeville ranks to attain a fair amount of success as a stage and screen actor. And if the son learned anything from his father, a shy, punctilious man who speaks of his career in terms of "moves made a little too late," it was to keep people at bay by beguiling them.

"I don't want to tell you about what pains or terrifies me," he admits, "because one of the things that is the mark, the currency, of an intimate relationship is revealing things about yourselves to each other that you wouldn't reveal to people you don't trust as much. If I spend all that currency on strangers, I'll go broke."

I had first met Alda two evenings earlier in an Italian restaurant, an hour before he was to screen a print of his motion picture *The Four Seasons*, which he wrote and directed as well as starred in. I was to see him for the last time six months later, long after his thoroughly wholesome cinematic exploration of middle-aged friendship had become the dark-horse hit of the year. In the months in between, I would watch him from the sidelines, amazed at his stamina and his ability to say little or nothing—in the nicest possible way—while he bantered with the reporter from *People*, chatted with an interrogator from *20/20*, and granted innumerable interviews to the press. After each of these episodes, he took me aside and made a valiant, but ultimately hapless, attempt to explain what had just happened, and who he really, *really* was.

That day in the Fox commissary was typical, Alda clearly most comfortable talking about subjects that have some ideological point.

He laments the "absurd" objections raised by censors in the first year *M*A*S*H* was on the air when a script called for use of the word "virgin," and notes with relief that *The Four Seasons* was rescued from an "R" rating when he decided to delete a four-letter word from a scene with actress Sandy Dennis.

"Maybe I sanitize everything I touch a little bit," he considers, anticipating criticism, "but that is *not* my intention." And then he wonders aloud if he has erred in letting *M*A*S*H* emphasize the comedic, rather than the dramatic, aspects of a medical unit's travails during the Korean War. He mentions the extensive preproduction interviews that were conducted with physicians who had served in actual MASH units. Much of what these medical personnel had to offer was never used, he says, and gives an example. It seems one veteran doctor recalled a unit being awakened one night by the terrified shrieks of a nurse.

"They all ran to see what was the matter," Alda recounts, "and she was in her tent screaming because a tapeworm was attempting to get out of her mouth—a long, long tapeworm whose head was poking out."

He sets down his fork.

"That to me has always been the essence of the *M*A*S*H* experience. Something so horrible that you *can't* escape from it. It's very deep inside of you and it's ugly. It becomes as intimate a part of you as the food you eat. It scares the daylights out of me from time to time and I'm helpless with it."

If this kind of horror has rarely shown up on the screen with actor-director-writer Alda, it isn't because he hasn't had personal knowledge of it.

"I'll never forget Alan's experience with polio," says his father, currently a regular on the TV soap opera *Days of Our Lives*. "I had graduated from vaudeville to the movies and had moved Alan and my wife out to Los Angeles to begin fulfilling a seven-year contract to Warner Brothers. It was 1943 and I was starring in *Rhapsody in Blue* and we had gone to see a movie when Alan—he was seven and a half—began to do a lot of coughing, sneezing, and wheezing in the theater. We thought he might have a bad cold. But that night when he wanted to go to the bathroom his little legs couldn't hold him up so I had to help him walk. The doctor came in the morning but there was no positive diagnosis. In those days not too many people knew what polio was."

The elder Alda phoned his stand-in on *Rhapsody* and the man and his brother helped the distraught father get his son down to Los Angeles General Hospital. Alan would eventually be examined by a number of specialists before the exact nature of his crippling illness was determined.

"We were envisioning a life of wheelchairs for Alan," says Robert, "when we heard about this controversial cure from Australia, which involved laying hot compresses on Alan's limbs. Eventually a physical therapist came in a number of times a week to attempt to reconnect the motor responses to his own will."

The heat treatments were the brainchild of a nurse named Elizabeth Kenny and Alan remembers them as being "excruciating." "They're blankets, cut up in pieces that fit over your arms and legs, that are dipped into a double boiler so they're scalding hot and then they're wrapped around muscles every hour to reduce the stiffness. It was awful. I would scream and beat the bed every hour on the hour. I also knew that they were helping me and I felt bad for my parents that they had to go through my pain."

Unlike Hawkeye Pierce on *M*A*S*H*, neither Alan nor his father have any medicinal quips to lighten the painful recollections.

The Aldas moved to a larger house in Hollywood, one that had a pool, and soon Alan was spending "eight to ten hours a day" in the water, exercising to prevent the deterioration of his muscles. Robert Alda thought he was living a nightmare—until he woke up one morning to the news that a child of his close friend Lou Costello had died in an accident. Realizing things could actually be worse, the senior Alda redoubled the vigilant monitoring of his son's therapy and as soon as the boy's limbs responded to treatment, he encouraged him to get up on horseback, try his hand at simple sports, strive to be active. Meanwhile, comics like Phil Silvers, Hank Henry, and Beetlepus Louis began showing up on Sunday afternoons to entertain each other—and Bob Alda's convalescing kid—with their hoary routines. Alan survived the illness with no physical impairments, but the father was aware that his son's contacts with the outside world had severely atrophied.

Alan had been in vaudeville and the Borscht Belt circuit since he was a baby. He even made his stage debut in the Catskills, sitting in a high chair in a skit presided over by comedian Joey Adams.

"Up until high school most of my friends were burlesque comics," says Alan. He was educated by private tutors through the eighth grade, and when he finally entered public school, it was only to discover that his classmates despised him.

"It was a shock. I was always getting beaten up," he says. "The kids would line up and take numbers—like in a deli. 'Twenty four! Sock him in the nose!' When I went back to school my father was a big star, and I was very extroverted and enjoyed being the center of attention with my jokes. I didn't understand the kids' language. I was too overbearing for them, and they found me as obnoxious as a baggy-pants comic."

Alan was bright, but indifferent to academic studies. He had asked his father if he could go directly from high school to the stage, but was advised to get a college education and do some summer stock on the side. He was packed off, and after a shaky start ("I literally slept through the entrance exams—I looked like the village idiot") matriculated at Fordham University at the age of sixteen.

His grades were strong enough in his junior year to enable him to go to Europe on an honors' program. He met a French-speaking Algerian girl in the Pyrenees and fell in love, "sipping wine in cafés and talking gibberish." In Rome he played the part of a young writer in a production of *Room Service*, and in Amsterdam he landed a role in a TV series that starred his father.

At 21, Alda married Arlene Weiss, then an assistant first clarinetist with the Houston Symphony Orchestra. The couple met in Manhattan at a recital and later attended a dinner party at which they had the good manners to eat the hostess's fallen rum cake from the kitchen floor. "We were the only two people who did it," Mrs. Alda assures.

The early years were hard. Arlene got a job teaching music in junior high schools while her husband paid the bills between acting gigs by working as a doorman, a cab driver . . . and a clown.

"He was a clown to attract customers to newly opened businesses—a garage in Brooklyn, a store in Manhattan that sold chicken parts," says Arlene with a wince. "The kids were hostile, wanting free balloons. I think they made fun of him."

One of Alan's earliest stateside TV appearances was a part as a rich kid on Phil Silvers's *Sergeant Bilko* series. Among his other early credits were a stint with New York's "Second City" improvisational troupe, and Broadway roles in *The Owl and the Pussycat, Purlie Victorious, Fair Game for Love*, and *The Apple Tree*. Before his 1980 motion picture success with *The Seduction of Joe Tynan*, he had appeared on the big screen in *Gone are the Days, The Moonshine Wars, The Mephisto Waltz*, and in the role of George Plimpton in *Paper Lion*.

But Alda's professional beachhead came with the development of the TV series based on Robert Altman's film *M*A*S*H*. Initially, he was unimpressed with the show and held out until the first day of shooting before agreeing to accept Hawkeye's olive-drab mantle. The show is now in its tenth season.

Huddled around the corner table in the otherwise empty Italian restaurant on Santa Monica Boulevard is one of the hottest trios to hit Hollywood in years: Alda, square-faced Marty Bregman (Alda's close friend of some twenty years and a top agent who helped to build the careers of such stars as Bette Midler, Barbra Streisand, and Al Pacino), and the pillowy Bobby Zarem, a wild-haired, bespectacled press agent whose masterfully orchestrated media blitzes for films like *Saturday Night Fever* moved both *Time* and *Newsweek* to dub him "Super Flack."

In between trips to the nearby buffet table for cold pasta and stuffed mushrooms, the three men are cracking jokes, slapping each other on the back as they anticipate the upcoming release of *The Four Seasons* and explaining how they all got to know each other. Bregman grew up in the same Bronx apartment house as Arlene Alda, so he's old-school. Zarem became Alda's Number One Advance Man after engineering a massive publicity campaign for *The Seduction of Joe Tynan*, a well-made but modest movie that received ten times the attention it might have attracted had there been no one to hawk it.

Everybody is thrilled but tense. Tonight is the first private screening of the final, scored edit of *The Four Seasons*. Only cast members and others closely connected with the film will be there, and nobody's quite certain if it was wise to let a reporter tag along. They're *sure* they've got a monster hit, but that doesn't mean they're *certain*, you understand—or at least that's how Zarem explains it in the car on the way over. He and Bregman are mildly terrified; they desperately want to triumph in Hollywood press and industry circles. Alda, however, is more concerned with being accepted by the general public, never forgetting that his fans have supported him whenever the Fourth Estate has shrugged. And he hates Hollywood. Period. So, logically, he refuses to concede that he has become a powerful and bankable presence there.

"I'm not aware of having power," he says. "At a certain point a few years ago I had an agent that kept coming to me every week trying to make me into a factory, telling me that all kinds of projects could be coming through my company and I wouldn't have to do anything. I would just collect the money. I tried to make him understand that I didn't want to be the Kentucky Fried Chicken of show business. I had become successful doing piecemeal work, and I also felt I would be as successful—more successful—than I'd ever dreamed of being, if I could just continue doing that."

As piecework laborers go, Alda is pretty prolific. After writing four *M*A*S*H* episodes and directing five for the show's seventh season, he spent a six-month hiatus starring in three films: *The Seduction of Joe Tynan,*

Same Time Next Year, and *California Suite*. That's working faster than Colonel Sanders or Colonel Parker, and in Hollywood, if you can turn out the product they pay you back with power.

"God, I feel *silly* being this nervous," says Alda, stalking back and forth as he hides in the looping room across the lobby from the private theater on the Fox lot where his film is about to be screened. Agitated, he knits his hands, plunges sweaty fingers through his hair, and sneaks peeks into the theater, as he hears members of the cast being greeted. Bregman pokes his head in to say that the lights are going down inside and we slip into the last row in the back.

The film is intended to be a slice-of-life glimpse at the interrelations of three middle-aged couples as they take four seasonal vacations together, examining the dynamics of their friendship, what holds them together as a group, and what keeps them apart from each other as individuals. The screening soon becomes an uncomfortable example of life imitating art.

Everyone laughs at the right moments but the reactions are restrained. It's obvious that each observer is evaluating his or her own contribution, from Arlene wondering aloud how well the prop photos she took for a segment of the film look, to Alan whispering how pleased he is that people laugh loudest at the laughter of characters who are amused by an off-camera sex scene.

Out in the lobby afterward, everyone mills around, emerging from self-absorption just long enough to shake Alan's hand or kiss his cheek.

"Alan, I really, truly adored the film," says costar Rita Moreno, who then insists rather strongly that a portion of the soundtrack is too loud. And so it goes.

Bregman mutters to Zarem that it was wrong to invite a reporter to this wake, and Zarem follows me into the bathroom to get my reading on the matter. Meanwhile, Alan works the low-key receiving line. For tonight these people are his public. And in conversation, as well as on the screen, he lets them off easy.

The next day I visit Alda at Fox, meeting him in his tiny bungalow office opposite Studio Nine, home to the main *M*A*S*H* "compound" set, a network of tents, operating rooms, and mess halls, surrounded by a backdrop of a mountainous landscape. In the center is the canvas-roofed shack shared by Hawkeye, buddy B. J. Hunnicut (Mike Farrell), and antagonist Charles Emerson Winchester III (David Ogden Stiers). We chat briefly and then he's called to work, confiding along the way as he crams for the day's shoot that he's been too busy with his film to learn his lines. As a result, he flubs and fumbles on camera but does so with high spirits, nobody appearing to mind. In the end, he catches on quicker than his cohorts, and proves to be the most commanding, and the most natural, presence in the scene.

"Alan's appeal is that he's very relaxed, just an average guy," says actor Jack Weston, who was directed by Alda years ago in an ill-fated NBC-TV comedy pilot, and then was reunited with him for *The Four Seasons*. "There is no difference between his demeanor as a director and his manner as an actor, which I find remarkable. I think that people go to see Alan in the movies and watch him on TV because they like *him*, the person, first, and then the character he's playing."

"I love people's ordinariness!" Alda exults during a break in the *M*A*S*H* shooting. "To be human is to be creepy some of the time. That's ordinary to me. That's also extraordinary, 'cause everybody's got an individual thumbprint. I don't think there are heroes. I think there are ordinary people who behave heroically at times. Therefore, everybody is capable of being heroic. I don't know about any famous heroes that I can get a handle on because they don't seem real to me. Take Reagan. The public persona that he presents is of a likeable person. But that's not saying much because that doesn't mean that you're talking about a *real* person."

The same could be said of the speaker: Alda suffers from his own camouflage, and so, possibly, do his biggest fans. His professional sense of *duty* toward a rigid wholesomeness saps the emotional strength of much of his work, especially his comedy. In the *M*A*S*H* operating room, the thoroughly moral Hawkeye cracks his black jokes to distance himself from the horror beneath his scalpel so that he's able to continue doing his job. Problem is, he tells those jokes so smoothly to his captive audience of medics and patients that the action soon becomes ritualistic, even precious, and we often wind up as far away from the horror as Hawkeye.

During another break in the *M*A*S*H* shooting, Alda stretches out on his character's bunk, exactly as he does on-camera. "My favorite thing here is the picture of Truman over my bed. I love the fact that Hawkeye would constantly wake up to a picture of the man who put him here."

The remark sparks a moment of introspection. "I just realized about a year ago what continued to interest me about the Kenny cure for polio," he says. "I was flying along in a plane and I was thinking about how hard it was to get people to care about the Equal Rights Amendment. I made the connection that my life was saved by this woman from Australia. She was a nurse who found out by accident that you could treat polio-afflicted children in this way. She was visiting kids out in the bush and she mailed a telegram to the doctor and said, 'What do I do?' and he said, 'There's not much you can do. Just treat the symptoms.' She thought that since the muscles were tight maybe heat would help.

"She personally cured hundreds and hundreds of kids in her clinic but for thirty years they told her, 'We're not interested. Doctors will run medicine. Not nurses.' Sexism not only kept her back, but also kept children all over the world from health. If she hadn't stuck to it and fought it and won, I might be dead now. Sexism is thought to be impolitic. It's not just impolitic—it can be lethal in some circumstances."

In 1979, Alda literally turned a cartwheel down the aisle as he approached the dais to accept an Emmy for a *M*A*S*H* script he'd written called "Inga." Its plot concerned a female-surgeon with greater surgical skills than Hawkeye. The story came about as a result of a dinner discussion with women friends about sexism. They vehemently disagreed with him on some points, and he found in the days that followed that he strongly disliked being disagreed with. He put things right by dramatizing the argument in "Inga," just as his support for feminist causes repays his debt to Elizabeth Kenny. Alda has an almost compulsive desire to keep his psychic slate clean, all karmic tally sheets balanced. Sometimes it seems like Alda is determined to be the nicest guy in America, and the inner frictions caused by this lofty goal permeate more of his work than he is willing or able to admit.

Jack, the quasi-sensitive, let's-get-it-all-out-in-the-open protagonist that Alda plays in *The Four Seasons*, is a man who loves to hear the sound of his own gently reasoning voice, someone who refuses to allow a problem to be resolved until he's convinced *he's* done the resolving. To the extent that the character is amusing, he is so because of the flamboyant intensity of his insecurity. It took Alda a long time to concede that he had not pulled Jack out of thin air.

"As I was doing it I would say to Arlene, 'This is a character trait for Jack. It's a lot like . . .' and I'd name somebody else. And she would say, 'What are you talking about? It's you.'

"For the next year while I was editing the movie," he continues, more intensely, "I started to drop a lot of those traits that I had owned up to in writing the script. Jack controls other people, but in a charming way. I finally acknowledged that I had these little techniques for controlling conversation. And it's a fear—it's not being *mean* to people. It's a fear that things aren't gonna go right or that people won't be happy, won't be entertained.

"I'll never be rid of some of them," he adds quickly, "but they're not all that bad. It's not like being an axe murderer."

When pressed, Alda eventually admits that there are other aspects of himself that found their way into the character of Jack. "Things that happen between friends in that picture have happened between me and friends." He cites as an example the disclosure by one of his friends in the film that he is going to file for divorce. Jack offers no solace, no comfort to his distraught buddy, only grating disbelief, followed by a scolding intended to provoke a guilty retreat from the decision to divorce.

"The divorcer," he says contritely, "is somebody I love and I'm very close to. The drive for friendship is as strong as any drive we have. You can get pissed off and separate from friends but you can't outgrow them. I think there's a certain unspoken point at which you commit yourself to a friend— only it's not like a marriage, where you commit yourselves formally and people come and fill up a room."

Carol Burnett, who plays Jack's wife, Kate, later tells me that when she fast read the original script she was surprised at the lack of depth in the characters she and Alda were to play.

"I talked about it with Alan and I said, 'You really don't know where they're at.' As far as Kate herself goes, I felt she was too perfect and there wasn't anything to play."

Kate evolved, at Burnett's urging, into a super-conscientious woman, whose very "goodness" means that she is frequently taken for granted by her husband and friends. She urged Alda to write a fight scene for the couple and, finally, he did.

Alda has difficulty, and a distaste for, discussing his own marriage and he makes it clear that he resents questions that force him to sum up the relationship in a few words. But when I happen to ask what he considers his greatest personal accomplishment, his response is swift and terse.

"I think marrying my wife," he says evenly. "And staying married and putting all the effort into that because it made me a better person and together we made three wonderful people—my daughters. It may sound a little trite, but it's the real reply to your question. What did you hope for," he adds eagerly, "when you asked that?"

The next time I encounter Alan Alda, he is sitting before a spotlight in a suite in the New York Plaza Hotel, dressed in a smart tweed sports coat and wool slacks, his knitted tie neatly knotted, speaking into a camera for his umpteenth *Four Seasons* TV plug, this one for *20/20*. He is droll and deferential, winning over his interviewer with his hair-trigger guffaw, while a *People* magazine reporter hovers nearby, taking it all in. He appears nervous only when asked about the Equal Rights Amendment.

"I didn't feel at ease mixing the film and the ERA during the taping," he says later as he rushes along the hotel corridor, en route to a photo session downtown. He has been on the road for almost two months, giving hundreds of interviews. Before he's through, he will have been around the world publicizing his picture. He says he doesn't mind. *The Four Seasons* is a huge success. It has appealed to both the middle-aged audience he felt he was assured of getting and the adolescent crowd that Hollywood predicted would elude him.

We keep in touch by phone. He reads me box office grosses, attendance records. Zarem also keeps in touch, making sure I'm aware of press response. Bobby notes that Aljean Harmetz, film writer for *The New York Times*, has done several pieces on the phenomenon of the film, pointing out that it was *The Four Seasons*, and not *Raiders of the Lost Ark*, that ignited the movie-going boom in the summer of '81.

Zarem and Alda and Bregman have done well. By Oscar time, the film will have opened worldwide. And the heretofore publicity-shy star will have appeared on the covers of *TV Guide*, *Ms.*, *People*, *The New York Times Magazine*, *McCall's*, *Ladies Home Journal*, the *New York Sunday News Magazine*, and *Redbook*.

"At the start of all this, the press people at Fox advised me that the two most important publications for me to appear in were *Rolling Stone* and *Playboy*," says Alda, sipping white wine in Bregman's plush offices. "They felt I had to be in those magazines to get the teenagers and the college kids in my corner. In the end," he laughs, "those were practically the only two places I didn't show up, and it made no difference whatsoever!"

Indeed. Alan Alda was for sale in the summer of '81 and everybody bought him.

His daughter Elizabeth enters the room with a girlfriend, carrying the poster of *The Four Seasons* that she has doctored so that it features sister Beatrice; Bea is turning twenty on Monday. But she feels there are bugs in the design. Dad gets down on the floor and focuses on the unfurled birthday gift. He suggests they consult with Mom tonight, and then make a trip to the art store near their New Jersey home. The girls leave. I'm about to do the same.

But first Alda takes me aside to review his criteria for a fairly reported profile, deciding I've probably fulfilled my journalistic duties. But what, I ask, about that business of the reporter "withholding" things that might "hurt" the subject? He breezily releases me from that obligation. One last question: How much of himself has he surrendered to the public this past season in exchange for vast notoriety?

"Enough. I knew it would be a transaction, a trade-off," he says. "I agreed to let reporters know just a little bit about me in exchange for their writing about the film."

Did he find any articles he read especially intimate or irksome?

"Most of it was fine. I didn't like the headline of the story in *McCall's* ['Alan Alda: Portrait of an Almost Happy Man'], little things like that. And there was an inference about psychiatry in the article in *The New York Times Magazine* that I didn't care for."

Was it untrue? Has he not been in therapy or analysis?

"Well, it was half true and half not. I don't want to get into it. What I found most enraging overall was the armchair analysis of me. I don't like that crap.

"One more thing," he says sharply. "I'm a little sick of this 'nice guy' tag that was hung on me all over the place. Like they put on the cover of *People*: 'Is there no dog mean enough to bite this man?' It's total bullshit. Robert Redford is an actor who also directs and writes, and also has a wife he's been married to for years, and lovely children too, and they don't stick him with that damned nice-guy label."

So what's the inviolable Alan Alda going to do the next time he has to market one of his film ventures?

He smiles, hoping to control the situation—in a charming way.

"Next time," he says sweetly, "I'm gonna be Redford and he's gonna be me. Okay?"

Michael O'Donoghue:
The Clint Eastwood of Comedy

Actor, songwriter, author, poet, broadcaster, television and film writer, and arguably the most influential humorist of the last 30 years, the darkly comic Michael O'Donoghue had patiently auditioned all his life to be the focal point of a proper Irish wake. On November 8, 1994, he finally got the part.

Best known as one of the creators of *The National Lampoon* and longtime head writer of the late-night NBC-TV institution *Saturday Night Live*, O'Donoghue died suddenly at 54 of a cerebral hemmorage. His wife Cheryl Hardwick, a musical director for *SNL*, was by his side.

Shortly afterward, Cheryl picked a Saturday evening for Mr. Mike's memorial party, draping their exotic West 16th Street apartment in Manhattan (which could have been Dr. Caligari's rumpus room) in black tulle, hanging the negatives of O'Donoghue's brain x-rays over his vacant desk, stocking the Zebra-skin wet bar in their former boudoir with champagne and beer, and inviting chums from *SNL* and elsewhere to stand on chairs and tell stories about "O'D."

Chevy Chase arose to recount how O'Donoghue had guessed his fortune one day in a taxi cab: "Michael told me, 'Someday, you'll make a mediocre movie star.' I don't know how to say this, but I loved Michael and I'm crushed that he's dead."

This soliloquy inevitably summoned memories of the *SNL* opening monologue that O'Donoghue fashioned for guest host Chase on November 13, 1985, which executive producer Lorne Michaels nixed well before airtime:

> *Chevy*: Right after I stopped doing cocaine, I turned into a giant garden slug and, for the life of me, I don't know why. Hi, I'm Chevy Chase. Have you noticed that, in the years since I left *Saturday Night Live*, my eyes have gotten smaller and closer together so that they now look like little pig eyes? Why? Again, I don't have a clue. As I was saying to Alan King the other day at the Alan King Celebrity Tennis Tournament, "Alan, I need more money. What I can't fit in my wallet, I'll eat or I'll shove up my ass, but *I must have more*!" And when I looked in the mirror, my eyes were the size of Roosevelt dimes and had moved another inch closer to my nose. "What is going on here?!?" I exclaimed. . . . Still—the fans showed up for my last movie—*The Giant Garden Slug's European Vacation*—a movie any man would be proud of. . . .

Michaels, whom O'Donoghue long accused of simply hijacking the O'D-directed cast of *The National Lampoon Radio Hour* for his own shrewd network TV purposes, stood up to say of the man: "I loved him deeply. And it would embarrass him as much as it embarrasses me to say so."

At that moment, one happened to recall a certain postcard—also authored by O'Donoghue in November '85—in which Michael imagined a sound-bite sized *Meet the Press* parry-and-thrust with his old boss:

Question One: "How much *are* you getting paid, Lorne?"

Question Two: "Even so, is it worth dragging your dick in the mud every Saturday Night?"

Truth is, it was a rare pleasure being the brunt of O'D's serrated sarcasm. Long before the notoriety of Hunter S. Thompson and P. J. O'Rourke (both of whom were admirers) O'Donoghue's writing, repartee and on-camera characterizations aimed for the bullseye behind the bullshit.

"Michael always knew the right targets," said screenwriting partner Mitch Glazer shortly before the wake. "Michael had real social concerns and was very moral, but he was also a sucker for a good joke. His 'nothing's sacred' sense of humor was based entirely on how good the joke actually was. If you were really funny, *then* all bets were off."

While no fan of cheap sentiment, O'Donoghue loved the expensive sort, and the many fetes, recitals and holiday theme parties he threw with wife Hardwick (also a composer for the Children's Television Workshop) were the chic downtown social events of the '80s and '90s, featuring guest musician-friends as diverse as James Taylor, Paul Shaffer and Diamanda Galas. In 1982, O'Donoghue celebrated a Top 10 country hit on RCA with his song, "(Single Bars and) Single Women," as performed by Dolly Parton. And in late 1991, O'Donoghue and Hardwick hosted an historic reception-recital for Leon Theremin, inventor of the pioneering electronic instrument that bears his name; it was the 95-year-old Theremin's first appearance in America since 1938.

An occasional screen actor with roles in such comedies as *Manhattan* and his own *Mr. Mike's Mondo Video* (both 1979), *Head Office* (1986) and *The Suicide Club* (1988), O'Donoghue was also the author of several humor books and editions of his wry poetry. He was working at the time of his death on an epistolary novel called *Letters from France*, and was more than a year into a monthly column for *Spin* magazine, called "Not My Fault!"

The O'Donoghue profile that ensues was assembled over some six months in 1979; said to be the source of more admired quips than any wag since Oscar Wilde, Michael was excellent company. More than anything else, O'Donoghue was a writer of meticulous modus and sublimely efficacious style—but no amount of goading ever got him in the mood to publish a collection of his letters to friends (and foes), or an anthology of his vast output of fiction, poetry, sketches, film and TV scripts, plays and comic prose (much of it penned for his private pleasure and defiantly unpublished, filling rows of carefully categorized file cabinets in his lodgings).

When this writer was asked to offer a reminiscence at O'Donoghue's wake, I decided to refute the calumny that Michael was a curmudgeon/ crank who had no affection for children by offering the following excerpt from a recent note he'd sent my wife and me regarding our newborn boys:

August, 1994

As for the twins, I think you should tell them that they were born triplets and one died—the brightest, prettiest one, needless to say— and drop hints that they were somehow responsible but, when pressed for details, just mumble, "I don't want to talk about it now. Maybe someday, when you're older." Then burst into tears and run from the room.

Of course, whatever their shortcomings, always compare them unfavorably with the dead triplet—"Betsy."

And occasionally Judy should set an extra place at the table and then blurt out, "I'm sorry! What could I have been thinking?!" and then slip off to her room and refuse to come out for days. Trust me on this. It will build character.

—X,
O'D

Herewith, by way of farewell, are a few more excerpts from a random sampling of faux-elegant O'D missives (in most cases stickered "Aerphost" and sent from O'Donoghue and Hardwick's second home, a country manor called Garraunbaun House in Moyard, Connemara, Ireland) that regularly turned up in the mailbox, addressed to this writer and his spouse, who had fondly dubbed Michael "The Only Snake in Ireland":

August 23, 1988

The Irish R.M. is just as much fun as you promised—sweet, gentle and witty—filled with antique argot such as "black as the inside of a cow," and the like. Violet Martin, one of the authors, came from this region and lived close to here in Oughterard. *Letters from France* goes well and, when completed, should get me kicked off the planet.

There *are* snakes in Ireland as enclosed ("Magic Snakes. 6 pieces— light at end—will form into a large snake—will not bite") will attest. *Warning! Do not believe the package! They will bite and are very, very poisonous!* I don't know how they can allow such dangerous—*Oh my God.* One got out of the package—a large one. It's slithering across the rug. It's crawling up my le

July 16, 1989

Here's an Ould Irish phrase you may find useful—"A concert for the deaf," as in "Last night during dinner, Paddy gave a concert for the deaf." It means Paddy farted a lot. Truly a land of poets.

—X,

O'D

June 18, 1990

Ireland Must Be Heaven Because My Mother Was Killed In
A Head-On Collision With A Speeding Cement Truck There

—Music hall ditty

Come see us anytime. There's always room in the turf shed for you (provided you "pull your weight," of course). Judy, unfortunately, will have to sleep with the caretaker.

—X,

O'D

"The only snake, etc."

St. Patrick's Day, 1991

Let's see. . . . Did you know this quote from Mike Tyson: "I like to hurt women when I make love to them. . . . I like to hear them scream with pain, to see them bleed. . . . It gives me pleasure." Foreplay is just a right cross.

Let's have dinner. We can talk about Mike Tyson's love tips—"Get in close and work the body!"

. . . All best,

O'D

August 22, 1992

"Wrap the green flag round me boys,
And shove me in a hole.
The drinks are on the house tonight,
I'm finally off the dole.
Another Mick potato to be planted in the ground,
So drag me to the graveyard, boys,
And wrap the green flag round.
Farewell to County Limerick
Where the River Shannon flows
And the fields are filled with heather
Just as purple as my nose. . . ."

And then the old guy vanished. One second he was there, sitting on a mushroom, stroking the feather on his little green cap and *Poof! He was gone!*

Just kidding. The song, of course, is from that movie about JFK—*Years of Lightning, Day of Drunks*. And there was no old guy. And it wasn't his feather he was stroking. . . .

Garraunbaun. Late afternoon. The sun has sunk so low it's smoking cigarette butts from the gutter. I swear, this country is on a ten-thousand-year coffee break. They finished putting up the stone fences and said, "Christ, Paddy, that outta keep the dinosaurs out. Now let's go to the pub and drink heavily until men have colonized Mars."

It's raining. There's nothing to watch on TV but game shows—*Priest for a Day*, that sort of thing. . . . In closing, let me leave you with an Irish Prayer:

May the road rise up to meet you,
May the wind be always at your back,
May the sun shine warm upon your face,
The rains fall soft upon your fields,
And until we meet again,
May God hold you in his hands,
And squeeze you 'til the piss runs out your ears.

Whatever,
"Irish Mike" O'Donoghue

In one of O'Donoghue's last letters from Eire, arriving in the early autumn of 1994, he offered his own critique of his comedy, contrasting it with that of old-school figures like Bob Hope:

Here's a book by Bob Hope (*They Got Me Covered*, 1941 edition) you might find interesting, obviously slapped together by his writers—chock full of "gags" about how ugly he is, how unfunny he is, what a poor lover he is, etc.

I've never gone for the "me like a schmuck" self-deprecating style of comedy (essentially a Jewish conceit), preferring how ugly *you* are, how unfunny *you* are, what a poor lover *you* are. It always seemed braver to me. And what really frosts my balls is the "we're all schmucks together" style. Eek.

—X,
O'D

THE INTERVIEW

"**H**ELLO? YES, THIS IS MICHAEL. You wanna do an interview with me? The day after tomorrow? Why, that's my day of rest! Well, okay, I'll cooperate—but I'll be doing a lot of drugs; I'm not giving up *that* part of my Sunday.

"Besides, I've got a lot to talk about. I got an idea last night for a book of poetry called *Jesus May Love You, but I Think You're Garbage Wrapped in Skin.*"

I arrive at O'Donoghue's New York West Village town house on a chilly afternoon, and he admits me with a polite handshake and then a fatherly pat on the back.

"Have a seat, old boy," he says, pointing to a green velvet couch. "Do you want some coffee? No? Well, I know you folks in the People's Temple are very strict," he dead-pans, and then laughs heartily. He's wearing a baggy pair of brown corduroy pants, belted tightly at his tiny waist, and a dark green pajama top with white piping. Shuffling around in slippers as he nips from a snifter of brandy, he seems nervous but eager to communicate.

"I have to get myself some coffee in a second," he mulls, his round, dark sunglasses firmly in place, accentuating his pale visage and further reducing a balding head no larger than a honeydew melon. "I took a Quaalude—half a Quaalude—which makes me honest. I don't have time to censor myself. I've always thought that truth is the ultimate lie; human beings aren't capable of understanding it, quite frankly. It dazzles 'em. But you can ask me any question you want if you ask it honestly. Cock size, anything, I don't care." He smiles encouragingly.

I figure I'll begin by asking about his book of poetry, but before I can, he insists I listen to a song he wrote at four this morning. As he hastens to recall it, I realize that he may have been up since then.

"Oh, this is a fucking beauty, this song! Let me see if I can put it together. It's called 'Blue Morphine.' I don't have a melody for it, so let me see if I can just talk it." He begins to recite the lyrics, occasionally lapsing into a surprisingly mellifluous croon:

> I'm flying too close to the moon
> What is the light that dreams are lit with?
> Will it be over soon?
> Falling like angels cast from, the sky
> Only blue morphine can teach us to fly
> Blue morphine.

It goes on like this for a while," he bubbles, "and the last refrain comes after some really hot saxophone."

Falling forever, shadows and smoke
Death is a lover, and love is a joke
Blue morphine.

"It's a bit on the negative side," he concludes with a beaming grin, "but when you make those major dream breakthroughs at four in the morning. . . ." He cancels the thought, striving ahead: "I had a dream one time, a real hot religious dream in which I was the baby Jesus, nude.

"I've always wanted to be Jesus," he continues. "Let's face it, any Irishman has. A lot of my humor is like Christ coming down from the cross—it has no meaning until much later on."

Michael O'Donoghue, 39, is perhaps best known as the originator of some *Saturday Night Live* skits in which he depicts the possible reactions of the Mormon Tabernacle Choir, Tony Orlando and Dawn, and Mike Douglas to having long steel needles thrust into their eyes. If your response to that kind of slapstick is an irate "That's not funny, that's sick!" then you're at least getting the point, so to speak, of his wanton wit.

On *Saturday Night Live*, he often appeared before the cameras in the sinister, sunglassed persona of "Mr. Mike," telling one of the "Least Loved Bedtime Stories" in which, for example, he reduced the hippity-hoppity antics of B'rer Rabbit to "random acts of meaningless violence." It seems his public comic sensibilities are identical to his private ones. He confides with a bleak snigger, "There's no difference between Mr. Mike and me. He rose out of a dark emotional situation I was in. The sunglasses came out at the same time. It was a time of *snakes on everything*." Michael is now remembered by his former *SNL* coworkers as "a certified nut case," an unbelievable, hilarious, sick bastard" and "a true comic genius who will someday surpass Mel Brooks and Woody Allen."

"Yes, there are a lot of things in life safer than comedy," O'Donoghue counsels with a smirking swallow. "But let's face it: when that sniper on the highway catches you in his sights, you're not thinking about statistics, eh?"

Does he have any philosophical thoughts about comedy?

"I always think about anything that gets a rise out of *me*," he says with a wink. "I look at comedy with, not a jaundiced eye, but rather a *cancerous* eye. I once wrote an ad for *Saturday Night*—which *did not* get on the air—for a wonderful new product, Spray-on Laetrile. The ad started with a girl telling her boyfriend, 'Gee, Jim, I'd love to go to the dance with you tonight, but I can't. I have cancer.' And he says, 'Aww, come on honey! Haven't you heard about Spray-on Laetrile? One little *pssst* and you can kiss cancer goodbye!'

"I never wrote or pandered to a market. I never made the stupid mistake of saying, 'I'm the New York sophisticate and I like this joke, but the pig masses in Crib Death, Iowa, will never understand it because they are such *filth*.' So I never did a Carol Burnett and wrote down to anyone."

The voice is overly calm, modulated to simulate a gracious, albeit tentative, benevolence. He sounds like a mellow late-night FM disc jockey who slits little girls' throats each evening before he reports to work.

"Excuse me," says O'Donoghue, abruptly rising for more brandy. "I think I forgot the question. Kitty Carlisle, do you want to field this one?"

"Life is not for everybody," O'Donoghue rules, and he admits he needs some extra encouragement to face the task. Over the years he's experienced a number of severe "emotional reversals," as he calls them, ranging from a brief ill-fated marital fling to a glut of career disappointments. "So I got myself some dark glasses," he says. "And then once inside them, I felt a lot better in the hidy hole and didn't want to come out for a long time. Tried to come out a couple of times while I was working for *Saturday Night*, but I didn't make it. I couldn't stand the fluorescent lights in the NBC offices." But somehow the glare of Hollywood seemed less harsh.

In the summer of 1978, Woody Allen asked O'Donoghue, sans his seaweed shades, to play a small part in his forthcoming motion picture *Manhattan*. Things were looking ever upward for Michael, who had just left *Saturday Night Live* to create three late-night specials in association with *SNL* producer Lorne Michaels. Working with a staff of young writers that included Mitchell Glazer, Eve Babitz, Dirk Wittenborn and *National Lampoon* alumnus Emily Prager, O'Dohoghue concocted a teleplay based on the lives of fashion models, a sci-fi horror epic about rampaging roaches entitled *The War of the Insect Gods* and *Mr. Mike's Mondo Video*, a comedy takeoff on the sleazy early Sixties oddities-of-the-world film documentaries.

O'Donoghue assures me he was genuinely thrilled to get the chance to present his comic vision en masse and (hopefully) unadulterated to the nation's TV viewers. But, hey, it's not as if *everybody* gets invited to appear in one of Woody's films, and the man *did* win a shitload of Oscars for *Annie Hall*, so we shouldn't mind if Michael puts on a few airs and rhapsodizes just a *trifle* too much about his "crucial" role in Woody's current cinematic masterwork, eh?

"I play Diane Keaton's old boyfriend, Dennis, who's this asshole film director that Woody destroys to get to her. You know, there's always a paper tiger in these urban love affairs.

"I play the macho lead and—*get this*—I'm the male sex symbol. It's an interesting role because I've never been in a movie before and there was a heat inversion in New York the week we shot my scenes. I got terrible migraine headaches, so I had to take massive doses of Percodan. Consequently, I could barely remember the lines, the shooting, anything, because it was all one narco haze.

"I was really outclassed on the set, I really got nervous. In a Chinese restaurant scene I finally conceded to myself that I was dying on camera, so I began eating as I spoke; a cheap device—yet it works!"

On the day *Manhattan* opens in New York, I purchase a copy of *Time* with Woody Allen on the cover and read it while I stand in line for two hours to see Michael O'Donoghue's screen debut. Fifteen minutes into the picture he pops up during a big cocktail-party scene in the sculpture garden of the Museum of Modern Art. Bella Abzug is concluding some sort of fundraising spiel when Isaac Davis (Woody) strolls up to speak with writer Mary Wilke (Diane Keaton) and her creepy, spectral date, Dennis (Michael!).

> DENNIS: [*To Isaac, mildly irritated*] Er, excuse me. We were talking about orgasms.
>
> ISAAC: [Meekly] Oh really? Well, sorry. I didn't mean to butt in. . . .
>
> MARY: [*To all assembled*] Give me a break! I'm from Philadelphia! We never talk about things like that in public!
>
> ISAAC: [*To Mary, quizzical*] You said that the other day. I didn't know what the hell it meant then, either.
>
> DENNIS: [*Self-absorbed*] I'm just about to direct a film of my own script, and the premise is this guy screws so great . . .
>
> ISAAC: *Screws* so great?
>
> DENNIS: [*Nodding coldly*] . . . Screws so great that when he brings a woman to orgasm she's so fulfilled that she dies, right? Now, this one [*indicating Mary*] finds this hostile.
>
> MARY: [*To the world*] Hostile? God, it's *worse* than hostile. It's aggressive-homocidal!!

ISAAC: She *dies?*

MARY: [*Laughing nervously*] You'll have to forgive Dennis. He's Harvard direct to Beverly Hills. It's Theodor Reik with a touch of Charles Manson.

BYSTANDING PARTY GUEST: [*Blankly, to no one in particular*] I finally had an orgasm . . . and my doctor told me it was the *wrong kind.*

Although it gets some of the biggest laughs of the movie, the whole strange exchange is over in a flash and O'Donoghue never reappears. So much for the Percodan Method school of acting.

Indeed, there is enough of Michael's own comedic perspective in the scene that he could have written it himself. Dennis has the detached, offhandedly evil aura that O'Donoghue sometimes likes to affect, and the other characters are full of the same pathetic liberal psycho-prattle that he loves to parrot. But he is much more complex than the singles-bar existentialists who Dennis epitomizes. Believe it or not, Michael's a somewhat charming guy who actually *likes* people—or several of them, anyway. As *Saturday Night Live* producer Lorne Michaels puts it, "Michael doesn't really believe that the human race is a lot of quivering scum. He just says he likes to feel that way because it gives him the nervous energy to get up in the morning."

There's another reason why Michael's brief appearance in *Manhattan* is so indicative of the man. All his crazed Percodan performances, the scenes in the Chinese restaurant that were probably his best stuff, ended up in the dumper. Michael O'Donoghue is a legend around the publishing and television industries not primarily for the things he's done that have reached the public eye, but rather for the, er, *unusual* body of work that has never gotten past the Bowdlers, censors and other assorted arbiters of taste in this country. Needless to say the expurgated material was pretty exotic fare. And then there's the slightly disturbing day-to-day behavior of O'Donoghue himself. . . .

A dropout from the University of Rochester, O'Donoghue first attracted attention while a contributor to the now-defunct *Evergreen Review*, in which he published bizarre, funny plays with names like "The Automation of Caprice" and also wrote a lurid comic-strip parody named for its scantily clad superheroine, "Phoebe Zeit-Geist." The strips, later collected in a book, became a cult favorite and paved the way for a volume O'Donoghue authored in 1968 called *The Incredible, Thrilling Adventures of the Rock* ("It only took twelve minutes to read"), whose sales were as slim as its story line. Shortly thereafter, he slipped ("like swamp gas," according to former colleague P. J. O'Rourke) into the Madison Avenue offices of the *National Lampoon* and there generated such broad strokes of parody as "Tarzan of the Cows," "Battling Buses of World War II" and "Underwear for the Deaf." When the Lampoon organization branched out into radio, records and books, Michael helped write the successful *National Lampoon Radio Hour*, cocreated (with one-time *Lampoon* editor Tony Hendra) the famous *Radio Dinner* album, and compiled an *Encyclopedia of Humor*. The last effort is perhaps best remembered for an entry called "The Churchill Wit," O'Donoghue's somewhat suspect minianthology of the jauntiest off-the-cuff quips by the late former prime minister of England:

> When the noted playwright George Bernard Shaw sent him two tickets to the opening night of his new play with a note that read: "Bring a friend, if you have one," Churchill, not to be outdone, promptly wired back: "You and your play can go fuck yourselves."

It was not by accident that O'Donoghue acquired this distinctly jaded outlook on humanity.

"A main influence in my life was the rheumatic fever I had when I was five," he reveals, "and I stayed inside the house for a year. Now this *has* to be a negative turning point in a child's life, and so consequently I got into working in scrapbooks, stamp collecting and so forth.

"Also, I developed a concept of 'others,'" he adds wryly. "For instance, you are one of the others and the things that make you one of the others are that you don't feel the same things that I do, or even think the same things. I have a difficult time understanding others, their wants, their desires."

Michael Henry O'Donoghue describes his childhood as that of a "weed bender." Born on January 5th, 1940, to Michael James Donoghue and the former Barbara Zimmermann, he grew up in rural Sauquoit, New York, located some seven miles from Utica.

"My grandfather's name was O'Donoghue. He came to this country from Killarney. On the boat ride over, he dropped the 'o' in the ocean, as the Irish are wont to say, but I put it back. My dad worked at a munitions plant, Remington Arms, during the war and then some white-collar job in industry. He's very smart, jovial, with a good warm sense of humor. My mother is Welsh-German, a mean woman, and I get most of my search-and-destroy humor from her." Michael also has a sister, Jane, who is five years younger, with whom he is "not on good terms."

O'Donoghue admits he was "not a very popular kid" during his years at Sauquoit Valley Central High School, despite his involvement in the band, Chess Club, Library Club, baseball team and especially the Dramatics Club (he was president).

"It was *not* a good period of my life," he recalls. "I was what was called a *nork*, a real creep, and the local girls certainly agreed, since I didn't have many dates. But the thing was that I was so damned bright that the other kids really couldn't keep me out of their lives.

"There was one boy, whose first name was Barton, who was pretty bright and even well liked, and he would have been tough competition for me, but he drowned in the lake during the freshman picnic. I remember everybody in the class was watching the police dredge the lake, but we hadn't eaten yet and I was hungry. I grabbed a sandwich and the gym teacher started hitting me, yelling, 'You monster, you *monster!*' Hell, I thought you could grieve and eat at the same time.

"I was very unhappy in high school, but in college I wisely pretended to be another type of person—suave, confident, popular—and I got away with it!"

O'Donoghue majored in English, with a minor in philosophy. At one point, he became immersed in Oriental religions and says he contemplated retreating to a monastery. After being kicked out of the university "for having a bad attitude" Michael migrated to California and attended both San Francisco State and the University of California at Berkeley. "I was leaning toward writing at that point," he recalls. "I started a magazine out there called *renaissance*—with a small 'r.' You know, one of those quaint literary rags with lots and lots of woodcuts. I ran it with a man called John Bryant; he'd published Charles Bukowski's poems and a lot of Gary Snyder's. Bishop Pike helped us out. Seriously. Very nice man. Gave us the key to the Episcopal Diocese office up on Nob Hill so we could type out the magazine there. We were always afraid he'd see what was in it. This was around 1960 to 1961. It's sad about Pike's disappearance; they found his jockey shorts in the desert. Worst way to go I've ever heard of—no dignity.

"Around this time I was working for the *San Francisco Examiner* as a reporter trainee—worked in the wire room, did everything. I was fired 'cause I got into a fight in the city room. I grabbed the man's tie and pulled him across a desk. I was gonna hit him with a lead typebar, which really can leave some kinda *Tom and Jerry*-type indentation in the skull, but someone stopped me."

Shortly afterward, O'Donoghue returned to the University of Rochester in quest of a teaching degree, but quit after six months. He subsequently sold *Life* magazine by telephone, peddled shrubbery and then costume jewelry door-to-door and worked as a credit manager for the Sherwin-Williams paint company. He also started a theater group called Bread and Circuses and worked as a disc jockey for WBBF-FM in Rochester. He had a classical music show at the radio station and also did the hourly newscast, which he would often hideously distort by expanding the worst tragedy of the day—an earthquake, plane crash, etc.—into a long, grisly lead story, while scarcely mentioning any of the other news events.

Sometime before fleeing to New York to toil as a freelance writer—he says he can't remember exactly when—he married a woman who already had three kids, toward whom Michael had difficulty relating. In a matter of months, the honeymoon and the marriage were over.

One evening, while I'm sharing an Italian dinner with Michael and his *Mondo Video* writing staff, the talk turns to O'Donoghue's past. Dirk Wittenborn begins needling his boss about his "great affection for children," specifically O'Donoghue's "baby-sitting technique" during the short-lived period when he served as a stepfather.

"Come on, Mister Mike," says Dirk with a mischievous grin. "Tell us again how you used to get the baby boy to stop crying at night.'"

"Now *Dirk*," O'Donoghue cautions lightly with a queer twinkle in his eye. "Let's *not* go into that."

"Oh no, Mister Mike, you're not gettin' out of this one! What he used to do," Dirk tells me, "is that he would go into the baby's room each night with a loaded revolver . . ."

". . . And I'd fire off a round or two—always into the ceiling—just to get the little fella to quiet down." O'Donoghue minimizes the story with a nonchalant shrug. "Gave him quite a start but it always worked. How else was I supposed to stop the kid from crying?"

"A truly brilliant writer but a very difficult character," says *National Lampoon* editor-in-chief P. J. O'Rourke. O'Donoghue was one of the original *Lampoon* editors when the humor magazine was founded in April 1970. O'Rourke has great praise for Michael's talent, especially "his gift for combining the heroic with the banal, as in 'Tarzan of the Cows,' and his stellar sense of black humor." But like other staffers at the *Lampoon*, P. J. was often weirded out by O'Donoghue's explosive temper.

"Michael had a short fuse with everything. He'd do stuff like, if the office phones didn't work quite right—as office phones never do—well, one time he beat one of his phones to death with a cane, smashed it to pieces, then went over to the next office, picked up the phone, called the phone company and screamed, 'The phone is broken! Get right over here!'"

All of this is retold with great affection and an almost involuntary wistfulness. Compared to the *Lampoon*'s first golden era (generally acknowledged to have been from 1970 to 1974), the legendary suite of offices now contains all the tumult of a sanitarium.

"Michael was like the Cardinal Richelieu of the *National Lampoon*; he was definitely the guiding light," says Anne Beatts, a former contributing editor to the magazine and now a writer with *Saturday Night Live*. She and O'Donoghue were an item near the end of their *Lampoon* days—both left in 1974 after an argument with chairman-publisher Matty Simmons—and they were known around Manhattan for their Gatsby-like attire, Beatts usually turned out in sleek Thirties dresses and Michael sporting a white tropical suit and matching slouch cap. Anne was working with Michael and John Belushi on a skit for the *Lampoon Radio Hour* called "The Nazi Doctor Doolittle" when the end came, and she is still bitter about the magazine: "*National Lampoon* is and was for boys of all ages—a good magazine for people with zits."

In retrospect, O'Donoghue places a higher value on his tenure there. "The *Lampoon* was hot in those days," he contends. "I think we could have kicked the hell out of the Algonquin Round Table the best day they ever lived. There was a long wait between quips at that damn potsy Round Table!"

During the O'Donoghue era, however, the *Lampoon* editors seemed to spend most of their time kicking each other.

"I still love him," says Simmons, "even though he won't talk to me. There was always fighting and wild outbursts from him and he was forever not talking to most of the other editors. And vice versa. His writing was absolutely hysterical but it would attract some strange outside reactions.

"I'm in my office one day [April 6, 1972] and I get a call from the kid in the mailroom. He says, 'Mr. Simmons, there's a box here for Michael O'Donoghue and I don't like the looks of it.' So when O'Donoghue came in, I said, 'Michael, let's open this box that just came in but let's open it *carefully*. So we took it into his office, looked inside and there are these sticks of dynamite. He turns white, green and orange. Then he picks up the phone and calls George Plimpton."

From there, Plimpton picks up the story. "Michael phoned me after he opened the dreadful package—I'm a demolitions expert, you see—and I told him that you could eat the dynamite and even hit it with a hammer and nothing could happen—provided the nitroglycerin had not leaked out and crystallized on the outside . . . which of course it had."

The building was quickly evacuated and Madison Avenue was closed off from Fifty-seventh to Sixty-third streets while a police bomb squad descended on the premises and removed the deadly package. The culprit turned out to be a pro-Donoghue prankster, who mailed along the blasting caps several days later.

"Incidentally," Plimpton adds, "Michael and I have an organization called the Dynamite Museum, which Michael originated. Its purpose is to keep people on edge. It serves as an explanation for all the terrible unexplained things that happen in this world, especially those with a humorous side to them. He and I are members of the museum, as are several to other more sinister people whose names we never mention. . . ."

As Michael himself points out, his comedy is about "the tortured little shadow areas we hide from our friends." But he is not above exploiting *any* painful situation for the sake of a laugh.

"You want to know what an incredibly funny, sick, nutty guy O'Donoghue is?" Matty Simmons asks. "Let me tell you, Michael was once sitting in my office when his father called and explained that as the result of some unfortunate occurrence, Mike's mother had just had to have her toe amputated.

"His father said, 'Michael, there's something terrible I have to tell you.' And O'Donoghue said, 'Oh. What?' His father said, very sadly, 'Well, your mother lost her toe.' Michael paused for a second and then he said, 'Did you look for it behind the refrigerator?'"

As O'Donoghue makes himself some coffee in his cozy little kitchen, I roam around, examining the glut of gimcracks in his apartment. Next to the fireplace in the living room stands an armless, battered little girl mannequin clothed in a misshapen dress who is gazing longingly out the window. Nearby is a large stuffed bear wearing World War I-vintage aviation goggles. Crammed everywhere in this room and the adjacent den is a dusty array of stuffed game, including various fowl, foxes and a pinched-face owl.

Michael wanders out of the kitchen, and assists me in my reconnaissance.

I am contemplating the Frankensteinian cluster of hatter's heads in the center of the case as Michael begins petting a nearby mummified ocelot. There is, somehow, a certain kinky poignance to the image, a notion not lost on O'Donoghue, who begins humming what sounds like a love ballad.

"What's that song?" I ask.

"Oh," he says, "it's called 'Cancer for Christmas.'"

"Huh?"

"'*Cancer for Christmas*,'" he repeats, explaining that he wrote the song for the 1978 *Saturday Night Live* Christmas show. "I was booked to do it at the end of the program, standing in a tableau with fake snow falling behind me, but they wouldn't let me. I thought it was time we showed the dark side of Christmas. Hell, I've had a bunch of relatives *die* over the holidays. It was a true act of censorship." He tilts his tiny head to one side and sings his heart out:

Cancer for Christmas
Blue lights on the Christmas tree
Yule log burning on TV
It's cancer for Christmas
Here's a brand new Timex
With a lifetime guarantee
Don't kiss Mommy on the lips
And don't sit next to me.
Cancer for Christmas
Plastic reindeer in the yard
The cleaners sent a festive card
With holiday greetings
Santa's bringing sacks of morphine
And some cigarettes
Time to call the Bide-A-Wee
And give away your pets
Play the tapes of "Silent Night"
Sung by Patrice Munsel
Wouldn't count on New Year's Eve
It's time to say farewell
We'll drink a cup of cobalt yet to
auld lang syne.

O'Donoghue's files are filled with outlandish material that the executive censors (Herminio Traviesas, Ralph Daniels and James Ottley) in NBC's Standards and Practices office have refused to okay for telecast. One such deletion was "Great Moments in Sports," a skit intended for the *SNL* show hosted by Fran Tarkenton, in which Bill Murray portrays Lou Gehrig delivering his heartrending 1939 Yankee Stadium retirement speech. "A little while ago," Murray/Gehrig tells the crowd, "I just found out that I have a fatal disease." Long pause. "Perhaps you didn't understand what I just said [*screaming*]: *I'm gonna die! And I'm so scared!* A year from now all you dumb jerkoffs will be sitting here watching some stupid baseball game and I'll be *dead*!!!"

Murray/Gehrig quickly becomes hysterical and must be dragged, kicking and screaming, from the field. The segment was rehearsed and ready to air, but the censors shook their heads: it ended up in the dumper. Likewise, a commercial for "Tarbrush, a toothpaste for Negroes"; a sketch in which Charles Manson (played by O'Donoghue) is carving his Halloween jack-o'-lantern and begins stabbing the pumpkin repeatedly; and innumerable "Weekend Update" news scripts, including the following rough gems:

> In an attempt to modernize its services, the Catholic Church has introduced something new into Communion. In addition to dispensing the host, priests will now also dispense a "cohost" which symbolizes the body of Mike Douglas.

> What will the smart, fashionable woman be wearing this fall? From California comes the answer—a lovely floor-length Chowchilla coat. Chowchilla coats—made from the matched skins of twenty-six [*kidnapped*] schoolchildren. They're not in the stores yet, but it's only a matter of time.

> And in a related item, FBI Director Clarence Kelley denied rumors that the bureau's entire investigation into Dr. Martin Luther King's death consisted of asking a Ouija board, "Who shot the monkey?"

But O'Donoghue says his favorite expunged rib tickler was this proposed exchange between "Update" hosts Jane Curtin and Dan Aykroyd (which Michael submitted under the pen name of Edith Wharton):

> JANE: How long does it take to cook a baby in a microwave oven? Exactly fifty-five seconds per pound, claims Mr. Nils Nickleson of Median Strip, Arizona, who turned this small fry [*baby projected on the screen behind her*] into a small roast in only eight minutes and fifteen seconds.

> DAN: Jane, to that let me simply add, "Well done!"

"I tried to use a Jonathan Swift/Modest Proposal argument with the censors on that last item," says Michael, "but they didn't buy the literary cross-reference."

Looking over the blue-penciled material, I note that there are tasteless potshots and ethnic slurs of every stripe . . . but no gags against the Irish.

"Oh, the Irish are a little dim," O'Donoghue demurs. "Someday I want to return to my ancestral home to piss on the Blarney Store, but basically the Irish are a race that is closer to the angels than to the apes."

When I ask whether his current project, *Mr. Mike's Mondo Video*, will be a fit network entertainment for viewers' living rooms, he changes the subject, promising a screening the following week of the raw footage of *"that soufflé of trash."*

A wild-haired O'Donoghue, bent into a resolute slouch by the weight of his thick camel's hair coat, is pacing the floor of a drafty loft in New York's East Twenties, raging about a media skirmish that is in the offing.

"We give up nothing!" he bellows to his staff as he stalks amidst a bewildering sprawl of video equipment, a cockeyed checkerboard of TV screens displaying various cold blue images of himself. This is the workshop where *Mr. Mike's Mondo Video*, three months into the writing and production stage, is finally being assembled. The air is electric with high-tension, editing and bitter feuds as Michael's coworkers psych him up for an impending meeting this afternoon with the NBC censors. It seems that NBC harbors strong reservations about the bulk of the hour-and-a-half program. Objections center on such segments as "Celebrity Deformities," wherein Dan Aykroyd probes the skin of his webbed toes with a Phillips head screwdriver to prove the authenticity of his claim: "I am a genetic mutant."

Also offensive to the NBC brass is "American Gals Love Creeps," a sequence in which heavily made-up vamps like Gilda Radner, Carrie Fisher, Margot Kidder, Deborah Harry, Laraine Newman and John Belushi's wife, Judy Jacklin, whisper their uncontrollable affection for "guys who miss the toilet seat," "men who smell their fingers," "fellows who drink too much and can't get it up" and "guys who sneeze in their hands and wipe it on their pants," the sultry testimony culminating in the admission: "When I reach down and feel a firm colostomy bag, I know I'm with a *real* man."

Personally, I found *Mondo Video* to contain some of the most uproarious comedy material I have ever seen, full of O'Donoghue's sick-o flair, but certainly no more prurient or shocking—with the exception of a 1928 peep show entitled *Uncle Sy and the Sirens*—than such *SNL* staples as Dan Aykroyd denouncing Jane Curtin on "Weekend Update" as an "ignorant slut."

(O'Donoghue is not the only new comedian who has had difficulty tailoring his humor for television. After ABC gave Andy Kaufman $100,000 for his own ninety-minute special, the network executives refused to air the completed show, which began with Andy urging viewers to turn off their TV sets.)

Nonetheless, the network is balking at broadcasting the show—presently four months late and $100,000 over its $275,000 budget—and O'Donoghue is fit to be tied.

"Damn those *cretins*," he booms. "I took the 'Dancing Navel' routine out didn't I? I met them halfway! What were they expecting from me? *Porky Pig Takes a Trip*?! Well, here's what we do: if they try to touch another frame of film, we cry rape, call them Philistine muck and then throw a brick at anything that moves!"

Coattails flying, he tears out of the room with video cassettes of the show, ready to do battle with the brass. I run after him and catch him at the elevator. What happens, I ask, if NBC refuses to run the show?

"Well," he says, now surprisingly calm, "I've always got my poetry, and Gilda is recording one of my songs, 'Let's Talk Dirty to the Animals' ["Up yours, Mr. Hippo, piss off, Mr. Fox"] on her forthcoming album. If we can't sell the show to cable TV, it'll just have to be a cult cassette."

Is America ready for a piece of business like Michael O'Donoghue? That may depend on his ability to prepare us for his hard-sell technique. Or perhaps the real problem is: Can Michael strike a truce with humanity long enough to win a few more allies? He confesses with a low chuckle that his favorite one-liner is, "Laugh, you assholes!" But one wonders if, in the end, we should be taken in by all this sardonic patter. Is Michael O'Donoghue really humor's answer to Dirty Harry or is there, deep (deep) inside, a trace of tenderness, a *shred* of decency? Well, judge for yourself.

"Success, comedy, all these things are great," he tells me during our final morning together." But what I care about most is my haiku and my work with the little deaf kids on Sundays.

"I want to end up like Oscar Levant!" he cracks disparagingly. "I want to end up a terrible actor with a lovely tremor of the hands, shaking to where I can hardly get the cork-tipped cigarette up to the crooked old mouth. I've already got a silk dressing gown like his, and I *hope* you noticed the blood stains on it. If I keep on popping pills, I hope to be found floating dead in the pool one day; hopefully one where I can see the bottom."

Soon afterward, in the TV column of the *Washington Post*, NBC Vice President Herminio Traviesas is quoted as vowing that *Mondo Video* will only hit the air "over my dead body." A network spokesman later denies that Traviesas ever said such a thing, issuing the following statement: "NBC has no air date at this time to present *Mr. Mike's Mondo Video*. The show has not been given an air date due to broadcast standards problems."

At present, O'Donoghue and mentor Lorne Michaels are fighting NBC to run a slightly toned-down version. Barring that, it may be sold to cable TV, the movies or be cut up into palatable segments—a tragedy, in my opinion—and aired, at intervals, on *SNL*. The fate of O'Donoghue's fashion models and *Insect Gods* scripts has not been decided.

Meanwhile, Michael is in final negotiations with Paramount Pictures to write *and* direct some of his own films, while his script for a sci-fi epic called *Planet of the Cheap Special Effects* has been bought by United Artists.

"Michael, you're the Woody Allen of the Eighties!" his agent told him during May, 1979, negotiations with the film studios. There was a long pause. "Does that mean," Michael replied, "that I have to wait another year?"

Walter Cronkite:
Walter, We Hardly Knew You

ARCHIVE PHOTOS

Although Walter Cronkite, often called "The Most Trusted Man In America," had warned the CBS management for two years that he was serious about stepping down as anchor and managing editor of the CBS Evening News when he turned 65 in November 1981, they didn't trust him. As a result, in the final negotiations over the transition, Cronkite agreed to depart in March 1981 so that Dan Rather could more comfortably assume the new duties which were already being analyzed in the daily press.

Contrary to divisive TV scuttlebutt, however, the decision never had much to do with the parallel ascendance of Dan Rather. The public had been well-prepared for Cronkite's departure for months, particularly after sentimental floor reporter Charles Kuralt closed CBS coverage of the 1980 Democratic National Convention by startling Cronkite and cuing footage of Walter's own coverage of the Democratic Convention in 1952:

Cronkite (1952): Hello everyone. Here we are again, in Studio A, our CBS Television control point for the Westinghouse coverage this time of the Democratic National Convention. From the International Amphitheater in Chicago, four-and-a-half miles out of downtown Chicago, out here in the stockyards, Democrats are due to begin their national convention in just a few moments' time. The first session could contain some interesting developments, perhaps even a little fireworks. Governor Adlai Stevenson. . . .

Kuralt (1980): That was the opening moment of one of the first conventions you covered on the air, Walter. And now that we are in the closing moments of the last one you'll anchor on the air, your colleagues around here have elected me to say something to you and to give you something. This old microphone, mounted here on a block of wood, is the one you spoke into 28 years ago to tell people in this country what was happening at the Eisenhower and Stevenson conventions of 1952.

You can press a button on the back of this thing and hear yourself reporting those conventions, if you're ever in a mood to do that. (*Laughter*) And on the front, there's a little plaque that says this: "Walter Cronkite. For three decades you enriched the political process and taught a generation of Americans how men get to be president. The people of CBS News are the luckiest of your fans. We got to work with you and be your friend." . . .This comes not only from [Bill Leonard] the President of CBS News and all the CBS executives; it comes from every page and messenger and editor and writer and camera crew, and from all of us who, at the end of our reports at all these conventions down the years, have been proud to say, "And now back to you Walter." And now back to you, Walter.

Visibly moved by the surprise tribute at 12:25 a.m., Cronkite got a tentative grip on his composure and answered, "Charles, thank you very much. I didn't expect that. I really would kind of maybe preferred it hadn't have happened on the air like this."

Then Cronkite acknowledged and thanked colleagues on-site, great and small, ranging from Eric Sevaried, Jeff Greenfield, Bill Moyers and James

Kilpatrick, to his researcher Ruth Streeter and *CBS Evening News* producer Mark Harrington. At 12:28 a.m., he stiffened and turned detached, stating, "This is Walter Cronkite, speaking for all of CBS News, saying from Madison Square Garden, good night."

Many of those Cronkite toiled with during that 1980 presidential race are now gone, including Sevareid, who died in 1992, and Charles Kuralt, who died in 1997, while Cronkite has spent the years of his semi-retirement hosting science specials, writing his memoirs, and sailing his 47–foot yawl, the Wyntie.

When he reviewed the great events he witnessed as a CBS anchorman, he confessed some misgivings about his renowned sign-off—"And that's the way it is"—saying it "suggested an infallibility that we didn't have and I certainly didn't mean to claim."

Interviewed by Charles Osgood on *CBS News This Morning* in January 1997, Cronkite offered a blunt insight into the private perspective his peers had on the medium of television, revealing that Sevareid and Edward R. Murrow considered radio more respectable than the TV.

"They actually felt it was below them," said Cronkite, "that it was some kind of show business, which it was and is. . . . Then they found out it was important."

THE INTERVIEW

Buzzy is dead.

Word has just come from the doctor, and as the sad news is passed among the family members and friends mingling on the lawn (including the guest of honor, columnist Ann Landers), the party turns somber. The host, an avid sailor, dons his captain's cap and calls for a moment of silence as he lowers the stars and stripes. Then he approaches the small saluting cannon that complements the forty-two-foot yawl moored nearby and fires a lonesome, booming volley into the sea.

And that's the way it is, at a chic summer cocktail party on Martha's Vineyard in 1979, on the day that Buzzy, Walter Cronkite's seventeen-year-old springer spaniel, has passed away.

A BRILLIANT, SENTIMENTAL, often eccentric man whose prowess at television journalism is as well known as his idiosyncrasies are private, Walter Leland Cronkite Jr., 64, gained some of his seminal broadcasting experience as an announcer in a bookie joint. During his first day on the job, the college-age Cronkite gave a phony live-action account of a race before delivering the results. His irate boss bounded over and roared, "What the hell do you think you're doing? We don't want entertainment; we just want the facts."

Cronkite has been striving to provide just that since he debuted as anchorman-reporter for *The CBS Evening News* in April 1962, when the nightly newscast was a mere fifteen minutes. In September of the following year, *The CBS Evening News with Walter Cronkite* became television's first half-hour daily news broadcast. His terse but benevolent basso delivery has underscored, and thus made more digestible, such events as Nikita Kruschev's first visit to the United States, the funeral of Winston Churchill, the assassinations of John F. Kennedy, Dr. Martin Luther King Jr. and Robert Kennedy, and the riots at Attica State Prison.

As a closet romantic with a burning ambition to rocket to the moon, Cronkite has covered every manned space shot since Alan B. Shepard's craft lifted off in 1961, and he has earned Emmys for his reportage on the Apollo 11 moon landing and the flights of Apollo 13 and 14.

When the grandfatherly Cronkite angrily denounced the Chicago police as "a bunch of thugs" after they roughed up CBS correspondent Dan Rather on the floor of the 1968 Democratic National Convention, or when he wept while announcing that President Kennedy had been felled by an assassin's bullet, it was a jarring display of emotion from a man who seldom loses his reserve—and it instantly summed up the mood of a nation that relies on and reveres him for his stalwart place in our shifting culture.

Courted by the powerful (the Shah reportedly once sent him three boxes of cigars and a jar of spoiled caviar) and accredited by the powerless, Cronkite remains an elusive presence—even, it seems, to members of his own family (he has a son and two daughters). When I ask twenty-three-year-old Walter "Chip" III how he would describe his celebrated dad to someone who had never met him, he responds, "I don't think I know him well enough to answer that, but he's a nice guy, very respectful, very humble about his thing."

Walter Cronkite was born in St. Joseph, Missouri, on November 4, 1916, the son of a dentist. His earliest journalistic endeavor was sportswriting, which coincided with his forced retirement from Houston's San Jacinto High School track team after he developed painful shin splints. Unable to compete, he wrote about the team and eventually covered general news for the school paper, the *Campus Cub*. While a journalism major at the University of Texas in Austin, he wrote for the college paper, the *Daily Texan*, and labored as a stringer for the *Houston Press*.

"In class he was rather quiet," recalls his journalism teacher, DeWitt Reddick. "I suspect he did his assignments in a hurry, and perhaps turned in first-draft stories in his reporting courses, but they were good enough to get by without caustic criticism."

Cronkite left college in his junior year to work full time as a reporter for the *Houston Press*, did a year's worth of radio work in Kansas City and then signed on with the Dallas bureau of United Press in 1939. He stayed with the wire service for eleven years and became a distinguished foreign correspondent during World War II, covering such pivotal engagements as the Battle of the North Atlantic, the war in North Africa and the Normandy beachheads in 1944. After the war, he served as UP's Moscow bureau chief for two years. Then, in 1948, he moved to Washington, D.C., as a broadcaster for a group of Midwestern radio stations before joining CBS News.

Speaking of the man he is about to succeed as anchorman and managing editor of *The CBS Evening News* fellow Texan Dan Rather says, "Walter Cronkite is ankle height above everybody else—not just shoulders above, waist above, but ankles above. Walter expanded the role of anchorman by going out himself and getting very important, exclusive interviews. No one should underestimate what Walter has done in demanding that our evening coverage include a lot of foreign news. That's not always easy. During the Vietnam War, he was a correspondent and insisted that that kind of reporting, that standard of excellence, be in *The CBS Evening News*, even when it wasn't leading in the ratings. His influence on people, including me, has been enormous."

Walter Cronkite (his coworkers fondly refer to him as "the Gorilla" because he usually gets what he wants) agreed to this interview one balmy afternoon last summer while munching popcorn in the living room of his home on Martha's Vineyard. The session took place in his office cubicle in the New York studio where he does his newscast. Seated at a desk littered with books and magazines, he occasionally paused to survey the three silent television sets—tuned to CBS, ABC and NBC—suspended above his door. Always in shirt-sleeves, his cuff links bearing the familiar CBS "eye" logo, he spoke slowly and purposefully, frequently smoothing his thinning hair in a nervous gesture and popping hard candies into his mouth.

When will you be leaving The CBS Evening News?

There's no firm date, but probably in mid-March. That's the earliest they think they can let me go. I wanted to get this next president inaugurated. I almost wish I were not going for another year, because it's going to be a fascinating news year. How revolutionary the changes are really gonna be is a big question, and I'd love to cover that story.

You've spoken with Ronald Reagan several times; what do you think of him?

I've always been impressed with the man personally—for his friendliness, warmth and interest in whatever subject you want to take up with him. He does not have a great depth of knowledge about many things, which he acknowledges. But he promises to get the answers, and he has for me when I've sought them. I think that on the basis of his Sacramento record, we can expect a reasonably efficient executive-office routine. We'll have to wait and see how pragmatic the campaign promises were. With the mandate and the number of senators he carried with him, he's got an opportunity that few administrations have had in recent history—not since Franklin Roosevelt, really.

Do you agree that his show-business background played a significant role in his success?

Yes, very definitely. His appearance, personality and ability to speak helped. I think Carter may be far more of an ideologue than Reagan, but the basic Reagan speech is not very strong on practicality; it's philosophical and appealing, and it's populist.

Do you think Carter was a more practical man?

No, I don't think you could say that. Reagan may be better at organizing a staff to get things done than Carter was.

I closely monitored your coverage of the 1980 Democratic and Republican conventions. You scored several coups, such as your interview with Gerald Ford at the Republican convention, and then with Reagan immediately after his election. Whether you like it or not, you have a lot of power; you're one of the best-known men in this nation and are regarded more highly than some presidents. Do you think your celebrity status influences the events you cover?

I suppose popularity is measured by ratings. If a broadcaster is known as the leader because of ratings, then that's where people most want to be seen and heard, so there's no question that there's an advantage. Going beyond that, the advantages of fame, both national and international, are great in helping to reach people by telephone and getting appointments with them.

Now, in the disadvantage column, I cannot do anonymous reporting. I can't go into a mob scene and sense the mood and the attitude of the crowd. I can't conduct man-on-the-street interviews or even get reactions that I can be sure are honest, because they know who I am.

Well, anyone could be dishonest with you. It's been said that Lyndon Johnson decided to forgo a second term after hearing you disavow the Vietnam War. Don't you think your celebrity influences or perverts events?

Not as an individual, I don't think so. I do think that the presence of television cameras and known reporters means that things might change a bit— TV cameras perhaps a little more than print because of the greater impact of television. If reporters are present, people are gonna react so as to get their side of the story told or to get the best possible image. This question is an all important one, and it is also indicative of something that should be made clear. A lot of the questions raised about television's power and influence on events have applied throughout history to every mass-communications medium—most particularly print, because that's the medium we've had the longest. What makes TV particularly interesting to people today is its more pervasive influence.

Television is a very intimate and swift medium in terms of relaying information and symbols. How do you feel about the early TV announcements that Carter lost the election, and do you think that they kept people in the Southwest and West away from the polls?

I think there's that possibility. Although my feelings are shared by a great number of people in television, they're counter to surveys done by the broadcast industry, which indicate that early returns and projected returns now being done through computers do not affect voters. CBS ran two such studies in 1956, and there was an industry study in 1964 of Western voters that indicated that they were not affected.

Now, I don't believe that, you see. Frank Stanton, president of the Columbia Broadcasting System in '56, ordered the first study because he was disturbed that we were going into this prediction business—er, not predictions but *analysis*. When he got the results back, he didn't believe them, although he had spent a lot of money getting them. So he said, "Let's run it again." And they did.

I still believe that it's *got* to have some effect. But that's not our responsibility. It's a *power*, I admit, but it's not a responsibility. If you want to put a sociological light on it, we are sharing with the public, exactly as the news business should, information that up until now has been the province of just a few political operators. With their little black book and their rule of thumb, they've been able to get enough figures together to say, "Hey, we're coming out of Cuyahoga County 100,000 light. We've gotta put pressure on downstate. We've gotta put pressure on Nevada. We've gotta get California." And they can work like this without the public being aware of *why* the pressure was on. Now the public *is* aware, and I think that's an advantage.

So, what should be done about the possibility that these early projections influence elections? Well, they should change the *law* and have a common closing time for all the polls across the country, and then no election results would be reported until all polls were closed.

But there's another point here. Public-opinion polls and your own projections on election night aren't hard news. They are speculative.

Pollsters would argue that polls aren't speculative. They call it factual reporting [*pause*], and it is, I guess. The pollsters say, "Here are the probabilities and I'll give you a sample. This sample of 1,400 names would produce a three-percent probability within a six-percent range." So that's mathematical, and I don't see why the media should be taken to task for using every tool possible to report political trends, political feelings, public attitudes. You see, this is the old business of beating the messenger for the message. Society and the political establishment have got to use that information to do their job better. If it's felt that it's an impingement on the free political process, then the politicians ignore it. That's all.

I'd like to clear up a controversial question concerning an incident during CBS' early Watergate coverage. After supposed pressure from the White House, CBS chairman William Paley reportedly told you to restrict or condense the amount of air time devoted to an ongoing Watergate report.

We indeed planned two early Watergate pieces. There was no planning on the amount of time we would spend on them. I'm very proud of these pieces, as they came out. Katharine Graham and the *Washington Post* are given a great deal of credit for making the Watergate investigation possible, and Woodward and Bernstein did a far better job and were getting a lot more information than our investigative team. But everybody was dropping these bombshells without any kind of coordinated story on how an event last week fit in with today's story. People weren't getting the big picture, because local newspapers weren't carrying the story day by day. I found it impossible to follow right at that desk out there [*points to center of adjacent newsroom*] and in Washington when we were immersed in it. So I said, "Let's do two good-sized pieces and trace the whole thing back—start with the burglary and go through everything we know up until today."

Like hitting a mule over the head with a board, you've got to first get people's attention, and we got it. "The first piece was a blockbuster, and it took half of the broadcast or more, which was an *extraordinary* devotion of time to a single story. The next day, Richard Salant, who was the president of CBS News at the time, told me that it was a good piece, but he was greatly disturbed with the length of time given to it, because the evening news was *not* meant to be a documentary broadcast of a single news item.

So we had to shorten the second one. It disturbed the producer of the piece, Stanhope Gould, a great deal. And I was particularly disturbed over the thought that this might have been dictated from somewhere else. I asked about that and was assured that this was not so, that it was purely in-house news-division criticism.

Did you ask this of Salant?

[*Murmuring*] Uh, there's some confusion about that in my mind.

Why some confusion?

Because, as we reconstructed this later, I insisted it was Salant [*nervous laughter*], and others say it was not. I don't know, I thought it was him who buzzed me up, but I'm not sure, so I don't want to lay the accusation at the feet of a great man—probably one of the greatest gifts to free and unencumbered-by-pressure journalism.

For years I went along saying there was no pressure from anywhere else. Since then, I have read various "revelations" about Charles Colson's pressure on Paley, and that Paley had indeed asked Salant, "Is the attention given to this story really worth it? I'm getting questions from the White House, pressure from the White House."

I don't know that this is so, but Salant would handle a thing of that kind just as I think he did handle it. He never told the news department that we were doing anything wrong, that the text should be changed in any way, but he said it was possible to placate top management by cutting the time, and that's the way we did it. I don't think that is so heinous, because we got everything said that we wanted to say.

What was your first scoop as a newspaperman?

If you mean in the sense of getting the story first *and* exclusively for at least one edition, I guess it was while I was on the *Daily Texan*. I got an interview with a young man who had shot his parents to death. They were prominent people; his father was a state judge. I was there when he was caught, and I managed to have some words with him. It was just luck, like most scoops. But part of luck is being prepared to take advantage of it. My lines were pretty well laid with some cops, and they tipped me that they might have him out on the grounds, oddly enough, of some institute for the deaf and dumb in Austin. So I dashed out there and it turned out to be the case.

What did you ask the suspect?

[*Laughing slyly*] Well, I hope I avoided the television question of "How do you feel?" I don't *think* I asked that. In those days, there were no restraints in talking with arrested individuals. The Supreme Court decisions hadn't come down yet. They didn't read a card outlining a person's rights. So I asked, "Did you do it? *Why* did you do it?" He allowed that he'd done it and didn't know why he'd done it. He regretted that he had, but the boy was out of his skull. I don't mean on dope or anything. He was a mental case. It was not a substantial or meaningful interview in any sense.

How did all of this make you feel?

Well, I felt a sense of elation. I had gotten to him, and I didn't think anyone else would. We managed to get a few quotes in that morning's edition. I haven't thought about it in forty years, not until you asked me the question.

In your career as a newspaper reporter, what are you most proud of?

Anybody who's spent thirteen or fourteen years in print journalism has a lot of stories he thinks were inwardly satisfying as far as preparation, understanding and diligence. I'm proud of a couple of pieces I did very early on in my press-service career, like one about a New London, Texas, school that blew up and several hundred children and teachers were killed. It was a major disaster. I think I was the first press-service correspondent on the scene, but not of my own initiative. I was sent out of the Dallas UP bureau.

Although they poured the real heavyweights of United Press from all over the nation into the story, I got two good feature stories. I wasn't writing the leads, by any means. I was about twenty-one. In Dallas, I was a legman for other lead writers, but on my own I did sidebars, and I was very proud of two of them. One asked the question *why* in the different ways that question could be asked: why the school blew up, why they tapped that particular gas line to get fuel. The religious question was written on a Sunday: why this should happen to this community, why it should happen to innocents—children.

Are you religious?

Not in the formal sense of regular attendance at services, no. I have great questions about an almighty being.

Do you ever pray?

[*Grimly*] In desperation. At really critical and very personal family things usually, like the health and welfare of my children.

Your fame must place a unique sort of stress on those close to you. For instance, your daughter Kathy once went so far as to change her last name for a while.

Part of that was on the advice of a Hollywood agent who thought she'd do better with another name. It also inspired her to write a book, which will be out in March, about the pressures on children of famous people. It's interviews with these children.

Did she ever describe the pressures of being a Cronkite to you?

[*Somberly*] Yeah. She gets tired of being introduced as Walter Cronkite's daughter. I think my other children feel the same way. The business of hitch-hiking on somebody else's identity is disturbing to them, which I can certainly understand. Although they're all too kind to say this to me, and I don't think we've discussed it perhaps as deeply as we should, they're probably living up to an *image* of what I am that they know is not quite a true one. I'd like to think that they respect me. I hope they do. But they've got to see a lot of clay mushing through my toes . . . and my ankles.

What do you feel was the greatest crisis you've faced in your life, either on a personal or career level?

The greatest crisis, on a career level, was in 1964, when CBS removed me from the convention coverage.

They replaced you with Robert Trout and Roger Mudd. Why?

Well, the first reason was that the ratings were poor, and the second was that I was a scapegoat for the new management; they had completely upset the old way of doing things and attempted to stamp the convention coverage with their own image—and it failed. So they put the failure on me.

What was the nature of this failure?

It was lousy coverage, terrible. And I was as bad as I've ever been. It wasn't quite the approach that was the problem so much as the technical facilities. I had done six conventions—'52, '56 and '60—and had practically engineered what was needed on the anchor desk and how we did it. Although we had gone through the desk fittings and how we were gonna communicate—all that was arranged in New York—I got out to San Francisco and was taken directly to the Cow Palace, where people said, "Oh, boy, we've got a great new plan!"

[*Sternly*] Well, it didn't work. The new communications plan didn't relate. They took away my desk assistant, who sits in the "hole" below my desk, regulates the flow of information and communicates where we're going next—[*irritated*] not what I am going to read on the air, as some idiot in New York wrote a month or two ago. People love to think that that guy in the little hole writes my material for me. I need that person for communication, and that's all there is to it.

Well, they hired a new assistant for me in San Francisco and put her *across* the room from me! I had no communication with her at all! I was sitting there just as innocent as the people sitting in the third balcony of the Cow Palace! I had no information flowing to me. [*Angrily*] And they were so inexperienced at that kind of broadcasting that they stood in the control room flying into fits every two seconds 'cause I didn't have some information they thought I ought to have. They'd come dashing into my studio between air time—while I was trying to listen to what was happening on the floor—with all kinds of complaints. [*Bitterly*] It was terrible, awful.

While anchoring the 1968 Democratic convention, your anger at the violent behavior of the Chicago police was very apparent. Likewise, your disaffection with the Vietnam War slowly became quite obvious. When did you decide the war was wrong, and do you think it affected your coverage?

I hope and believe my coverage in both cases was not affected by my personal feelings. This should be the mark of every professional journalist—to keep personal prejudices out of the news report. I decided, fairly early on, that people were not getting the full facts or being permitted to participate in decisions regarding the Vietnam War—and this was brought home by the fact that, in Vietnam, the military was preparing to use far more troops than the Johnson administration was saying we were going to commit.

What do you think is the gravest problem in the world today?

I think there are four major dangers to civilization, and the greatest is population. Stemming from that are pollution, depletion of natural resources, including food, and atomic proliferation. It's almost essential, if civilization is to survive, that we get a handle on nuclear armaments, and it should be serious disarmament, not just ceilings on nuclear arms, such as SALT II promised.

The only reason that SALT II had any promise—and it had great value in this regard—was that it was a *step* toward disarmament at some later stage. Presumably we had to go through SALT II to get to SALT III and IV and V. Now we see an administration in power that does not even believe in SALT II. Whether we ever get that disarmament is highly problematic.

Can I assume that you're a proponent of Zero Population Growth?

Oh, absolutely! I would acknowledge that we could tolerate something a little more than zero population growth, but as a catch-word goal Zero Population Growth is something to be supported and encouraged.

As a UP correspondent, you covered such harrowing stories as General George Patton's rescue of encircled troops at the Battle of the Bulge in 1941, as well as the Nuremberg trials of Göring, Hess and other Nazi war criminals. On the scene, a good reporter is as percipient as he is dispassionate. I would like to hear your reflections on these two difficult assignments.

Well, Patton's feat in turning around the Third Army, which was then facing the Germans far south of the Ardennes, and throwing it within a comparatively few hours against von Rundstedt's forces in Belgium, was one of the greatest of the war. He proved then what a remarkable tactician he was, and the value of a disciplined army.

As for Nuremberg, there has been much criticism over the years that the trials were the imposition of *ex post facto* justice on a beaten enemy, but I've always felt that they represented an effort to establish a juridical precedent for a system of world order before the outbreak of another war—after which, clearly, it would be too late.

You've known so many presidents, from Truman to Reagan. For which president did you have the highest personal regard, and why?

I have found things to admire, and things to dislike, in each of them. It's hard to choose, but possibly it would be Truman, for his guts in making tough decisions and sticking with them.

On the other side of the fence, what contributions do you feel Edward R. Murrow, Chet Huntley and David Brinkley, Howard K. Smith and John Chancellor have made to TV news?

I would say they have been—or are—serious, dedicated journalists interested primarily in the obtaining and presentation of the truth. But Murrow helped more than any other individual to raise the standards of broadcast journalism to a level equal to and sometimes above that of daily print journalism. The others have helped keep it there.

Why did you ask that your fan club be discontinued in 1974 after about five years of existence?

Oh, I never approved of the fan club in the first place. I don't think news people ought to have *fan clubs*. It smacks of show business and all the things that are wrong with television news. It's just not right.

Do you think you've been guilty of showbiz?

No, quite honestly, I don't. That's what I mean by holding the line. Some critics suggest that I am an old fogy about the use of graphics, and that ABC is doing graphics more brilliantly than we are, and that I've dug in my heels against this sort of thing. That's not true. I don't think for one minute that the use of graphics is show business. It's audio-visual education. I'm all for it, *if* it's used to enhance an understanding of a story you're gonna cover anyway. I do not mean to suggest that I am opposed to photojournalism and do not acknowledge that we are a visual medium. We should not *ever* turn our backs on a good picture because of some exalted idea that it is not the most important news story of the day. But underlying all the things we do with pictures and graphics and two-way communication and mini-cams is the attempt to communicate in a half-hour the maximum amount of news that is of *importance* to that viewing population. If we have to drop important news for a picture story, then we have to weigh carefully what we're up to.

I am most proud of doing everything I could to hold the line of journalistic professionalism in television news—giving it a professionalism, I hope, that it either didn't have in the early days or that it is now constantly threatened with *not* having by show-business pressures. Television news is always in *danger* of slipping into show business. Too many local stations have already done that.

I assume it's no accident that The CBS Evening News *is broadcast directly from a working newsroom, as opposed to a set.*

No accident at all. And it's a great handicap to us. A good still photographer wouldn't take a portrait in that room. That's a low ceiling; you can't get a high enough light in it, and our lighting people cry and cringe. So I look *flat*; not nearly as handsome or pretty as I'd look if we'd go to the studio upstairs. On election night, when we're up there with the big lights and sets, it's ten times better visually.

But CBS can't afford to give us a newsroom in a studio setting—and *I* insist on being where the news is. I'm not going to be divorced from this newsroom for an hour and a half each evening in order to go to a set somewhere. If we had a set, I'd have to leave here at 6:15, and normally I do a lot of editing and some writing between six and 6:30. I put on my jacket at 6:29:45. Last night everything changed in midbroadcast.

Is it true, as Abbie Hoffman states in his new book, Soon to Be a Major Motion Picture, *that your decision to trade your eyeglasses for contact lenses on-camera was a result of a written suggestion from him?*

No. The switch to contacts was dictated by the fact that on-air lighting caused a reflection in my reading glasses.

What do you see as the differences in style and approach between yourself and your successor, Dan Rather?

I think the changes in the broadcast will be more gradual than revolutionary. I gather from what little I've talked with Dan about it that he has no plans for overturning the present system. In time, there may be some changes. We've done the best *we* can to balance the assignments and the problems, but he may have a different view on that.

As for style, we each have our own. At the moment, I would describe Dan as having more vigor, a little more attack on the news, which is good. But there's no difference between us in dedication to the kind of job that has to be done, and in devotion to integrity, keeping the thing as unbiased as possible. I think Dan is that way, or he wouldn't have been selected for the job.

Everyone seems to have an "inner age," that is, an age one perceives oneself as being. How old do you feel you are?

[*Laughing*] Well, I'd say I'm about thirty-five.

Why does sailing appeal to you?

What all sailors have said since time immemorial: it's the challenge of nature, the *oneness* with nature, the ability to work with nature and hopefully *conquer* it. Also, it's provided a marvelous escape valve for getting away from the telephone and the pressures of city life. I can cast off in a boat and really put the world behind me.

You were once an avid auto-racing buff and occasionally got behind the wheel of your own Lotus. How did this hobby emerge?

Like any red-blooded American boy, I had always been interested in cars, and I used to race jalopies around an abandoned race track in Houston. But I could not afford, in either money or time, to do more until later years. When a little more of both became available, in the post-World War II boom, I bought my first sports car.

Everyone from Laurence Olivier to Joe DiMaggio has done TV commercials. Would, as The New York Times *recently speculated, "the most trusted man in America" ever consider endorsing a product?*

I cannot at present imagine doing that.

You are generally regarded to be part of a noble tradition of American journalism that encompasses everyone from Edward R. Murrow and H. L. Mencken to Walter Winchell and Ernie Pyle. How did you feel as you stifled tears when your staff presented you with the microphone trophy at the close of the Democratic Convention coverage?

Proud—and embarrassed.

Do you have any regrets?

[*Firmly*] About the only thing I regret is not being smart enough to say to all these people in the company who have projects and write and do everything else that the biggest job in the world is to put out *The CBS Evening News*, so *don't bother me*!

Dan Rather:
What's News in the
Eye of CBS' Storms

I f his job as successor to Walter Cronkite has been a wild ride, an unanticipated prelude to Dan Rather's promotion to the post left him well-prepared. Rather had flown into Chicago's O'Hare Airport in November 1980, hailed a cab to author Studs Terkel's house in town, and sat back in the car to read when the mumbling cabby allegedly became abusive and veered onto a major thoroughfare at 75 mph.

A frightened Rather waved out the window for help, flagging down a passing deputy sheriff and another motorist, who gave chase, ultimately cornering the cab against the curb.

The hackney driver was charged with disorderly conduct and "refusing to let a fare out." Police dismissed his accusation that Rather had tried to welch on the fare, and the driver was released after posting $35 bond pending a court appearance. "This is a very minor problem," said Rather. "Don't be too hard on him."

Rather continued on his appointed rounds, left the Windy City intact, and lived to laugh about the incident. Months later, on March 9, 1981, Rather replaced Cronkite as anchor of *The CBS Evening News*.

But other bizarre incidents dogged the anchor, such as the moment in Miami in 1987 when the *News* had a six-minute blackout in the midst of Rather's annoyance that CBS tennis coverage had intruded on his broadcast. Rather's 1988 mugging by a man yelling "Kenneth, what's the frequency, Kenneth?" was no less strange. (The mugger was later identified as one William Tager, a paranoiac arrested and convicted and now serving a 25–year prison term for murdering an NBC employee.)

The rock band R.E.M. later turned the obtuse "Kenneth" exclamation from the strange encounter into a popular song from their 1994 *Monster* album. For his part, Rather was sportive enough to sing the lyrics to R.E.M.'s "What's the Frequency, Kenneth?" on *The David Letterman Show* in 1994 as the house band offered accompaniment.

"I have a great deal of respect for the man," said Michael Stipe of R.E.M. afterward. "Nobody in our office contacted his office and said, 'Nothing personal, Dan.' As far as he knew, we were completely sending him up with that song."

The worst was yet to come. For 23 awkward months ending in May 1995, Rather was compelled to share his anchor spot with Connie Chung, the less-qualified Chung never equaling Dan's unquestionable confidence in the job—or assisting in CBS' longtime ratings battle with NBC for the No. 2 spot behind ABC's *World News Tonight*.

When his 15th anniversary as anchor arrived in 1996, Rather was publicly assured by the CBS brass that his place at the network was secure. And if the anonymous on-camera surfaces and dove-gray backdrop he initially inherited from Cronkite had long since been replaced by a huge, half-circle mahogany and suede desk and a living scrim of high-tech monitors and newsroom bustle, Rather still seemed to suit the task at hand.

By 1997, the gray-haired Rather, born October 3, 1931, was 66—two years older than Cronkite was when he agreed to bow out—but CBS still maintained it had no plans to replace him. Indeed Dan signed a $7 million contract extension that will keep him at CBS News through 2002. Whatever else fortune holds, Rather had finally beaten the odds, the oddballs, and any other human or mechanical obstacles in his path.

As Rather assured in 1981 we sat and passed an afternoon talking in his office overlooking West 57th Street in Manhattan, "I'm a pressure player— I'd better be."

THE INTERVIEW

"MAY I KISS YOU?" shrieks the elderly woman, and before Dan Rather can answer she has thrown her arms around her heartthrob with such a vengeance that her straw hat and his headphones are knocked to the floor of the 1980 Democratic Convention. Rather smiles weakly at his aggressive fan and stoops to retrieve both. Luckily, he was not on the air at the time.

"Er, sorry about that," he hurriedly says into the phones in his courtly Texas twang. "Had a little problem here. I, ah, strongly suggest you get cameras over to the New Jersey delegation immediately."

He shakes off his embarrassment, adjusts his simple charcoal suit and gropes through the wall of humanity that separates him from the good delegates of the Garden State.

Everybody's having difficulties getting around Madison Square Garden tonight but few are finding it as problematic as Dan Rather. With the exception of Ted Kennedy (and Walter Cronkite, who's safely ensconced in the CBS broadcast booth), Rather is the most popular figure in the house. If Cronkite ever decided to make a bid for the presidency, Rather would make a fine running mate.

Unlike Democratic incumbent Jimmy Carter, Dan has the weather-worn good looks of a Jack Kennedy (although he lacks Jack's easy grin), is a fine speaker with a mildly self-deprecating wit, and he's honest to a fault. Only trouble is that Rather wouldn't be interested in the job.

But it's not for lack of ambition—an innate quality that has kept him traveling three-quarters of every year since he joined CBS' Houston affiliate in 1960. Cronkite admired the job Rather did covering Hurricane Carla in 1961 and he was offered a correspondent's post at $17,500 per annum. Now Rather's got Cronkite's job as anchorman and managing editor of the *CBS*

Evening News, and an $8 million contract. At 49, he's one of the highest paid newsmen in the world, yet Dan's still obsessed with knowing which way the whirlwind is blowing, whether reporting on the turbulent Nixon administration or unwinding in his free time by reading about bygone acts of God.

He says the Bible is his favorite book (especially Gideon's). While in college he was almost fired from his first good job—DJ for a tiny Texas radio station—when he inadvertently let a recorded gospel-hour sermon skip on the turntable for twenty minutes in mid-exhortation, the preacher repeating, "Go to hell! Go to hell!" He once attended an early morning meeting with CBS chairman William Paley wearing, accidentally, one brown shoe and one black shoe. He has described covering the Nixon White House as "trolling on the beach for coins that have fallen out of people's bathing trunks." When he filled in for Walter Cronkite in 1975, a woman phoned him and demanded to be told the "truth" about Cronkite's "death." He says he loves his job and calls himself "a child of the road."

"I like to lead, and I want to be the best reporter of my time," Dan Rather says bluntly. But that bold statement is underscored by a nagging notion that he is far from his ultimate goal. Muckraking for *Sixty Minutes* has kept him on the move for years, but his new job is about to change that.

"Last year I was gone eight months of the year for *Sixty Minutes,*" he says. "There hasn't been a time since I've been with CBS that I haven't traveled." The reduction in travel will be a tough adjustment for Rather and probably a welcome one for his wife, Jean, and their two college-age children, Robin and Danjack.

Another problem Rather has been grappling with is his emergence as a media star. As he struggled to cover stories while *he* was a story, it seemed possible that his promotion may have saved his career.

Dan Irvin Rather is the son of Irvin "Rags" Rather, a pipeliner by trade, and his wife, Byrl, whom Rags met while she was a waitress in the Travelers' Hotel in Victoria, Texas. He grew up amid a flurry of newsprint, since his father was a manic newspaper reader with a temper to match. As Rather notes in his autobiography, *The Camera Never Blinks* (written with Mickey Herskowitz): "There was a constant harangue about newspapers in our house. My father would read something in the *Houston Press* that riled him and he would shout, 'Mother, cancel the *Press.* We're through with that paper forever.'"

Young Dan was less inclined to blame the messenger for the message, and while he did not consider a career in journalism until he was near the end of his schooling at Sam Houston State, he had often daydreamed about being the radio announcer for the roller derby punch-outs at Houston's City Coliseum.

Several decades later, while covering the 1968 Democratic convention in Chicago for CBS, he found himself on the losing end of a slugfest with Mayor Daley's security forces. The scuffle was captured by the CBS camera as Cronkite urged Rather to get some medical attention.

"Don't worry about it, Walter," cracked a shaken Rather. "I'll answer the bell."

And he always has, whether covering the assassination of John Kennedy in Dallas, the civil rights movement in the South, the war in Vietnam, the White House during Watergate, or some corporate negligence in Virginia. The epitome of a tough but gentlemanly reporter (his coworkers complain that he's so courteous it drives them crazy), he nevertheless succeeded in making the best enemy an ethical newsman could have: Richard M. Nixon.

Our talks took place in Manhattan in Rather's *Sixty Minutes* office, which overlooks the barge-filled Hudson River. In his shirt-sleeves and striped suspenders, he was usually stretched out on his couch with an unlit cigar, fidgeting with a needlepoint pillow—a gift from his wife—that was inscribed: ALWAYS IS NOT FOREVER.

When I asked him what it meant, he blushed, saying,"I must keep that between Jean and me."

The other two eye-catching objects in the neat, book-filled room were a stuffed armadillo doll and a New Yorker cartoon showing a man and his scowling wife watching TV. "Give the man half a chance," her husband is saying. "You can't expect him to be as avuncular as Cronkite practically overnight."

Do you think that your fame inhibits you in your work?

Sometimes yes and sometimes no. It does cut both ways. I do have a small quarrel with the word *fame*. Fame is not a word that's applicable, in my judgment. One can be and should be famous for some remarkable accomplishment: You invent the polio vaccine, that's fame and it ought to be; you paint like Edward Hopper, that's fame and it ought to be; you write music like Aaron Copland, that's fame and it ought to be. You do television, even at a sustained, high quality of excellence—that's not fame.

At the 1980 Democratic convention, I saw a woman ask if she could kiss you on the cheek, and as she did, she knocked your headphones off.

I'm so awkward and uncomfortable in those situations. I've never learned to handle them well. They detract from and inhibit what you're doing. But there is the other side of that. When you call people and say you're Dan Rather of *Sixty Minutes*, you're much more likely to get through. You can work faster, more effectively. Also there's a matter of trust, which is the single most important thing a reporter can have. People see you doing stories on the air and they say, I gotta tell somebody about what I know is happening. And they call *you*. You gotta love it when somebody calls or writes and says, "I'm trusting you not to reveal my name, not to tell who I am." It is a direct result of your reputation, deserved or otherwise.

Could you take an incident in which a noted anchor man's mere presence aided his facility to report the news?

The Republican convention this year would be perhaps as good a case study as we've had recently. I think Walter Cronkite's interview with Gerald Ford was a tour de force. But asked the same questions by Jim Smith from Casper, Wyoming, I don't think Ford's answers would have been much different, if any different. The difference might very well be in the quality of the questions and how the interview was handled. Walter Cronkite asked the right questions at the right time, and he paced the interview to keep Ford from leaving any number of times, or from turning to Mrs. Ford and that kind of thing.

Ford had obligated himself to appear on all three networks. It was the luck of the draw that he was on CBS that Wednesday night. It wasn't arranged at five o'clock that afternoon, it had been arranged *days* ahead of time. As a matter of fact, we at CBS were a little put out that we weren't getting him first. He had a sweetheart arrangement with NBC, for which he got paid a lot of money, and they got him first.

The second factor was the quality of Walter Cronkite's information. CBS News crawled all over that story. Beginning at eleven o'clock in the morning, we knew what Gerald Ford and other people would have preferred that we did not know—that Ronald Reagan had said he wanted Ford as a running mate, that Ford had agreed to continue discussing it, and that Kissinger was brought into it during the day.

Fortunately, not a lot of this had seeped out. Ford himself said that he was surprised that CBS News knew as much as it did. By the time Ford got to the anchor booth, Walter had this information, and Ford was faced with only two choices. He either had to lie or, at the very least, deal in sophistry before 40 million people and run the risk of being caught, or he had to tell at least *some* of the truth.

But this would have been true whether the interview was with Walter Cronkite or Leslie Stahl [White House correspondent]. Those things all go into that equation, and that's what leads me to say, in that instance, and I think in most instances, that while there may be an element of truth in what you've said about such persons as Cronkite bringing very special reputations and quality to an interview or an event, it's a small piece of a much more complex situation.

I don't think many people realize that often the reporter who reads the news also did the legwork and wrote the script. Do you write your own scripts for Sixty Minutes?

At *Sixty Minutes*, I work with five other people—reporters and writers. Sometimes I write all of the script, sometimes next to nothing. Most times it's the damnedest amalgam you can imagine.

But there're a lot of games played with writing in this business—for publicity purposes and advertising purposes and general bullshit *purposes*. You will hear someone say from time to time, "Joe Blow writes all his own newscasts." If Joe Blow is not the best writer in the house, it would be better if he concentrated a little less on copy.

I'm told there's been controversy about Sixty Minutes *and other news organizations' use of "reverses," which are on-camera questions retaped after the interviewer has gotten the answer. Explain what reverses are.*

A reverse is a technique of using one camera and you still get, on air, the ideal effect. If you have only one camera you keep that camera for the most part on the interview subject, not the interviewer, and you film the whole interview with that camera trained on the interview subject. Now what a reverse is, is after the interview is over, you then take a camera, move it around to the other side and refilm the questions.

Under ideal circumstances—and frequently the circumstances are ideal— what you have is a room in which you have one camera filming the picture and sound of the interview subject, *and* one camera trained on the interviewer, Dan Rather. And that's the ideal circumstance, and frequently that's the way it's done and there's no problem with that in anyone's mind. Let me say that we at *Sixty Minutes* are among the only people who consistently and regularly still do this.

So on Sixty Minutes *you don't use reverses?*

We sometimes use reverses if we only have one camera in that room, as opposed to the ideal circumstance of two. The reason most people don't use two is that it's an added noise factor and an extra lighting situation, or because the room is small. It also doubles cost. It's rare, for example, in a regular news piece that it's shot with two cameras. If you have only one camera, you keep that camera for the most part on the interview subject, not the interviewer. Then you take a camera, move it around for Dan Rather or Mike Wallace, and then you have Wallace or Rather repeat the questions.

Standard film and tape technique, whether it be news or anything else, is that you see the person asking the question, and then you see the person answer the question. You don't have to do that with every question but it gives the viewer some sense of where you are, you know, so the eye would follow the interview.

CBS News policy—and this is not the same at all three networks—but our policy is that the interview subject should *remain* in the room when you're doing that. And the purpose of that, of course, is to ensure when you're using this technique that the questions are the same. There are very few fireable offenses at CBS News but one fireable offense is to do a reverse that is not a true and accurate reverse.

So far as I know there is no controversy in this, but some people are looking for something—anything—to pick at. In other words, when we finally do a piece and it's on the air and they don't like it for whatever reason, if our facts are accurate and they can't attack that then they try to on subjectivity. Among the lesser ways they can attack it is to say, "Well, goddamnit, they used a confusing reverse technique." I would argue it is neither complex nor confusing.

Frankly, I consider it total unadulterated bullshit, because the interview subject is in the room when we re-ask the question, if indeed we *do* re-ask the question.

You have a contract as anchor man for a set period of time?

Yes.

Can you say how long a period of time it is?

Not beyond saying it's a long time. I have several points to make: I'm a pressure player—I'd better be. At this level, you either don't get here or you don't stay here unless you have demonstrated that you are. Those of us who are in it know what you can control on your best days and what you can't.

A lot of people see journalists as ambulance chasers.

There's a lot of truth in that. I'd like to make it otherwise, but that is the way it is.

I'm always reminded that so much of what is considered news is negative. Three-quarters of journalism is disclosing evil wherever it comes up; the *banality* of evil if the job is well done. The good reporter, after he chases an ambulance, does something else, he makes three or four other telephone calls, and he wears out a little shoe leather finding out why the ambulance was necessary in the first place. To me that's what separates the good journalist from the other.

About the fact that so much of it is bad news, we haven't done a very good job as journalists in explaining that to people. It has a great deal to do with the definition of news and human nature. You and I know that if you lean over the back fence to your neighbor and say, "What's news?" the news is, "Well, I paid my taxes. Joe across the street paid his taxes." But if he says, "Well, Mr. Jones down the street, the IRS was down there today and arrested him for income tax evasion," you say, "Hey, did they?" That's news. Someone says, "Hey, Ford Pintos, when hit in the rear, explode into flames." You can't very well run a headline that says Ford Fairlanes, when hit in the rear, *don't* explode, because nobody's interested. That's not news. News is that in which people are interested, which people *want* to know, and *need* to know.

Who's gonna decide? Somebody has to make a judgment. That's one of the things which people such as myself have themselves to do. If there's a fire down the block and Mrs. Smith races in to pull out somebody else's child, that's a positive good, and a good story. My point is that it's got to be something out of the ordinary. Boosterism is considered news less now than it once was. That's one of the positive things that journalism, along with the rest of society, got out of the Sixties and Seventies.

I would also say that the truth is always good news, however painful. It's better to know the truth as soon as you can, rather than delaying it. Because the price of not knowing or refusing to face it or accept it compounds. If you don't face the truth about Vietnam in 1963 and 1965, it's going to cost you more to face it in 1969 and more to face it in 1972.

People are always critical of the press, they sometimes presume that an expert gets sent to the scene, but that's not always possible. You're our eyes and ears. At the same time you're human, too.

I'm acutely aware of how often I fail. I don't think anybody can be involved with daily journalism without constantly being humbled by how many mistakes you make.

I often said to myself, particularly in the early stages, I don't know whether I'm the right person to be doing this, I don't know whether I'm up to this. Yes, I'm a good reporter, yes, I'm an experienced reporter and I have confidence in my skills, *but*, do I know enough to cover this? Well, whether you know enough or not, you're *it*.

Accuracy is the first law. I would say that fairness is its twin. But you can know all the facts and still not know the truth.

That's right.

We were reminded of that during the McCarthy period. I am constantly grappling with: How do you make your own experience work not just for you as a reporter, but for the viewer and listener?

I've heard you described, and I would agree, as being very aggressive. People have said that as a compliment and also as a criticism. The classic case was your Watergate-era exchange with Nixon, in which the president asked if you were running for something, and you said, "No sir, Mr. President, are you?"

Aggressive is not my favorite word as applied to myself. I do believe in hustling. I think the criticism of it is fair. I'd like to believe the praise is fair as well. It is my style, that's what I set out to be, that's what I want to be, and with no apology, while fully recognizing that it has its shortcomings.

Has the incident with Nixon dogged you over the years?

Yes, but less each year. The reaction of the majority is positive. That has not always been true. At the time I'd have to say it was pretty evenly split. There are people who now want to talk about it who say, "I still think you made a mistake." They come from a variety of directions, all the way from people who still think Richard Nixon was terrific, to people who read what Nixon and the people around him did as terrible, but they think I made a mistake approaching him in that way as a journalist.

I respect all of that but generally speaking now *what I* hear from people personally is, "You were right on the story, even though I hadn't thought so at the time," or, "Whether I agreed or disagreed with what you did, it took guts." Most of it is now positive but I repeat that it has not always been thus.

But if I'm going to err, I would much prefer to err on the side of too much hustle than not enough. I recognized early that to be at my best, to give myself any chance to be my best, I have to get up early, stay late and keep my concentration high.

Give me an example where this kind of legwork paid off.

One example is a story *Sixty Minutes* did on Kepone. Kepone is a chemical, originally manufactured by Allied Chemical Company and then by a smaller company called Life Sciences in Hopewell, Virginia. Kepone gave the workers bad nervous problems; it affected them mentally, made them sterile. Workers had it on their clothing. And if they were not careful about washing their hands, they might ingest it. Even if you were careful, it might fall off your hair—that kind of thing. It didn't take a lot of energetic coverage to get that much of the story, but we kept asking questions.

By continuing to pursue it, it turned out—and a court later established this—that Allied Chemical had a chemical that it knew could be injurious to the health of workers. It stopped producing that chemical under the name of Allied Chemical Company. One of the key people from Allied Chemical Company set up Life Sciences in Virginia and started producing this stuff. Well, you see where this was going.

See, you don't stop with what is ostensibly true, you don't stop with a *piece* of truth. You keep pursuing it. Sometimes the energy can lead you past something. There is a school of thought that people who take the Dan Rather "push" approach and flat out go for it aren't careful. They're not as thoughtful.

Can you think of a situation where the Dan Rather approach didn't work so well for Dan Rather?

Yeah, and I'm not proud of it. When I first got to Vietnam—this was in late November or December of 1965, pretty early on—I wanted to be where it was happening. I put a high premium on that, and I tried to charge forward all the time. Certainly I didn't want to sit around in Saigon and listen to the "follies"—the official military daily briefing—and that kind of bullshit. But in my determination not to, I erred by staying in the field, where, well, just to keep on the go and survive consumed so much of my energy and time that I didn't pull back often enough and just *think*.

Now as to specific stories, we had the first television pictures of the defoliation program. They were using slow, propeller-driven aircraft; we flew on those missions, and I think that to this day, the only public-access film of it that exists is CBS News film.

But after we had flown those missions and had filed our report, I did not take myself away and say, "Okay, this is what I've seen. What are the long-range ramifications of it for Americans, for the Vietnamese, for the war?"

Was this Agent Orange?

Yes, but I didn't know that at the time! If I had stopped to think, I might have been able to find it out. For one thing, just *getting* it consumed an awful lot of energy—to get it out, to get it shipped, to get it on the air. This is something I think a lot of people outside journalism don't understand. We have difficulty with depth in television, and that's what I'm referring to.

How about the controversy over the reporting you did in Afghanistan? One columnist described it as grandstanding, in the sense that you were dressed up in native clothing.

I don't understand criticism of my Afghanistan story, and I certainly don't agree with it.

How did you come to dress in the native attire?

That's the only way we could get into Afghanistan in March 1980. I had talked to a lot of people. The question was, *what's* going on in Afghanistan? How can you have 80,000 to 100,000 Soviet troops in there, with reports of fighting on a mass scale, and nobody in there seeing it?!

We did have people going into Kabul, which was considered a big thing—just to get around the airport and get some grab-shots for two hours was considered a major accomplishment. It was damned difficult to get in there. But then you say, "Never mind going into Kabul, how do you get into the heart of Afghanistan?"

So how did you?

What you do is, you have to have a guide; you have to have somebody who knows Afghanistan very well. You have to have somebody who can help you get across the border from Pakistan or Iran.

This was pre-hostages [the U.S. Embassy workers in Teheran were taken hostage on Nov. 4, 1979] when we started, and then the Iran side of it closed down and we're waiting in Iran to find a way to get across the border. The Pakistani authorities did not want people going in there because they didn't want to be accused by the Soviets of any number of things. And the Soviet puppet government in Afghanistan doesn't want you in, so the only way is to get an Afghan who knows the territory very well, and then look for a border crossing.

At one time, we asked somebody, can you parachute in? "No. Suicide. Forget it, you can't." Can you drive in? "No, you can't drive in. You can only *walk* in."

The answer: Let's *go* to Pakistan, let's go to Peshawar, where the refugees are coming in. I knew from previous war coverage that one important source of information is refugees. I also knew that the last thing you want to do is talk to people who speak English. The information frequently is suspect.

In Afghanistan, it's tough because Farsi is the main language, and it's indecipherable. If you go to Peshawar, first you try to find people who have been there and who might be willing to go back. You try to get *their* confidence. They want to know if you have been in combat before: "How do I know that you aren't going to just jump up and start screaming and yelling?"

Then you have to disguise yourself, which isn't easy, let me tell you. You've gotta grow a beard: if you don't have a beard in Afghanistan [*snaps his fingers*] you're marked right away as an outsider. So keep your gear down to a low weight; make yourself up insofar as possible to blend in with other Afghans. In our American contingent we had six people, including sound man Peter O'Connor and cameraman Michael Edwards and two Afghans.

Did you come close to getting caught at any point?

Yes.

When?

Not long after we got there, we were trying to film some Russian aircraft, and we got, amazingly, within 200 or 300 yards of the end of a runway where Soviet aircraft were. But by getting that close, we almost got caught.

What happened?

Somebody from the nearby village, a very suspicious bicycle rider, came by and started asking questions about what we were doing and then rode away. And the people we were with said very quickly, in translation, "We'd better haul ass," and we did haul ass, and it was a good thing. We just barely got out of there in time.

There were several of those things when we were up on the mountaintops, when we did the scenes at night. Just before we got to the top of one mountain, I found myself thinking, "This is it, we've had it, we're found, and they're either going to kill us or capture us right here."

Were people following you?

No, this was a case of helicopters coming back from a mission. They were flying very low, and there was no place to hide. It was a very rocky terrain. Now the Afghans had told us that if that happened in any place, become a rock. What they did—and we followed suit—was quickly freeze on the ground, pull their blankets over them and play like rocks. The helicopters came in at such a low altitude that I was convinced they had seen us. And I felt that they were either going to land right there, or they were going to make a sweep around and start strafing the area. But by becoming rocks, we saved ourselves.

After working as a White House correspondent, how much solid information would you say the average citizen gets?

Well, they get a lot, but not enough. Any White House correspondent—no matter how good—can find out only a small portion of what is actually going on, and when he attempts to convey even that small portion, there are the usual problems with time, with clarity and with, frankly, the viewers' attention. I always tried to convey information that people watching every night could accumulate. If one watched carefully and listened carefully, more information would accumulate than you could really convey on any one broadcast.

Can you think of one particular time when you obtained information from a source, and the president or a member of his cabinet was really taken aback by the fact that you had this information?

There was a time fairly early on in the Nixon administration when a school bus filled with black students was overturned in South Carolina, and the whites beat on the side of this bus with ax handles. It was a bad, *ugly* scene.

Now President Nixon and the White House were in a dilemma. They were busy building on the foundation of their Southern Strategy from 1968, looking forward to the 1972 elections.

Therefore, the president did not want to place himself in a position of condemning. Instead, the vice-president, Spiro T. Agnew, was instructed to make a carefully crafted statement that would put the White House on record as saying something about the incident in at least a mildly critical posture, but at the same time containing code words and phrases that those who were working politically in the South could point to with a wink and say, "You know where our heart is."

Now, I knew several people in the White House, Nixon men to the core, but they couldn't stomach this. They thought it was wrong morally; they thought it was wrong politically.

I went around asking questions: "*What* the hell is going on around here? If the president of the United States can't condemn this kind of thing, what kind of country are we? What kind of president is he?" And I would find people who would say, "Well, look, I'll tell you what's happening, but I can't be quoted by name. It would be fatal. . . ."

And they wanted me to be very careful how I attributed it, and under questioning, they explained what had happened. I told the story, and everybody with or without human decency was shocked, for his or her own reasons, that it came out.

Let's talk about the Kennedy assassination for a minute. Just recount when you first heard that he had been shot in Dallas—the events of that day and of the next four days.

I did not have the primary responsibility to cover the presidential trip. That's very important in terms of what effect it did have on me and how things went down. I had the overall responsibility of making sure that our logistics and coverage were what they should be. I had been down in Uvalde, Texas, to interview former Vice President John Nance Garner—"Cactus John"; we were having several belts of good bourbon whiskey, and he was being photographed with Miss Texas Wool. When I heard the news, mentally and emotionally I went into a special place that I believe many reporters know, that I know I had known before. Right away you say to yourself, this could be a big story.

How would you describe that place?

It is where your training as a reporter moves you, insofar as is humanly possible, to set your own emotions aside and concentrate on what needs to be done.

I've heard reporters say that people on the outside often take this to be a callous process.

This is why any number of people, including my brother, whom I talked to that weekend, and my wife, asked, "What are *you* thinking, how are *you* feeling?" Looking back on it, I know exactly why I said [things that] struck their ears as callous. I didn't want to talk because the emotions that most people were feeling—those things hit, but they didn't hit me until ten days to two weeks after the story.

Had you had any significant contact with Kennedy before his death?

I had interviewed Kennedy at the 1960 Democratic convention in Los Angeles. This was before I came to the network. I was working in a local station in Houston, KHLU, as a correspondent for Corinthian Broadcasting. We were determined to interview Kennedy and positioned ourselves and waited for hours protecting our position, elbowing people out of the way. And he came sweeping by, and I stuck a microphone in his face and fell off the table.

It was a ridiculous interview, if you could call it that. After waiting all that time you would have thought I had a list of really good questions but I didn't, and I asked him, "Do you intend to campaign in Texas?" Since he was there already, how stupid of a question can you get? Anyhow, he said, "Yes, of course," and gave me a little political spiel. I asked him something about the vice-presidency in which he was noncommittal and not very forthcoming, and then he swept on.

Walter Cronkite was very complimentary of your work in Dallas in the aftermath of the Kennedy assassination. Did he ever communicate that firsthand to you?

Yes. Sometime well after the events of that weekend. My recollection is sometime near the end of the following week. Note that when Cronkite compliments—Cronkite does not regularly compliment people—that he is from a school that believes that if you do a good job, that's expected. That's what you're paid to do, so what's the big deal. He's sparing with compliments;

he's a generous man but his managerial style, if you like, is to be sparing with compliments. If you get a compliment from Walter Cronkite it *is* a big deal. And that was a big deal to me.

It came in what form?

A telephone call from him. Which is generally the form in which Walter Cronkite compliments someone.

What was the essence of the conversation?

The essence was "I thought you did a hell of a job." It was a short conversation, matter-of-fact and professional. I felt wonderful. (*Laughs*) There are plenty of times when people compliment you and you know and felt that you didn't deserve it. But with Walter, he's smart enough to know that as well. The great thing about Walter was that he would keep a regular line of communication going with his reporters and we'd talk regularly. If he doesn't want to compliment the person then they know that it's just an application of what we call "eucalyptus aura," which is just a CBS expression for some kind of stroking.

I can't remember another time, until the Nixon years, when I had such a telephone call. It was a different conversation, more along the lines of, "Do you need any help? I know you're under a lot of pressure. I'm here to help you. You're doing a hell of a job."

What's the most horrific assignment you've found yourself in? It might not be a big news story per se.

Covering Martin Luther King for the first time had a profound effect on me. I was not very well prepared; it was a tremendous education for me in a hurry.

The first time being when and where?

Albany, Georgia, 1962. King and some others—Andy Young among them— had taken on a very difficult chore.

What about the experience had the greatest impact?

First of all, the overall environment was more violent than anything of its kind that I had ever been associated with.

I had not seen, for example, a group of blacks walking down the street and a group of whites come seemingly from nowhere and beat the hell out of them and then disappear, and nobody—other than the blacks—being very excited about it.

I had not seen, white *or* black, hundreds of people arrested for nonviolent protest. To me, it was as if one had landed on another planet. A lot of it had to do with my parochialism, with my outright ignorance and insensitivity.

The other thing that had a profound effect on me was King himself. In the midst of what seemed to me a kind of miniholocaust, he had this ability to know where he was going, what he was about, what he was trying to do. His tranquility is the thing that I remember, a remarkable inner peace. He was absolutely convinced that what he was doing was the right thing. He knew that it would be a long march, not just the march of that day in Albany, but a long overall march. I thought that was remarkable.

What was your most intimate contact with him?

I interviewed him almost daily. I had conversations with him regularly, and not always in a formal interview. He was accessible. It was to his political benefit to be accessible. I remember walking into a scene in Albany—and I don't know the details—but something no good for King and his cause had happened. There was chaos all around.

It was difficult to get in; staff people were running around shouting and making telephone calls. He was at the very center of this. Finally we were getting him and saying, "Need to talk for a minute." He stopped everything he was doing; he turned, and when he looked at you, you had his *full* attention. This is not always true of people. He stopped and said, "So you say you need something. What is it you need?" "I need the answer to the following two questions."

I don't even remember what the two questions were, but I remember he drilled me in the eyes, he listened to what the need was and answered the questions. And there was a softness and a gentleness that impressed me. Then, as soon as he felt that I had what I needed, his attention turned to someone else.

How did he unwind?

He'd take himself off with some of the younger people on the staff—whomever he liked.

I think he almost always unwound in church. He was a great orator, we know. What we may not know is that the oration itself was a kind of therapy to him. He could really lay himself all out if he was making a sermon.

There were plenty of times in which he was making a sermon on automatic pilot because it was a sermon he'd made dozens of times before; he didn't even think about the words, he was miles away.

But when he was in church, I had a sense that a lot of his frustration came out.

He also liked to eat. He'd go to a good rib place, and he could smile. Frequently, the only time you would see him smile was at mealtime.

Which of the presidents you've covered was the most forthcoming?

Boy, oh boy. The answer is *none.* I suppose the instinct for forthrightness was probably stronger in Ford and the people around him than anybody in my experience, but I don't want to overstate that. It wasn't much, but comparatively, there was more with him.

With which president did you have the closest contact?

Johnson. That was not something personal with me; in general, Johnson was by far the most accessible. He had supreme confidence that if he could simply talk to you man to man, he could convince you of anything [*laughing*]. Now, he was wrong about that, but he sure believed it.

Can you think, then, of an instance in which you had close contact with him along these lines?

When I came back from Vietnam—this would have been in late 1965—I was assigned to be CBS' White House correspondent. Bill Moyers said to Johnson, in effect, "Rather's been to Vietnam, he's been on the ground there, and he's had firsthand personal experience there. You ought to talk to him."

Somebody called me and said, "The president would like to talk to you about Vietnam." I came in, and we did have a conversation. Part of it was in the Oval Office and part of it in the small anteroom off the Oval Office. Johnson liked to move; he was restless. He'd tip his chair and get up and move and walk around and say, "Come with me here and there."

We talked for the better part of an hour. He began with, "I know you've been in Vietnam; I'd be interested to know what you saw, what you heard, what you think."

What did you tell him?

Among other things, I told him that the war just wasn't working. Also, he asked me whether I had seen Viet Cong units or North Vietnamese units.

He listened, he seemed interested, and he had comments. He talked some about whether I'd been along the Cambodian border, and how much fighting there had been along the Cambodian border.

I had seen a lot of our equipment bogged down, and I said that it struck me as foolish to try to use armor under those circumstances. And he said something to the effect of, "Well, who the hell are you to second-guess experts in armor and whether it ought to be used or not used?!"

I said, "I can only tell you what my eyes saw and what my mind registered, which was that that wasn't the best use of that kind of equipment."

Was the Johnson who declined to run again very different from the one whom you sat with in those rooms?

Yes. When I sat with him then, he felt, rightly or wrongly, that his time, his administration, was in its ascendancy. When he announced that he wasn't going to run again, it was clear to him and to all those in the White House Press Room that, for better or worse, his time was ended.

Did you ever meet with Nixon in a similar fashion?

The only time I had anything I would consider to be meaningful conversation with President Nixon was about fifteen or twenty minutes after I did the one-hour interview with him in the Oval Office in January of 1972. To everyone's surprise, he hung around afterward.

Did he say anything to you directly?

Yes. He smiled, and it was not that tight political smile that is so commonly associated with him. And he said, "You know, there was one question and only one for which I was not prepared." He paused. "And I don't think I handled it very well. And that was the last question."

The form of using *Ms.* rather than *Miss* or *Mrs.* in addressing women was coming to the fore, and I had asked him if he was considering doing that on White House correspondence.

He regretted that his staff hadn't raised with him the possibility that he might be asked that. He was very proud of the fact that his staff had anticipated almost every area of discussion.

Did he say or do anything else that might give some indication of his general modus operandi?

I remember him saying that he always considered himself a beast for homework. He prepared himself for the presidency, for the difficult job he'd ascended to, but of course, in the end, even *he* was overwhelmed by the amount of reading and, er, homework [*nervous laugh*] that he had to absorb!

The Last Good Sport

Muhammad Ali:
"I Am the Master of My Destiny"

A brave man was destined to win, and a bully was doomed to lose. In April 1997, Zaire President Mobutu Sese Seko was losing control of his country, a corrupt 32–year reign propped up by Cold War politics finally lumbering toward collapse. An opposition army was closing in on Kinshasha, the capital of Africa's third largest country, and the rebels were led by Laurent Kabila, a stubborn loyalist of the late Patrice Lumumba, the leftist independence leader whom Mobutu usurped three decades earlier.

A world away, in Los Angeles, former heavyweight boxing champion Muhammad Ali, the beleaguered figure whose October 30, 1974, "Rumble in the Jungle" against George Foreman had once been coopted to bolster Mobutu's regime, was triumphing anew: Director-producer Leon Gast's *When We Were Kings* documentary of Ali's knockout victory in Zaire was about to win an Academy Award.

A month later, Mobutu would flee the country. Ali, meanwhile, would continue a U.S. tour endorsing research funding for the Parkinson's disease he'd been diagnosed with back in 1984. That tour took Ali to Capitol Hill to endorse bills in the Congress and Senate, which would give the National Institutes of Health $100 million to fight Parkinson's. And so the champ would walk the same corridors where he had once been hounded and reviled for his principled refusal to fight in the Vietnam War, even as Mobutu's misrule had simultaneously been praised by legislators merely because the dictator gave access to Western mining companies and shunned pro-Soviet neighbors.

The demise of Mobutu, who was suffering from prostate cancer (from which he succumbed on September 7, 1997), had been forecast since the summer of '96, when growing unrest stemming from the multi-party politics Mobutu was forced to permit, fueled a fierce seven-month battle to overthrow him.

Even as such forces of retribution were converging in Zaire, the power of rehabilitation was alive in Atlanta, Georgia, as Ali made an electrifying appearance at the 1996 summer Olympiad, his arm trembling but true as he lifted the flaming baton to light the Olympic torch.

Afterward, Ali's office in Berrien Springs, Michigan, was deluged with calls, faxes and e-mail, including a grateful message from a woman who said her husband, disabled by Parkinson's, had been housebound in shame until viewing Ali in the televised opening ceremonies for the summer Games. Afterward, he went out and proudly told people on the street, "I've got Muhammad Ali disease!"

Witnessed by an estimated 3 billion people, Ali's moving gesture as a veteran Olympic gold medalist (Rome, 1960) was followed by several months of high school visits to spread the message of a pamphlet of his inspirational prose, *Healing: A Journal of Tolerance and Understanding.*

On February 11, 1997, Ali and his fourth wife of 10 years, Lonnie (who had known him since she was a child in their native Louisville, Kentucky), attended the world premiere of *When We Were Kings* at Radio City Music Hall in Manhattan, a capacity crowd giving the man a wet-eyed, foot-stomping standing ovation afterward.

Like the raw personal courage it so rousingly evoked, *When We Were Kings* was one of the most inspiring films of the 1990s, a testament to the incalculable impact of leadership by example—as well as the acute loneliness anyone must be willing to withstand to fulfill one's personal destiny.

Watching from the audience as Ali smiled from the stage and waved, throwing kisses, this writer remembered how, six months after his victory over Foreman, Ali had extended a kind personal invitation in March 1975 to revisit his Deer Lake, Pennsylvania, training camp.

"Wasn't that a heck of a thing, a nice article," he said of the accompanying story, rising from a bench in his locker room to hug his guest in welcome. "That was beautiful, man," he added regarding the verbatim presentation of his "I Am the Master of My Destiny" prophesy. "You got it word for word. Because in the end I said that once you blow on the spark of mastery, that glow will turn to flame, and on the night I meet George Foreman, my light shall be bright. And that's what happened!"

As Ali toweled off and dressed for lunch, having completed a morning of sparring with Larry Holmes in preparation for an upcoming bout with Chuck Wepner, a phone call came from singer Gladys Knight. Ali cradled the receiver against his shoulder as he donned sports clothes, listening as Knight explained she and her new husband would stop by the next day. She also mentioned she was about to star in her first film, a romantic drama set in the Alaskan oil fields, entitled *Pipe Dreams.*

"So you gonna make a black movie?" said Ali. "Outtasight. But look here, Gladys, do a *good* movie. Don't be talking about 'motherfucker' and calling women 'bitch' and have one titty hanging out and all of that stuff. Don't make none of them kind of black movies.

"All of our movies pull our people down and ain't nothing to be proud of, with all kind of dope, El Dorados, and sisters cursing, half-naked. So whatever you do, I hope it's clean and ain't nothing to lead our people into a lot of dope and filth, you know. Because I don't represent that; I got a lot of honor and fame for standing up for black people, not Uncle Tom-ing, not selling us out, and not doing nothing nasty."

Ali's tone was gentle, brotherly, but he was in dead earnest. As with virtually everything he ever vowed, Ali would keep faith with his own advice to Knight and avoid any project, cinematic or otherwise, that played into the entertainment industry's pandering greed or its recurrent racist cynicism.

After he said a warm goodbye to Knight in '75, Ali turned to Holmes, manager Angelo Dundee, and his guest and grinned almost sheepishly, saying, "Isn't it amazing what I tell people? Ain't I something? There'll never be another me."

THE INTERVIEW

I F FOURTEEN PAGES of a scratch pad could contain the passions of a man, these did. Late on an August afternoon in 1974, after a full schedule of sparring and roadwork as the then-challenger for George Foreman's heavyweight crown, Muhammad Ali sat down on the back steps of his private cabin at his nearly deserted Deer Lake, Pennsylvania, training camp. Gripping the lined pages of the yellow pad, which were covered with a purposeful scrawl, the 32–year-old Ali explained that he had been unable to sleep the previous night and had gotten up in the early hours of morning to write. It was two weeks before he was due to leave for the world championship bout in Kinshasa, Zaire, in which Ali hoped to regain his title.

Scanning his lengthy jottings, his strain-hardened features lit with a boyish resolve, Ali said he was thinking about making this manuscript his definitive pre-fight statement, to be delivered just before he boarded the plane to Africa. Several days onward, at his airport press conference, the boxer would blurt a diverting burst of prose for the press but, surprisingly, it was not the almost prayer-like diary of thoughts he'd shared in seclusion.

"I'm still working on this," he'd quietly said that waning August afternoon, "but I'm gonna read it for you now." And then Muhammad Ali, alone and tired, began to recite the future as he saw it against the rustle of the Pennsylvania woods:

"I am the master of my destiny.

"My present fight with George Foreman is the reflection of my past fight with Sonny Liston. Destiny is not what is already made; destiny is what we are making. Many people think that we are in the hands of destiny, driven in whatever direction life desires or wills, but really, we are the masters of our destiny, *especially* from the moment we realize this fact. Man is responsible for his rise and fall.

"There is a hint of this in the Bible, in the principal prayer taught by Christ, in which he says, 'Thy will be done on earth, as it is in heaven.' It is a psychological suggestion to mankind, to make it possible that the will of God, which is easily done in heaven, should also be done on earth. If we study my fight with George Foreman, we will understand that it is not the qualifications, the enthusiasm, the energy that counts in this fight, but also the design, the plan already made. And according to that plan, I have to go through my destiny.

"The question of destiny can be better explained by the picture of an artist meditating a design as he has it in his mind. The first stage is to create the design in his mind; the second stage is to bring it out on canvas, and when he draws his picture on the canvas, it may suggest something to him that he had not originally thought of in his mind.

"When George Foreman meets me, he will see something, he will experience something that *he has not thought of in his mind*! When the artist has finished the picture, he will see that it is quite different from what he had originally thought it to be: and when George Foreman finishes meeting me, he will see that I'm quite different from what he originally thought I would be.

"When all has been designed beforehand and the fight begins, it will receive a totally different situation from the picture. Something that was lacking may have been added to it, and in this way the picture is improved. For there are two kinds of artists: The one who paints the plan, which has been made in his mind, on the canvas; and the other, who takes the suggestions from the picture itself as he goes on painting.

"The difference is that one is merely an artist and one is merely a master.

"There is George Foreman, who is driven by the hands of destiny. He does not know where he comes from, nor does he know where he is going: He is placed in a certain condition in life. His boxing ability is limited and imperfect compared to mine, and, on the other side, I represent the unlimited and perfect state and style of boxing. That is why Christ has said, 'Be ye perfect even as your Father, which is in heaven, is perfect.' It means I not only inherit from my earthly parents, but I, Muhammad Ali, inherit a creative power which comes from Almighty God, Allah himself.

"Ninety percent of the world cannot imagine me whupping George Foreman. They are capable of recognizing victory as long as they can see it according to their view, but the moment that they cannot clearly see that victory anymore, then they are defeated. In other words, that which we call defeat is a word in our mind. We cannot be the winner; we cannot be victorious; it is not *visible* to us, and therefore my fans and enemies cannot understand it and therefore they say for me it is The End. But is there anything that ends, or is there anything that is destroyed? The answer is no. All these words are our *illusions* of the end, destruction or defeat.

"These are our own *illusions,* our own conception, which is only true as long as we have not seen or recognized the power of God. Those, like myself, who have realized in themselves the possibility of victory in their lives—they are victorious and they improve themselves. But the one who thinks, "I cannot make it; George Foreman is too tough; he is too strong; he hits too hard," that person comes under his own suggestion and he naturally becomes weaker every day, and he will never be able to accomplish defeating George Foreman.

"But one, such as I, who realizes that life begins with *spirit,* he says, "What does it matter? There is no human being that I'm afraid of! I am the greatest boxer in the world! The present image of George Foreman doesn't bother me at all!"

"So it is never too late for us to improve. There is always scope for the man who wants to improve himself. But for the man who is contented with himself, or who is so discouraged that he does not want to improve— he falls flat. There is no way for him to accomplish anything in life.

"So a man, such as Muhammad Ali, who is a responsible and reliable man when the cards are down, has a control over his situations and conditions. Such a man is greater than a thousand men and boxers who may otherwise be gifted, but don't have this particular gift— being able to control his situation and his conditions.

"Boxing fans cannot imagine to what an extent the power of the mastermind can accomplish things in the ring. They cannot *imagine*! But I do it behind the scenes, not in the gym.

"Those who do little, come forward and say they can do much; but those who can really do, say little.

"Every soul here on earth is here in order to accomplish a certain purpose. But when he has reached mastery, from that moment on one is chosen by God to be used as a tool and instrument to accomplish a certain specific purpose. Every single human being is a kind of a raw material which destiny uses. The mastermind is a finished instrument which destiny handles to accomplish a purpose, and in my case, my purpose is to promote the religion of Islam, as taught by the Honorable Elijah Muhammad, which preaches freedom, justice and equality for the so-called American Negro.

"So do not be surprised, therefore, when you reach Zaire and see 100,000 people rooting for Muhammad Ali while George Foreman is

the champion. Be not surprised when you hear the words of
Muhammad Ali still being cherished after three and one-half years of
exile from the ring and defeat by Ken Norton and Joe Frazier. Be not
surprised when you see the *personality* of Muhammad Ali still powerful after so many years of being before the public, thanks to Almighty
God, Allah Himself.

"It is because of my life's experience in the world of success and
failure that I have so many followers, and am known to the people of
the world, because what I did was *real*; it was true and it was brave. I
did what I thought was right—freedom, justice and equality for the
Black man in America—and I always will remain the same. Mastery
not only means accomplishing the things of the world; it is that with
which a person fulfills his purpose in life.

"The spirit of mastery is like a spark, and blowing continually upon
it one can blow it into a blaze. So people of the world, do not be troubled by what my outer skills look like compared with George
Foreman's. Do not look at the outside for, in reality, all my power is
within and it is not seen by the human eye. If I keep this idea before
me and blow on the spark of mastery, then on the night that I fight
George Foreman the flame will rise and victory will become clear and
my power will be indeed great!"

A man's character may best be judged by the adjectives
which he habitually uses in conversation.

Rev. Joseph Tuckerman, 1813

I am the greatest!

Cassius Clay, 1964

I am the greatest boxer in the world!

Muhammad Ali, 1974

On October 30, 1974, under a humble roof of tin in Kinshasa's Stade Du
20 Mai, while trainer Angelo Dundee and buffoon Bundini Brown screeched
and howled over the tumult of 50,000 lunatic Zairians for an explanation of
why their man wasn't shuffling, and while George Foreman lurched about
the ring trying to sort out Dick Sadler's directives as if they were a roadmap
he was unable to refold properly. Muhammad Ali used the ropes the way a

pinball wizard uses the bumpers and wrought one sweet eighth-round number on that Texas streetpunk's head.

Against all odds, Ali won.

And why not? Ali was the man who brought boxing back from the dead and gave professional sports its first massive youngblood transfusion since Babe Ruth. He seized the reins of a bandwagon while it was still a stagecoach and, through the dynamism and charisma of his uniquely ostentatious nature, guided into the sports arena a team of maverick stallions (like Joe Namath, Reggie Jackson and Derek Sanderson) hauling an opulent new era of exceptionalism. Under Muhammad Ali's tutelage, the promotion and distribution of public athletic contests became superbusiness and its principals elevated to the status of statesmen. His purses, totaling an estimated $34 million, were the solid groundwork that made it possible for athletes— most specifically, black athletes—to win equitable contracts and collect Rolls Royces like trading stamps.

Moreover, Ali's haughty, unbridled bearing lent encouragement and impetus to a worldwide generation of blacks demanding human dignity, self-determination and the right to their own singularity. When he refused induction into the Vietnam-era army, he legitimized and inspired thousands of similar personal protests.

He kicked open windows nailed shut in the backrooms of boxing, and let a fresh, invigorating wind dispel decades of cigar smoke and skullduggery. Ali's antics and wry epigrams, his sculptured, caramel physique and his fat mouth transformed sleazy slugfests into glittering, elegantly visceral events that drew to ringside kings, presidents, Broadway and film luminaries, Pulitzer Prize-winning authors and thousands of outrageous high rollers and minions.

"You love me and you hate me 'cause I talk too loud and too much," he told an often begrudgingly attentive public, "but you all come up and ask me questions like I was a senator.

"I put on a good, clean exciting show; I make boxing an art, a science. Nobody can beat me and nobody deserves to. I'm gonna be the first black fighter that people will look at and say 'There's a wise, wealthy man with property, businesses and two million dollars in the bank.'

"I'm the greatest, the fastest, the prettiest, the dancin'est heavyweight boxer in the world, and you know it!"

Cassius Clay, a.k.a. Muhammad Ali, came dancing into prominence during the Camelot years of John F. Kennedy's New Frontier.

In the early '60s, the United States, watched over by a boyish, Promethean president, his comely wife and a staff of the "best and the brightest," believed itself possessed of an unassailable integrity with infinite potential for creative growth and good-will.

It was a period of self-induced innocence and unsettling incongruities; we had an active Peace Corps and a just as active Central Intelligence Agency. We had Freedom Rides and the Bay of Pigs.

William L. Shirer's *The Rise and Fall of the Third Reich* was a runaway bestseller, second only to the New English Bible.

Films like *West Side Story*, a homogenized version of streetlife in Spanish Harlem, were capturing Oscars while venereal disease and violent crime among juveniles were continuing in an upward trend that had begun in 1957.

Two U.S. helicopter companies, totaling 400 men, were sent to Vietnam, the first direct U.S. military support for Ngo Dinh Diem's crumbling regime, and James Meredith was enrolled, at gunpoint, as the first black student at Ole Miss.

Civil wars were shattering inconspicuous lives: Belgian miner Albert Verbrugghe suffered machine gun wounds in the face and the death of his young wife during a roadside inspection of his car by UN troops outside of Jadotville in the Katanga Province of the Republic of The Congo, an embattled country in Africa that would later be renamed Zaire.

Grim realities were something folks were reluctant to turn and face. Turmoil and upheaval were rife at home and abroad, but Americans, distracted by prosperity, felt they were in capable hands and so they went off chasing rainbows.

The fight game was not the pot of gold: a murky, obviously manipulative, blood-sucking carnival under the control of racketeers and the underworld cabals. The greats were gone. Jack Dempsey was now a restauranteur specializing in thick steaks and blarney; Rocky Marciano had retired undefeated, and anyone who didn't know the tragic story of Primo Carnera could get the gist by forking over $1.50 to see *Requiem for a Heavyweight*.

The public knew that prize fighters, like crooked policemen, were low-class, backdoor aspirants to an altar of affluency, and there was a severe limit to the malarkey the public would put up with from them. With no one as gentlemanly, capable and self-effacing as Joe Louis to recommend the sport, the whole unsavory business was in an advanced stage of decay, languishing under the reign of pallid titlists like Floyd Patterson and the in-the-ring deaths of Davey Moore and Benny "Kid" Paret, which inspired a young folksinger named Bob Dylan to write a protest song advocating the abolishment of boxing.

Patterson was a likeable, even gallant figure: The first boxer ever to lose and regain the heavyweight title; but he fought opponents no more deadly than ancient Archie Moore and "Ingo" Johansson. Gifted with lightning hands of minimal wallop, he was, in the final analysis, a spidery, overly polite, peekaboo fighter with a bumpy complexion and a bad habit of permitting matchups with bums to retain his hold on the title.

And then there was pig-faced Sonny Liston, a union goon, headhunter and jailbird, twice convicted of armed robbery and assault with intent to kill. He had two moods: grim and murderous. When his turn came, he wore the heavyweight crown the way a pimp wears a porkpie hat.

The battle plan of the body politic was calculated optimism, and Patterson, Liston and colleagues were vivid reminders of all that was lackluster across the New Frontier.

Like him or not, the loudmouth from Louisville was at least a change of pace.

First known by the slave name of Cassius Marcellus Clay, a moniker he shared with a Roman gladiator, he was every blessed thing that boxers were not then and still are not—handsome, witty, flamboyant, unscarred—and possessed of an entertaining and provocative personality. A true champion, he fought the meanest, the toughest, the most skillful pugilists in the fight game and left them lying on their backs. Brimming with quips and smart-alecky conversation, he was a sportwriter's dream.

"Boxing needs me," Cassius revealed to a reporter before his 1961 match with Willi Besmanoff. "Boxing needs fighters who talk a lot.

"A fighter today brings two or three girls with him to a fight. In olden days a fighter'd go back in the woods to train and drink tea without sugar in it, getting mean. Today, temptation is abroad in the land. There's more pretty cars and you can get them cheap—five dollars down. Everything's a dollar down, there's a liquor store on every corner and a rock 'n roll show in town every week.

"Ohhh, but when he's in training, Cassius Clay goes to bed at *nine*. I'm eating them lima beans, collard greens, okra, tomatoes and spinach. Most guys eat crackers and soda pop and expect to stay in shape. But not Cassius Clay, he's a determined man. When he lays a man down, he's supposed to STAY down.

"I should be the champ when I'm twenty-one. You writing that?" They were.

Clay was a darling of the electronic age, welcomed by any host on whose television program he deigned to appear. He once popped onto *The Tonight*

Show to deliver what he called the world's shortest poem:

Whee!
Me!!

Last August, I met Ali at Fighter's Heaven, the training camp he built in the Pocono Mountains. He had been working out daily since June in preparation for his challenge to George Foreman's title in Zaire, then scheduled for September 25.

As my car mounted the hill, a big alabaster sign with red block letters rose into view, "Muhammad Ali's Training Camp."

An arrow pointed across the road to a precipitous driveway. On the ride up the incline, I passed construction in progress and clusters of log cabins. At the top was a small, unpaved parking lot hewn out of a mossy mound of earth and pine. Perhaps fifty people were strolling about, chatting with each other, snapping pictures, eating picnic lunches on large boulders on which had been painted the names of boxing greats. A little boy was running in furious circles in a gravel courtyard formed by cabins containing the gym, messhall and bunkhouse.

A bowl-bellied man I recognized as Drew "Bundini" Brown, Ali's long-time valet and witchdoctor, called out to the boy. "Little Muhammad!" he yelled. "You not gon' get nowheres that way!"

The crowd grinned and took more pictures as Bundini, a black man with asphalt skin, lowered his brutish head and charged at the bouncing kid, who scampered off in hysterical laughter. The child ran to a statuesque, strikingly beautiful black woman with long, braided hair and dressed in a flowered dress that flowed to her sandletops. "Mommie!" he shrieked, throwing his arms around her legs.

The scene was not what I had expected. I gazed about the rustic complex in search of sunglassed hoods in sharkskin suits with bulges in the armpits. The best I could find was Angelo Dundee, Ali's trainer, stretched out on a piece of slag with "Sugar Ray" emblazoned on it.

He was regaling two of the tourists, a Chinese man and his son, with anecdotes. They seemed to be having difficulty following Dundee's galloping discourse.

"You know how Muhammad prances around the ring," he laughed. "Well, outside the ring he can't do any of these popular dances. Not a step. No way. Would you have figured that? You wouldn't have, would you?"

The man and his son smiled broadly but said nothing.

I turned idly to my right to see Ali strolling down from the parking lot, flanked by two husky black men, all three dressed in pastel sports shirts, slacks, heavy brogans. He smiled at the buzzing fans, mussed a little blonde kid's hair and went into his dressing room to change.

Ali worked out for two hours that day, pleasing the gallery with double-time rope-skipping and fancy speed bag rhythms. He was naked when I entered his cramped dressing room. There were several mirrors in the small area and he was pivoting, checking himself out in their reflection, chopping the air with tensed arms.

In the gym he had given the crowd, especially the ladies, a good show. Muhammad Ali knows how to angle his arms to get the maximum definition out of his biceps when he punches the bouncy speed bag, and he has long since perfected a type of shoulder roll that causes the muscles that fan out from his spine to ripple in brilliant symphony, the fleshy ochre keyboard of a runaway player-piano.

A female wire-service photographer was visibly impressed. Twice she lifted her camera away from her face and stood there in an extended, unashamed stare.

Ali sat down on a green couch in the corner of the dressing room, toweling the profuse sweat that jeweled him from head to foot.

He spoke just above his breath, deliberately, as if to himself. Sportswriter friends had warned me that he might rant or ignore me, but I found him uncommonly polite. He answered in minute detail, and offered additional particulars on things like his diet, which consisted entirely of fish and steamed vegetables. "Fish don't tire you to eat," he told me, "and I take a lot of fruit, like peaches. There's a peach tree orchard over the hill. I go into it when I run and I reach up in the trees sometimes 'n steal the peaches."

What would be his strategy against Foreman?

"To whup a man like George Foreman you need the speed and hands of a lightweight, and there aren't any heavyweights in history that can rank themselves with lightweights, except maybe me. I'm the only man alive who can take him."

It was a throw-away answer, something he'd blurted out a dozen times before. We both knew it. I was about to rephrase the question when he spoke up again in a barely audible, downright melancholy voice.

"It's difficult to advise a man how to defeat George Foreman or anyone else," he murmured.

"I can't easily tell a man to do what I do, because can't many humans do what I do as a heavyweight boxer. That's not bragging, it's just true . . . but

I'll tell you, you got to get your legs in shape to take the body punches. Jabbing and moving is part of it. When you're at arm's range, you beat the man to the punch and get out . . . Foreman can't jab like me . . . he don't know how. After five rounds, he'll be equal with you . . . he'll be tired. Five rounds is tiring for a lightweight.

"It's complicated. I say that in the fifth round his resistance will be low and he'll be irritated . . . embarrassed. He's been puffing after his latest victories. You've gotta be tricky and not tire yourself . . . you've got to make him pour it on. If you can get to the point where you can make him pour it on and he don't stop you. . . ."

His face was stony, deep in expressionless concentration. After a while I watched only his eyes. They had an odd, point-of-tears look, totally out of kilter with the stoicism his taut features sought to portray.

Ali's last words to me were spoken so softly, I had to strain to hear them. "I have the advantage," he mused, "because George Foreman has never tasted defeat. He just doesn't know how it feels." I was startled. His tone so sad, it bore no resemblance to the overweening prattle I had grown up hearing him spout.

Disconcerted by his behavior, it wasn't until the night of the fight, midway through the fourth round, that I flashed back to that moment and realized Ali had, two months earlier, frankly disclosed his entire strategy for whupping George Foreman.

All I could think about at the time were those eyes, Muhammad Ali's eyes, welled up, distant, downcast. How, I wondered, does a man become so profoundly sad?

Cassius Marcellus Clay, Jr. was born on January 17, 1942, into a middle-class family in Louisville, Kentucky, the son of an insecure sign painter and his doting wife. By his own admission, Cassius didn't do anything but lounge around the house eating snacks and napping for his first twelve years. His younger brother, Rudolph Valentino Clay—his father obviously had great expectations for both his boys—breezed along in similar fashion.

Odessa Clay, a loving and extremely generous woman, asked very little of either of her sons, especially Cassius. A willful, dominating personality even then, he was not the kind of kid one could easily order about.

"When he was young," Odessa Clay recalls, "he always wanted to play with children that were older, and he wanted to be the boss. And he called his little brother his baby. If I had to punish Rudolph, Cassius would run and hit me and say, 'Don't you whup my baby!' And he'd put his arms around

Rudolph and walk him away and say to him, 'She better leave you alone.'"

Despite all the free, unhassled time at Cassius' disposal, the Clay household was not the most pleasant place to be. Cassius Clay, Sr. was a frustrated fine artist, a man plagued by an overblown estimation of his own limited talents. He often went on raucous drinking jags, during which he railed against the white devils for preventing him from becoming a famous painter, and administered severe beatings to his wife and sons. Court records in the Louisville City Hall show that Odessa Clay preferred charges against her husband on a number of occasions. Clay, Sr. also has a record of arrests for disorderly conduct, reckless driving, and assault and battery.

He was not entirely hateful, however. When business was going well, he laid off the bottle and was kind, considerate, very likeable. At such times there was also a strange turnabout in his racial pronouncements, Clay boasting about the white blood in his family tree, which he claimed originated with one-time Secretary of State Henry Clay.

Clay, Sr. shared his wife's propensity for spoiling the children; one day he came home with a $60 bicycle for Cassius. The boy hotdogged the shiny new bike around the neighborhood for two days. On the third, while his back was turned, someone made off with his fancy wheels. Cassius wandered into the nearby Columbia Gymnasium, a hangout for amateur boxers. Crying and furious, he approached Joe Martin, a Louisville cop who ran the gym.

"If I catch that boy who took my bike," he raged, "I'll whup him good!"

Joe Martin warned that if Cassius was gonna start throwing hands, he'd better learn how. He took the spunky brat under his wing and taught him all he knew. Eager to escape from home, Clay accepted an onerous regimen that kept him, except for sleeping and schooling, at the gym around the clock.

"A boxer has something to do every day," Clay would later explain. "Go to the gym, put on the gloves, and box. In the streets there wasn't nothing to do. The kids would throw rocks and stand out under the street lights all night, running in and out of the juke joints, smoking and drinking."

Martin produced a local TV boxing show on which Cassius began to appear regularly. His poor grades in school became permanently miserable; in class he sat with his feet on his desk and drew the back of a jacket on scraps of paper, enscribing "Cassius Clay, World Heavyweight Champion" across the shoulders.

"During lunch hours and times like that, I'd imagine I could hear my name announced over the loudspeaker as the champion," Clay once confessed.

These reveries would soon be interspersed with visions of romance. During the Deer Lake visit, while finishing up the lunch of broiled chicken that Odessa Clay had prepared for us, I asked Ali about the other women in his life. When did he first discover girls?

He seemed mildly startled by the personal question, but replied with great tenderness.

"It's fun to remember your first this-and-that in life. You know, the first time you did a certain thing. One of the first things I can remember very well from the days when I was growing up is the first girl I ever kissed. Her name was Areatha Swint. I walked her home from high school on this particular day. I guess I was about 17 years old at the time. She was a pretty girl and lived in a complex of apartments, with her apartment at the top of this long flight of stairs.

"I was walking her up those stairs, and suddenly I just turned around on one of those steps, so that I was standing facing her with my back to the stairs that led up." He swallows slowly, the muscles rising on his neck. "And we kissed.

"But after she gave me that kiss, don't you know that I *fainted*, and fell back down the stairs, all the way down. Whew! I'm telling you, I fell out. Don't laugh! I was gone. Even though I landed on my head, I didn't feel nothing. She came running, patting my wounds, and asking, 'What happened? Oh, what happened?'

"I got shy, and embarrassed, and I jumped up and ran all the way home, which was two miles away," he insists in his rolling Kentucky cadence. "I ran so fast I beat the bus! After that, I just kept training and fighting, and didn't look at no more girls for a while.

"And I didn't ever get a chance to kiss her again," he concludes with a small smile. "It's too bad, but I was too scared."

Sounds like she left a serious impression; it's a pity he can't go back for her. "Boy," he nods, meditative, his neck muscles in relief, "that would be something. . . ."

"My relationship with Cassius was one that certainly could be rated as 'G'," says a giggling Areatha Swint Eubanks, 33, now the strikingly pretty mother of four and supervisor of the Department of Research and Evaluation for the Louisville Board of Education. "I remember him as a witty, shy boy, always a perfect gentleman and a bit of a practical joker. When he fell back on the stairs, I at first thought he was kidding, but when he landed so hard I realized it wasn't a joke.

"I was fifteen or so when we first met. We both attended Central High School and met on the night the school was holding a variety show. There wasn't any pot or drugs back then, and if you smoked a cigarette or had a can of beer you were really on to something. The variety show was definitely the social event of the season.

"After the show I was frightened to walk home by myself, because there had been a purse snatching in the neighborhood of Beecher Terrace, where I lived. I was standing by the school steps when a person called out, 'There's Cassius Clay. He's a boxer! He's the one to get you home safely.'

"He walked me home, chattering all the way. That was the start of a long series of talks on my front porch and sessions watching television and baby-sitting together. So many of the things he vowed to do while sitting on my porch, he has gone on to do. Besides saying he would some day be champion, he also said he wanted to do things to help the poor, and I believe he's kept his word.

"I remember another story about his winning the [National] Golden Gloves title," she adds sheepishly. "He got a big trophy and a gold pendant with a diamond in it. He kept the trophy but he gave the diamond pendant to me. Three or four days later, there was a knock on my door and I opened it to see his brother Rudy standing there. I asked where Cassius was and then I saw him out in the yard hiding behind a tree. His mother had told him to get the pendant back, but he was too shy to ask for it himself, so he sent his brother."

If he was hesitant as a boy friend, he was vehement as a fighter, and with Joe Martin as his mentor, he won a gold medal in Rome at the 1960 Olympics.

If Clay sometimes seemed a bit too caustic and overbearing, he was at least a clean-living, patriotic young man. A Soviet newspaperman approached the black American boxer after the gold medal presentation, asking him how he felt about the racism that he, despite his achievements, would again be subject to when he returned home.

"We've got qualified people working on that and I'm not worried about the outcome," Cassius allowed. "To me the U.S.A. is still the best country in the world, including yours. It may be hard to get something to eat sometimes, but anyhow, I ain't fighting alligators and living in a mud hut."

He was eighteen years old at the time, a pepper-tongued kid with a gangly, rail-shouldered frame that had yet to fill out into the robust striations of a heavyweight. So enraptured had Cassius been with his Olympic success and its attendant cynosure, he could not bear to remove the gold medal hung on his neck in Rome for months after the Games. He wore it around Louisville like a scarf out-of-season, and even to bed.

Cassius Clay ended his association with Martin in 1961. A group of Louisville businessmen, headed by Bill Faversham, were eager to underwrite his burgeoning career for fun and prestige. Martin wished to continue coaching Cassius, but Clay, Sr. hated the white patrolman for providing his son with the guidance he could not. He refused to lend his consent to any contract that had Martin's name on it.

When the Louisville group made their offer, Mr. Clay protested, but then signed the papers, probably to spite Martin. The terms were generous: a six-year contract with a $10,000 bonus that paid Cassius $333.33 a month, plus 50 per cent of his winnings the first four years and 60 per cent thereafter. In addition, a trust fund was set up, available to him at age 35, into which was deposited 15 per cent of the purse from each fight.

His therapeutic hobby now a lucrative occupation, Cassius celebrated by purchasing a pink Cadillac.

The Louisville group was honest and sincere. Their management of Clay was a stroke of good fortune that rarely befalls boxers, or many other athletes for that matter.

Faversham first sent Cassius to San Diego to study the manly arts with Archie Moore, but the two did not get along. Clay kept insisting he could whup the old man.

Angelo Dundee, who trained fighters of the caliber of world light heavyweight champion Willie Pastrano, was called in from Miami to bring Clay along.

"He was like a puppy dog when he first came into my gym," Dundee remembers. "Leaping around, wanting to take on everybody, he wasn't there two days when he wanted to climb in the ring with Pastrano.

"And you had to fool him a little bit to teach him. When he did something wrong you complimented him on what he should have done. He'd say, 'Yeah. yeah. I'm good at that,' and the next time he'd do it the correct way."

Clay was first pitted against the likes of Tunney Hunsaker, Herb Siler and Jim Robinson, tenpins content to topple for a sawbuck; but Cassius vervefully toyed with them. Many fighters look upon their early cinches, called "barneys," as mere fodder for their egos, but Cassius took the bouts seriously, letting the clowns think they had a chance against him so he could hone his parry, his footwork and his deadly right hand. When they were frustrated and flailing, he'd coldcock them.

The novice soon graduated to the harder stuff. His first real competition was Alex Miteff, an aggressive Argentinian of wide experience. Miteff almost decked Clay with a ferocious right cross in the second round of their 1961 meeting in Louisville. Dundee's boy was staggered, but stayed on his feet and came back for a knockout in the sixth with a terse right stab of his own.

He was on his way: All that remained to be sharpened was his stage presence. Ali now has an insatiable appetite for attention, for the press and the touch of the crowds; he absolutely cannot function without it. Back then, Clay was outgoing, talkative and smart-alecky when the Fourth Estate came calling, but always exercised some restraint. He didn't believe he could carry his normal bonhomie undiluted in the spotlight and get away with it.

Gorgeous George, the hambone wrestler, was the man who supplied the final shove. A few months prior to his duel with Miteff, Clay appeared on a Las Vegas radio program with Gorgeous. The host spoke first with the rising star from Louisville, asking about an upcoming bout with Duke Sabedong. Clay gave a confident, though hardly effusive account of himself, saying that surely he would kayo the six-foot-seven lummox. (It proved to be a difficult fight for him, the first time he would go ten rounds.)

The host then turned to George and questioned him about a match he had in the works. The wrestler exploded in mock fury, jumping up and down and pounding on the table so hard that it upset the microphone. "I'm gonna kill him!" he promised.

"Why, why . . . they shouldn't even bother to hold the match! It's a waste of my time! He's a dead man!" From there, Gorgeous launched into a lengthy and graphic description of the exotic dismemberment in store for his opponent.

Clay was impressed. He prevailed upon Dundee to accompany him to the match and sat, thoroughly charmed, while the plump wrestler cavorted through his bogus routine.

"Ain't he sumptin'!'" Cassius kept saying. "Ain't he sumptin'!"

You know the rest. He went on to make Gorgeous look like George Gobel. And the planet ate it up.

"They all must fall in the round I call."

Newsmen remember with fondness the autumn afternoon that Cassius Clay appeared in the downtown Chicago press headquarters for the first Liston-Patterson fight. After making certain that there was a representative present from each of the wire services and every major publication ("Anybody here from *Time* magazine? Nobody from *Time*? Awww. . . . Where are they?"), he bade them sharpen their pencils for a bold prophesy.

"Gentlemen," he told the hushed assembly, "I have a poem:"

It was that night in the Coliseum
That's when I annihilated him.
I gave him a lot of sand

The one they call the old man.
He was old and I was new
You could tell by the bombs I threw.
I had left jabs to fire like pistons
They were twice as rough as Liston's.
The people cried, "Stop the fight!"
Before Clay could put out the light.
He was trying to remain the great Mr. Moore
For he knew Clay had predicted four.
I swept that old man clean out of the ring
For a good new broom sweeps up anything.
Some say the greatest was Sugar Ray
But they haven't seen Cassius Clay!

One month later, 1 minute and 35 seconds into the fourth round of their match, Archie Moore's crafty chin got in the way of Clay's right hand and the old man melted under the hot lights like a fudgsicle.

The fight game now had an attraction who was something snappier than a thug or a furrow-faced punching bag, and the box office reflected the public's tremendous curiosity. Unlike the toe-to-toe stylists of former days, Clay relied on a jab-and-run boogaloo fashioned from the fine points of associates like Willie Pastrano and Luis Rodriguez.

Clay was both loved and hated for his stylish dexterity in the ring, and his antics on the boulevard, but he was conscientious about pleasing those who enjoyed him. A day or so before each fight, he would shut himself up in his hotel room to fill pads of paper with his signature. Bringing the pads along on public appearances, he'd tear off a strip whenever someone requested his autograph.

Gaseous Cassius would turn up in the unlikeliest places.

Training in New York in January of 1963 for his fight with Doug Jones, he appeared one afternoon at the Bitter End in Greenwich Village, a surprise entry in a poetry contest. Dressed in a tuxedo, he squatted down in the midst of the Beat Generation and offered to recite from some volumes of his own deathless prose. "Ode to a Champion" lumbered along thusly:

Marcellus vanquished Carthage
Cassius laid Julius Caesar low
And Clay will flatten Douglas Jones
With a mighty, measured blow!

The contest ended prematurely when the man in the tux declared himself to be the winner. "It's no contest!" he roared.

Clay defeated Doug Jones on points in their ten-rounder in Madison Square Garden, a verdict received with hoots and projectiles, one of which knocked a ringside photographer unconscious.

At the final bell, Clay's rubbery arm was raised by the referee and he was instantly drenched by a torrential downpour of roasted nuts, some of which he scooped up, threw in his mouth and chewed.

"There ain't no such thing as love for me," he said later. "Not while I'm going for the championship. But when I get that championship, then I'm goin' to put on my old jeans and get a hat and grow a beard. And I'm gonna walk down the road until I find a little fox who loves me for what I am."

He got that championship in Miami Beach in the winter of 1965, when Sonny Liston, torpid from the shuddersome pain of a rent bicep tendon, failed to answer the bell for the seventh round. Still, the champion's road to fame and foxes turned out to be a long and treacherous one. It was a prodigious affection the public had for Cassius Clay, but it ended when Clay did what the rest of the country was struggling not to do: He opened his eyes and grew up.

Black men were being thrown from moving buses for daring to take a seat in the front, and getting their heads rammed into the spigots of "Whites Only" water fountains when they tried to sip from them. Racial incidents were mushrooming into a ballet of evil. Watts and Harlem burned. Police sicked dogs on peaceful marchers in Little Rock; high-powered hoses were trained on guiltless children in Selma; electric cattleprods were thrust into the stomachs of pregnant black women in Montgomery.

(Some eight years later, the megalomaniacal dictator of an emerging African nation took the same expedient approach to solving a crime wave in the capital city of his country. There was a giant public relations scheme underway, a spectacle that would put his domain on the map. He didn't want the throngs of anticipated tourists getting any unfavorable impressions, so he sent his soldiers through the streets to arrest indiscriminately whatever wretches, criminals and troublemakers they could find and herd them into a soccer stadium. Forty-seven of the hapless souls were executed and the rest were set free to pass the word: Crime doesn't pay in Kinshasa.)

Cassius Clay saw the panoramic falsehood of freedom-and-justice-for-all in America, and he began to jab at it, strike out against it, shout its oppression onto the front pages and the Seven O'Clock News.

"America is supposed to mean freedom, isn't it? What white people don't understand is that it's the hurtin'est thing in the world to be black and live in a ghetto. You prove you're a man by throwing bricks. If you're reasonable and intelligent they don't respect you for it, they roll over you."

A loquacious nigger boy on the loose was one thing; a veracious black man quite another. The public suddenly realized that the point-blank voice had grown deeper, more resonant, threatening.

Hours after his victory over Liston, the new heavyweight champion made public his conversion to the Nation of Islam, announcing that he was changing his name to Cassius X. (Elijah Muhammad later revised it to Muhammad Ali.) He had become a Muslim, one of those serge-suited, terrifyingly independent black men like, well . . . Malcolm X.

It was an outrage. In the patrons' minds, they had paid good money for a minstrel show, and here the genial darkie had stalked onstage, unbuttoned his spats, wiped away the white face and lit into the orchestra swinging his banjo like a club.

Muhammad Ali was compelled to adopt a role he unconsciously held all along: the lonely crusader.

Originally classified I-Y by his local draft board (because he had repeatedly failed the Army intelligence test due to poor reading skills), Ali was mysteriously reclassified I-A shortly after announcing his devotion to the Black Muslims. Living in Houston at the time, he was summoned to the U.S. Army Induction Center, where officials gave the 26–year-old boxer two chances to comply with his draft call.

"We will address him as Muhammad Ali when we ask him to take the one step forward to be inducted," said a presiding officer. "If he refuses, we will then ask him under the name of Cassius Marcellus Clay, Jr."

"I'm not going to war," the young Muslim told the American people. "No Viet Cong ever called me nigger."

A hundred deals were offered him. He would never carry a rifle or enter a free-fire zone. The Army would send him on an exhibition tour, just as they had Joe Louis, sparring on aircraft carriers and in quonset huts. His answer was a flat no.

"Louis was a sucker," said Ali. "He was the one without courage, not me."

"If I pass this test, I'll come out stronger than ever. I'm being tested by Allah. I'm giving up my title, my wealth, my future. I've got no jails, no power, no government, but 600 million Muslims are giving me strength."

Within an hour after Ali declined both opportunities to take the symbolic step, the mighty New York State Boxing Commission took the unprecedented measure of revoking his license, thus denying him his constitutional right to make an honest living at his chosen profession.

J. Edgar Hoover got into the act, bugging Ali's phone conversations, including several with a sympathetic Dr. Martin Luther King.

Ali was barred from the ring pending the outcome of his trial: guilty until proven innocent. He was eventually convicted of draft evasion and sentenced to five years in prison and a $10,000 fine. The conviction was appealed.

In the meantime, Muhammad Ali sought to regain his boxing license. The N.Y. State Commission said no, contending that he was a felon "who had not yet paid his debt to society." It was the brazen persecution of an uppity, assertive black man—especially since the Commission had previously seen fit to certify a wide array of highly, questionable citizens, including convicted murderers, sodomists, arsonists, confidence men and child molesters.

Ali was aghast. If he couldn't box, he couldn't breathe.

Most of his bank account exhausted by legal fees or siphoned off by the Muslims, he retreated in 1967 to a modest home in Chicago, with his second wife, the former Belinda Boyd. Ali met her in the Muslim-owned Shabazz Restaurant in Chicago, where she had been a waitress. He had divorced his first wife, model Sonji Roi, eight months earlier because she would not abide by the tenets of the Muslim faith, among them the ban on mini-skirts. Belinda bore him two daughters. It was a quiet existence. Ali ached to disturb that quiet.

With nothing to do but wait, he was forced back into the lazy lifestyle of his childhood, loitering in a circuit of haunts in the black section of Chicago, among them the Shabazz Restaurant on 71st Street, the office of *Muhammad Speaks* (the Muslim newspaper) over on 79th and Champlain, and LaTees Beauty Parlor and Barber Shop on South Drexel.

Television reporters and magazine writers would come to the house to do stories on his predicament and he would brush them off by stepping quickly into his car. "I'm too busy for you now," he'd apologize. "I got a dozen important things to do."

He was lying. He'd cruise around Chicago until the reporters left. From time to time, whenever he'd spy a full sidewalk, he'd stop the car and jump out, hollering, "Where's Jimmy Ellis?" or, "Where's Joe Fray-zjuh?" A crowd would gather and Ali would spar and joke with the folks until their thrilled expressions waned. Hopping back into the car again, he'd speed away in search of another unsuspecting audience. The man killed a hundred afternoons doing that.

When the word spread that he was dying off the vine, invitations to speak at colleges began to appear in the mail. A generation of draft bait wanted to hear him tell his story. He accepted—he needed the money. The lecture tours became a dry run for the day when Ali would retire from boxing and become a Muslim preacher. That is, if he wasn't retired already.

If the campus speaking engagements didn't provide him with enough of a chance to lash out at his tormentors, further opportunity arose when he appeared briefly on Broadway in the title role of *Buck White*, a musical satire-drama about the Beautiful Allelujah Day Organization (B.A.D., for short), a black political group of dubious conviction. Ironically, the play opened on December 2, 1969, the day after the first drawing of the national draft lottery. In the second act, a bearded Ali, his hair grown into a substantial afro, looking every inch the African prince, delivered a chillingly appropriate soliloquy:

> . . . I'm talking, I'm talking, I'm talking about history, history fifty thousand years ago, and it seems like today, because today man is filled with useless laws. . . . Lord knows, a Whitey obeys laws. He drinks his water from pure white fountains, excremates that good food he eats in lily-white toilets, and he walks the white sidewalks and tells us that Law is a thing he created that teaches him against death. But the walking mud of Mississippi is staining those shoes. Your life is the most precious thing you'll ever have . . . so crush those useless laws and let man create his own universal form so that men can stand and walk their own little dark areas in life!

In 1970, his draft conviction was finally overturned; a Supreme Court decision had extended conscientious objector status to those unwilling to serve in the Armed Forces on solely religious grounds. He was, again permitted to practice his profession throughout the world.

After a three-and-a-half year suspension that saw his peak years dissipate into mist, Ali had the courage to begin the slow, painful road back to the heavyweight championship that was still rightfully his. He took on all contenders: Jerry Quarry, Oscar Bonavena, Joe Frazier, Buster Mathis, Jurgen Blin, George Chuvalo, Al Lewis, Floyd Patterson, Bob Foster and Ken Norton.

Frazier emerged the victor in Super Fight I, but it was difficult to tell the winner from the loser; Frazier was in and out of the hospital for ten months, with a rock garden of facial welts and rumored internal injuries. Norton busted Ali's jaw, but Ali came back six months later to avenge that mortifying defeat. Next was a rematch with "Smokin' Joe" Frazier, and Ali settled that score with a triumphant 12-round decision, inspiring one ringside loyalist to scale a "No Smoking" sign onto the canvas at the final bell.

People seemed a little bit friendlier the second time around. The country had turned against the Vietnam War; too many of their sons had been killed or disfigured or driven into expatriation. Ali was welcomed back by a sea of smiling faces, white and black, that regarded him as a hero. He again gave them the show they all craved.

Ali insisted, against Dundee's advice, on strolling up New York's Fifth Avenue on the raw and gusty December morning before his fight with Argentine Oscar Bonavena. Hundreds fell in step behind him as if he were some funky Pied Piper. He paused in Saks to try on a matador-style cape, which he then removed and floated about as if fighting a bull. A bull named Bonavena.

That evening he chose to ride the subway from his hotel down to Madison Square Garden, his presence on the train causing a near-riot. He greeted fellow passengers with his left hand, because in his trusty right he clutched a paperback book, *Wishes, Lies and Dreams, Teaching Children To Write Poetry*, by Kenneth Koch.

On page 158 of the book is a poem entitled "I Wish," written by a fifth grader, very near Ali's age when he wandered into the Columbia Gymnasium.

It begins:

> I wish I was a Super human being.
> I wish I could see what happened long ago.
> I wish I could go anywhere I want to.
> I wish I was a genius.

And concludes with:

> I wish I could make it snow, rain and make it sunny.
> I wish I could do everything in the world.

Zaire: Wed., Oct. 30, 4:44 a.m. Central Jungle Time. President Mobutu Sese Seko Kuku Ngbendu Wa Za Banga, forty feet high, resplendent in pin-striped silver abosco and ocelot cap, a full-color cross between Mao's mammoth portrait in Peking's Tien An Min Square and the five-story Times Square Winston Man who blows taxi-sized smoke rings, beamed his toothy, laser grin down upon two rather large men being paid what in the end boiled down to $208,333.33 dollars a minute to pound the bejesus out of each other.

Only one man was earning his pay: the pretty, sylphidine one in the white silk trunks who was resting on the ropes and then sling-shooting devastating left-right combinations when it pleased him. The other guy, the burly fellow in red, the one who'd just been pummeled six times in the face and was stumbling around the ring like a drunk looking for the keyhole, was about to fall down on the job.

"Aleeeee . . . bomayeee . . . Aleeeee . . . bomayeee . . . Aleeeee . . . bomayeee. . . ."

After it was over, Belinda Ali removed the Foreman button she had been wearing, a jab at her husband for a pre-fight quarrel, and wept uncontrollably.

In a sprawling palace on a faraway hill, President Mobutu was watching an instant replay of the fight—a replay that demanded all the juice used for whatever communications equipment was functioning, hence the sounds of silence around the press compound. Mobutu wanted to see the fight because his television picture had gone fuzzy after the first ten minutes.

Nothing had been going right for him. His grand public relations scheme had forfeited a mountain of front money, been ridiculed from Toledo to Timbuktu, and the fearless leader himself had gotten more bad press than Lieutenant Calley.

And then the rains came. Rains of wrath, a message from Allah to the nonbelievers, thick wet blankets of monsoon fury, short-circuiting everything, filling photo dark rooms and dressing rooms with two feet of water and red clay, buckling the corrugated tin roof over the now-empty ring and carrying away the lush multi-colored flowerbeds on the palace lawn. . . .

All that had stood between Ali and immortality was a lug named Foreman. It was a minor matter for the man who had palsied that gruesome bear Liston, reduced British heavyweight champion Henry Cooper's head to a hunk of pink and red marblecake, upended the invulnerable Bonavena and out-pointed, out-maneuvered and out-classed the infernal machine known as the Federal Government.

We didn't believe. We judged Muhammad Ali by the same worldly standards that we use to measure ourselves. But Ali is different from any of us. A figure of uncommon intensity, he is repeatedly capable of what is referred to in the world of sport as The Last Full Measure, as if Allah really is his cornerman.

"If defeat doesn't destroy most athletes," Angelo Dundee once told me, "then the boredom of constant training will eventually do them in."

Somehow, Ali found a way to conquer those inevitabilities. The record speaks for itself: Incredibly, he has peaked three times in his long career as a professional athlete.

This becomes doubly remarkable when one considers how, during the course of his nearly twenty years in the public view, Muhammad Ali has endured an unrelenting barrage of venom, disparagement and miscomprehension on a scale which few less vulnerable public figures have known.

It was right there in front of us: The possibility of his successful comeback loomed like a colossus. Instead, we pitied him, mourned his untimely passing.

Foreman didn't win a round.

Halftime at a Kentucky Colonels game in Louisville, Muhammad Ali is getting the hometown hero's welcome; everyone he's ever known is on hand, even Areatha Swint Eubanks. Wearing a neat Sunday School suit, he stands on the sidelines in the spotlight while a young white woman extols his virtues. She announces that Ali is going to sponsor a boxing school *right here*, so that other kids will have the chance he had. And then introduces Joe Martin, the man who started Ali on his road to fame.

White-haired and distinguished looking, Martin steps from the darkness and extends his hand. Ali takes it in a firm grip and turns away, first into the spotlight and then towards the stands on his left.

The look is there again, in his eyes: the look that had stunned me into silence at Deer Lake three months before. For the second time, he is Heavyweight Champion of the World, but the man whose hand he holds has seen him cry like a baby. Ali had done it all, yet there are regrets that the years embarrass. How often he must shadow box with them.

But the crowd cheers, wildly, adoringly, stomping on the bleachers. He's back. Ol' sad eyes is back.

Home Movies

Raquel Welch:
Rumba with a Red-Hot Anachronism

"I don't have any time to do all the things I'd like to do, so I only do them when I make a movie," is how Raquel Welch summed up the gap between her personal and her professional life during an afternoon's worth of talk in her Beverly Hills home at the peak of her movie stardom in the late 1970s.

Welch's statement could explain why she left San Diego State College to chase film stardom, quickly landing the bit part of "College student" in Elvis Presley's 1964 picture *Roustabout*. But it carried a poignant air of diminished possibilities when her cinematic options (given a portfolio that included such mid-career attractions as *Shoot Loud . . . Louder . . . I Don't Understand; Le Fate, The Biggest Bundle of Them All* and *Lady in Cement*) had dried up after she was compelled to sue over her lost lead in *Cannery Row*, the part of the wisecracking prostitute being given instead to younger actress Debra Winger. Welch won her court case, but Winger had done well in a role for which Raquel seemed ill-suited.

Critics' persistent contention that Welch can't act remains demonstrably untrue, as she made clear when she starred in *Right To Die*, the 1987 NBC-TV dramatic special about a woman who was a victim of Lou Gehrig's Disease. Nonetheless, the sense of Welch the actress as continually being in the wrong place at the wrong time for the wrong reasons has reinforced her voluptuous presence as the entertainment industry's perpetual poor fit. Welch spent much of the '80s and '90s doing rather convincing commercial pitches for diet drinks and promoting exercise videos and fitness products.

As a result, however, when she replaced Julie Andrews on Broadway in *Victor/Victoria*, reviews for her portrayal of a woman masquerading as a man masquerading as a woman were unflattering in the extreme. *Variety* reported that only 50 percent of the seats for the play were sold during the week preceding the announcement that the Welch edition of the show would close prematurely on July 27, 1997. Although *Victor/Victoria* producer blamed the "traditional" mid-summer dip in theater ticket sales on the Great White Way for the abbreviated run, the restoration of the Times Square theater district was bringing record numbers of tourists into that legendary precinct of Manhattan.

Still, the New York press also acknowledged the stage-door crowds Welch drew each night as she left the theater. There was an audience for Raquel as herself, a living monument to obstinate flair personified.

THE INTERVIEW

Only last week she was simultaneously on the covers of no fewer than eight European magazines. *The German Quick* has put her on its cover nine times since January, and the French *Lui* recently ran 14 pages of her photos and hailed her "old-fashioned, hot, sensual return to the curve." There is only one flaw in Raquel's career so far: No one has seen her movies.

Time, June 24, 1966. Just prior to the release of *One Million B.C.*

THERE ARE FEW THINGS in this world more intense than the total awe of a little girl, and still fewer that command it the way ballet can. When eight-year-old Raquel Tejada was smitten, it consumed her to the edge of exhaustion. And this was before she enrolled in classes. "It's really difficult, isn't it?" she worried during the lonesome two-bus journey from her suburban home in seaside Bay Park Village, California, to enroll in the dance school. "But it's so exciting," she thought, "there is just no way not to do it."

For many impressionable girls, the lure of *les pantoufles de danse* finds its focus in the person of a prima ballerina, whose feminine form has been sculpted into an instrument of the will. But the gangly Tejada girl—known to neighborhood kids as "Bird Legs"—had no such paragon. Instead, she drew inspiration from the elderly ex-dancer who taught her class. Looking back on the period, the adoring pupil cannot remember a single tender word ever having passed between them, yet this matriarchal teacher became a profound catalyst. So profound, in fact, that the hard TAP! of ballet mistress Irene Ishim Clark's darkwood cane as it counted out pliés still resonates in Raquel's adult ears.

"Oh yes, there was once this wonderful woman," Raquel recounts, "who was so inspirational that she first brought my dreams into perspective. Most of the women, when I grew up, wore their hair very short, but she had her gray hair down past her waist. And she had this face that was very beautiful, but you didn't know it was beautiful in the beginning. Irene—I never dared to call her Irene—had this amalgamation of incredible purity and classicness, and something valiant too.

"I didn't get to know Irene Clark so well. It was impossible to kiss her ass. I suppose there was a certain amount of competition in her class, but you had to be extremely honest about your effort."

Years afterward, Irene Clark would be approached by a reporter wondering if she could recollect anything about her now-famous student. The aged instructor mulled it over and replied that, as a little girl, this familiar film star had shown great aptitude for the dance.

"But there was no humility in her approach to art," said Ms. Clark of Raquel Tejada Welch. "She enjoyed attention too much—and she know how to get it."

She's aimed everything she's got at her quarry: two cold auger eyes that could bore through bedrock, as well as a headlight-sized set of breasts, dun-colored with dark ochre nipples, sternly directed from behind the camouflage of a diaphanous tennis blouse.

"No!" she booms. "I'm not ready to talk just yet!"

Her palms slap the leather tops of her thigh-high spike heeled boots as she rises from the opposite chair. Stalking to and fro, straining the snuggest pair of Levis ever stretched across a mammal, her diamond-hair features are framed by a wooly new hairdo she calls "L'Animal" (after her just-completed French film of the same name).

"You want something to drink?" she snaps, cornering her still-seated visitor. "Seven-up?" Getting an assent, she swivels smartly and struts across the gloomy, antique-filled living room of her mock-Tudor Beverly Hills mansion. Her guest's gaze moves from the savage sway of her ripe derriere to a bright silver bas-relief hanging on the wall opposite the grand piano. It's a female torso, split down the center by a sleek strip of plate glass—the perfect mannequin for the storefront of some *Clockwork Orange* massage parlor. I've really got to get out of here.

The opening strains of Steely Dan's *Aja* album explode from hidden speakers, rattling the windows in the poolside sun porch as the hostess returns with two tumblers of soda. Setting them down slinkily, she lowers herself backward into an adjoining chair, her laquered fingertips drawn slowly lapward from either side of those highway-length legs. It's a tightly choreographed tease from a grainy Edie Adams TV cigar ad.

"This is a gas-up period for me," she states rawly, extending her gams as if to gamely block the exit. "Nobody can be prolific interminably without a gas-up period to gain strength inside."

Uh-huh.

"You can't give something you don't have. You can't give love if you don't have love. You can't create if you have an impotence. That's the only thing I'm interested in: giving out creatively."

Does that mean we can't open a window a crack?

Her Fearless Fosdick jaw drops into a frigid smile. She flicks her taut pink tongue against the edges of her upper incisors. And laughs selfishly.

When the lady of the house is in charge, nobody may relax without permission, the underlying gripe being that the lady so rarely feels she's ever in charge of anything.

At the moment, she seems a far cry from the uncertain sex kitten who headlined a high-powered press conference in 1975 for the American Cancer Society. With public concern over cigarette-related illness escalating and the Surgeon General intensifying his warnings to smokers, Raquel seized the spotlight to announce she was the new annual National Crusade Chairperson. A male writer stepped forward at the briefing to coyly inquire if Ms. Welch's abundant bust had any bearing on her suitability as field marshall in the fight against lung cancer. Stung by the sexist swipe, she burst into tears.

Such pent-up emotions, one discovers, often smolder just below the surface of her cool, collected demeanor. It's understandable; this woman has drawn some uncommonly vicious fire during her 17-odd years in Hollywood. While progressing, so to speak, from a seedy mid-'60s bit part as a hooker in *A House Is Not a Home* to such meaty roles in the hay as a seductive Yaqui Indian opposite Jim Brown in *100 Rifles*, the whip-snapping slave driver in *The Magic Christian*, a convenient cowgirl in *Bandolero!* and the queen of the roller derby in *Kansas City Bomber*, she has been treated to an unprecedented critical razzing.

The few crumbs of compliments usually fell into the "second-rate Sophia Loren" or "Jane Russell retread" category, and time has done little to dilute the snideness.

This week's Los Angeles edition of *TV Guide* promised that Raquel would "display her anatomical charms" on a Late Show edition of a 1967 insomniac's savior called *Fathom*. When your film heroines are such "versatile," "serious" actresses as Katherine Hepburn, it's not easy to take professional comparisons to Mount Rushmore and/or the Grand Tetons. Nonetheless, she persevered against all odds to accumulate a solid seven-figure bank account and install herself as one of the precious few sex symbols of either gender who works steadily—even in an era when her Stone Age-svelte persona has been eclipsed by the scrubbed-down California frailty of a Farrah Fawcett. Most amazing of all: Don't expect any unappareled *Playboy* gatefold "garbage" from this cinema siren, because Raquel Welch never has and never will appear in the altogether. They broke the mold after this gentlewoman and a lot of Hollywood users have been emptyhanded ever since.

Welch, 37, is an easy target; and if the truth be told, she brought it all upon herself. (Imagine accepting the role of Lust—in *Bedazzled*, 1967—in order to dish out double entendres like "Would you like hot toast—or *buttered buns?*") Still, she doggedly seeks recognition as a serious talent—and there are signs that the climate may be growing more hospitable. Raquel was praised for her supporting role in *The Last of Sheila* and won the 1975 Golden Globe Award for Best Actress in a Comedy or Musical for her portrayal of the comely, bumbling Mme. Bonacieux in *The Three Musketeers*. (And she showed superb comedic savvy in the sequel, *The Four Musketeers (The Revenge of Milady)*, nearly stealing the movie from co-star Faye Dunaway.) Meantime, Las Vegas has welcomed her into its main rooms as a top-billed singer/dancer, and she's been getting more offers for work above the caliber of *The Oldest Profession,* *Shipment of Tarts* and *Mother, Jugs and Speed.* Where once she had an on-set reputation as "distant," "tough" and "a bitch," she now is described as "fun," "accommodating" and even "delightful." But a word to the wary: Even her good friends call her "Rocky."

All things considered, I expected to find the last (?) of the great screen goddesses in good spirits. Unfortunately, the barrages of ridicule have taken their toll, and this strikingly beautiful woman has transformed all the absorbed hurts, insecurities, denials and self-deprecating impulses of two decades into a tangible force field. While she is not openly hostile, she shows scant warmth as a conversationalist, and her crisply modulated parlance quickly becomes the eeriest contrivance ever encountered. As one who genuinely admires her guts and feels she has great potential as a comedienne, I am nonetheless completely drained and unnerved after only 15 minutes in her presence.

Suddenly aware that I'm fighting a powerful urge to excuse myself politely and leave, I sigh expansively, kick back, and put out of mind the fact that my clothes are sopping wet with nervous sweat. I mean, this woman is *cranky.*

"Well now," I say, pressing on. "Let's talk about something positive. When was the first time you can remember feeling pretty, the first time you were pleased that someone noticed?"

"I don't know!" Raquel barks, her arms akimbo. "I don't know. That just seems so *redundant* to me and it's *immaterial* too."

"For a sex symbol?"

"OK," she says testily. "I don't know exactly when it was. I'm sure I felt pretty before I was pretty. I'm sure I felt pretty when I was a little baby— and not because somebody smothered me with kisses or something. I think I always created in my mind the thing that I wanted, the way that life was supposed to be, and so I don't remember, you know?"

Fidgeting, she throws her head back and pulls her frizzy orange-brown mane away from her face to expose a short, ropy neck and the stiff right angles of her profile. There is no subtlety in her heavily tanned countenance, no surprises beyond an unnecessary caramel veneer of liquid makeup. Hers is the same blunt, unlined mask you've seen in a thousand movie stills.

Outside, the pale yellow sun of early afternoon pours down. Her attention wanders to the ragged mutt dozing on the lawn beside the pool . . . and then both boot heels hit the brick floor in exasperation.

"I *know* I had a lot of compliments when I was a kid," she asserts, glaring. "And of course I didn't really—meaning that of course I had insecurities and stuff like that. The overriding goal was not to be pretty, but to live a different kind of existence, on a dream level! 'Dream' is a funny word; people think that it doesn't have anything to do with reality but it does, in a sense."

What kind of dreams was she dreaming, say, as a child?

"It didn't come into focus for a long time. I just knew that I liked anything that was positive energy—and that magnified emotions. Most of the time it had to do with music and dancing. Irene Clark gave me that, I think.

"Funny," she muses. "She just died, and I found out when her daughter, who was a friend of mine as a child, came to one of my shows in Vegas. When I'm singing and I pass along the apron of the stage, I *see* the faces; I always remember everybody in the audience, mostly their expressions, and six months later I pass them on the street and know they were in my audience. I saw Irene's daughter, sang a line to her to be sure it was her, and then found out about her mother when she came backstage afterward. It was so sad.

"Anyways, a lot of great challenges for me have been in taking a disadvantage and turning it into an advantage. I've taken so many situations that were totally negative, offered almost no opportunities, were filled with a lot of prejudices, and literally turned 'em around so that they at least were something of some *qua-li-ty.*"

She leans back, arms tightly folded, waiting for the next question.

"Give me an example."

"Examples? I'll give you some examples! *Kansas City Bomber* was a milestone for me, in a way. This young man from UCLA came and left this screenplay by my door. Somebody read it in the house and said, 'You know, this is really a good idea.' I said, 'Is it really? I'd be happy to read it. It's just that I read so much *junk.*'

"I don't know; it's like wading through the gutters: You see a lot of trash and you almost miss the few pennies lying there. So I wed—or *waded*—through this trash and there was this wonderful idea. They said I was too good-looking for it and I said, 'No! Come off it! That's not what it's about!' These roller derby girls, the people watch them 'cause in some way they represent something about their *own* sexuality. They're acting out this thing that is at the elementary, juvenile basis of Americana. Good girls and bad girls get out there and knock each other around, cream each other in this violent show.

"The whole thing that doesn't make it quite legitimate is that a lot of it is 'pre-ordained,' shall we say. What the skaters do takes an inordinate amount of talent, but because it's not a legit sport, that means it's all bullshit. But they love it! I had to know what these girls were really like. And, of course, there were some that were dykes—but there were some that truly were not. Even the dykey ones were real nice. At least the ones I met.

"But I learned to skate for the part. I busted my ass. They built a track for me at MGM and I spent a coupla months down there, every day, skating for two, three hours. I broke my wrist at one point. I had bruises the size of grapefruit. I had to have intermuscular cortisone shots all the time—but I did it.

"As you can see," she rules vehemently, "I'm not a great, big muscular chick, as the world would have you believe. I'm rather petite; fragile, in fact.

"But I've always felt good about doing a lot of physical things, I guess. I liked the first time I had to learn to ride a horse for a movie—I think it was *Bandolero!*, and then I did it again for *100 Rifles*. I found out that I'm a crappy rider in a saddle. It must be my father's Bolivian blood, but I can ride great *bareback*, with one hand on the mane.

"Those are the fun things. The acting was always a real pain. I was always thinking, 'Oh God, these lines are so terrible!' At the first part of my career I didn't know enough to go ahead and change the line without asking. I used to go the director, very meekly and say, 'Do you think. . . .' I wanted permission for everything! Because I thought that those people were in control [*righteous guffaw*] but the point is that they are *not*.

"Have you seen my new film, *Crossed Swords*?"

"No."

"Don't bother."

In an attempt to keep this discussion alive, she is asked if she's done anything recently that proved rewarding before, during and afterward.

"I just did the film with Jean-Paul Belmondo called *L'Animal*. It was a huge hit in Europe but hasn't been released here. It's an adventure, a comedy with slapstick. We both play stuntpeople who are lovers. And my character is similar to the one in *Three Musketeers* in that she's very vulnerable to this man and his charms. But he's one of the great cock-ups of all time; can't do anything right. So she always gets pissed. It's like *Taming of the Shrew*. One of the best scenes is where he falls out of a plane. I have to go after him in a parachute and he tries to rape me in midair."

I smile, and she pauses, flashing a suspicious stare, then proceeds.

"As actors, there were certain things Jean-Paul and I had to accept about one another, because he's French and French men are chauvinistic people. But Belmondo is a French Humphrey Bogart, with a lot of the old [*she averts her eyes and shows a clenched grin*], the old. . . . *Ummmmmm*, yeah. He's got *it*.

"Jean-Paul does that muscled, athlete walk [*she rolls her broad shoulders awkwardly*] so that you just know, when he's walking down the street, that he could take care of any sit-u-a-tion. That way, that manner, it's terrific, full of energy, and it's also very chauvinistic and macho. And I like that!

"And I've got my style too!" she beams. "I mean, I like to strut my stuff. On good days, I'm pretty hot at it. And when I'd come on the set he'd really pay attention.

"I'm so physical!" she chirps, her interest growing. "I mean, I'm a well-traveled, intelligent and successful woman who knows all about what it's supposed to be to assert yourself in life, and have an identity, and all the slings and arrows of outrageous fortune.

"I love to do the stunts in my films. I want to do those ducks and rolls and come up firing my machine gun! Like on this French film, one of the first days on the set I got to shoot his machine gun and I was having a great time doing it. I said to myself, '*God*, Raquel! You're enjoying this violent act *waaay* too much. This is not right; you *know* it isn't right.'" She breaks up in giggles.

"Now I understand where all those weirdos get off on carrying firearms around, because every once in awhile in a movie they'll hand me a gun. I mean, I don't own a gun myself! I'm a different person when I'm working."

I'm conscious at this moment that my clothes have finally begun to dry out, as Welch takes up an imaginary machine gun, holds it fast between her iron thighs . . . and commences firing.

"Wooo! See, my work gives me a license to forget my feminine consciousness, to grab up a machine gun [*the first weapon presumably spent, she seizes another, arches her back and lets it blaze*] and get it shooting like crazy and watch the *fire* come out of the end of it! I mean, I *know* it's a phallic symbol and all that, but what the hell! It gives you such a sense of power! It's not impossible for any woman to understand what that's about!

"Say, you know what it is about anybody in a position of power? There's always that ability to *intimidate* other people. And they always wonder if you'll use your power in an abrasive way or however. And I've had that same feeling about people *I've* worked with, so it doesn't have anything to do with me individually.

"People I work with have this image of me: that I am a superstar, formidable. Will they be able to please me? But I want to please them! And get *into* my role! They say to me, 'Are you sure you wanna take this fall?' And I say, 'Oh sure! Just get me a mattress to fall into!'

"See, I have so much energy to expend that *any-thing* physical for me—that helps me express myself—is a help. 'Cause otherwise I just talk and pretty soon it sounds like a train going down the tracks and the words keep coming: Dut-dut-dut-dut!!

"It's a little frightening. I mean, there's just so much of me!"

Seeing her now, it's hard to imagine Raquel Welch as a shy slip of a girl. What was fun for her back then?

"I don't like questions like these," she snaps. "That's probably why I'm always so awkward in these interviews. Why can't we just talk about my work? I prefer to do that. All I know about that type of stuff is that you must have a vision in mind. That's all I know. When you try to verbalize it, it just fucks everybody's head over.

"You're putting me in a head-space I don't think I want to be in, but I can tell you that there used to be a lot of victories, little victories for me as a child. There was never a great sense of accomplishment, however, or joy. I was always just on the way to something. I never used to rejoice about it.

"I'm very self-critical," she stews, seemingly irritated at having to say it. "I don't think I used to take joy in my own success or the good things that I did. I always used to just look at them to see what it *meant*.

"People who don't know *what* they want don't know what to *try*," she states, almost bitterly. "Probably it helped that I always knew what I wanted. But nothing was ever a breakthrough to me. Could we talk about something else?"

There is an old story that when Raquel Welch decided at the age of 21 to stage an assault on Hollywood, her mother threw a copy of *The Carpetbaggers* at her daughter and roared: "Read this! And tell me if that really is the kind of career you want!" Raquel reportedly took her parent's advice, poring over every word, and returned much later to announce that the book "had been a tremendous help."

The story is true. But what I always wondered was: What's a nice mom doing with a copy of *The Carpetbaggers*?

Raquel Tejada was born in Chicago on September 5, 1940, although she is sometimes inclined to claim the year was 1942. She describes her father,

South American-born aeronautical engineer Armand Tejada (Spanish for "Spears of Clay"), as "a Bolivian tyrant," Josephine, her Scottish-English mother, "was the strong one."

"He *looked* to be the strong one but she was the real strong one—just like a rock," their daughter declares. "She had enormous flexibility but he was unyielding. It was *his* way or no way. Or, it was that he had an idea of how things should be, and they could never live up to that."

When Raquel was two, the family relocated to Bay Park Village, California, near La Jolla, and she grew up (along with a younger brother and sister) basking her olive skin in the California sun. During her years at La Jolla High, she landed a lead role at 15 in the local Mexican festival and got a summer-stock part as an Indian maiden. On campus, she was a cheer-leader and active in the Class Council, Speech, Jazz and Drama (10, 11, 12) clubs. Initial notoriety came in the form of a slew of beauty contest titles: Miss La Jolla, Miss San Diego, Miss Con-Tour, and Maid of California. Her high school years were capped by marriage to classmate James Welch, by whom she had two children, Damon and Tahnee. During the time ('58–'63) that Raquel and James were man and wife, she pursued her acting ambitions with ever-mounting passion. Classes at San Diego State led to some local television work, including a sometime spot as a weather girl. When the fork in the road came for her and her husband, she deemed it "inevitable."

"I had my children and I *worked* at being married," she says wistfully. "It was not a successful marriage, it was a failure, so I left and eventually I came here to Los Angeles." She was a shade more candid in a 1970 *Playboy* interview: "I wasn't very happy with my first husband. Sex didn't work out too well for us; it was very clumsy and awkward in every respect. In fact, it was just boring."

Before moving to L.A., Raquel made a brief sidetrip to Dallas, where she labored as a cocktail waitress, modeled for Neiman-Marcus, and raised enough money to get a nose job. After that auspicious surgery, she hit Hollywood and thereupon fell under the spell of Patrick Curtis, an ex-child actor who had scored a job as Olivia de Havilland's baby in *Gone with the Wind* (by winning the Adohre Milk Company's Adohreable Baby Contest), been a member of Ma and Pa Kettle's movie brood, and played Buzz on *Leave It to Beaver*.

The two met in 1964, while he was a public relations man with the Rogers and Cowan firm. She shared a $70-a-month apartment with her two children and lived off an allowance from Welch, who was then a Green Beret fighting in Vietnam. Three weeks after their acquaintance, Raquel and

Patrick formed their own star-stoking enterprise, Curtwel Productions; sole client: Raquel Welch.

"I kept my first husband's name, not realizing it would become my professional name," she now confides. "But I don't know what I would have changed it to, anyhow. How many things go with *Raquel?*"

With Curtis at the helm (they were wed in 1967 and stayed that way until 1972), they turned on the adrenalin with swiftly escalating results: bikini pic in *Life*; part as stripping-happy beach bunny in a low-budget film, *A Swinging Summer;* billboard girl on ABC-TV's *Hollywood Palace*; named one of the ten most promising actresses by Hairdressers and Makeup Artists Guild at 1965 Hollywood Deb Star Ball; screen test for 20th Century-Fox that led to role in *Fantastic Voyage*.

After that last bomb, she was loaned to Hammer Film Productions in England to star in the project that changed the course of primordial poontang: *One Million B.C.* For those with failing memories, the film was a remake of an earlier stroke of leapin' lizard legerdemain. This time around, the plot centered on the complex interactions of the Shell and Rock families. "Rocky" Raquel played Loana Shell, if you follow, and had but two lines: "Tumak" and "Akita." The late-'60s movie-going public was as confused as you. Yet, the sight of scantily-clad Ms. Shell (37–22–35) caught on with a vengeance when the Hammer studio chose in 1966 to put the buxom cavewoman on their 11" by 13" Christmas cards. The resulting poster blowup has since become part of American folk culture, a critical college dorm forerunner to the Farrah Fawcett-Cheryl Tiegs closet door bakeoff.

By 1969, she was featured on the cover of *Time* in a story heralding her impending appearance in the screen version of Gore Vidal's novel about a male transsexual, *Myra Breckinridge*. The critics called it one of the most horrendous films of modem times. Raquel concurs, up to a point.

"I saw it recently and I thought my performance was quite . . . *arch*," she admits with an apprehensive laugh. "—But that's what it was supposed to be. It was not a good film. However, at the time it was being made it was quite innovative; a *brave* subject.

"But that was all aborted because of lousy, lousy management. The philosophy at the studio—and I told them it was wrong—was that any publicity is good publicity, so they printed every bit of gossip.

"They had *Rex Reed* in the cast," she recalls disdainfully, "and he went on the Carson show every night. We were working every day, seriously, with a great deal of commitment—at least I can speak for myself—and yet you'd think we were a bunch of children misbehaving! They also cast it too camp, and the subject already was camp. I think the director, Michael Sarne, wanted it to work, but he was double-crossed at every turn and they fixed his wagon. Boy! He'll be lucky if he can ever show his face in this town again!

"In fact," she adds confidentially, "I don't think anybody else gave a performance in that movie *but* me. I tried to hold it up single-handed! I honestly think to this day that nobody took it seriously but me."

No argument here. Raquel is asked what's new.

"Oh well, I'm very happy with some of the roles I've been getting offered this year [among them, "the girl" in *The Red Hot Ferrari*, with Roger Moore]," she insists. "I can feel enthusiastic and not apologetic about what I'm doing.

"What I'm really into these days is music—and singing! I've been singing other people's material for the last five years, and I'd love to do an album now, but I want to do it my way. I don't want it to be heavy breathing over disco tracks. I mean, I could always do that. I have no objections to doing: [*eyes shut, hands on loins*] 'Ba-by, uhhh, baby, uhhh, ohhh, uhhaaaa, oooh baay-beee. . . .'—It just bores me!"

I mop my forehead with my shirt sleeve as she goes on.

"Every time I find material I like, somebody else is doing it! So I thought, 'Well, you're about *five years* away from writing something yourself.' And then, in a flash, I woke up in the middle of the night recently and, without planning it, I wrote down a song! Talk about a fulfilling experience!

"It's not a love song, except, well, it turns out to *sound* like a love song. Except, well, it *is* a love song. I sang it into a tape recorder! It's crazy, isn't it? I wonder who could put it together for me? Burt Bacharach? He's doing some lovely things lately." Like squiring Raquel around Vegas during their recent engagement at the MGM Grand Hotel. Rumor has it they're dating.

"You know, if you're eclectic, like I am, you're always a little frustrated that you can't do everything in a given space of time. At one point years ago, I wanted to do short films, real shorties, like 3½ minutes, and take a song like Elton John's "Amoreena" from *Tumbleweed Connection*, and do this whole thing about this girl in this western cattle town! See, that song had lines like: [*She coos*] 'Rolling in the hay, like a puppy child' and 'The fruit juice running slowly, slowly, slowly down the bronze of her body.' You'd just have two people, all that hay, and a little cabin in the middle of a wheatfield!" She licks her thin lips pensively. "Some people know how to live right on the *land*.

"Hey, look, maybe that's not *realistic*," she submits, icily, "but, like, people told me for instance that I would not get away with doing the Eagles in

Las Vegas. But I did this skit about this girl who's on the street, doing *every-thing* there is to do, and we did 'Life in the Fast Lane' and 'Wasted Time.' And they loved it! Those songs have limitless possibilities! You could do a whole contemporary *West Side Story* based on that album [*Hotel California*]! But where are the minds to do it? Get Stigwood! Where's Robert Stigwood?! *Where is Stigwood?!*"

Stigwood remains elusive as dusk descends, but Raquel's dog has just fin-ished his nap and moved from the now-cool grass to a warm spot near the back door. Four solid hours have passed since Raquel jump-started this dia-logue, and the atmosphere has grown as stale as the forgotten sodas. An unspoken recognition of our mutual fatigue allows the flustered mood to ease into somberness.

I look across at the woman who has been an object of titillation and prurience for tens of millions of men and boys. A rugged assignment. But there has been one moment in her screen career, in a medium-sized, deli-cately rendered period role, during which she showed herself capable of dis-appearing entirely behind an exquisite modesty of spirit. The role was Mme. Constance Bonacieux, the naive neighborhood seamstress in Richard Lester's *The Three Musketeers*. And her screen apotheosis came as Michael York's D'Artagnan, the sorely tested novice swordsman, applies his timid heart to the task of seducing the married but neglected Constance.

Seeing only the best intentions in his wiles, allowing her perspiring, unkempt self to be tempted by this would-be rake, Welch imbues her needy character's response with the bittersweet glow of perfect trust. If only in that one transcendent film interlude, she proved she could forget herself in the service of an emotional truth, and be as admirable and radiant an actress as any woman might wish to become.

Anger and ego, however, have poisoned many an artist's hungriest aspi-rations. If Raquel could someday play any role, portray anyone, who would it be? Joan of Arc? Amelia Earhart? Annie Oakley?

"There is one lady I'd love to play," she says quietly, "I'll probably never get the chance, because Vanessa Redgrave looks like her. Except that I could, because I know how to do that; but no one knows that yet. Anyhow, her name is Isak Dinesen, whose married name was Blixen."

The late Danish Baroness Karen Blixen; pen name Isak Dinesen. When Ernest Hemingway won the Nobel Prize in 1954, he took time to say a few words of praise for "that beautiful writer, Isak Dinesen," asserting that she was more deserving of the honor. Like Hemingway, Dinesen had an enthrallment with Africa; living in Kenya for many years, managing a coffee plantation, she stored up the probations that would later become the prose of her esteemed books, *Out Of Africa* and *Shadows on the Grass*. Her difficult, courageous life *would* make a fine film, assuming such aspects as her father's suicide, her husband's betrayal, her love for a white hunter, and great personal strength in doctoring, mediating, and merely understanding the natives could be conveyed with an unHollywood-like percipience.

"I like, best of all, her sensitivity," Raquel says. "She's independent and strong-willed, but it's more that she's somebody who loves nature and people. What she's found through these people, and the way she allows the African people to share the substance of their lives with her, is what I'd like to put into a movie. She's not a missionary type, 'cause she's not out to convert anybody; she saw to it that these people were educated but not so their own heritage and culture were interfered with.

"Apparently someone owns the rights to her story," she murmurs. "I'll probably never get my hands on it, and if I do, they'll tell me I'm not right for it. So I'll find something else. . . .

"There's a picture of Isak Dinesen in the beginning of a book by Peter Beard, *The End of the Game*, that was taken when she was very old. It's a face filled with wrinkles, and such *strong* cheekbones. You get the feeling that everything she's experienced, that's gone into her, has made a kind of tapestry on her face."

Listening to this pragmatic soliloquy, while also trying to fill in the missing humility, one strives to picture Raquel Welch as a wise and wintry Isak Dinesen, or an Irene Ishim Clark. But the effort somehow stalls.

"The sex symbol thing is something that I now feel comfortable with . . . for the most part," she says haltingly. "For the most part, I do. But to say that has always sounded self-pitying or self-congratulatory.

"It has constricted me, has impeded my progress. But it's not something you transcend. Maybe it's something you . . . accept."

And yet, if people choose to be rigid or ungenerous about it, a sex symbol can never grow old.

"BULLSHIT!! BULLSHIT!! WHO SAID THAT?!!"

She is fuming, her nostrils flared, staring daggers at her guest. Just as quickly, she calms down.

"Excuse me," she says solemnly, "but I find the whole subject rather depressing. I don't want to discuss the pain, the agony, the *shit* I've been through. And it's too bad, because a sex symbol should be a thing of . . . joy."

There must have been some big disappointments over the years.

"Disappointments? *Dis-a-point-ments*.

Oh yes," she assures grimly.

She pauses, spreads her wiry arms in a wide arc, and then brings her long flat hands together at the tips, placing them against her pursed lips. Tilting her large head back at a harsh angle, staring into nowhere, she begins a stern, formal-sounding summary. During this pointed act of introversion, her voice drops gradually, lower and lower, until the last words are delivered in a gentle growl:

"You want to know about disappointments? Yes; sure you do. And I should know, because I've been there a lot.

"I'm an actress and I'm a celebrity; that's what I do with my time, as well as being a mother and a friend and a lover—and a human being. Professionally, there've been some people who got on my case *pret-ty* heavy in a *pret-ty* venal way. Why, I couldn't say. Maybe they saw a weakness that was vulnerable and they went for it. People are like that, you know?

"We're all animals. *In fact*. Sophisticated animals, but nonetheless animals. When animals travel in a tribe and they see somebody that's a little vulnerable, they go for her. And that's the truth. So that's what's happened to me. But who would you trade places with? Marlon Brando? Marlon Brando was called a genius 15 years ago and that's a terrible thing to live with.

"I guess you could call me 'The Enlightened Sex Symbol.' I don't see myself as a victim—and I have been—but it's not interesting to me. Life has a way of giving you a sufficient amount of pain and anxiety, so that you learn about it from all sides.

"How much you learn . . . *depends on how much you can stand.*"

Blues Brothers Confidential

Episode One: The Ballad of Jake & Elwood

Before the House of Blues, or The Blues Brothers *movie of 1980, or its* Blues Brothers 2000 *sequel, or even the 1978 release of the Blues Brothers' chart-topping, double-platinum* Briefcase Full of Blues *debut album, there was the Blues Bar, an unlicensed, derelict brick tavern at the corner of Dominic and Hudson Streets in the lonesome industrial canyons of Manhattan's Soho district.*

In '78, Universal Pictures gave John Belushi and Dan Aykroyd some money to finance the development of the script for *The Blues Brothers*. John used his share to lease a suite of offices at 130 Fifth Avenue to headquarter a creative partnership with Danny they dubbed Black Rhino Enterprises. Danny took his portion of the advance to establish—as he once had in both Chicago and Toronto—a cloistered after-hours haunt in which he and John could "gather their thoughts."

The ancient two-story building housing the intended Blues Bar was rented in the summer of 1978, its ground floor recast in superficial speakeasy style. Aykroyd and Belushi left its windows painted black as they'd been after the former watering hole for factory workers shut down in the early '70s. Each weekend following rehearsals and broadcasts of *Saturday Night Live*, they filled the long narrow room with non-paying friends and associates, beginning with a fete thrown for the Grateful Dead when they played on *SNL*.

The original Blues Bar (not to be confused with a spinoff pub Aykroyd and Belushi acquired three years later called Mickey's) had the best jukebox in New York City. Its choice menu included R&B, rock, and reggae selections running the gamut from Sam and Dave's "You Don't Know Like I Know" and "Goin' Back to Miami," by Wayne Cochran & The C.C. Riders, to Bob Marley and the Wailers' "Jah Live" and "A Message to Pork Eaters" by Tapper Zukie.

Belushi and Aykroyd usually supplied the liquor and Budweiser that fueled the place, though it was not unknown for all assembled to chip in to buy more when provisions ran low. Contrary to popular reports, the private hangout had no small cabaret-like stage, no sophisticated sound system, no frills of any sort (beyond the single flower Aykroyd regularly placed in a vase atop the porcelain ruins of the toilet in the otherwise fearsome ladies powder room, "Just so we have something nice for the womenfolk").

Actors, musicians, writers, models, family members, friends of friends, curious passersby, and the occasional exotic spillover from a strip bar further up Hudson Street formed the basic clientele. Unless it was the bitter depths of winter, the party inside the Blues Bar also regularly spilled out onto the wide public sidewalk surrounding it, dozens of people leaning against cars and motorcycles, discussing everything from Harley engines and movie deals to the collected works of Bobby "Blue" Bland.

Moreover, neither Belushi nor Aykroyd were adverse to loaning the entire premises out to their downtown associates. When the Greenwich Village-based *Crawdaddy* magazine folded in 1979, its orphaned staff asked the

Blues Bar's proprietors if their lounge might be borrowed for the night. John, whose first appearance on the cover of a national magazine (November '77) had been for *Crawdaddy*, and Danny, who'd written prose ("Heavy Metal Silence," January '78) for the magazine, happily obliged, ultimately joining in the festivities.

But as memory serves, an average night circa the autumn of '78, went something like this: Aykroyd usually showed up at 11:30 p.m. to unlock the premises (since Belushi, having hurried over earlier from his Morton Street apartment had forgotten his key) and by midnight the ritual bash was in full roar. Francis Ford Coppola would be tending bar alongside Danny and Atlantic Records executive Michael Klenfner, with Boz Scaggs, Belushi, Peter Aykroyd (Dan's brother), the members of ZZ Top and assorted *Crawdaddy* editors jamming on John's guitars and the other equipment always stashed in the corner to the left of the front door (a battered set of white pearl Ludwig drums, several bass and guitar amps, microphones).

Drifting through the capacity crowd of bikers, William Morris agents and assorted members of the Aykroyd and Belushi families would be the cast and crew of *Saturday Night Live*—including Michael O'Donoghue, a spectral sentry in his white straw fedora and a tropical suit over a pajama top with white piping, wearing sea-green sunglasses and smoking only the first few puffs of a brown Nat Sherman cigarette before extinguishing it with his black ballet slipper and lighting another.

O'Donoghue, a Playboy bunny on his arm, would whisper something mischievous to an appreciative Carrie Fisher as public relations man Bobby Zarem tried to divide the actress's attention. In would stroll Keith Richards, dressed in the same jeans and shirt he'd been sporting for the duration of the current Stones tour, making straight for the juke box with Ron Wood in tow. Gilda Radner, Judy Belushi and *SNL* writer Rosie Shuster would be leaning over the sagging bar on the right, gazing at photographer David Alexander's outtakes (pinned up around the mirror) from the session he shot for the *Briefcase Full of Blues* record jacket, while *Rolling Stone/SNL* writer Mitch Glazer dreamed up witty alternative photo captions for the images.

Elsewhere along the bar, members of the *Rolling Stone* staff would chat with Bill Murray, his brother Brian Doyle-Murray, Second City actor Tim Kazurinsky and an off-duty policeman. Huddled near them one evening were two Con Ed workers and a young couple who'd wandered too far from the West Village, these impromptu patrons wondering aloud how they could drink all night and have the bartender refuse their money.

Suddenly Keith Richards would spy the Tapper Zukie single on the record machine, punch it up, and as the reggae oozed out, the ad hoc band in the corner would take a break as everyone began to dance non-stop with the nearest possible partner.

Come 6:30 a.m., John and Judy Belushi would leave in a hired car, offering lifts home to assorted chums. At 7:30 a.m. the hired car would return to the Blues Bar, sent back on Belushi's orders to collect up any dawdlers who had fallen asleep on the bench lining the length of the tavern's left wall, and drop them off at their respective doorsteps.

That Saturday evening, the previous night's revelers would belatedly rise from their hangover beds and catch the tail end of NBC-TV's 11 o'clock news, while rummaging through cupboards and refrigerators for something to repair their tattered metabolisms. Around 11:30 p.m. Belushi and Aykroyd would appear on the TV screen, bright-eyed and eager, none the worse for the last 24 hours' wear, and wing through the cold opening of *Saturday Night Live* as another installment got underway.

The Blues Bar casualties watching at home would suddenly realize—despite protests from their throbbing heads—that a new morning of fun was about to commence. Thus, the local 24–hour pizzeria would duly be phoned for a recuperative delivery, its customers timing the interregnum to include a hot shower, and then at 1:45 a.m. all or most Blues Bar veterans would converge once more at the corner of Dominic and Hudson to do it all over again.

"Belushi," the actor was asked one October Sunday at 2 a.m., "how did you possibly find the energy between early Saturday morning and late Saturday evening to rise from the slab, do this week's show, and make it back here to the Blues Bar?"

He smiled, arched an eyebrow and answered, "Doing live comedy gives me the energy to do everything else."

THE INTERVIEW

HERE'S THE STRAIGHT POOP: every hapless hambone stranded in this sorry life should *at least* have a main squeeze who knows how to clean his clocks, an unholy soul band that this twosome can do the *Do* to, and a copacetic little gin mill where they can work this blissful bit of juju.

Now that's a sweet little vision, but it's *not* the Big Picture. The Big Picture, unfortunately, is that there is a wealth of chowderheads, mean-spirited stiffs and marginally adjusted jerks out there upon whom such a blessing would be squandered. I'm not trying to sit in anybody's lunch, so to speak, but some people in this world wouldn't know a good time if they chipped a tooth on it. For this reason, I feel at this moment that most of the people who reside in the totemlike town houses of Manhattan's moneyed Turtle Bay area should never be privy to a piece of heaven like Jake and Elwood's legendary Big Apple hideway, the Blues Bar.

You see, Turtle Bay is a cool, crusty enclave in the east 40s where every Saturday night soiree seems more like one of those reptilian Tuesday cocktail quip-a-thons where the icy hors d'oeuvres never get touched, where the tart white wine goes down like Janitor in a Drum, and where every chattering mannequin is auditioning for a fat cat's lap. "What a marvelous collection of contemptible crumbs," I'm thinking to myself when my good-natured chum, Miami, pulls me over into a corner and rules that it's definitely time to slip out of this mortuary and go where folks know how to get on the good foot.

"So wherezat?" I slur.

"The Blues Bar," he whispers desperately.

"Huh?"

"You know, Jake 'n Elwood's hangout."

"Jake and El—oh, you mean the Blues Brothers!" I say, brightening considerably at the memory of their unbridled treatment of "Soul Man" on *Saturday Night Live* earlier this evening. "They hang out at some place in the city? You mean there really *is* a Black Rhino Club?"

"Nah," he hisses, *"the Rhino thing is just a routine on the show. But Jake and Elwood get loose at the Blues Bar on certain nights—and tonight's one of 'em!"*

"Where is this place?"

"You'll see."

The ride to our arcane destination is a lengthy, bleary bumpalong through some pretty nasty neighborhoods. At last, we pull up to this forlorn little saloon with paint-blackened windows.

"There's nobody around here. This place has been shut down for years," I protest as Miami pushes me out of the taxi.

"That's what you think, joy-boy," he chuckles as he taps on the side door and barks, "Big Jake summoned us!"

When the door swings wide, I sober up in a hurry. Looming in the doorway is a big drink of water in a taut T-shirt and shades, the guy flexing biceps the size of my waist. It's Matt "Guitar" Murphy, one-time member of James Cotton's band and now thundering alongside Steve "The Colonel" Cropper in the Blues Brothers band.

"Come on in, Miami," Murphy laughs, "and bring your funny-looking pal. The beer's ice cold and we got a lotta nice *snug-geets* in here t'night."

"*Snug-geets?*"

"That's what Matt calls his women," my friend explains as we wade into an ecstatic dancing crowd that fills every inch of the small, cozy room. A jukebox stocked with every jump blues and R&B single of any lasting significance is blaring a Sam and Dave tune and the walls are plastered with faded snapshots of the Blues Brothers posed in front of most of the gas stations, roadhouses and jails between New York and Calumet City, Illinois. In the majority of the photos, the sunglassed group is either holding someone or being held, at gunpoint.

"Who *took* those shots?"

Miami looks at me like I'm a dunce. "Fans—who else?"

"*And who's asking?*" roars a voice behind me.

Shaken, I turn to face the Black Rhino himself, Joliet Jake Blues. Built big, badassed and close to the ground, Jake is decked out in his customary baggy black serge suit, sweat-stained white shirt and ribbon-thin black tie. Rising behind him is broad-shouldered Elwood, his younger brother, sidekick and silent confidant, who's a mite less formally attired in these wee hours, having stripped down to a sleeveless T-shirt and black vest. But both men are wearing midnight fedoras and shades that, even in the red light, accent their sinister barroom pallors.

"Is this clown a friend of yours?" an unsmiling Jake snaps at Miami, who nods cautiously, introducing me. "Well, I hope he came here to listen to the blues, get shitfaced drunk and fall down on the floor," Jake rules as Elwood shifts his stance threateningly.

I nod very cautiously.

"Well then," Joliet laughs, giving me a mighty bear hug, "lemme fill the biggest mug I can find for ya!"

Stunned, I stand amidst the melee as my hefty host hunkers over to the bar and tells Keith Richards, one of the guest bartenders (along with Richard Dreyfuss and Atlantic Records Senior Vice President Michael Klenfner) to fetch a tall draft. But the biggest jolt comes when silent Elwood steps forward, extends his hand and speaks, asking me if I enjoyed *Briefcase Full of Blues*. "S-s-sounded pretty decent to me," I sputter, and as we shake on it I notice a heavy gold chain trailing from his handcuffed wrist to a black leather briefcase. Suddenly, Jake is back with my beer and suggesting very strongly that I drink it in one gulp. As my eyes water from the effort both men vanish in a puff of truly rank cigar smoke.

"Jake and Elwood are two mysterious pieces of work," the huge, mustachioed Klenfner later concurs. "Either one is capable of appearing or disappearing at any damned moment, but silent Elwood's the queerest case—he's gone in a flash and nobody knows where the hell he went. Elwood's never too comfortable, especially around groups of people, but then he could be rolling around naked in a tub of whipped cream and still not feel comfortable. So he just splits. It drives me so crazy I've thought about getting one of those Batman-type spotlights to shine in the air at night whenever we need to contact him. Instead of a bat symbol silhouetted against the sky, we'd either project a giant pair of sunglasses—Ray-Bans No. 5022–G15—or his silhouette. I don't know, it's a problem I haven't solved yet."

Well, it must be the only one. Klenfner's new act has produced a runaway hit single ("Soul Man") and a platinum album that contains some of the most exhilarating music of an especially bleak winter. The Blues Brothers and their record have been dubbed a "novelty" in this disco-dominated era, and, considering its long heritage of work with blues and R&B artists, Klenfner is especially pleased their aggressive R&B sound triumphed on the Atlantic label.

"I think their second album is gonna do even better," he enthuses. "We've got the best band working anywhere, and on the road Jake and Elwood prove they have the chops to—"

"But Michael," I interrupt. There's one thing that bothers me about the Blues Brothers. I can't shake the screwy feeling that I've seen 'em some place before. I mean, exactly *who* are they? Jake, for example, looks a fuck a lot like John Belu—"

"Now *listen*," Klenfner says gruffly. "I don't know any more about them than you do. All I know is they sound great and act awful goddamned strange.

I'll tell you this: They're gonna be on the bill on the New Year's Eve show at the closing of Winterland out in San Francisco. Why don't you fly out? I can promise you a great show and a great time, but as for getting the Blues Brothers' inside story, you're on your own. Far as I'm concerned, what you *hear* is what they *are*."

"What a goddamned good band!" Bill Graham yells to Klenfner over the din of an afternoon soundcheck rendition of "Jailhouse Rock." Holding on to his own crumpled, gray version of a Blues Brothers hat, he darts around the vacant, drafty floor of Winterland issuing orders.

"So what the hell did you expect?" Klenfner bellows back as Jake and Elwood put the group through their paces. "Naturally we got the best!" At this point the band members are a well-rehearsed bundle of nerves. Few major reviews have yet appeared on *Briefcase* and the Brothers & Co. feel like interlopers on a bill that places their act between a short set and the New Riders of the Purple Sage and an all-night epic concert by the Grateful Dead. Camped on the sidewalk outside are hard-core Deadheads, and the only indications that this anxious hippie throng might have any familiarity with the Blues Brothers are a couple of dazed backpackers wearing battered plastic coneheads.

"Three hours 'til we open!" Graham shouts as the horns persevere. Led by Tom "Bones" Malone on sax, trombone and trumpet, the distinguished lineup (Lou "Blue Lou" Marini, tenor sax; Alan "Mr. Fabulous"' Rubin, trumpet; Tom "Triple Scale" Scott, tenor sax) is skintight by the second take when they're joined by Steve Cropper, Matt Murphy, keyboardman Paul Shaffer and the funky ballistics of bassist Donald "Duck" Dunn and drummer Steve "Getdwa" Jordan. Jake decides to grab the mike and leans way back for a growling assault on the "Jailhouse" chorus while Elwood punctuates the proceedings with some honkin' blues harp.

But in a finger snap it's a wrap, and the band mills around the hall as mammoth breakaway plastic bags full of balloons are hoisted to the ceiling in preparation for the New Year countdown. Meanwhile, Jake and Elwood have now dematerialized. It takes the rest of the afternoon to locate the dingy hotel room they're holed up in, but my reconnaissance pays off. Their reticence virtually dissolved by a late breakfast of tepid Muskatel and some overripe seafood, both open up for the first in-depth interview of their convoluted career.

"Elwood!" Jake howls, drawing his partner's catatonic attention from the high-school football game flickering on the TV. "How do you think the Blues Brothers are gonna do tonight? Do we have a chance against the Dead and all the Deadheads?"

Elwood hesitates before speaking, flashing me a wounded glance.

"Jake, I gotta say no way, man. They're gonna blow us off the stage."

"It's a nightmare," Jake agrees. "They'll be screaming, 'Grateful Dead! We want Garcia!'"

"'Get offstage, you swine!'" Elwood joins in. "'Get fucking *lost!*'"

"Oh no they won't!" scolds a shadowy female figure in the next room. She is laying out their black suits and slipping extra pairs of sunglasses in their breast pockets; Foster Grants for Jake, Ray-Bans (No. 5022–G15) for Elwood. I realize it's Jake's spectral spouse, known only as the Blues Wife. "You guys are wrong!" she begs. "They'll be screaming Colonel, Bones, Joliet, *El-wood!*"

"I'm not so sure," Elwood sighs. "Right about now I'd like a bottle of Night Train wine—with a little spike of Sterno in it—to cheer me up. But hell, that swill is up to a buck-seventy a fifth!"

"Key Largo was another great brand," Jake chimes in wistfully. "'Just one sip/And you will *know*/That you're on the island/Of Key Largo.' So what do *you* wanna know?" he asks, pointing a menacing finger at me.

"To begin with, the word is Universal is planning a Blues Brothers film, and Elwood is writing the script."

"The Scriptatron XL 9000 has to finish the script," Elwood recites mechanically. "It'll be the first screenplay by the amazing Scriptatron XL 9000; the first fully programmed script. It's almost half finished."

"But what's the plot? Some say it's the story of your veiled past."

"Yeah," Jake admits, scratching the bristly soul patch under his lower lip with a shrimp tail. "We play ourselves. Here's a simple synopsis: It starts with me getting out of jail after three years and I expect the band to still be together. . . ."

"He got three years on a five-year rap," Elwood interrupts. "Armed robbery at a gas station. I was driving but he took the rap because he knew I would string myself up if I went to jail. He did it for the *band*."

"Well, the band demanded their per diem," Jake explains, "so I had to rob the place! But anyhow, the film is about finding the band members and trying to get it all back together again."

"We hunt them down like cops, like *detectives*," Elwood bubbles. "We have nothing, a scrap of paper with their last phone numbers and a coupla old addresses. We discover that each one now has a different trip; a couple of 'em are living suburban lives, mostly working day jobs. We were just getting hot when Jake went in the slammer, drawing big crowds in highway drinking halls. Now we've re-formed to try again!"

"It's like *The Magnificent Seven*," yells Jake, "or *Force Ten from Navarone!*"

The liner notes on the back of their album jacket inferred that they grew up in orphanages, took a lot of grief from frustrated nuns, learned the blues from a black janitor named Curtis and staked out Calumet City, Illinois, as their stompin' grounds. . . .

"Right," Elwood confirms, "but that wasn't the half of it."

"Both of us were victims of heavy corporal punishment as children," he reveals somberly. "And there's a scene in the movie, in fact, where we go back to one of the orphanages to fulfill a promise we made to a nun. We're both sitting in these little school desks, and Big Jake's wedged in, he's stuck, and she whacks the shit out of us with a steel-edge ruler. She's like a kendo artist. She moves in on us, and then vanishes because Jake says the 'F' word in front of her! The school is named St. Helen of the Blessed Shroud Orphanage and the nun's name is Sister Mary Stigmata.

"There are blood references everywhere in the film and the halls of this orphanage are filled with the images of martyred priests, these grotesque statues of clergymen strung up years ago by pagans. It's a school for special children now but the subsidies have all fallen out from under it, the church won't support it anymore, and Sister Stigmata is really strapped for bucks. They're gonna ship her off to a mission if she can't keep up the rent.

"Now, she's the only family we have, see?" Elwood says passionately, "but she threw us out and said, 'Don't come back until you redeem yourselves! You're thieves and liars, so clear out!' It's a big Catholic guilt trip she lays on us, but we *are* thieves and [*big grin*] filthy-mouthed liars! So we come back and decide to do her a favor and raise some money for the school.

"We're pretty strapped financially at this point. I've got a job but I put most of the money into our car, the Blues Mobile, which is an ex-Indiana state police car with a 440 in it—from the pre-unleaded gas era. The speedometer just says 'certified calibration' and it's clocked for 140. All through the movie you'll see close-ups of the speedometer, the needle just banging in there at 130.

"We bought it at a municipal auction. We used to have a Cadillac, which I traded for a microphone, and Jake goes nuts when he sees this old Dodge I'm driving around in, but I soon prove to Jake how fast the Dodge is.

"And it helps during an incredible car chase at the end of the movie," he says with a sly wink.

"By the way, how did you assemble the original band?"

"It was agony, agony," says Jake, burying his fat face in his hands. "Elwood and I were a duo and when word got out we were forming a group, I got phone calls immediately, calls from heavy stars, saying, 'I wanna be in your band!' And it was a question of whether to assemble one or just get a band that was already established—some guys together for ten years so we could put 'em up there and let 'em just groove. I was thinking about getting Delbert McClinton's band, and Roomful of Blues, too. When we first resurfaced, Elwood and I did a gig at the Lone Star Cafe in New York in June [of 1978] with Roomful of Blues.

"But finally we just decided, 'Fuck the cost and the damage it will do to the feelings of people who aren't asked, and let's go for the best band we can get, *piece by piece.*' We got Bones Malone first and he recommended Cropper and Dunn. We really didn't know who they were," Jake snorts. "Then when he [Malone] said, 'You know, from "Knock on Wood" and "Soul Man,"' we said, 'Would *they* do it?!'

"I called them up, acting real arrogant," Jake recounts, "saying, '*Wellll*, all right Cropper, you're in the group but you're a rhythm. I'm guitar player—ya got that?' and he went [*meekly*], 'I *like* playing rhythm guitar; I don't like all that lead stuff.' So I said [*sarcastically*], 'Oh, you're hard to work with, aren't ya?'

"Then I called Dunn up and said, 'I never met you but I'd like you to be in a group—but I understand you don't get along with Cropper.' He said, '*Aw no*, we get along all right!' I was just giving them all kinda shit, bustin' their balls," Jake guffaws, slapping Elwood on the back.

"But they both said yes, and, uh, incidentally . . . they didn't know who *we* were either."

"Wasn't your first public reappearance on a 1975 segment of *Saturday Night Live* in which you dressed in bee costumes and played 'King Bee'?"

Their beads bob . . . warily.

"At that time, I'd do anything to sing," counsels Jake contritely. "So they got us into these stupid bee costumes. Boy, that was a dog performance."

"I'm intrigued by this long-standing affiliation with *Saturday Night Live*," I press them. "How close are your ties to the show? You know, the more I look at Elwood, the more he reminds me of Dan Aykr—"

"Well, gotta split now," they yelp in unison. "Er, hope you like the show tonight!"

I do, and I'm not alone. A shoulder-to-shoulder army of Deadheads rushes the stage when Jake and Elwood scramble on to a tumultuous fanfare of "I Can't Turn You Loose," Jake turning cartwheels as they erupt next with "Hey Bartender." The program is identical to the album, but it takes on a uniquely exultant tone as the group becomes aware that the audience knows every number.

Indeed, halfway through the set, Jake looks up to spy several willowy longhairs decked out in basic black getups identical to his own. A deafening salvo greets the familiar twanging lead-guitar intro to "Soul Man" and the victory is complete by the time the Brothers close with "'B' Movie Box Car Blues."

The group overruns the stage when they do their encore, and Jake's cartwheel choreography is out of hand when "Flip, Flop & Fly" segues into the unhinged "Jailhouse Rock."

Backstage afterward, the dressing room floods with wellwishers, and even a cantankerous old grizzly like Jake is so moved by the adulation that he removes his Foster Grants and presents them to a deeply touched young fan—although Joliet quickly replaces them with a spare pair he had stashed in his breast pocket.

The Jefferson Starship turns over its Airplane-era Victorian house on Fulton Street for a post-concert Blues Brothers party, but as the evening wears on, there are rumors among the 300-odd guests that Jake and Elwood won't show. Spirits are momentarily lifted when *Saturday Night Live* stalwarts Laraine Newman and Bill Murray stroll and stumble, respectively, in . . . followed shortly afterward by John Belushi and Dan Aykroyd, but disappointment blankets the crowd as it becomes apparent that 1979's conquering heroes will be a no-show.

Some critics have noted that the Blues Brothers' musical direction and their decision to record their debut LP live at the Universal Amphitheatre in L.A. bespeak a vitality and an unabashed sense of fun that is currently in short supply. Although their show consists entirely of a roundup of R&B and blues oldies, each was picked and refurbished with genuine enthusiasm. And sometimes their feelings for the music run still deeper. Stax/Volt veterans Steve Cropper and Duck Dunn say that it was a special thrill to resurrect some of their vintage material; the night before the band left for their ninenight stand in Los Angeles, Cropper listened to some Otis Redding records for the first time since Redding's death, Steve's eyes welling up with emotion at the sound of his old boss' searing vocals.

As a band, the Blues Brothers are a delight. As a musical force they are merely a friendly reminder of some great music that in recent years has largely been ignored or forgotten. There's more to popular music than the "preprogrammed electronic disco" Elwood disdains, and the Blues Brothers remind us of this fact with humor and spirit.

I wander upstairs for what proves to be a fascinating conversation with Dan Aykroyd, but feel a little badly because Joliet Jake had vowed earlier that we would have a last chat. I've come to realize that the positive energy emanating from the Blues Brothers is something of an elixir in these jaded times, and I'm pissed off I won't be getting another hit of it.

Wrung out and kinda bummed, I decide to drown my already sodden sorrows sometime around 4:30 a.m. by swigging from various bottles of champagne being passed around the mansion, and soon discover my depression is being cemented by an unexpected dose of acid. Cursing myself for forgetting what Bill Graham had advised earlier ("Don't eat or drink anything being passed around tonight if you don't want to trip"), I race around the house in mounting terror. Luckily, I collide with Cynthia Bowman, the pretty national publicity director for the Starship, who commandeers Michael Klenfner's waiting limousine and sternly instructs the bewildered chauffeur to take me back to the nearby Miyako Hotel, posthaste.

Grateful for the assistance, I lean out the window to thank her as the car pulls away from the curb and look up to see that her face has become a hideous kaleidoscope. I'm jolted speechless; I've never done acid before and the sight scares me out of my wits.

After a seemingly endless excursion through predawn San Francisco—during which I momentarily became convinced that the driver is a horned demon taking me, willy-nilly, down into the Stygian depths of hell—I find myself sitting outside the comforting Oriental familiarity of the Miyako. Somehow I make it to the suite on the thirteenth floor that I'm sharing with Miami.

"Fuck me dead!" I rage as he opens the door. "I got dosed by some low-life scuzz at the Blues Brothers party and now I'm tripping straight out of my skull."

Miami's jaw drops and he leads me in gingerly, telling me to lay down and try to remain calm while he makes a phone call. I am too distracted by the colorful streams of insects surging up the room's melting walls to get a fix on his telephone conversation, but minutes later the door swings wide and in strides a formidable slice of reality, John Belushi and his wife, Judy Jacklin.

To make a long story short, the Belushis, with whom I have only an acquaintance, stay with me for hours, John assuming a comforting bedside manner as we shoot the shit until I am exhausted enough to doze off with the help of Valium; his kindness reminding me of one additional thing every hapless hambone should have in this life: a couple of unexpected friends.

I never do see the Black Rhino again that weekend but I remember Belushi smiling at the tail end of my trip when I mentioned Joliet Jake's latest disappearance. "Aw, don't worry about it; I think you should have these," he said soothingly, placing something dark and gleaming upon the night table as I drifted into sleep.

When I wake up late that afternoon my head is full of questions. Squinting about, trying to get my bearings, the first thing I see is the San Francisco skyline reflected in a shiny object lying just across from my head. I blink and realize that it's the gift I was given the night before . . . Jake's spare pair of Foster Grants.

Episode Two: Messin' with the Kids— Dan Aykroyd & John Belushi

*J*ohn Belushi was born in the Norwegian American Hospital *in Chicago on January 24, 1949, at 5:12 a.m., the son of Adam Belushi of Qytetes, Albania, and his wife Agnes, a native of Akron, Ohio. John was the ham in the family's home movies, the leader of the bands (the Vibrations, the Ravens) he formed at Central Wheaton High with buddy Dick Blasucci (Dick and his brothers on guitars, John on drums), captain of the football team, and point man of a bogus aerial act he formed with Tino Insana and Steve Beshekas for Chicago's Second City comedy troupe called the Flying Benzeni Brothers.*

Growing up in a lower middle class Wheaton, Illinois, household that his mom described as "very European in outlook," John was the child who ran interference for the rest of his siblings, petitioning his conservative dad for permission to, among other things, speak freely at the dinner table.

As John recalled in 1978, "I used to tell my father, 'This is America, Dad, you're not in Albania anymore. You made it out and escaped to a free country. Let's enjoy that freedom, let's at least loosen up at home.'"

Belushi had a diverse career, excelling in improv comedy, winning a loyal following on radio in *The National Lampoon Radio Hour*, on stage in *Lemmings* and on television. He made just seven feature films during his brief (1978–81) Hollywood transit, including *Goin' South*, *Old Boyfriends*, *1941*, *Continental Divide* and *Neighbors*.

Bernie Brillstein, Belushi's manager, believed John's ideal roles were not as the broad and antic Bluto in *Animal House* but rather as the visceral but deeply vulnerable newspaperman he played in *Continental Divide*.

"If John wants to, he could be another Spencer Tracy," Brillstein once mused over a drink at the Blues Bar.

Belushi's comic partner Aykroyd likewise showed a strong gift for subtle drama, winning an Academy Award nomination as best supporting actor opposite Jessica Tandy in *Driving Miss Daisy* (1989). But of the dozens of movies (*Trading Places*, 1983, *Sneakers*, 1992, etc.) and occasional TV series (ABC-TV's *Soul Man* in 1997) Aykroyd appeared in after Belushi's death, Dan remains best known for his co-starring role in the two big-budget, blockbuster comedies he'd envisioned as vehicles for John, Bill Murray and himself: *Ghostbusters* (1984) and *Ghostbusters II* (1989).

For all the distance covered since, both Belushi and Aykroyd are rooted in the public's mind by the comradery they brought to their work together, most particularly with the Blues Brothers. Lighthearted, sincere, and unpremeditated, the seminal Blues Brothers performances on *SNL* and the blues-promoting tours and companion film that emerged from the initial notion took a lot of critical knocks, but participating artists like James Brown and Ray Charles saw it all quite differently.

"John was a loyal fan of rhythm & blues," Ray Charles told this writer in 1982, "and I know for a fact that the Blues Brothers movie and soundtrack got a hell of a lot of people back into R&B."

James Brown concurred: "When John and Danny invited me to be a part of the Blues Brothers film, they helped me get myself going again. I was going through a bad period at the time, having trouble getting my records released. John flew in to watch me cut my stuff for the soundtrack album. He knew I was having problems with my career and he said, "How can I help?" He was *there* for me, understand?"

Somewhere between the high-wire sketch comedy of Second City and the Blues Brothers persona that created the Hollywood stardom he first tasted in 1978 with *National Lampoon's Animal House*, Belushi lost both his resilient natural energy and his balance, and he fell, dying of a drug overdose in the early hours of morning on March 5, 1982. He was 33 years old.

John Belushi was buried in a bleak ceremony on Martha's Vineyard on a chilly, windswept day in the winter of '82. "He was our middle linebacker," said Mitch Glazer at the time. "In our minds he was invulnerable. We bought the myth of his strength. And, in a way, so did he."

When the spring came, fellow actor and fan James Cagney, John's neighbor on the island, conferred with Judy Belushi. He invited John's widow to comb the rocky shoreline of Cagney's Roaring Brook Farm and choose a fitting boulder on the beach for what became the headstone of John Belushi's final resting place.

THE INTERVIEW

My parents have a photo of Dan when he was about three and I was just a small protein unit, and in the picture he's riding a small motorcycle, carrying a machine gun, and wearing a cowboy hat. In other words, even then he had at least three characters going at once.

Peter Aykroyd, Dan's funny younger brother

EASTER SATURDAY 1978, 7:30 p.m.: *"Now what in the hell am I sup-posed to do with these claws?!"*

Portly, pissed-off John Belushi stomps down a gloomy hallway at NBC's *Saturday Night Live* studio in New York after rehearsing a skit due to air this evening called "The Thing That Wouldn't Leave." Dressed in washed out jeans and a baggy sweatshirt, with large floppy green claws covering his hands and feet, Belushi is as disgusted as the suburban couple (Jane Curtin, Bill Murray) he torments in the skit. Grunting a hello, he lumbers into his dressing room, plops down and bites a banana. Then he simultaneously swallows the fruit and spits out the peel.

"I'm not gonna wear these stupid claws, they're too weird, make no sense," he pouts, pulling them from his hands and throwing them against the door as Dan Aykroyd steps into the room. Dan is wearing a collarless, candy-striped shirt with elbow garters, red apron and straw hat. Tonight he will do one of his bizarrely credible pitchman segments, in this case hawking a new fast-food treat: barbecued bunnies.

"Hello there, Thing," he calls out affectionately. The appearance of Aykroyd is a welcome relief; with his bright, twinkling eyes, boyish face and courtly manner, he's obviously the saner of the two. As Belushi begins to bitch with great resonance about the raw deal—"bullshit money, no points, but I'm gonna be a fucking star anyhow, those cheap bastards"—he got for starring in some forthcoming film comedy called *National Lampoon's Animal House*, Danny and I have a pleasant chat about each other's plans for the holiday weekend.

I move further away from Belushi as he begins spitting pieces of banana peel at the *Animal House* poster taped to his mirror—*Sploff!* "Ha! Those motherfuckers!" I am about to broaden the range of my discourse with Aykroyd, who's been leafing idly through a magazine, when he suddenly comes upon an article on the penile transducer, a *Clockwork Orange*-inspired bit of hardware used in the treatment of sex criminals.

"Aversion therapy!" Aykroyd shouts with sufficient glee to knock his own hat off, then delves into the text with salacious enthrallment. I glance from one man to the other, increasingly unnerved as Aykroyd whoops at each psychosexual revelation and John twitches his claw feet and vents his anger with mounting velocity. I steal away, convinced that both actors are off the beam, but finally deciding that from the claws up, Belushi is, pound for pound, the more *alien* of the two.

Until I later learn about Aykroyd's feet.

It seems that the man has more in common with the Thing than meets the eye, by which I mean that, well, I don't know how to break this to you all, but there happens to be this thin membrane of skin tissue that connects his toes, specifically the second and third toes of each foot. As Danny phrases it, he's a "genetic mutant," but that sounds a trifle indelicate. Let's just say the Dan Aykroyd, the handsome, talented star of TV's *Saturday Night Live*, the hero of millions and an inspiration to youth . . . has webbed feet.

John Belushi is Everyman's superstar; Gilda Radner is America's sweetheart; Bill Murray is the oddball celebrity's celebrity, but Dan Aykroyd is a precise *blur*, moving slow enough to be seen clearly, but much too fast to be categorized.

Think about it. For more than 120 Saturday nights he's come into our homes and made acting on live television look *easy*. A comedic Lon Chaney, this Funny Man of a Thousand Faces has mimicked with unerring accuracy some of the greatest figures of our time. His Jimmy Carter sendup captures the president's ineptitude-masking fascination for folksy banality and quasi hipness with an unctuous schoolboy drawl and a Cheshire cat grin. Still more devastating are his impersonations of Richard Nixon, each nervous facet of this broken-down Cro-Magnon crook sharpened to a cutting edge, from Dick's apelike shoulder roll and phlebitic shuffle, to his chomping, jowl-quivering monotone and his mail-chute smile.

"I look at him as a bird of prey, with that hawk-lipped way about him," Dan asserts. "Tremendous magnetism. God, he's charismatic."

"Most comedians or actors will try characters out on you from time to time to see if they work," explains Michael O'Donoghue, a former *Saturday Night Live* writer/performer. "But with Danny, they just seem to leap out of nowhere. It's utterly startling because you think he can do anything; he can just make it up, fully realized, on the spot."

Aykroyd's night gallery of alter egos is voluminous, including such difficult subjects as Elliot Ness, Orson Welles/Citizen Kane, Julia Child, Clark Gable, both Scotty and Bones from *Star Trek*, plus such regional and/or dialect characters as curt Southern state troopers, randy Midwestern rubes, proud Aberdeen Scotch guards, mincing French waiters, and snobbish British theater critics—not to mention creations like Beldar Conehead, sleazy cable-TV personality E. Buzz Miller, and his Jorge Festrunk to Steve Martin's brother Yortuk in the "Czech Brother" routines.

"I had no idea the 'Czech Brothers' would be as popular as they are," says Aykroyd. "Steve had a character called the 'Continental Suave Guy'; I saw him do him in his act one night and I really enjoyed it. I went backstage afterward and I said, 'Listen, I do this Czech architect.' . . . I'd noticed a tremendous similarity in the rhythms of Steve's character and I said, 'Let's put them both together as Czechs who wear polyester shirts and everything!' It didn't work that well with the studio audience the first time we did it on the show, but then we got so much feedback from people who watched it on TV. Phew! Really blew me away."

Just as popular as the "wild and crazy guys" are the Coneheads. "The Coneheads were originally a drawing of mine" says Aykroyd with a low chuckle. "I was watching these heads on TV one night and I thought, 'Fuck, wouldn't it be neat if they were four or five inches *higher*?' I put the whole Remulak thing together with one of the writers, Tom Davis.

"We were gonna call them pinheads," he adds soberly, "but we decided no 'cause we didn't want to offend anybody who had encephalitis."

When Aykroyd wishes to offend, he does so masterfully, as with his huckster spiels for useless appliances like the Moth-Masher or the electric blender that liquefies uncleaned fish called the Super Bass-O-Matic. It's no accident that he's adept at duplicating the machine-gun, doggerel prose of TV-commercial pitchmen, having worked as one for a cable-TV station in Toronto, CITY-TV's Channel 79.

Aykroyd's most off-putting guise is that of Irwin Mainway, a crass, oily entrepreneur with a pencil mustache who possesses all the moral fiber of a doorknob. "He's the ultimate urban businessman—the true hawker," says Aykroyd in admiration. "Have you ever been to one of those joints where they auction appliances off the street? The guy has a mike around his neck and he talks a five-dollar clock radio up to thirty-three bucks! This is how Mainway started. He was one of those barkers and most of his goods were hot. Now he's evolved into a business executive and he goes on talk shows for publicity and to push and defend his really bad, harmful products: fur coats made from near extinct animals, a kid's toy called Bag o' Glass. . . ."

Mainway recently turned up on the consumer awareness program, *On the Spot*, hosted by the aggressive Jane Face (Jane Curtin). The discussion concerned the unusual menu for his school-lunch catering service.

> FACE: "Mr. Mainway, isn't it true that on last April 18th, the school children of this city ate a hot lunch composed almost entirely of pureed insects!"
>
> MAINWAY: "Hey, come on, gimme a break. I gotta find out what dese kids like!"

The same canny respect that informs Aykroyd's Irwin Mainway illuminates his stunning Tom Snyder. The rumpled tan leisure suit is there, and the volcanic horse laughs, aimlessly waving arms, and smug, pseudo-absorbed slouch. But Aykroyd also captures the desperation of Snyder's pursed-lip cigarette puffing, and the empty-headed "By gosh" and references to "the boys" that the perpetually ill-prepared *Tomorrow* host employs to buy time.

Snyder himself is so rattled by the way Aykroyd nails him that he recently attempted to confront the caricature by inviting an NBC page on his show to try to top Danny; and when that fizzled, Tom leapt in and sought to imitate Aykroyd imitating *him* with a bumbling compulsiveness that was as pathetic as it was spellbinding.

Aykroyd's ability to mirror and then expand on any character he chooses—prominent or not—borders on the soul-snatching power of *obeah*. Thanks to Dan Aykroyd, we know things about Nixon, Carter and Snyder that they themselves could not have shown us. And poor Tom; if he wanted to retaliate (i.e., save face), what he should have done was attempt to mimic *Dan Aykroyd*. But the Funny Man of a Thousand Faces is also the Man in the Shadows. Quite simply, none of us know who the devil Dan Aykroyd is.

Born in Ottawa, Canada, and raised in Hull, Quebec ("where Montreal sends its old gangsters to cool out") twenty-six-year-old Daniel Edward Aykroyd is the son of Samuel Cuthbert Peter Hugh Aykroyd, a Canadian government official of English-Anglican descent, whose lineage traces back to a fourteenth-century constable of Wadsworth, England, and the former Lorraine Gougeon, the Norman-French daughter of a farmer who also served as a Royal Canadian Mounted Policeman.

Described by younger son Peter Jonathan, 23, as a "seasoned bureaucrat," the senior Mr. Aykroyd rose from a middle-echelon post in the policymaking Privy Council to assistant deputy minister of transport for research and development. Careerwise, Danny headed in the opposite direction from his strait-laced father, cutting a footloose swath through various fine schools in Quebec and Ontario, among them the St. Pius X Minor Preparatory Seminary for boys and Carleton University in Ottawa. Both Aykroyd boys maintained an abiding interest in comic acting, and Peter followed Danny into Toronto's improvisational theater company, Second City. Danny's big pre-*Saturday Night Live* break was the role of a "Jackie Gleason antagonist-type" janitor in a Canadian Broadcasting Company TV comedy for children called *Coming Up Rosie*.

Upon meeting Dan Aykroyd, one is impressed with his gentleness, his deference and, where his various hobbies (motorcycles, architecture, armaments, aeronautics, almost anything involving intricate machinery) and profession are concerned, an overwhelming intensity.

This intensity is best illustrated by the on-location proceedings during Aykroyd's first day of shooting with *Coming Up Rosie*. Aykroyd arose on the morning of Friday the thirteenth and dutifully reported to the *Rosie* offices at CBC-TV, despite a killer flu and a temperature of 104. The first scene called for foreign secret agents to scurry through a car wash, and Danny, wearing a black hat, did so without hesitation. When he emerged from the other end—coughing, sneezing and sopping wet—much of the hat's indelible dye had been transferred to his face, where it remained for the rest of the day.

Undaunted, the black-faced Aykroyd completed the morning's shooting without complaint and then came back for more in the afternoon, the day's chores culminating in a key rooftop chase scene in which the tireless foreigners run an adversary around a skylight.

Overzealous to the last, Aykroyd decided to ad-lib a spectacular five-foot leap over the skylight. Regrettably, he sailed short of the mark and plunged through the wired glass to a warehouse floor some twenty-five feet below, hitting two light standards on the way down and landing on his ass.

The cast and crew were horror struck, with much shrieking and hysterics all around. Rushing to the shattered skylight, the cameramen peered in to see an unhurt, twenty-two-year-old Dan Aykroyd screaming back up at them *"Hey, you guys! Did you get the shot?!"*

After flying into San Francisco for the Blues Brothers show at Winterland on New Year's Eve, I was fortunate enough to learn that Belushi and Aykroyd were also in town for the event, the two taking a break from the L.A. filming of director Steven Spielberg's work-in-progress, *1941* (in which they play a pilot and a tank commander, respectively). I take a room—along with my cohort Miami—at the Miyako Hotel where John and Danny are staying and arrange to interview Aykroyd for a separate profile. He gives his tentative consent and then . . . nothing. He successfully evades me thereafter—until I persuade Belushi to intervene on my behalf.

"He's a little hard to pin down," explains John as we sit together in his suite, "and he's very suspicious of the press, but you'll have no problems now."

Sure enough, there's a brisk knock at the door and in hastens Dan Aykroyd, dripping wet and clad only in an orange bath towel. Nonetheless, his mind is now clearly made up. He pops a beer and props his webbed feet on a room service cart, calling happily for the first question.

"Say, I hear you've been playing a mean harmonica since your early teens," I begin.

"Since I was sixteen," he nods with zest. "I jammed with Muddy Waters once, too—but that was on drums. He was fuckin' great! It was at a club called Le Hibou, which means 'the owl.'

"Incidentally, John is the Owl too," he informs with affection, "and he's also the Bear Man, and the Black Hole in Space, and the Thing, and I also like to refer to him secretly as . . . *the Black Rhino.*"

Belushi, presently engaged in a heated phone conversation, cups the receiver and roars with considerable annoyance, "Did he say I was the Black Rhino? *Don't you listen to him!*"

"I have a company now called Black Rhino Enterprises," Aykroyd beams, suddenly speaking in a clipped, businesslike fashion. "Part of it is a T-shirt marketing thing. . . . Where the Black Rhino comes from," he confides, "is that I had a dream one night that I was living way up on this cliff in Canada, overlooking this snow-strewn waste. There was this snorting rhino chained in the backyard. And I looked at it and the face started to look a lot like Belushi," he giggles. "And he was snorting hard and ripping up the backyard and I went out and tossed meat to him. I placated him, helped him, and I realized [*his eyes glaze over goofily*], '*I need this force in my life.*'"

"But doesn't someone else share the same nickname?" I ask. "As I recall Jake Bl—"

"Belushi is *also* the Black Hole in Space," he overrules, "because, you'll notice, if you ever lend him a watch or a lighter or something, it goes through him into another dimension. You ask for it back five minutes later and it's gone and there's no way you can find it. Really.

"He's like a hurricane!" Danny proclaims with a ringmaster's flourish. "He's the Black Hole in Space!"

Belushi, still on the phone, makes an ugly face that dissolves into a big, sloppy grin.

Watching the two friends go at each other, their Frick and Frack relationship also incorporates elements of Abbott and Costello, antic patrolmen Gunther Toody and Francis Muldoon of *Car 54 Where Are You?* TV fame, and a slightly stoned out Huntley and Brinkley.

Usually Belushi pretends to be blasé about Aykroyd's ribbing, but actually he revels in it. When Belushi is in an especially ornery or obsessive mood, Danny will creep along behind his corpulent comrade as they go through the

day's activities, Aykroyd making loudly whispered explanations to onlook-
ers like, "*Ssssh! The Thing is feeding!*" or, "*Behold, the Bear Man rests!*"

Belushi usually gets his licks in when Aykroyd isn't around—or when
Danny's manic meticulousness backfires. "Here's the difference between
us," John tells me later. "See, I never carry any ID, no driver's license, no
passport when I travel, nothing. I couldn't care less. He always carried this
big ID wallet, big as a purse, that he kept *chained* to his belt at all times.
When he lost it I was laughing my ass off.

"He's Mister Careful and I'm Mister Fuck It. I can't always figure him out;
but whenever I'm around him I feel safe."

Actually Aykroyd is that and more, a batch of contradictions forged into
a willful, dependable whole. But it wasn't always thus.

"My brother and I were hellions," Aykroyd says with a smile, picking at
some leftover Japanese food scattered upon the room-service cart.
"Incorrigible. All through school there were discipline problems with me particularly. I was a chatty little sort. The Fat Mouth in primary school. I've had
a solid relationship with my father for years, even though there was a lot of
corporal punishment there as a kid. Many belt whippings. We deserved it.

"You know how parental units are," he laughs. "My mother always had
friends that she wanted me to see: these prim, nice little girls and correct-
speaking guys. Eventually, I found out these people were as delinquent and
corrupt as I was. When you got down in the basement with them, they
wanted to crack open a bottle of whiskey same as you."

Young Dan Aykroyd's first memorable brush with alcohol and delinquen-
cy occurred while he was in the seminary.

"One night we blew down to Massena, New York, in the Thousand Islands
area, 'cause you could drink in New York at eighteen. But, uh, I was fourteen
at the time. We bought this vodka, went into this field, and suddenly out of
nowhere there was the ringing of shotgun shells. This farmer was running us
off his land. So we jump back into the car and go to a hamburger joint. The
fucking place filled with cops with their guns out and they grab us, take us
down to jail. My parents thought it was over for me at that point."

They weren't far wrong. Shortly thereafter the seminary superiors tired of
his "late-night vandalism, skipping mass, fucking off" and expelled him. He
completed his high-school education in a coed Catholic school in Ottawa.

"My friend, there were much better men than me there to serve the
Lord," he clucks. "We were all supposed to be little angels, little priests. But
we'd put on our polka dot mod shirts, Wildroot creme oil, Beatle boots, and
cut loose.

"In my main years in high school I wore a flattop, butch-waxed, with no hair on the sides. Then I got into the Beatle phase; went through a slight greaser phase and then finally long and unwashed—my hair *and* me."

And things got even hairier when Aykroyd reached college. "He and his friends—a gang called the Black Top Vamps—lived in old houses in Ottawa and it was just like *Animal House*," says brother Peter. "They used to have parties and they'd go into the same shopping plaza every weekend with beer cartons, order filet mignon from the meat counter and just fill the boxes up, slip them past the girl at the cash register and leave."

During this period the multifaceted Aykroyd played harp in several bands, notably Top Hat and the Downtowners.

"In its day, the group was like Dan Hicks and His Hot Licks," says Danny. "I was into jazz first, Art Blakey, Erroll Garner, Mingus and Thelonious Monk. Then I started listening to blues and stuck with that. I don't really have broad tastes for modern music and I don't like disco too much, although 'Le Freak' by Chic is nice. My tastes are narrow, see. The first record I ever bought was *Hymns of the Army, Navy and Air Force*.

"But I liked playing in the Downtowners. I had a great friend in the band who was also an acid dealer. He always had bundles of hundred-dollar bills."

Apparently Aykroyd has had many such companions.

"The guy who put my life on a different path was my friend David Benoit. I love him dearly. He's a low-class merchant seaman—by his own admission. He turned me on to music, let me smoke my first joint, introduced me to a woman I had a little thing with when I was fourteen, and awakened me to the hip scene around '67 in Ottawa, this whole underworld I never knew existed. I decided I was dropping out and I've never looked back.

"The most profound night of my life, the turning point, was the night we went out in a stolen Cadillac with this guy called Ray the Green Beret. Ray was an ex-Green Beret who'd ripped this Cadillac off in Wisconsin and driven it north. I got high that night and met George the Thief, a crazy French Canadian, and ultimately I just started to hang out with these people.

"'*I yam a teef! I yam a teef!*' That's what George used to say, and that's all he used to do. You could always obtain any amount of fenced goods through him. I still see these people and probably will associate with them for the rest of my life."

Up until his college years, Aykroyd's dad did his best to divert his sons from a life of slovenliness and iniquity. "Industry—the old man was big on that, ya know?" he tells me. "I mean, for my twelfth birthday I got an electric lawn mower to do the lawn for my father. That was my present, with a bow on it and everything. Thank you very much, Dad, thank you *very much*.

"He had me out at thirteen, working. I worked as a warehouseman, a brakeman on a railway. During college I drove a Royal Mail truck. But I'm glad I did that blue-collar stuff. My father would pull strings for me. He always knew somebody somewhere and he'd hear about these weird jobs.

"I was a dial reader on a runway load-testing unit. I almost got killed one night at Toronto International Airport when a DC-8 took off and grazed the station wagon I was riding out to the site in. Man, it was heavy.

"The best job was one I took at seventeen in the Northwest Territories surveying a road. We were up in an isolation camp. It was heavy work but you could really enjoy the territory: the crows, white wolves, bears. We used to skin and roast ground squirrels on a stick and they tasted just like chicken. A fabulous little rodent. *Sooo* tasty. Whenever we were low on Spaghetti-Os we had no choice.

"I was up there in the wilderness with Indians: Cree, Blackfoot. Jeeze, it was a great summer. But it gets tense up there. The drinking was heavy. Mounties up there don't wear uniforms 'cause it's so far north nobody's gonna check on them. And there was this one young cop up there, a real eager beaver we'd see when we'd come in and drink with the Indians and local townspeople of Fort Simpson. This young cop, he'd dance with the Indian girls and hang out, wearing a corduroy suit and cowboy boots, and then half an hour before the dance was over, he'd go back to the RCMP detachment and put on his hat, bring a fuckin' paddy wagon back and bust the drunken Indians, *everybody*. He was just the worst. You know, actors and sheriffs, for centuries, have never gotten along."

With one notable exception.

"My buddy Marc O'Hara and I, for three years we ran the best bootleg booze joint that there ever was in Canada, the Club 505 in Toronto. This was on Queen and River streets, and some of the cops we met on that beat who'd come in and ask us what we were doing we still know today as friends.

"You could drive by on the street and look in and see all these people drinking and we were just protected and covered for three years by whatever karmic umbrella.

"I'd work at Second City at night and run the bar from one a.m. on. The 505 Club was completely furnished with old Forties-style couches and plush armchairs, a barber's chair. All scavenged and scrounged. We slept in lofts, above whatever crept on the floor at night. It bordered on serious squalor at times.

"I remember I went down to the 505 once to take a shit. I sat down on the toilet and I was reading and I heard this scrabbling in the bottom of the bowl, this slushing about. I thought, 'Must be flushed water going from the back of the tank into the plumbing system,' so I continued reading. Finally I looked down into the excrement that lay there and a rat was clawing its way up the side of the bowl, its jaws just *inches* from my vital parts.

"Lorne [Michaels, executive producer and creator of *Saturday Night Live*] and I had met at the 505 one quiet night when it wasn't open. He sat in the barber's chair by the fish tank and he talked about what he hoped the show would be."

When the cast was being chosen, Michaels asked Danny to come to the auditions.

"I came down from Canada with this guy named Dan Hennesey who was working on *Coming Up Rosie* with me. We were gonna sing this song we'd written about Jimmy Hoffa for Lorne, but the audition was a real cattle call with 200 people. I spent a minute and a half in the room, saying hello to Lorne, and then a friend of mine and I took off to California. Lorne called me and said, 'Come on, ya gotta come back!' And that was it."

"It's always been my understanding," I object, "that Michaels was very skeptical as to whether he could tame you and Belushi."

"Well Lorne *wasn't* sure about John and I," Danny admits. "I met John in Second City, and we were a little cocky and thought we didn't need it [the show]. I was cutting out a good wedge in Canada and I had the bar going, which was important to me and quite prosperous. Life was comfortable."

Since that time, life for Aykroyd has remained comfortable, although he's sometimes made things uncomfortable for the higher-ups at NBC.

According to one of his writing collaborators, Aykroyd got pretty infuriated with an NBC executive in 1977 for not paying him as both an actor and a writer for his work on an *SNL* special. "Danny took it as a point of honor; he was always fighting the NBC people. So what he did—he was *angry* at them—was get nails and paint and stuff, and outside of this guy's office and door he nailed and printed stuff onto the wall, which had references to the cabala, psychic numbers and stuff. The phrases he made up were the things that some subway psycho would scrawl on a wall.

"He must have worked for hours on this thing; the place was a mess. He really terrified that whole wing of NBC. And, really, it was just Danny figuring out what would scare people the most. God, I thought it was funny. I'd like to see him do more of that kind of thing on the show. It was a monstrous practical joke."

"It was *not* a joke," Belushi later tells me. "They took $400 out of his pay-check—money he should have gotten—and didn't tell him beforehand. You don't do that with Danny. So being a really smart guy, he thought up this thing to fix 'em real good, and he wrote, 'I am the Devil, I am Beelzebub!' on the walls in red and all this very satanic stuff, just to freak them out. And it worked. He was mad at them and they deserved it.

"They couldn't understand why he would do something like that, but I could understand it. And they'll think twice," John sniggers sardonically, "before they take money out of *his* pocket again."

Another thing Belushi says he can understand is Aykroyd's unfrivolous interest in UFOs, mysticism and psychic phenomenon.

"When Danny and I drive cross-country, we always look for UFOs, and I've gone up to his dead grandpa's farmhouse with him to wait for his ghost. Danny said he had seen it before, and I believe him. We used to turn the lights off and wait. He said it started as a green glow. . . ."

"My grandparents used to have séances," says Peter Aykroyd, "and our dad passed the interest along to Danny and me. In our house it was just something that was accepted as viable. We never had séances but they were very regular at my grandparents' house when Dad was in his twenties, and my grandfather had a whole accounting on paper of his séances, who came through and what was said. He had photographs of the people who appeared in the room.

"Our father still has an interest in mysticism. He definitely rubbed it off on us, and we were always very interested."

As to the notion that his older brother is an excitable boy, Peter merely feels that Danny's sensitivity is miscomprehended.

"He's a real approachable guy in his own way, you know? And he really creates relationships quick with people because he has a way of, like, interrogating, like a cop. When you answer all the questions about yourself, you suddenly get the feeling: 'Gee, he knows me, therefore I know him.'"

The more one knows about Daniel Edward Aykroyd the more it seems there is to know. Beyond each door in his makeup is another door, slightly ajar, that opens on a room leading to still another. The complexity of the man is staggering. Yet certain constants emerge from the fabric of his web-footed personality.

"I don't want to wax poetic about it," says Michael O'Donoghue, "but Danny gives you a real solid bounce. You feel he's really there and you can trust him."

"You wonder how everybody on the *Saturday Night Live* show seems to handle the pressure," Peter Aykroyd muses, "and Danny, he seems to deal with it like it's a nine-to-five gig: 'I walk in, I write my scenes, I do my thing, I get out.' When things get bigger, as with the *1941* film, I think he can deal with it because *1941* is just another clear-cut job. He sets his own timetable.

"Now he's starting to get recognized on the street, he's going to become a personality. In the ego sense, I think he can handle it real well; no problem. I guess people don't handle stardom because of some insecurity and he's pretty damn secure."

Later in the evening I find myself sitting with Aykroyd in a quiet room on the top floor of Jefferson Starship's Airplane house in San Francisco as the New Year's Eve bash for the Blues Brothers begins to wind down. Danny is ruminating on a variety of subjects ranging from the invention of stucco paint, to the genius of car customizer Ed "Big Daddy" Roth and the flaws in the design of the NASA space shuttle, when his clever, curly-haired girl-friend, *Saturday Night Live* writer Rosie Shuster, ambles by. They speak briefly, and when Shuster departs Danny's talk turns to their relationship.

"Lorne [Michaels] and Rosie were married," he volunteers softly, "and—it's so strange—I go out with Rosie and have been for a while. We're an 'in-house' group over at *Saturday Night* and, hey, I'm a hetero, ya know? When you spend twelve, thirteen hours together at a stretch writing that show, there's a physical attraction and a magnetism sometimes.

"You know what I mean," he says, nudging me playfully, and then turns to watch Rosie bound down the stairs to the second floor. "She's a good girl," he says, a little sad. "Life is a funny deal."

I am finally beginning to feel that I understand this Man of a Thousand Faces when he dons another one, abruptly shifting the topic of conversation to, of all things, crime.

"I took a lot of crime-related courses in college," he says stiffly, as I gulp from a bottle of champagne offered by a passer-by.

"I took a course in criminology, one in correctional policy, one in deviant psychology. It was a program heading toward a career in prison classifica-tions. I worked for the penitentiary service as one of my summer jobs and wrote a thick manual—it may still be in use—on personnel placement for the solicitor general's facility in Ottawa.

"There's always gonna be crime; I mean, I *know* this. I saw the graphs for Canada over a period of ten years on the flow of prisoners and recidivists and there's no bell curve there. It's either a holding pattern or it gradates upward."

"Why is that?" I ask, still uncertain why he brought it up.

"It's simple," he says with the curt detachment of a prison warden. "It's

Robert K. Merton's sociological theory; probably the most tangible bit of knowledge I've gotten from *all* my training: the theory of 'illegitimate means.' When people from low-income groups see a TV or a car advertised they usually don't possess the legitimate means to get it. Frustrated, they have to resort to illegitimate means; so they pull a cheap job, a heist, a robbery, maybe break a pete."

"A pete?"

"Yeah, a pete, a safe."

"Hmm," I mull, beginning to wonder whether Aykroyd isn't trying out a new character on me. "Did any of this data/experience rub off on you?"

"On me? Well, I'll say this. My grandpa was a Mountie, and I have my experiences through research, among other things. I've noticed that in street crime, you have officers always forcibly restraining suspects that are being arrested. But in any situation where the criminal has a *skill*, as with a good pete man, there's a moment between the arresting officer and the skilled criminal when it's all over and he's been caught and everything relaxes. There's *no* tension any longer and they light cigarettes and share a nice smoke.

"At this level, you see, they're kindred spirits; part of the same huge business. It's an art, a *craft*, an industry like any other!

"But say," he says with a sudden smile, offering me a joint as he slips on a pair of Ray-Ban No. 5022–G15 sunglasses. "So what did you think of the way we played 'Jailhouse Rock' tonight?"

John Travolta:
Separating the Dancer
from the Dance

A generation who came of age in the late 1970s may have revered John Travolta for his physical dexterity and dance floor grace in Saturday Night Fever, Urban Cowboy and Grease. A subsequent age group must have cringed at his decision to exert himself during the mid-1980s in lame movies like Staying Alive, Two of a Kind, Perfect and The Experts.

Children who liked his second-banana style as the dad in the Look Who's Talking "talking baby" comedies of 1989 and 1990 were surely startled in their adolescence by Travolta's raw-edged talent in *Pulp Fiction, Get Shorty, Broken Arrow, Phenomenon, Michael, Face/Off, Mad City, She's So Lovely, Primary Colors* and *A Civil Action*. However, direct contact with the actor himself would tend to make one push Travolta's fluctuating standing in his profession into the background, thoughts of the peaks and valleys of box office currency replaced with more stark impressions of Travolta's tough-minded desire to excel at any risky task that drew his attention.

In conversations before the filming of *Urban Cowboy* in 1979, Travolta mentioned how he'd discovered skiing while shooting *Saturday Night Fever,* immediately advancing in the sport when the stunt man joined a group of the cast members on their second trip to Mammoth Mountain in California's eastern Sierras.

"I was on the expert slope and I just fell the whole way down," he explained, "and I was so angry at the stunt man for taking me up there— but I still ended up liking it. I'm physically able and agile, so I, with the proper instruction, can adapt pretty well."

In September of '79, this writer had a brief brush with Travolta's penchant for jeopardy, having quietly slipped onto the closed set for *Urban Cowboy,* dressed in boots, jeans and faded Western shirt similar to those worn by dozens of extras. Wandering, unquestioned, through the vast Gilley's saloon off dusty Spencer Highway in Pasadena, Texas, I watched beside the camera crew for several days as Travolta worked through both his intricate dance sequences and his mechanical bull-riding sessions.

In the evenings after each day's shooting, the sleek black vinyl hydraulic bull for the film was removed, and the two older, uglier, carpet-covered bulls for regular patrons were repositioned. The whiskey-fed tension among Gilley's release-starved working class clientele was considerable, and found its focus in frequent bar fights, in the testy undulations on its dance floor, and in the ritual that combined the two: riding the bulls.

One night I rashly made the mistake of pulling on the requisite rawhide riding glove and entering Gilley's bleacher-encircled indoor arena to twice try my luck astride the bull. The first time I approached the bull's burly operator, I handed him my ticket without comment, and managed to stay on the machine for some 90 seconds of its furiously lurching, inflexible punishment. The second time, the ride was half the duration of my first, and downright brutal. The operator revved the bull to buck with such force that his rider was tossed straight up above the contraption like a ragdoll, right side landing hard against the raised steel hand grip at the pommel of the saddle. The now-whirling contraption then flung its rider out past the surrounding mattresses and into the folding chairs before the bleachers. Nine months later, my right ribs were still tender and sore.

While it's unlikely Travolta was ever treated similarly, one had some call to admire the craft the New Jersey cowpoke had brought to his role.

"I trained three weeks to a month on that darn thing," Travolta later consoled with a laugh. "At the beginning of the movie the bull is slower because people are learning—it goes from speeds of 1 to 12—but at the end of the movie we're riding it at 12; and it was exciting 'cause the people who hung out there said I had ridden it the best of anybody when they were watching the scenes being filmed. I rode it at *maximum* speed for the rodeo contest at the end of the movie—you bet I did," he added solemnly. "It was wild, but it had to be."

Another example of Travolta's self-willed tenacity was the three weeks the serenely stubborn actor spent in intensive training at the American Airlines School in Texas in the early 1980s enroute to graduating from mere credentials for flying a single-engine plane to acquiring a private jet pilot's rating from the Federal Aviation Administration. "Flying is my major activity outside my profession," he explained at the time.

Such absorption came in handy in 1992 as Travolta was guiding his Gulfstream Two executive jet from Florida to Maine at 39,000 feet on Thanksgiving eve, his eight passengers including wife Kelly Preston (wed on September 3, 1991) and their son Jett (born April 13, 1992). While passing over Washington, D.C., at a speed of 600 miles per hour, the plane suddenly lost all electrical power. Travolta sent a "Mayday" message that reportedly precipitated the temporary closing of the runways of the Dulles, National, and Baltimore-Washington airports as he groped with flight controllers' assistance to aim his plane toward an emergency landing at the nearest possible facility. He proved to be an excellent flyer undersuch stress, staying calm throughout the dire crisis, which climaxed when landing with all four of the craft's tires exploding on impact.

The harrowing incident recalled something Travolta confided in '79 regarding the strain of preparing for *Urban Cowboy*: "There was a certain hazard or threat, aside from the entertainment value of it, that I could see in these things. It's a movie, but it's real. That's the quality of the experience I always hope to touch."

THE INTERVIEW

K EEP YOUR DISTANCE FROM THE STAR—*or face being fired immedi-ately.* This is the stern ruling that has come down to the rank-and-file extras. Not surprisingly, there is something sinister and smoldering in the manner of many of the local, on-set "expendables," all of them dressed in tight, dirty jeans—the pale young women, slump-shouldered and sullen in frayed halter tops, their sour-faced men stalking back and forth in washed-out Western shirts. Standing stiffly in their midst is John Travolta, his one-way eyes as piercing as a raven's, wearing a sleek, black cowpoke get-up accented by the splash of scarlet in his two-tone satin shirt.

There's a movie being made here called *Urban Cowboy*, based on a 1978 *Esquire* article by Texas-born writer Aaron Latham. It's a contemporary, boomtown Western, a farmboy-meets-girl romantic fracas that ultimately figures around the mechanical bull sitting defiantly in one corner of Gilley's, the world's largest honky-tonk, a three-and-a-half-acre, prime-for-brawling saloon nestled in the dingy heart of Pasadena, Texas. The bull, a rock-hard hunk of bucking and swiveling hydraulic might, was devised to toughen the timing of rodeo bull riders, but country singer Mickey Gilley and partner Sherwood Cryer installed this one to cool off the club's shit-kicking clientele—mostly drugstore cowboys who labor by day at nearby petrochemical plants.

This afternoon's shooting schedule concerns the film's climactic bull-riding contest, wherein Bud Davis (Travolta) challenges archrival Wes Hightower (Scott Glenn), a sinewy ex-con with "real cowboy" rodeo credentials, who has diverted the attentions of Bud's rambunctious bride, Sissy (Debra Winger).

The club's noisy air-conditioning system has been shut off to avoid interfering with the sound technicians, and the sweltering environs have been suffused with musty artificial smoke. To make matters worse, today's ration of beer is Gilley's own, not the far superior, long-necked Lone Star the extras had previously been served—an indiscretion greeted with grunts of "What's this, cow piss?" It is all the camera crew can do to hold back the Gilley's regulars until the day's shooting is in the can. Paramount is struggling to place a frame around a frame, so to speak, and the filmmakers can't help editing these people's lives in the process; and they, in turn, can't help openly resenting it. (In order to keep the club open during Paramount's four-month-long cinematic bender, the management of Gilley's has insisted the movie folk clear out every night no later than seven.)

There's an undeniably spooky aura about the way Travolta looms on the sidelines of the "bull ring," somehow shutting out the environs, even angry glares surging down from the bleachers created around this strange arena. Nevertheless, there is an informal posse among the Pasadena-area talent, who occasionally crack clumsy jokes about the "Texas ways" Travolta has yet to assimilate. When one cocky local fella summons up the courage, he blurts out that he's heard Travolta, who is reported to be hog-wild about aviation, is actually scared shitless of flyin'! No one offers Travolta a hearty Texas backslap to diffuse the gag. He smiles and gamely murmurs, "Lies, lies." But his timing is off, and the uneasy instant is swallowed up in the silence.

"The first night I went down to Gilley's with Travolta, we slipped in a side door to show John exactly what it looked like," director James Bridges later tells me. "Before we could stop him, he was on the dance floor. He had a beard then, and nobody noticed him. But the minute we were in the 'hot' area around the bull, people began to recognize him. There were catcalls, the redneck honky-tonkers baiting him while their girls screamed with excitement. A little too much macho tension there.

"I was in there one night when there were fifteen fights," Bridges continues. "I was there one night when somebody's eye was gouged out. And I was there when Steve Strange [who runs the bull machine] threw a guy on the bull. He said to me, '*Watch.*' And he took the controls and threw him up in the air. The guy's back fell against the plastic base of the bull and he split his head open. There was blood everywhere: Everybody thought he was dead. They got him up after about fifteen minutes. Steve walked over, laughing, poured beer on the base to wash off the blood, then looked around and said, '*Next.*'"

When I mention all of this to Travolta afterward, he falls silent for a moment, stares off into space, then looks me squarely in the eyes.

"The people who hung out there were ready for a fight, definitely." Travolta agrees. "But I liked it 'cause I got a real charge out of that *danger.*"

"You have got to play the cowboy, you know: it has certified all the major stars," says James Bridges matter-of-factly. "McQueen, Newman, Brando—they all had to play that American hero to solidify their careers forever."

The cowboy brand placed on Travolta in *Urban Cowboy* seems more matinee idol than hard-bitten buckaroo. From the moment he clambers onscreen, all the way through to the staccato punch-out that precedes the film's happy ending, *Urban Cowboy*'s photography evinces a near-adoration of him. Hell, there's one upward pan—a slow, sensual boots-to-cheek-bones assessment of the star—that lies somewhere between reverence and violation.

"It was an absolutely conscious approach," explains Bridges. "When you're dealing with a star like John Travolta, there is a commodity to be captured that does not have anything to do with the role he's playing. And because of his incredible celebrity, his visual image does have more impact than his acting. I guess you could say it was an enormous asset I had to conquer.

"He's become one of my best friends," Bridges adds. "I think that incredible success and incredible attacks on him have made him a more interesting person. He's bright, vulnerable and tough; he's a contradiction. He reminds me so much of Monty Cliff."

Bridges says that Travolta "doesn't believe in indulgence or method acting. He is a total professional who believes in form and structure. His work is clean.

"That toes-to-face shot, where you see him from the bottom up in Gilley's, John suggested that whole shot," says Bridges. "I was setting up a different sequence, and he said, 'Let's try one of these.' It's a shameless movie-star moment."

Truly, there is a different John Travolta making movies these days than the one who soared in *Saturday Night Fever*. He has developed the instincts to exploit the charisma that moved New Yorker film critic Pauline Kael to dub him "an original presence." Professionally, he has become as insulated as a working actor can possibly be, and after *Urban Cowboy*, he hopes to control his career even further through his own production company. As for the mystery surrounding his personal life, it can be no accident that after years of extraordinary press coverage, we've learned precious little about *who he is*.

And so, when Travolta, 26, ambles into Joe Allen's in Los Angeles for an informal lunch, it isn't surprising that he exudes no particular panache beyond a boyish likability. He arrives alone, as he will for subsequent meetings, driving himself to each rendezvous in his Mercedes. He shakes my hand, plops into a chair opposite mine and puzzles over the menu, trying to decide whether he should eat something nourishing or go straight for brownie cake topped with whipped cream. (He eventually opts for the latter.)

Relaxed in faded jeans and matching jacket, well-worn boots and a snug blue T-shirt, he wryly unfurls his long arms and offers himself for inspection. "Beer," he explains, playfully poking the bulge above his belt.

After a few minutes of unfocused banter, I ask him how he would describe himself on the phone to someone who had never seen him before.

"That would depend on the day," he answers.

"So, what if somebody called today?"

"I'll think about that," he demurs, scratching at his three-day-old beard, "and maybe before the end of the interview I'll give you a better-spoken answer than I can think of right now."

For the remainder of lunch we debate the virtues of the West Coast (he recently purchased a home in Studio City and owns a ranch in Santa Barbara) versus the East (he grew up in Englewood, New Jersey). After our meal, we ride over to the nearby offices of Front Line Management, the headquarters of Irving Azoff, who produced *Urban Cowboy* with Bob Evans. The place is deserted, and as the copper sun creeps down behind the Hollywood Hills, we sprawl out on the overstuffed couches in Azoff's comfortable inner sanctum.

"You've had enough time to consider my question about your self-image," I remind him. "Now I'm calling you on it."

"Well," he says timorously. "I'm a person who likes to be inspired and likes to inspire; I like to exchange that flow. And I'm unsettled, anxious, passionate, compassionate, hungry, excited, disappointed. I go through the gamut of emotions a lot: I trust very easily and mistrust very easily. I'm clear, confused, analytical, and add another one—cautious.

"I guess I put a lot effort into wanting people to admire me, like me, love me," he asserts. "But I don't want the constant battle of trying to make it happen. If I could just have more confidence about how *I* feel about a subject. I'll hold on strongly to what I believe, and then someone comes along and I want to understand him and duplicate him so much that suddenly I let his viewpoint really affect me. It's the damnedest thing, because I don't like myself when I do that.

"I really have to work at getting new goals, because pretty much everything is attainable at this point." He absently rubs a shine into a fancy silver and gold belt buckle commemorating his role in *Urban Cowboy*. "Like feeling proud of myself: I really cherish the days I have that kind of feeling. It's so foreign to me. I'm an emotional person who tries to intellectualize my feelings. Often, people are so success-oriented that they skip that step of acknowledging the success they've obtained. And then they go downhill again and have *never* acknowledged their success."

"*Saturday Night Fever* turned you into a cultural icon. What was your reaction to the impact of the film?"

"I think with *Fever*, people were evaluating my impact more than they were my acting. As for *Moment by Moment*, God, you would have thought we had committed murder or something! It was, like, *serious trouble*.

"And the weird thing," he continues with a sigh, "was that everything in my life up to that point, well, I don't know of a career that had gone more smoothly and successfully than mine. *Welcome Back, Kotter, Carrie, The Boy in the Plastic Bubble* [a made-for-TV movie], *Saturday Night Fever* and *Grease*—they were five major strokes that were 100 percent all right. Unfortunately, at the very peak, when the lights were on full and everybody was waiting—*Moment by Moment*. Boom. Failure.

"Then I read the script for *Urban Cowboy*, and I wanted to check out Gilley's and the bull. It seemed like something new to me, with a rough element that made it exciting. The bull riding, the dancing, the dangerous atmosphere—it had all the right elements. It was a one-shot project and I made my own decision, took my *own* risk."

"Both *Cowboy* and *Fever* are movies whose central theme is that of a young person's rites of passage," I say. "The success anyone has with making that transition to adulthood determines the success of everything else he or she ever does."

"You know," he says softly, fidgeting, "if I can have a conversation with someone who won't judge what I have to say, he has me as a friend. Honestly, I don't judge other people. But then, there are very few people who I feel vice versa with, who I can say anything to that's in my heart."

He leans back, spent, his arms limp in his lap. But his eyes dart wildly around the room, as if seeking a safe place. "I keep on thinking there's gonna be that effortless day when everything is in sync, when it's much easier to accept the lows with the highs and there's no longer this endless search for harmony."

The baby in a six-child household, John is the son of Sam "Dusty" Travolta, the former coowner of a Firestone tire outlet in Hillsdale, New Jersey. His mother, Helen, an actress, director and acting coach, died of cancer in 1978.

"He was always very shy. I'm the same way," says John's father, a kindly, reticent man. "He was very, very curious. He wanted to know the answer to everything, like, 'How far up is the sky?' and 'Why can't you make me an airplane that can fly?'

"He loved flight and airplanes, involving himself in anything connected with them," Dusty continues. (John now pilots his own twin-engine Cessna 414.) "But he was also a good dancer, and he played basketball at the CYO. He could have been a helluva football player, too. He was an excellent mimic. He would take one of my cigars, make believe he was smoking it and do a pretty good imitation of me."

As for John's attraction to show business, his father recalls that "as a kid, he saw a production of *Gypsy* and loved it, so he bought the soundtrack to the

Broadway show. He used to go down to the cellar and play it all day, memorizing every part. My wife had trunks and trunks of old costumes down there, and he'd use them to rehearse all the parts—the men's parts *and* the women's parts, everyone from the chorus dancers to the newsboys. Then, when he was ready, he would invite my wife and me down to see his little show. But he would *never* let the kids see this. His brothers and sisters teased him a lot.

"See, Johnny was always real skinny, and his older brother Joey gave him a nickname—'the Bone.' I'd come home from work and Joey, who was always cracking jokes anyway, would say to me in front of Johnny, 'Hey, dad, what's left of a chicken after all the meat is gone?' And I'd laugh and say, 'Why, the bone.' Johnny would get very upset and hurt, thinking that Joey *and* I were making fun of him."

Rumors have been circulating for some time that John is feuding with Joey, a moderately successful actor and singer whose style and mannerisms resemble John's.

"It's not true," Dusty counters, "When Joey got married recently, John paid the whole family's way out to New York for the wedding and put us up in hotels. Johnny would go all-out for any member of the family, and vice versa."

"I generally get a positive feeling from my family," says Travolta when I ask him about how they've reacted to his elevated status. "But I'm too smart not to know that it affects them in a negative way, too. I've been so busy I haven't really talked with them to find out—probably because I don't want to.

"Joey came into the business after I was established, and I think he's gotten out of it more or less what he expected to, and that was to make a living at it and be recognized somewhat, and I think he's attained that. I don't know if he's shooting for what I have."

Travolta was about twelve when he went public with his acting ambitions, sleep-walking through school so he could concentrate on the Actors Studio workshops held in Englewood. He eventually landed a role in a Studio production of *Who'll Save the Plowboy?*, went on to appear in summer-stock productions of *Gypsy* and *Bye Bye Birdie*, then decided to quit school and pursue his passion full time in the Big Apple.

"My father didn't want me to quit," says Travolta. "My mother said to him, 'He's sixteen and should be able to make his own choice.' So there was a deal that I could be out for one year." He never went back.

Travolta soon met up with manager Bob LeMond, who placed him in a series of upscale commercials; he did about forty, including spots for Honda, Hagar slacks and Mutual of New York. He got a supporting role with a touring company of *Grease*, a singing-dancing snippet in *Over Here* and a bit part in the 1975 horror film *The Devil's Rain*. Just a few months later, Travolta tested for, and won, the part of Vinnie Barbarino in a new TV comedy series, starring Gabe Kaplan and Marcia Strassman, called *Welcome Back, Kotter*.

"We didn't ever miss a *Kotter* episode," says Mr. Travolta. "My wife used to get so mad because people would ask if John was the Vinnie Barbarino character—meaning, was he a dumb kid? I wouldn't say he was a brain, but he was no *dope*, either."

"My mother was outwardly emotional," says John, "and I was the kind of kid who liked to play on people's emotions, so in order to get my way, I'd threaten her with frightening things, like, if I didn't get to go to Chicago in an airplane to visit my sister, I would jump out the window. Seeing her react strongly was satisfying to me as a kid. I'll give you one more example that has a little more bite to it. I said to my mother when I was six years old that if she didn't cook me chocolate pudding, I'd cut off my weenie—and she made the pudding, fortunately."

Helen Travolta developed her own strategy for dealing with her conniving offspring. Mindful that young John was awestruck by James Cagney ("the *only* one outside my family who was a main source of inspiration"), she would pretend to telephone Cagney, saying to John, "Jim here wants you to do as you're told!"

"Okay!" Travolta recalls replying in abject terror. "Does he, does he *like* me?

"I was, of course, afraid to get on the phone," John assures me. "I don't know whether it was because I'd be afraid it wasn't true, or whether I'd be too damned inhibited to talk to him."

"Ah yes, it's a sweet story, isn't it?" says snowy-haired James Cagney with a rumbling chuckle. "She encouraged him by using me as a symbol and she did that with both his training at home and his work as a young actor."

Learning several months ago that Cagney was at his Beverly Hills residence, Travolta contacted Marge Zimmermann, Cagney's longtime friend and aide, who invited him to meet his hero at Cagney's St. Patrick's Day party. Rubbing shoulders with Pat O'Brien and a host of other old-timers, Travolta (who's half-Irish) blended in well with the ballyhoo and blarney.

"I did a dance for him," Travolta says, blushing. "As a matter of fact, I did the dance from *Urban Cowboy*, a little hoedown that resembles an Irish jig of some sort."

John wound up spending the night there, and repaid the hospitality by inviting Cagney, his wife, Frances, and Marge Zimmermann up to his ranch for a long weekend.

"We did a lot of walking, talking about my past and his past, his viewpoint on acting and mine, and watching movies, his and mine," says Travolta. "Basically, *being* with him was what I always wanted to do; I just wanted to know him. His movies were mainly city-type movies, but I found that his heart is really in the country. He showed me a walk he did in *Love Me or Leave Me*, in which he played a gimp, and I was dying to know how he did that walk up the wall in *Yankee Doodle Dandy*."

"To me," says Cagney, "*Saturday Night Fever* was just another film—but John's acting is always very fine. Impressive. I saw the *Cowboy* thing too, and he's as straight as can be in it, a very convincing job. When I was visiting him, he was very self-controlled, you know. That seems to be his way. There's no furor to the boy, no fanfare. He seems very direct and even-tempered all the time—and good to talk to, because he's got an excellent mind. But in the time we spent together, there was no great display of affection by him."

With at least one exception.

"In the mornings up in Santa Barbara," Marge confides, "John would always ask me, so timidly—he's so like a little kid that you have to remind yourself he's not—'Can we wake up Jamesy now?' I'd go into the guest bedroom, wake Mr. Cagney, and then John would go in and lie on the bed next to him and shyly talk and try to make him laugh with all these cute remarks."

"I was in my *glory*," Travolta says, reflecting on the experience. "Ironically enough, we're maybe the only men in history who have been in a dramatic role that we also sang and danced in. Him with *Yankee* and me with *Fever* and *Grease*."

Notwithstanding its inaccuracy, when I repeat the remark to Cagney and outline the extent to which he was a direct role model, rather than a mere symbol, for his adoring fan, he is taken aback.

"Oh?" he exclaims. "I didn't have any idea John felt that way about me. And, er, I guess I *was* able to act, dance and sing—although my singing was always a little questionable. I had to be able to do the three without any serious trouble, because that was my bread and butter."

"John, he's got plenty to learn," Cagney quietly concludes, "but he will. And *then* he'll use it correctly. When I saw *Cowboy*, I said, 'The kid's got it all.'"

It wasn't always thus. In 1974, when Travolta arrived in Durango, Mexico, to do *The Devil's Rain*, he was, in his own words, "so depressed I just felt like nothing could work right." He had been in analysis for about nine months and was disappointed in himself for "choosing negative people to be around. I just wanted to be more consistent with feeling good; I didn't want it to be such a darn roller coaster."

In Durango, he met actress Joan Prather, now in the cast of the popular ABC-TV sitcom *Eight Is Enough*.

"He was in need of friends," Prather recalls. "He was depressed, as was I, and we were the only two young people there, really. It was a very lonely time for him. The friends he had were using him as a door wipe, to put it bluntly. We were together for three months, but I wouldn't call it dating. We were just the very best of friends. I'm very stable, and I could see that he also wanted to be that way. I had taken all my [Scientology] materials and books down to Durango with me, because I thought I'd have a lot of free time.

"One day Johnny got very ill with the flu. In Scientology, we do a thing called a 'touch assist,' which makes you get better much faster. It's not magic. If you have a broken bone, it'll heal in two weeks instead of six. So I was giving him this assist, and in the middle of it, he looked at me and said, 'This is the first time anybody's ever really helped me without wanting anything back for it.' I started showing him my [Scientology] books, and he just couldn't read enough of them.

"I was really supposed to be in *Saturday Night Fever*," Prather adds, "but it didn't happen. You see, the story line of the film was *our* story as friends."

At this point, it should be noted that after five years as a Scientologist, Travolta is "CLEAR," a term designating that, in the eyes of the highly controversial Church of Scientology, John is in "a state of supra-human awareness and ability." "Cleansed of unwanted feelings and mental images" is how Travolta puts it, adding that the organization's use of the word *church* is "figurative."

"Basically," John explains, "you go into it because you want to handle some problems. It has no barriers on what it is."

But there are some barriers in Scientology: for instance, against journalists and government agencies that inquire into its instructional procedures, business administration and policy-making structures, especially those of the self-descriptive Guardian Office—one of the organization's twenty-one departments.*

---

*According to a Pulitzer Prize-winning series of articles by Bette Orsini and Charles Stafford of the *St. Petersburg Times*, a 1965 policy issued by founder Lafayette Ronald Hubbard designates as "fair game" anyone who "actively seeks to suppress or damage Scientology or a Scientologist by suppressive acts." (Federal investigators obtained documents showing that the church has an enemies list that included Edward Kennedy and Jackie Onassis.) The penalty: "May be deprived of property or injured by any means by any Scientologist without discipline of the Scientologist. May be tricked, sued or lied to or destroyed." Hubbard revised this directive in 1968: "The practice of declaring people fair game will cease. Fair game may not appear on any Ethics Order. It causes bad public relations. This P/L [policy letter] does not cancel any policy on the treatment or handling of an SP [suppressive person]."

The church maintains that it has been subjected to "thirty years of documented government harassment," and that Dianetics, its complex and costly approach to mental health, is quite simply "a therapeutic philosophy and practice which enables a person to think for himself and enjoy a more creative life." All this press-release prose aside, the IRS, FBI and Justice Department are investigating the church's claim to tax-exempt status and an array of alleged dirty tricks, including break-ins and character assassinations, much of it emanating from the church's branch in Clearwater, Florida—a center Travolta visits for advanced courses. [In 1993, the Internal Revenue Service granted the church tax-exempt status; in February, 1998, *The New York Times* reported that "Church staff members remain under criminal investigation in connection with the death of a Scientologist at a church facility in Clearwater, Fla. in 1995."]

At present, nine members of the church have been sentenced to jail for such crimes as conspiring to steal government documents, theft of government documents and conspiring to obstruct justice. (The convictions were appealed.)

"Why," I ask Travolta, "is Scientology such a controversial creed?"

"The only thing I can say," he replies, "is that anything powerful usually does create an effect or conflict in some way."

"Not because of anything specific to the nature or operating methods of the church?"

"I don't think so. I don't think so."

"How about, say, the way the church and members of its hierarchy conducted themselves after they moved to Clearwater, under the pseudonym of the United Churches of Florida?"

"No," he says, his voice dropping to a whisper. "I don't know much about that."

Prather, who has done a television commercial for Scientology, dismisses the charges as a "put up" orchestrated by the FBI and the city fathers of Clearwater.

After speaking with dozens of people who have known or worked with Travolta over the years, two virtually unanimous outlooks emerge: (1) everyone is charmed by his kindness, cherishes the time they've spent together and longs to be close to him: (2) few of these people feel they truly are, and it nags at them.

What those nearest to him seem to value most is his unique sense of humor.

"He's a terminally silly person and nobody ever knows it," Marcia Strassman maintains. "I think the thing he used to love about *Kotter* was that it was one place where he could play. He'd walk onto the set and it was like he was home, because we didn't think of him as a superstar. So he and Gabe used to do these two kids. Gabe was Jeffy and Johnny was Billy. The two of them could go back, like, twenty years. They would chase each other all over the studio. It was just hysterical."

Strassman also recalls getting a "touch assist" from Travolta one day on the *Kotter* set: "I was in the dressing room, I had a headache and John came in and said, 'What's the matter?' I told him and he went, 'Wait a minute, I'll give you a touch assist.' And I went, 'I beg your pardon?'

"What a touch assist is, is they touch your knee, your arm, all over, and what it's supposed to do is put your mind on what they're touching and you forget your headache. He finished and said, 'Well, do you feel any better?'

"I said, '*No!* You've been touching my knee for an hour and a half now and it's been real annoying—and I *still* have my headache!'"

"He has a whole comedic side to him that no one ever sees," Joan Prather reaffirms. "When you talk about the joy of entertaining, he was like that. Like a little kid. He used to do a great imitation of Elvis. We'd be waiting outside the church, and he would do 'Hound Dog'—any of Elvis' songs. And he'd have it down so perfectly! You couldn't stop laughing! He really loved to have a good time, or he *can*, or, I mean, he used to, anyway."

You know, John had two deaths in the time we were doing *Kotter*," says Strassman. "And those were the only two times I've seen Johnny upset. He'd just get real quiet, very quiet. I mean, if you know him really well, his face is an open book."

Travolta met Diana Hyland in 1976, when she was cast as his mother in *The Boy in the Plastic Bubble*. The blond, effervescent Hyland was forty years old and terminally ill with cancer. Travolta was twenty-two. They had been together for approximately one year when she died. Travolta has said that if she had lived, they would have gotten married. Before she died, he promised Diana he would remain close to her now six-year-old son, Zachary, and he has.

The following year, Travolta's mother died after a long bout with cancer.

"I had a real dichotomy in which I had great success and at the same time great sorrow and tragedy," Travolta says, shaking his head in disbelief. "A lot of people got frustrated when my grief and tragedy were publicized. They were saying, 'Because you're famous, suddenly your loss is more important than our loss.'

"My mother was really compassionate and helpful when Diana passed away. She had a big understanding in that area. I think that a lot of people, by the time they get in their sixties, have really experienced a lot of death."

"She would have killed for him," states Strassman, who came to know Helen Travolta well during the four-year run of *Kotter*. "And if you love someone that much, it's always someone you have problems with, you know, because she wanted him to be a success so much. I'm sure that was a problem for him for a long time, but he adored her. And when *Saturday Night Fever* happened, it was like Helen took a deep breath and said, 'Okay, I can die happy. I've seen him get what he deserves.'

"When his mom died, everything just sort of sagged," she adds. "He could finally admit he was tired and just say, 'I can't.' It's very hard for Johnny to say 'I can't' about anything."

As a result, despite months of preparation that included French and etiquette lessons, he withdrew from his next scheduled film, *American Gigolo*.

"I was in a pretty bad state of mind," Travolta says. "I was really feeling the loss of my mom. Plus, *Moment by Moment* had just been released and had created a negative storm. I really wasn't emotionally fit to do any movie."

One might have expected Travolta to have been upset when his father remarried six months after Helen's death ("There was some initial friction from all the kids," says Dusty), but his public reaction was a selfless one: "I just absolutely want him to be happy."

The last time I encounter John Travolta, there is a timid knock on the door of my suite at the Santa Barbara Inn, an elegant, oceanfront hotel-and-villa complex. The door swings wide and there he stands, alone, in his familiar boots and Western jeans, the beaming *Cowboy* buckle peeking out from under his unbuttoned brown suede sport jacket. "Until I get a new character to play with," he explains, "I usually hold onto the last one, almost like schizophrenia."

The jacket and a thin suede tie are concessions to the management should we decide to eat in the stuffy downstairs dining room. But we immediately agree that room service is the preferable option and order a third of the main courses on the sizable menu, in addition to a surfeit of Mexican appetizers and a generous supply of beer.

The staff, alerted to the presence of a prominent visitor, delivers the copious order with comical swiftness. We settle down to the motley banquet, spread out on a great oval table next to a flickering fireplace. The setting is a festive one, but for some reason Travolta is intense and grows increasingly contemplative.

There is a strange wistfulness about this young man who appears to be immune to the effects of fame. He speaks with great bemusement about his

career advisers' suggestion that "a person in your position" should not purchase a modest home in unglamourous Studio City (he did anyway). And
he cannot understand, after having perused some 300 scripts over the last
year, why he is unable to find a single property with which he feels comfortable. Throughout our talk, there is sadness in his voice and flashes of
fear in his eyes.

Travolta confesses he is extremely apprehensive about the reception to
Urban Cowboy, but he seems more intent on discussing Cagney.

"Sounds like you've made a friend," I say as I drain a bottle of Dos Equis.

"You bet I did," he says. "And I'm gonna spend as much time with him
as I can, because I think he enjoys being with me and I'm proud to be with
him."

I am pondering the profound affection Travolta has for Cagney when,
recalling John's recent personal losses, I suddenly see their relationship in a
morbid light.

"Where," I ask, "do you think people go when they die?"

He stops eating and leans forward, framing his face with his palms.

"I think—I hope—they go on to another body," he murmurs. "I have a
feeling of having done this before; I've been an actor before. I don't know
where or when. I know I have a very strong feeling for aviation and had
something to do with it before. It seems too familiar, this business and aviation; my affinity for it was at too young an age, and too strong."

"Awhile back," I say, "you told me you enjoyed certain kinds of danger.
It's been said that trying to love may be one of life's greatest dangers. What
do you think love is?"

After a long pause, he says, "To me, when it's felt the rightest, it's just
wanting the other person to *survive*, wanting them to do well, endlessly.
Maybe it has something to do with selflessness—but I don't mean that it
ever comes before yourself. You have to have that feeling toward yourself,
too.

"The thing is," he implores, "they always *do* survive. Meaning that I
believe they go on. I don't believe a spirit is capable of dying. [*Firmly,
almost to himself*] It's not *capable* of dying. What I think is the most frustrating part is that they're not here with you in this lifetime anymore, so you
can still have the love toward them, hoping whatever they choose and whatever they do in their future, that you're still giving them that love—and
they're getting it. There's, like, a dance of the spirit that we don't see.

"It's the only thing that saves me from total disillusionment in life," he
says, gripping the table. "It's the only thing that made me want to keep

going, because if I didn't believe that, I don't know how much I could deal with the setup in this business, this life. I just don't know. . . ."

"The idea that your loved ones still exist. . . ." I muse. "Do you ever say things, now, to your mom or Diana?"

"Yes," he says with a fragile smile. "I will speak things to them. But what I end up doing is dreaming about them all the time. A night never goes by when there isn't one of them in some part of a dream.

"It's interesting," he continues, self-absorbed, as the fire's glow fills his smooth face and glints off his silver buckle. "They're always very much alive in those dreams, like their deaths never happened, and there's a great satisfaction, because I *believe* those dreams when I'm in them. It's almost too incredible. Like last night, I had a dream about my mother. We were in Chicago, and my sister Margaret and I were in the back of a car talking and having a great time and *she* was there—there was no doubt about it. It's the only time when they can live again in full life . . . but it's so hard.

"When I wake up, it's always such a disappointment, almost like it's *all* been reversed." He looks into the fire, his eyes welling up. "It's as if my realities are dreams and my deepest dreams aren't yet realities."

Goldie Hawn:
Private Goldie

"T*he toughest time in my career? Well, I wrote a poem about it," said Goldie Hawn in the winter of 1981, as she sat crosslegged on the bed in her home in the Pacific Palisades. Hopping up, she went to a nearby desk, rifling through its drawers until she found her personal journal from the mid-'70s period in question.*

"I was feeling so frustrated back then," she said, plopping herself back on the bed, "with no work, and nothing to focus on. So here's my poem; I'll read the last few lines:

Please take all these fragments
And give them a life
Prepare me a canvas
To paint with my knife
Make it all fit
Into one whole creation
And give some meaning
To my consternation.

"I suffered for too long," she moaned, "but four months later my consternation unraveled." The reason was a phone call from director Colin Higgins, who offered her the lead opposite Chevy Chase in a property she'd once tried to option called *Killing Lydia*. The film was now titled *Foul Play*, and it restarted a career that had been sliding downhill since she appeared in an ill-conceived mess in 1976 called *The Duchess and the Dirtwater Fox*.

At the moment, however, Hawn was the foremost female box office star in the nation on the strength of her performance as *Private Benjamin*. The film not only went on to become a huge international success, but spawned a spinoff 1981–83 CBS-TV series (that featured actress Lorna Patterson and the film's original commanding officer, Eileen Brennan).

Most significantly, *Private Benjamin* got Goldie Hawn nominated for an Oscar, ensuring her status as one of the most in-demand actresses of the next two decades. Ultimately it landed her starring roles in *Seems like Old Times* (1980), *Best Friends* (1982), *Swing Shift* and *Protocol* (both 1984), *Wildcats* (1986), *Overboard* (1987), *Bird on a Wire* and *My Blue Heaven* (both 1990), *Deceived* (1991), *Crisscross, Housesitter*, and *Death Becomes Her* (all 1992), and her acclaimed comedic triumvirate with Bette Midler and Diane Keaton in *The First Wives Club*, as well as *Everybody Says I Love You* (both 1996).

Yet Hawn was struggling with a more disconcerting predicament in 1981 than her periodic status as a job-seeker. Repairing her world after a second failed marriage, the 36–year-old actress was also assessing her long-range romantic prospects as a single mother. Unaccustomed to dating, uncertain anyone would want to take on the burden of keeping company with a prominent personality who had two small kids in tow, she was feeling oddly marooned by the high-powered circumstances *Private Benjamin* had created for her.

At the time Hawn was unaware that within the year she would fall in love with actor Kurt Russell, and that she and her son and daughter would move in with him to create a new family, which endures to this day. (Hawn and Russell also have another pre-teen child, Wyatt.)

Thus, the point at which this profile was reported was actually epitomized by the other poem Hawn shared at the close of the interview, read by Goldie in the tiny interlude between the time she fed her kids dinner and then readied them for bed. Standing in their empty playroom, she opened her journal and recited:

The lines upon my face
Are happening with grace
It's just the sags I find
Disturb my piece of mind.

Just then her daughter Kate bounded in, dressed in her pajamas and carrying a finished portrait of her mother, her parent's blond hair and big eyes preserved in bright finger-paint circles of yellow and blue.

"Mommie, I'm making pretty pictures for you!" Kate squealed.

"Yes you are," Hawn answered softly, "the ones that matter most."

THE INTERVIEW

"I WANTED TO GO FOR THE *THROAT*," says Goldie Hawn with a lusty giggle, recalling one of many battles she had to fight in her new role as executive producer of her own films. The subject is *Private Benjamin*, the surprise comedy hit that has ratified her current status as Hollywood's top film comedienne—one of the best, according to some critics, since actress Carole Lombard. "The people connected with the film wanted to take out the wedding party scene in which Judy Benjamin went down on her husband [Albert Brooks] in the car. They felt it was unnecessary and would turn a lot of people off."

The story she is recounting is, er, not the sort of thing we are accustomed to hearing from blond, blushing Goldie Hawn, but then, it's become increasingly obvious that we knew precious little about the lady to begin with.

"Sexuality," she continues, "is, of course, the worst thing you can show in a picture. You can cut off a woman's breast in some bloody, violent film, but you can't film a man making love to it.

"I wanted the scene in there because I wanted to demonstrate something about Judy's character—that basically she was someone who didn't have much self-esteem. She wasn't able to say, '*No.* I don't want to do this. I'm in my wedding gown. It's our wedding night. I'm embarrassed.' What she valued most was having a man take care of her. She was prepared to be a doormat.

"There was no tenderness involved, so the scene showed his character *and* hers. She pleaded briefly, realized, 'Okay, I have to do this,' and then she went down out of the frame. The script was written for *me,*" she says with finality, "and I had a clear vision of what I wanted."

("Goldie wanted to linger on that scene for a long time," director Howard Zieff told me later, "and she wanted to let people see the back of her head in her husband's lap. I objected to that, and I guess I was afraid of the scene anyway, in that I didn't want the audience to squirm during it.")

"We fought for that scene and won," says Goldie, "but then, in the final cutting, they wanted to edit it before her head even went out of the frame! A bunch of us said, 'This isn't going to work. It ruins the joke and you don't get the impact.' So we got a little bit of what we wanted, but I still would have been happier had she stayed out of the frame longer."

Still, Goldie's not exactly crying in her Amaretto. Strolling around the expansive bedroom of her colonial home in the Pacific Palisades section of Los Angeles, a tumbler of the liqueur in her hand, she exudes a hard-won confidence. Particularly satisfying to her was the process of developing *Private Benjamin* with writer-producer friends Nancy Meyers, Charles Shyer and Harvey Miller.

She also showed a bold agility when it came to doing business with the film studios.

"The fact that Goldie herself took *Private Benjamin* around to the studios was unusual," Howard Zieff points out to me. "She and the script were an instant package, and she had a lot of pull as a result of her performance in *Foul Play.* Everybody with sense knew she had become *the* hot film comedienne."

"*Foul Play* made over $50 million and put Goldie back in the film business," adds Stan Kamen, Hawn's longtime friend and agent. "She's always been smart in terms of making sure she held on to her loyal TV audience by doing a special every eighteen months or so, but *Foul Play* [which was released in 1978] paved the way for *Seems like Old Times* and *Private Benjamin.* She could finally show the world her sex appeal, comedic timing and vulnerability."

But she could not necessarily display her personal sensibilities. *Foul Play* established Hawn as a bankable star, but it also exploited a safe, boy-girl (in distress) formula. *Private Benjamin* was considered too provocative.

"It was, for some reason, a big deal for people in this town to accept Goldie as a Jewish princess—let alone one who grows to be independent and aggressive," explains Charles Shyer. "The mentality was: stick with what works."

"The studios wanted to keep her a lovable victim," says Nancy Meyers, "or keep her in a *Laugh-In* bikini with *Love* painted on her belly. One studio head called Goldie and said, 'You're making one of the biggest mistakes of your career with this film.'

"Other studios offered us more money for the script, but we went with Warner Brothers because [theatrical and feature division president] Bob Shapiro didn't just want to make a 'Goldie Hawn' film. He believed in the character."

But Arthur Hiller, the first director, did not. "He didn't want to depict Judy or her parents as Jews," says Shyer. "He felt it could be construed as anti-Semitic, which we four all found ridiculous. So he gracefully stepped aside."

Meyers recounts ruefully that in November 1979, "We had a week to find a director or the film would have to be shelved, because of Goldie's prior commitment to *Seems like Old Times*."

"One day, Goldie, Nancy and I saw Howard Zieff on the Warners lot," says Shyer. "He called me later and asked, 'What are you doing these days?' I said, 'Funny you should ask' and offered him the picture. He took it, thank God."

"I liked the original script," says Zieff, "but *meeting* Goldie was the deciding factor for me—I was totally charmed by her, which is also what made her a good executive producer."

(The feisty foursome recently agreed to collaborate on another film, which will be made—once they write it—over the next two years or so. Shyer will direct, Hawn will be executive producer and Meyers and Miller will act as producers.)

"Goldie's ability to get the studio's attention in order to get a little more money for a scene, etc., was significant," Zieff observes. "She is, without question, a very persuasive person—and it's because of her great charm, not because of any pushiness. People on the set and from the studio were forever telling me how *charming* she was, and frankly, I got a little tired of saying, 'Yeah, yeah, I *know!*'

"Also, cooperation on all sides was important because we were on a very tight schedule. We had only six or seven weeks to prepare for filming: to find all the locations, both here and in Paris, to build all the sets and to cast all the parts. Goldie worked with the writer-producers, and she would also do things like read with auditioning actors and actresses, which is not common; it's often tough to get a star to do something like that. Therefore, we could immediately see the great chemistry between her and Armand Assante, who played her French fiancé, and with Eileen Brennan, who was so good as the sergeant in charge of Judy's barracks.

"For big battles," says Meyers with a laugh, "we always said, 'Send in the Babe,' and Goldie would go in and make people understand our logic rather than simply intimidate them."

"If we, for instance, disagreed," says Shapiro, "she stood firm and argued but also knew how to compromise. From the time I got involved in the film in February of 1979, the single most impressive thing about Goldie Hawn was that she never, *ever*, used her status as a star to win a point."

"I just stuck to my guns," Goldie says. "There were differences of opinion, but I didn't back down too easily, and this was hard for me, because I didn't want people to see me as a bitch."

When the film was first assembled, it ran three hours and one minute. Before its premiere, Zieff had to toss one hour and twelve minutes of the movie "into the trim barrel," as he puts it, "and it was like killing my children."

What made the editing so painful, he explains, was the hilarity of many of the deleted scenes, most of which took place in France.

"We had to cut a wonderful scene in which Armand, who plays a gyne-cologist-obstetrician-playboy, is lecturing on a new method of delivering babies at a college you were supposed to believe was the Sorbonne. Goldie, as Judy, is auditing the course, and the interplay between them was uproar-ious. And there was another scene in which Goldie is left in Armand's house for the first time while he leaves to play soccer. She must stay there and listen to his telephone answering service. All these women keep calling, leaving their numbers, and she gets more and more bugged!

"In the end, all of the necessary points were made, and I was satisfied, but nobody, of course, knew what a hit it would become; it was just released as product. But we knew from two very successful screenings in Denver and Chicago that we would have a good response. When Warners saw that, they *really* got behind the film, and Goldie worked very hard on the promotion."

"After grossing $60 million, the film is still going very strong," says Bob Shapiro with undisguised delight. "It will be released in foreign markets in the spring, and a handsome TV sale price will further increase its coffers. It will be a very, very profitable movie. I'd like to do one or two Goldie Hawn pictures a year. That would make me one very happy man."

"I cannot be anything on the screen that I haven't seen or felt myself—I can't pretend," says Hawn of her acting technique. "I have to have, or to find, something in my own experience to draw on." But she says she was never a Jewish princess like Judy in *Private Benjamin*. "As a child, I wasn't spoiled or protected too much, but I understood the character, having known people who were somewhat like Judy. I liked the fact that Judy was a directionless Jewish girl who didn't know from the army at all. It was a big canvas for comedy, but also a chance to say some things I felt about women.

"We all get rained on, but a Jewish princess would see herself as being *drenched*. A princess is someone who thinks she is better than anyone else, privileged, and that the world owes her something. *I don't buy that*," Goldie says firmly. "And I don't like people who don't work for what they want or get. I'm not afraid—without breaking character—to let my real feelings about a film situation show on camera."

"She's a fine actress because she is so natural," says Chevy Chase, her costar in the romantic comedies *Foul Play* and *Seems like Old Times*. "She never went out of her way to be any different than she really is, except to add whatever ingredient—rage, sorrow, fright—was needed to make a scene work.

"When we were filming *Foul Play*, doing that insane car chase up and down the steep streets of San Francisco, I could barely see through the lighting and camera equipment mounted on the hood of the car. Goldie was truly terrified, having once been in a serious car crash, and it really helped to make the whole sequence much more believable."

("I was in this awful car crash on the West Side Highway in New York City in 1965," Hawn says. "I woke up in the hospital, and the doctor said it was a miracle we all survived. Afterward, I went through a long period of severe anxiety—I couldn't even ride in a car that I wasn't driving.")

"The two words that describe Goldie best are *endurance* and *resilience*," adds Chase. "There was always some mild chaos going on with both films, but she would always maintain her composure—except to laugh at herself. She was continually surrounded by an entourage—all these little kids and dogs and family members and somebody hemming a dress that she'd gone shopping for earlier in the day. The key thing to remember, however, is that the woman is no disorganized kook. No matter how much seems to be in disarray, Goldie, in her own wonderful way, has got it *all* covered."

"This is the single toughest time in my life," Goldie says bluntly, hunched over in baggy denims on a couch in her living room as the dusk gathers outside. "I'm thirty-five, and now I'm gonna have to learn to *date* again!" she says, referring to her pending divorce from Bill Hudson, her second husband, after five years. "If I ever had a life plan, I saw myself as happily married. I never saw myself as single, with children, and frightened. I mean, waking up alone to a screaming child sometimes really scares me. And then one of the kids [Hawn and Hudson have two children: Oliver, four, and Kate, almost two] will wonder why there aren't *two* of us at home, and all I can say is, 'Honey, I'm here; let's get it done together.'

"It's a terror!" she yelps, lighting another in a succession of cigarettes. "So now what do I do, already?!"

What indeed? Though it's tough to see past the prismatic appeal of Hawn's flamboyant personality, beneath this pseudo-wacky eruption is a sturdy, worldly-wise resolve. "Handle it right!" is her constant, clipped soliloquy.

Over the last twenty-odd years, Goldie Hawn has survived a spate of snap judgments, from those who decided (wrongly, as it turned out) that the seventeen-year-old Goldie was too green and goofy for the lead in a Williamsburg, Virginia, summer-stock production of *Romeo and Juliet*, to the Burbank executives who deemed her incapable of transcending her bikini-cum-body-paint "ding-a-ling" blackouts on *Laugh-In* to garner anything in the movie world but dizzy blond-type bit parts. She now has thirteen feature films to her credit, including a humble debut in a dancing sequence in the Disney studio's dismal *The One and Only Genuine Original Family Band*, her Oscar-winning performance (Best Supporting Actress) opposite Walter Matthau in *Cactus Flower*, her big breakthrough in *Foul Play* and her present box-office blitz.

While it took more than serendipity for her to gain major television exposure—a chorus spot on an Andy Griffith special led to a role in a brief CBS series called *Good Morning, World* and, in turn, a three-show trial from *Rowan and Martin's Laugh-In* producer George Schlatter—it certainly didn't hurt matters when she flubbed her straight lines with such charm that Schlatter immediately signed her to a long-term contract.

Freakish good fortune runs in the family tree. Goldie's father, Edward Rutledge Hawn, is a direct descendant of the youngest signer of the Declaration of Independence. Initially dismissed as "a peacock" and "excessively vain and weak" by future president John Adams, twenty-six-year-old Edward Rutledge of South Carolina did vacillate a bit on the subject of independence. Thomas Jefferson later joked that the savage influx of horseflies swarming around the silk stockings of Rutledge and his colleagues in the summer of 1776 had much to do with the speed with which they made up their minds and scrawled their way into a hallowed place in American history.

But, like Goldie, her ancestor was greatly underestimated by his contemporaries. Edward Rutledge went on to fight bravely in the American Revolution, serve in the South Carolina legislature and become governor of the state.

"And you know," Goldie says with a smirk, "if my Presbyterian father hadn't married a Jew [the former Laura Speinhoff], I would have been qualified to end up as some horrible damned member of the D.A.R.!"

Godlie Jeanne Hawn was born on November 21, 1945, in Takoma Park, Maryland, a Washington, D.C., suburb. At the age of three she was enrolled in the Roberta Fera School of Dance, and it was not long before she was also taking lessons in voice, piano and acting. By the age of ten she had danced in the chorus of a production of *The Nutcracker Suite* with the Ballet Russe Monte Carlo.

"It was not, originally, my decision," Goldie says of her early plunge into showbiz. "Nevertheless, I enjoyed it, and it became a part of my life. When I was seventeen, I had my own school in Maryland: Goldie's Dancing School. I guess I was just industrious. I taught ballet and handled everything."

"I admit that I introduced the idea and encouraged her," says her mother, "but she grew up in a music and dance environment and just responded to it very positively. She was also very athletic; she swam on the school team and was a cheerleader in junior high school. If she had to choose, she would always go to dance class rather than go swimming.

"Uh, you see," says Mrs. Hawn awkwardly, "Goldie's teen years were also a difficult time for her. She was a late bloomer, and not quite as developed physically as the other girls. She didn't do much dating."

"I was very, very flat-chested," says Goldie. "I had absolutely no shape. It's a wonder I don't have a horrible inferiority complex, because I was someone who sat in the corner at all the dances—and most everything else, too. Even at spin the bottle I never had much luck! Once, in my early teens, I had a Halloween party and we played the game, and on my turns, the bottle never pointed to a soul! I'm telling you, I was a *sloow* starter.

"I tried out for cheerleader in ninth grade and got it for one year, but even *that* didn't help. And then I fell in with a bad crowd—or tried to—and I'd hang out smoking cigarettes and would cut my homeroom to put on eye liner, but it was no use.

"I mean, sure, I wore falsies and all, but still you're made fun of, and some guy says, 'Hey, your mother know what you're wearing under *there*?' What it does to a girl who's trying her best to be attractive to the opposite sex is devastating. The first time I kissed anybody, I was sixteen and in this car with this guy I hardly knew, and, *ugh*, it was a disappointment, too. In the middle of it, all I could think was, 'God, what a *bore*. Is this what it's about?

"I once said to my mother, in tears, 'I don't have any titties!' And she said [*soothingly*], 'But honey, you're very young, and you'll get older, and those boys, you're not gonna be able to keep them from your door. You'll have to beat them off.'

"To this day," Goldie says, "I haven't been beating them off [*shrieking giggles*], and I hope you'll pardon the pun!"

Having gotten a taste of the outside world during her summer-stock stint in Virginia, Goldie hit the Big Apple.

"I was studying dance and working the go-go circuit," she recalls. "It was grim and hard and not very profitable, but I would not trade the time spent in that world for anything, because of what I saw.

"Bad experiences are not necessarily totally bad," she counsels with a shrug. "Especially if you get over them. I learned from the bottom, looking around myself at the dregs of society, having both men and women relate to me purely as a sexual creature, coming on to me, propositioning me.

"I never danced topless, but I worked some *dives*. At least I always knew I was a very good dancer."

The go-go and chorus-girl grind took her to New Jersey, back to New York, then on to Anaheim and Las Vegas. The pace was punishing: usually four shows a night, each a feverish hour-and-a-half revue (if it wasn't feverish, you were fired).

Something had to give—and it did.

She had a nervous breakdown.

"I was living in L.A., alone for the first time," she recounts slowly. "Suddenly, I was making tea for myself at night and wondering what mattered. I was so upset, I was always throwing up in some bathroom.

"And then came seven years of analysis, and lots of soul-searching, and lots of honesty, and lots of bullshit. And I eventually came out of it. It's really an alienation from the family and tough on them [*giggling nervously*]— and tough on spouses, too.

"Sometimes you outgrow old friends, and there's nothing you can do about it, because you *cannot* turn back. If I realized anything from the experience, it was: one, that I would never have anxieties like those again; and two, I would *not* share a common sensibility with certain friends ever again. These kinds of realizations, especially if you're a sensitive person, are very hard to accept, and it's also hard to demonstrate this awareness by having to confront that person. But you *do* it."

During this period, Goldie married (in 1968) Gus Trikonis, a dancer who aspired to be an actor and a director. In 1969, she copped the Academy Award for her first major film role and felt "so hollow; it came too soon, too easily." In 1973, she did three debilitating films in one year, and her marriage to Trikonis simultaneously self-destructed. In an effort to restore herself, she began traveling with sister Patti, friends or by herself. Her personal manager, Art Simon, wanted her to work, however, and litigation ensued.

The situation seemed to brighten in 1975 when she met Bill Hudson of the Hudson Brothers. Although long separated, Goldie did not file for divorce until she and Bill planned to wed. Trikonis demanded a $75,000 settlement from Hawn under the California community-property law. "I was hurt," she said at the time. "He never supported me a day in his life."

When she and Hudson married in 1976 in the backyard of her childhood home in Takoma Park, Goldie was "joyfully" pregnant. Three months after the wedding—a month late by the doctor's count—Oliver was born.

For a time, things were good with Hudson. Then Goldie's static career slowly began to accelerate, while Hudson's hit the skids.

"After I had my first child," she recalls,"I started to get itchy about going back to work. My career had not been flourishing by any means, partly by choice and partly not. I had made a decision earlier to turn down all pictures offered to me, though I was not being offered the cream, either. At the two-and-a-half-year mark, I was open to things, and I was offered stuff like *Superman*, but I didn't want to do it. I was wondering exactly what I was gonna do. There didn't seem to be anything tangible to look forward to, careerwise. An actress, when she's not being sought after, is merely a lump of protoplasm."

"Mom! See! I got you some potato bugs that you could put in your bedroom!" says blond, beaming Oliver Rutledge Hudson as he bursts-through the front door and scurries over to the couch, clutching a weed-filled jar. His face is mottled with dirt, and he is shadowed by an equally grimy little boy named John, who is the son of Goldie's friend Joan and is Oliver's "best friend in the *whole* world."

"That's great!" says Goldie, her enthusiasm rivaling her offspring's. "Potato bugs to put in my room; I like the idea of that! Shall I leave them here, or do you want to go and put them up on my bed? Upstairs?"

Oliver nods at the latter suggestion and leaves the room.

It's late afternoon at the Hawn residence (Hudson has possession of their Malibu beach house and joint custody of the children, who live with Goldie during the week), and I'm still trying to get my bearings after a half-hour in the hectic household, whose antiques-crammed rooms lend it an aura closer to that of a Connecticut farmhouse than a movie star's California manse. Katie and her toddler companions are following their own errant muses into various corners, and Oliver and John can be heard demanding bananas and cookies in the kitchen. Casual order is imposed by Goldie, a middle-aged housekeeper named Teresa, and Carol, a thirtyish governess/extra pair of eyes. But Goldie is clearly *the* lady of the house, and when her son comes back sobbing after being denied a between-meals snack, Goldie embraces him and says with a tenderness underscored by no-bullshit finality, "Hold the phone; it's not that important. You'll have a nice dinner soon." He calms down.

Reflecting Hawn's heritage as well as her own distinctive predilections, the living-room decor is a mix of oddball stuffed animals and sentimental *tchotchkes* dominated by Early American folk art and primitive paintings. When I ask her which of these possessions she could least bear to lose, she reflects for a few seconds and then shows me a painting that hangs by her front door. It is an American primitive of a child with piercing blue eyes, dressed in a ruffled gown and one blue slipper—the other clutched in the child's hand.

"I bought this painting in 1971 while I was doing *Butterflies Are Free*," she says quietly, "and I could not bear to lose it. There's something very pure and profound about it. The child resembles both of my children, *and* my father, too. I love the fact that I see this child whenever I enter or leave the house.

"I have this naive, idealistic attitude toward life," she offers when we've settled back on the couch. "That's why I buy these simplistic, romantic paintings. And I enjoy being with a man who has an artistic point of view. What a shame," she says, her face suddenly flushed with sadness, "you always meet people in the business."

"Neither Gus nor Bill," I observe, "was doing as well as you were during your marriages."

"I honest to God *try*, at least, to leave my career problems outside my door," she says. "But in the end, *that* didn't even work, so either it's money, power or fame. They all work against you, unless you find a man who is absolutely secure in who he is.

"Personally, I have few excesses; I'm not a coke head, I don't drink too much; I guess I do smoke a lot. But being well balanced, being someone who has the ability to look at the problem objectively, is not necessarily an asset.

"I have my own problems that people have to buy when they fall in love with me or when we hitch up in marriage—I come with my sack of goods, too. But forgetting that, the other things that are—or seem—bigger than both of us are success, power and money.

"It's hard enough on a man when a *woman* has these things, and it's very difficult—almost impossible—to maintain a balance of power in a relationship. And it's the saddest realization that I have ever had to come to in my life. With women's liberation and all the great strides that people are making, basically we are having the same problems, and I'm confronting them head-on right now.

"Having my kids know how much I love them is so important to me. When I was a little girl, I dreamed about a woman who lived on our street in Maryland, and she was very scary to me. With her hooked nose, she looked like a witch. In my dreams, I remember her as someone walking around being threatening—someone who was gonna get me. I want my children to feel wanted, protected."

Judging from her general tone whenever the subject arises, the things Goldie says about her children, she could just as easily be saying about herself.

"It was very rough on her when she suddenly became a big star," says her mother. "Her marriage was breaking up, and thirteen people would run up to her in the supermarket; she lost her sense of privacy and security."

Much of Goldie Hawn's film persona is of a piece with her personal experiences, and that loss of privacy and security, that vulnerability, is a quality with which many moviegoers can readily identify.

"Absolutely," Zieff agrees. "Yet even when she's tough, you're sympathetic. But it would be difficult to cast Goldie as a negative force; that would be like trying, in the old days, to make Gary Cooper into a villain."

Unfortunately, the actions Goldie takes to fortify her world are the same ones that invite the greatest jeopardy.

"I'm not anxious to get back to work," she offers. "Having worked so hard over the last two years, I feel drained, played out; I need to get back in gear. I'm not a goal-oriented person; I'm more *project*-oriented. Do you know what I'm saying? I certainly have an aggressive spirit when it comes to getting something I believe in done, but I don't sit home and immediately think of what I should do next: 'Well, I should make this move now. . . .'"

We walk to the playroom and find Kate and Oliver on their knees before the TV screen, happily painting their coloring books and waiting for Goldie to come on the screen in a cable-TV interview program.

Goldie gives Kate a big hug and kiss, and then stands expressionless as the silver-haired host, film critic Charles Champlin, introduces a glamorous-looking Goldie and describes her "great triumph" with *Private Benjamin.*

"Private 'Mommy' Benjamin," Oliver corrects with annoyance, as a clip of the film is shown.

Afterward, Champlin asks his guest, "Is the Goldie Hawn we see very close to the Goldie Hawn that you see . . . when you go home?"

Goldie frowns at the phoniness of the segment and shuts off the TV.

"I think I've OD'ed on looking at myself, listening to myself on TV or film," she says to no one in particular. "It's not healthy."

At that moment, Oliver leaps up and hands me his finished painting.

"I want this to be for you!" he says, and Goldie squeals with delight. "Ollie! What a nice little son I have! What a wonderful thing to do for someone!"

She lifts him with a loving nuzzle and carries him up to bed, Carol following with Kate, good nights and goodbyes exchanged all around.

An hour later, I'm in the car with Goldie and her friend Joan, heading down Sunset Boulevard to see a movie. Goldie sighs and mentions Oliver's gift to me, how touched she was by his gesture.

We reach a red light and she brakes, looks downward pensively, and says to both of us, "The other day, Oliver gave me this star, and I just had to ask, 'Is this for being a movie star or for being [*long pause*] a mommy?'"

The pause is unsettling. The light changes. Goldie, glassy-eyed, gazing straight ahead, speaks, her voice just above a murmur.

"He said, 'It was for being a *star mom.*'"

And then she hits the gas.

The Homecoming:
Bette Midler in *The Rose*

"**E**verything seemed to fall apart," said former Army ordinance worker Fred Midler, 71, talking in his home outside Honolulu, Hawaii, in 1979. He was recalling the Sunday morning of December 7, 1941, when the Japanese bombing attack on Pearl Harbor changed his life forever. "I was under the impression it was simply maneuvers, although it looked rather realistic. The average civilian hardly knew what was going on until after the announcement came over the radio, and then we had a difficult time adjusting ourselves, believing that such a thing could happen."

Midler was previously stationed in Hawaii during half of his 1930–33 hitch as an Army ordinance specialist. He had returned alone in 1940 when the U.S. civil service advertised for experienced laborers in munitions plants and storage magazines for Oahu's military installations, later sending for his wife and children. The son of Rubin Midler, who ran a tailoring shop in Paterson, New Jersey, Fred later resumed his prior profession as a house-painter after World War II, striving under contract to the U.S. Navy. The experience of Pearl Harbor had hardened his view that life was best lived with few frills and fewer wants, given the seeming inevitability of sudden, dire losses.

"We had no difficulties, we couldn't complain at all—that is, the people working in the Defense Department made very little sacrifices," insists Fred when he looks back on the Midlers' spare post-War existence. "We were comfortable despite the fact our apartment was a converted barracks."

His wife shared his resigned outlook—although his two daughters did not. Yet all might have been well in Fred Midler's simple, ordered life, but for the birth on December 1, 1945, of a third little girl her mother named Bette.

"I didn't want any luxuries," added Fred docilely, explaining why the Midlers didn't have a TV set until 1957 or a phone until 1962. "I personally couldn't accustom myself to luxuries. My wife seldom went out and bought things, she always made dresses and the things the kids needed. We had all the basic conveniences; but Bette didn't stay here long enough to enjoy it."

Bette Midler was bent over the sink in the kitchen of her rented Los Angeles home, giving herself a mayonnaise shampoo on the 1979 afternoon of the last in our three-month span of East and West Coast interviews. The talks were in preparation for a profile that would be published just prior to the October '79 premier of *The Rose*, a film for which she earned an Academy Award nomination as Best Actress.

"Mayo's the greatest; it makes your hair shine!" she hollered with a laugh, kneading the gooey dressing into her scalp as she glanced up at her visitor. Bette may have had an early reputation for being controlling and image-conscious, but during this journalist's many encounters, her vulnerability was rarely under wraps.

Wrapping a towel turban-style around the touseled viscous mess, she seated herself in the kitchen and fixed lunch as she detailed the fundamental divergence in her dad's orientation and her own: fear vs. freedom, safety vs. fulfullment.

"My mother used to give a little shove in the pants to my father, but he wouldn't be the leader; so it was a very closed life for her," said Bette, disclosing why she had to depart Hawaii and prove to both herself and her parents that the world still held greater promise. "She was one of those mothers who'd say, 'Don't take candy from strangers,' but beyond that, 'Don't look at anybody, don't talk to anybody, don't walk on that side of the street, don't go through the cane fields!' She was completely fear-ridden, in a place that was really glorious and free-spirited.

"I find myself suffering from the same problems—of really loving to be with people but fearing maybe they won't like me, you know? And isolating myself because of a funny kind of a fear that really shouldn't exist."

The Rose became the first step away from Midler's former life as a stage performer and recording artist, the singer feeling increasingly trapped in an airless professional corridor between the two disciplines while tied to a constrictive management relationship.

The torments depicted in the often intensely unglamorous *The Rose* were liberating for Midler, enabling her to show every side of her essential nature. The approval it drew changed her, making her "stronger and more resilient." She severed her old management ties, and following a minor setback with the movie *Jinxed* (1982), she met and became friendly with Martin von Haselberg, a successful commodities trader turned producer/performance artist under the stage name Harry Kipper. They became romantically involved in 1984 and married in December 1985, her new husband urging Bette away from film drama and into the more natural realm of comedy.

Midler reemerged with a string of well-attended screen attractions, including *Down and Out in Beverly Hills* and *Ruthless People*, both of which were released in 1986. She also spent much of her free time that year nursing and making peace with her dying father Fred. The care of her younger retarded bother, Daniel, long looked after by her dad, now fell to her older sister, Susan, a health-care executive trained to teach those with severe special needs.

Midler's next movies were *Outrageous Fortune* (1987), *Big Business* and the animated *Oliver & Company* (both 1988). She was now under contract to Disney/Touchstone pictures, with her own production company (All-Girl Productions) and a two-year-old daughter she took time off to raise. Midler later did well with *Beaches* (1989), whose soundtrack yielded the No. 1 hit, "Wind beneath My Wings."

Among her films in the 1990s were *Stella* (1990), *Scenes from a Mall* (1991), *For the Boys* (1992), which gained her another Oscar nomination for

Best Actress, *Hocus Pocus* (1993), and the 1996 box office smash, *The First Wives Club,* which cast her with co-stars Goldie Hawn and Diane Keaton, as well as *That Old Feeling* (1997).

Midler also won an Emmy for her performance on the final installment of *The Tonight Show Starring Johnny Carson* in May 1992. In addition, she notched a No. 2 hit in 1993 with "From a Distance," from her *Experience the Divine—Greatest Hits* album, besides appearing in an acclaimed 1993 TV production of *Gypsy.*

"I love my flaws," a smiling Midler had advised back in November 1979 as we bade each other goodbye on the gusty Manhattan corner of Fifth Avenue and 60th Street, the actress without makeup and bundled in a woolen cap and bulky sweater. "It's my illusions and fears that embarrass me."

THE INTERVIEW

S HE IS STRANDED IN A WHIRLWIND: exhausted, alone and so wound up and strung out and shitfaced drunk that her self-image has shrunk to the size of a tiny, fallen dime that she can't even *attempt* to stop on, let alone locate on the filthy phone-booth floor. Slumped to a halt yet driven forward, all the psychic brake linings are burned through. But she has so *damned much* to do tonight; so many things are demanded of her by so many feverish faces.

For the Rose, soul-wrenched rock singer nonpareil, it all comes down to one hard reality: Somewhere out in the vast pitch, Rudge, her insatiable *motherfucker* of a manager, wants her to perform. Right this minute. And the added fact that she's lost and terrified in her hometown makes her private hell complete. So she spills out her kit bag, finds another dime and calls the only two strangers who can do absolutely nothing to help: her parents.

This scene is the centerpiece and true climax of *The Rose,* Bette Midler's long-awaited cinema debut, and the ensuing conversation is perhaps one of the most heartbreaking ever captured on film.

"Mom? Yeah, yeah, it's me," Rose entreats with a croak. She is calling from a forlorn outpost next to her high-school football field, and while the squad wraps up its practice under the lights, this ragged rock queen, the woman who many years earlier had allowed the home team to gangbang her on the fifty-yard line, now takes a last simpering stab at being a little girl. But there is no consolation coming back over the wire, so she hangs up and ties off and sinks into a smack-induced murk as the booth's windows fog up. Seldom has Hollywood depicted disjunction and despair with such mundane clarity. And what makes the scene so sad is precisely this awful ordinariness, the undramatic realization that, for Rose, shooting junk is merely the next most accessible option. Scarcely even a choice.

"Unrequited love is a subject very near and dear to my heart," says a reflective Bette Midler, 34, as she nurses a glass of white wine in the dining room of Manhattan's legendary Algonquin Hotel. "I have a whole well of inspiration when it comes to that." Unrecognized by the well-heeled young socialites and overdressed dowagers who amble by, Midler goes on to describe both the plot of *The Rose* and her character in vividly personal terms. I express surprise, noting that gossip columnists have been reporting that the movie is a thinly veiled *roman à clef* about Janis Joplin's epic self-destruction.

"The truth is, it's a story about a girl who happens to sing and has a need for the great love of an audience," Bette says. "I love that shit, I love to bare my breast.

"My own family household was fairly violent," she offers. "I'm not talking about whipping each other or anything, but we did feel very strongly about things, and we expressed ourselves in very strong terms. Yet there was a lot of thwarted emotion. My father was always right, never wrong. It was simple: He was the loudest and the oldest and the heaviest. It was usually him against us. My mother tried to be a soothing influence, but she wasn't very successful at it. There was *that* kind of passion."

She jumps to the subject of her songs in the film, explaining that she had chosen its two most riveting numbers—"When a Man Loves a Woman" and "Stay with Me"—because "they're songs I always identified with. I was determined just to be genuine, and *good*. I didn't want anybody to dump on me. I didn't want to have anybody calling me names. You know," she says with a wounded grin, "how they do that sometimes. . . ."

Indeed, in all of rock & roll, few stars have made a bigger initial splash than Bette Midler, only to peak and fade with astonishing swiftness. In the space of only two years, she rose from a camp curiosity at Manhattan's Continental Baths to the nationally acclaimed headliner of a lavish New Year's Eve bash at Philharmonic Hall in 1972. She was a frequent guest on *The Tonight Show* and made the cover of *Newsweek*; her percolating remake of "Boogie Woogie Bugle Boy" blasted out of radios across the nation. But her one smash album, *The Divine Miss M* (1972), was followed by four comparatively sparse-selling offerings, the best of the lot being *Live at Last*, a two-record set that contained a bit of the electricity of her stage shows. How she managed to plummet from this pinnacle remains a mystery, the blame usually laid on a temperamental Bette, a tempestuous Aaron Russo (her manager of six years, now out of the picture) or both. Regardless, the furor was over by the end of 1973.

"'Being laughed at' is not the phrase to describe what happened," Bette says woefully. "I was *snickered* at. That was much uglier."

As it happens, *The Rose* is likewise steeped in trauma. Its plot is nothing so much as the story of a young woman's fear-ridden homecoming, in this case a confrontation between a hard-drinking, low-living rock star on the slide and the dingy past she is striving to eradicate. Rose wants to quit the business "for at least a year," as soon as she musters up the courage to play a huge outdoor concert in her hometown. Obstacles abound—from Rose's need to overcome her lesbian inclinations and try a little heterosexual tenderness with an AWOL army rounder (played to near-perfection by Frederic Forrest) to her wavering resolve to end her symbiotic relationship with Rudge (Alan Bates).

Although flawed, the film succeeds as a vehicle for Midler, showing her range as a singer and comedienne, but most importantly, her potential as a serious actress. In other hands, Rose could have come off as a repellent bitch, but Midler manages to bring a human dimension to the role without resorting to gauche grandstanding or bathos.

"When Janis passed on," says Midler, "there was a script that came to me called *Pearl*. I was really shocked by it. I didn't know Janis, but I thought she was treated irreverently. It wasn't that it was a bad script; it was just the idea of not letting this person alone, especially so soon after she died."

During this period, Russo and Midler tried their damnedest to locate a suitable film property for Bette. The ongoing quest provided several years of grist for the Hollywood gossip mill: "She's doing the life of Dorothy Parker! Helen Morgan! Zelda Fitzgerald! Sophie Tucker!"

None of the projects ever materialized.

"Just idle speculation" was the way the slightly rotund Russo dismissed it one winter afternoon some two years ago. "She's not gonna do Ethel Merman or Janis Joplin. I don't think that Bette's fans, the people who really love her, want to see her play someone else," he said heatedly, then proceeded to contradict himself.

"George Furth and Joan Rivers are writing one, an all-out musical comedy," he enthused. "She's not playing Bette Midler. Lilly Potts is one name we're thinking of for the character. It's about a superstar and the relationship between her and her manager."

Russo went on to boast of the film deal Midler signed with Columbia, how she would have her own production company and that screenwriter

Arnold Schulman (*Love with the Proper Stranger, Goodbye Columbus, Funny Lady*) was at work on another effort, "tailored" for Bette, about an avid autograph collector. But less than a year later, there was a reshuffling of executives at the studio and the wolf was suddenly at Divine Pictures' front door.

"They decided we were not a happening thing," says Bette, "and they sort of asked us very politely to give up our grand offices and go."

Undaunted, Russo and Midler found their way to Twentieth Century-Fox and producer Marvin Worth, who now had possession of *Pearl*.

"By this time, I was worn out," Bette recalls, "but I wanted to do films. I felt I had a contribution to make. Aaron called me up and said, 'Why don't you look at this again?' I read it. I said, 'These are the elements I'd like to keep: I'd like to keep this person a rock & roll singer, and I would like to keep the sorrow and a certain amount of self-hate, this constant seeking of hers for approbation. Everything else has to go.' And that's what they did. It's a fine framework to hang the songs on, something to hang the character on. We did a lot of improvising."

As a result, the statement that emerges transcends the tenuous Joplin connection and comes compellingly close to being Bette's own story. The monstrous star-manager relationship is at the center of the film. And while specific scenes may or may not reflect real life, Midler and Russo, throughout their many troubled years, had retained a stubborn attachment to this particular cinematic theme. They seemed to relish the sense of drama created by their bond, however suffocating it grew to be. It is perhaps no accident that the tie was finally broken only after it was played out on screen to its horrific finale.

"Our relationship was so much sicker than anything in that film," Midler assures me. "Aaron was very protective of me—in his way. He made a lot of enemies on my behalf. You see, we had a personal relationship at the beginning of everything, and when our personal relationship foundered, it tainted our professional relationship. I was so dumb; I didn't think that'd happen. He was so overbearing, and he kept me very isolated, kept the bad stuff away from me and a lot of the good stuff, too.

"For a long time I never saw people backstage, never read anything about myself, never had fun. And he would have a magazine article about me in his hand as I was going onstage and I'd say, 'Oh boy, lemme see that!' But he'd say, '*No*, I don't want you to read it now or later. It'll only upset you.' Long, long afterward, I would find out it said bad things about *him*, not me."

In fairness to Russo, Midler concedes that, unlike the mean-spirited Rudge in *The Rose*, who does his best to pull his overwrought star through a contractual knothole, "Aaron *never* forced me to work. I can be very lazy and temperamental that way, and I guess he indulged me." Midler did, in fact, take a year off (1974) and did not perform again until Russo organized her well-received *Clams on the Half-Shell Revue*.

"We were just two bullheaded people going at each other like crazy," she says, recalling that their low watermark occurred during and shortly after the record sessions for her 1977 *Broken Blossom* LP.

"I was in the studio *forever*," she groans. "I had lost a lot of confidence along the way—and I had a lot of help in losing my confidence. But I would have to say that the absolutely lowest point came when I was on the road the last time with Aaron [Europe and Australia, in 1978]. I knew that if I didn't get out at that point, I would never be happy again.

"I used to do shows, and no matter how good they were, it didn't matter until *he* told me it was okay. And he used to withhold this approbation from me all the time. *That* game. And that's a real horrible mindfuck to get into. I was pretty messed up there for a long time. I don't know why—emotional retardation, I guess. He was the only one I trusted. I started out with a lot of people around me and eventually they all left, and I was alone with Aaron. If it didn't go down the way he wanted it to go down, there was no joy in Mudville."

"I'm sorry, but I don't want to speak to you at this time," says Russo when I later ask him for his side of the story. "You know me, you know how I am," he sighs, alluding to our long conversations in the past. "When I talk, I shoot from the hip. But that's only when I choose to shoot. I just don't want to now."

As Bette and I order dinner, I think aloud about her appearance last May on *Saturday Night Live*. Poured into a sleek white dress covered with jagged black spots, she had treated the studio audience to a disco-driven rendition of "Married Men," the single from her latest LP, *Thighs and Whispers*. She resembled some manic she-devil—half woman, half jungle cat—as she slithered and snarled to the torrid dance tempo. Ruffling her unruly blond tresses, Midler carried on with vintage vigor, supported by a phalanx of backup singers whose garish costumes (satin wedding gowns, black tails) and cocky grins were of a piece with the Divine Miss M's trademarks of hot flash and sassy trash. But when she stepped from the shadows for her second song, her racy attire had been replaced by a simple black smock and tights, and there was a vulnerability in her humble demeanor. She stated she wanted to do a song written by her friend Tom Waits, and in a strained, doleful voice she began to sing "Martha:"

Operator, number please, it's been so many years
Will she remember my ol' voice, while I fight the tears . . .

Although rather bleak, the ballad is not terribly different from many of her more somber torch songs. But there was an underlying grittiness to her tone that had less to do with performing than with simple grief:

I feel so much older now, you're much older too
How's the husband, how's the kids,
you know I got married too
Lucky that you found someone to make you feel secure
We were all so young and foolish, now we are mature . . .

Creeping into the second chorus, her voice faltered, and the camera caught a tiny sparkle in her eye, a glimmering pinpoint that grew steadily into a tear:

I was always so impulsive, guess that I still am . . .
I guess that our bein' together was never meant to be. . . .

As the plaintive music subsided, Bette clutched the microphone, mascara running down her cheek. The dark eyes glazed over and her face fell into a pained expression so distant that I wondered if she remembered where she was. It was an altogether curious vignette, profoundly moving yet equally perplexing.

"That song calls up a lot of deep things for me," Bette sadly admits as she picks at her Caesar salad. "That night on the show, I was thinking about my mom. I lost my mother this year, she had leukemia for a long time, cancer of the liver—and of the breast, incidentally, when I was a kid. She suffered most of her life.

"She just thought I was *it*," Midler says, brightening for an instant. "She thought I was so funny and so adorable; she just loved all the excitement. She used to say I was the only thing that brought her joy." Bette explains that Ruth Midler and her husband, Fred, moved from Paterson, New Jersey, to Honolulu in the early Forties and settled in a converted military barrack in the midst of the sugar-cane fields of the rural Aiea area. They subsisted on the modest income Mr. Midler earned painting houses and doing civilian work with a U.S. Navy ordnance detail. Ruth, meanwhile, escaped their threadbare circumstances through a consuming interest in Hollywood films and movie fanzines. She went so far as to name all three of her daughters—she also had one son, Danny—for her favorite screen stars: Judy (after Garland), Susan (as in Hayward) and Bette (in tribute to Davis).

"Eventually, she and my father bought a couple of houses and fixed them up and had tenants," Bette says. "They were small-time landlords. My mother was extremely talented at it and got a real kick out of that, yet she did it all from her own house. She never had the nerve to go out and get a job; she was *totally* house-bound. She wanted to be in the world the way other people were in the world. She was just a housewife, but she wanted to take part. And she loved all the Hollywood whoop-de-do.

"She got no satisfaction any way she turned. She was afraid and she wanted my father to shield her, yet he refused, so she resented him for that. And that made it very, very rough. The Depression had a terrible impact on them. They were terribly frightened that they were gonna lose everything. I think that's why she was so charmed by me. She saw that I was taking a chance and wasn't a total failure. Whenever I think back on it now, I think of this Carl Sandburg line."

"What line is that?"

"You know," she says, "the one about 'dreams stronger than death.'"

Caught off-guard by Midler's sudden intensity, I stop to consider this woman seated next to me as she orders after-dinner coffee. There is little outward indication of the great charisma and convulsive energy she exhibits when she steps before the footlights. She is diminutive (five feet one) and deceptively frail-looking. When she is somber or sour, her rubbery features harden into a forbidding mask worthy of a Gahan Wilson cartoon, but when those huge eyes flutter their mystic fanfare, and her awesome, mugging smile is on the move, rising on that mammoth proscenium of a mouth like some radiantly toothy orchestra, well, as the lady herself would say—I mean, it just *melts you down hon-ee.* And then there's her tight little frame, a stripped-down bumper car of a body with the biggest headlights in the arena, bustling and spinning and battering away at the opposition with short spurts of gleeful abandon, then long surges of head-on savvy.

Growing up as the only chesty Jewish *haole* in a hostile world full of Samoans, Japanese and a host of other South Pacific nationalities, Midler rapidly developed into a sharp-tongued fireplug, defusing her enemies with a lightning wit and winning them over with an open heart. By the time Bette graduated from high school (she was class president and valedictorian), she had earned a reputation as a first-rate clown, a second-rate amateur shoplifter and a fledgling folk singer as part of a female vocal trio called the Pieridine Three ("It means, 'like a butterfly'"). A bit part as a missionary's wife in the George Roy Hill-Walter Mirisch production of James Michener's *Hawaii* strengthened her hunger for the spotlight, and she departed Hawaii in 1965 with $1,000 in savings (she left $1,500 more behind, "just in case"). At length, she arrived in New York and took a room in the Broadway Central Hotel, begged for bit parts on and off the Great White Way and survived by doing filing at Columbia University, selling gloves at Stern's department store and go-go dancing at a bar in Union City, New Jersey. Her first break was landing the title role in Tom Eyen's off-off-Broadway production of *Miss Nefertiti Regrets*, followed by a part in Eyen's *Cinderella/Sinderella* and the role of the Red Queen in *Alice through the Glass Lightly*.

Next came a three-year run in the Broadway production of *Fiddler on the Roof*, first as a member of the chorus, then as the eldest daughter Tzeitel. "It was great the first year. It was great the second year. The third year it got a little unnerving 'cause I couldn't get a raise, I couldn't get another job, and I was auditioning all the time. See, by that time, *Fiddler* wasn't where it was at: it was the Beatles and marijuana and *Hair,* and Janis Joplin. All of a sudden people my age were happening, and I just wanted to see where, and *if,* I could fit in."

Her last significant theater stints were a brief appearance in an off-Broadway musical called *Salvation* and the double role of Mrs. Walker and the Acid Queen in the Seattle Opera Association's 1971 production of *Tommy.*

Deciding to concentrate on her singing, she made her solo debut at Hilly Kristal's old club (he now owns CBGB), doing a fervent version of "God Bless the Child." After she appeared to raves at the Improvisation, the club's owner, Budd Friedman, booked her on *The David Frost Show*, *The Merv Griffin Show*, *The Tonight Show* and at the Continental Baths for sixteen weeks. She attracted the interest of several record companies, eventually being signed to Atlantic by Ahmet Ertegun. Bette (now managed by Aaron Russo, the former owner of Chicago's Kinetic Playground rock palace) became the brightest new star in the music industry. It should have lasted, but it didn't.

To put it politely, Bette's brush with success has been no day at the beach, and she is now poised on the brink of what will either be a triumphant comeback or her most ignominious defeat. But if Midler has had difficulty surviving her recent troubles, it has been no less difficult outliving her early years, and coping with the painful threads that bind the two.

"I'm a lot like my mom," says Bette after her coffee arrives, fixing me with a piercing gaze. "I guess that's why I leaned on Aaron so heavily for so long. I have to give him his due. I had this dichotomy of a tremendous *wanting* and yet this gigantic fear. He was a leader and he really did lead me.

"See, my mother was the most negative woman. Hypertense. I saw this misery, this incredible misery that she could not force her way out of, this loneliness and bitterness. But I adored her because I saw in her this somebody who was trying to get out, who had a dream that unfortunately never came true."

Bette refers to her father as a "minor tyrant. He would scream and carry on," says Bette. "He thrived on it. My sister Susan and pa, they'd have terrible riles. She used to call the cops on him! He used to *piss her off.*"

"He didn't like us wearing makeup and we had a curfew, some ridiculous hour like ten o'clock," Susan Midler later tells me. "And if you weren't in the house, you usually got locked out. Us sisters were always sticking up for each other, and sneaking each other in the window at night."

A petite, attractive woman, Susan, 35, works with the disabled and mentally retarded and now lives in the cozy West Village apartment that was Bette's throughout her early theater career.

"It was hard," Susan says of her cantankerous father. "If he was angry, he let you know it right away, so we would take that anger and try to turn it around and make him laugh at himself."

Whatever it was that was eating at Fred Midler, he found a constructive outlet for his dogged contrariness shortly after the birth of his youngest child, Danny, who was diagnosed as retarded following a postnatal illness.

"The public-health authorities, the social workers, wanted to put Danny away," says Bette angrily. "But my parents wouldn't hear of it. This doctor told my mom that Danny's tongue was too long, and he would have to cut it a bit in surgery. And because the doctor cut it, Danny lost the power of movement there. In other words, the doctor severed some nerves, so Danny wasn't able to move his tongue anymore. So now he can't chew, he doesn't talk quite right.

"At that time they didn't have public-school classes for retarded children, so my father taught him. He used to come home from work at about four o'clock every day and sit him down in the rocking chair to teach him to talk, read, write and add.

"Pa would start off quietly, but by the time 4:30 rolled around, he was *screaming* at the top of his lungs out of frustration, and Daniel would be crying. He's not so retarded that he doesn't know it. But eventually Danny did learn. It took a lot of love for my father to do that. Or some heavy guilt.

"I think," says Bette, "there are certain things you have to pass through in life in order to come out on the other side."

But there were other sorrows in store for the Midlers. Judy, the eldest daughter, gave in to her own restless urges a few years after Bette had, and she migrated to San Francisco, where she did office work briefly before resettling in New York City. By all accounts the prettiest and brightest of the Midler girls, she was fluent in French, fascinated with filmmaking and was considering a career in set design or directing when she was killed at the age of twenty-five in a freak car accident. Bette took it upon herself to notify the family, and when the telephone rang back in Hawaii, Susan answered.

"I gave the phone to my father," says Susan. "Bette spoke to him first, and then it was passed around to all of us. It was a nightmare. I don't think my mother ever got over it. Then when my mother passed away, it took its toll on all of us. The chemotherapy for the last couple of years was really rough. Bette made her very happy with the things that she had done, and reading some of the articles about her, and fan mail, and talking to fans on the phone, things like that made her very happy. But dad is very lonesome now. It's just him and Danny [now thirty-one] in his little house. I can imagine what he's doing right now. . . ."

I've just been working on some machinery out back," says Fred Midler when I phone him. "My success is rather limited," he asserts with a muffled, nasal chuckle. "I enjoy repairing it, but I enjoy cussing it out when it doesn't work, too."

"Looking back, how would you evaluate the years you spent raising your children?"

"I'll tell you the truth about that particular period," he murmurs solemnly. "I was too busy chasing after the buck. I left everything to my wife. I didn't pay much attention to the children.

"I used to have some terrible arguments with Bette, and I regret most of them. I tried to be too strict with all of them. Bette liked more of a free-lance life—doing the things most of the normal children did, like dancing and theater and movies and things of that nature. I was a very conservative person and I couldn't see it."

"Still, you did spend a lot of important time with Danny."

"That was when he first started out," Fred Midler says with a hint of bitterness. "I don't do it anymore, because there's just so much you can do with that sort of thing. I believe he's reached his capacity. We had to talk to a psychiatrist from the mainland, a harsh man who believed in shock treatment for alcoholics, and he insisted there was nothing wrong with Danny and he was simply lazy mentally. He shouted at the boy, who was scared something terrible from the shouting alone, and I followed that method. My wife jumped all over me for shouting at him that way."

"Are you pleased with Bette's fame?"

"I'm still astonished at her success," he says meekly. "I don't understand it, I never expected it. I still don't believe it."

"Have you ever been to any of her concerts?"

"Truthfully? No, I haven't. I'm not a fan of pop music, no way. As long as she's happy, I'm happy. I try to divorce myself completely from her and let her do as she will.

"I remember Judy, she also was a real hard driver; she would fight for her rights for anything. I was in favor of that stuff up to a certain degree. After that I say a woman should be a woman, stay at home. It was very bad losing Judy. As I understand it, an auto came out of one of those indoor garages and smashed her right up against the wall. Mutilated her completely. The funeral directors wouldn't even permit us to view the body. As you get older, you realize that it all comes down to the final stage."

Bette does not share her father's resignation. There are, however, traces of his willfulness in her, just as she evinces a strain of her mother's insecurity. But the qualities she inherited are the same ones that impelled her to seek a life apart from their world.

"I'm telling you, it's better to be isolated from family sometimes," Bette says vehemently. Family is so hard; it's your intro to the world, this microcosm that sometimes can be so *fucked*."

She shrugs with an uncertain chuckle.

"I think that's how I get away with singing those strange off-the-wall ballads that are about that particular kind of weirdness, like John Prine's 'Hello in There' and James Taylor's 'Millworker.' They tell you in black and white terms about somebody's baggage, they give you someone's saddest stories. By the time my mother died, she had isolated herself so *completely*—the Naked City, then there must be 8 million songs too. Any joy I get in singing them is probably borne of despair."

Bette's mood lifts and as we leave the restaurant she rhapsodizes about her parents' colorful quirks, notably their habit of accumulating mountains of knickknacks and junk. "The stuff was gonna stay there come hell or high water, and so it *did*," she says, giggling at the memory of the thirty-five nonworking lawn mowers her dad had squirreled away on the grounds of their home. "We also had twelve refrigerators on the lawn. He's like Mr. Fix-it, Mr. Handyman, except he's not very good at it. One day the roof was leaking, so rather than hire a roofer, Mr. Midler gets up there with his tar paper. He didn't have a roller for it, so what does he haul up there? One of his lawn mowers! I came home from New York one day and there he was on the roof, mowing the shingles flat!"

Laughing uproariously, we hit the street and walk up Fifth Avenue in the direction of Bette's hotel. The sidewalks are fairly empty at this late hour, and we stroll along in peace, window-shopping and chatting. The sight of a bookstore reminds Midler that her own flippant scrapbook of memoirs, *A View from a Broad*, is due to be published this winter by Simon & Schuster. As she is telling me that the project was conceived during her last European tour, her spirited discourse is interrupted by two young, homeward-bound waiters still wearing their uniform vests.

"Hey!" one calls out to Bette. "Where you *been*? What you been *doing*? We don't see you so much anymore on TV or anything."

"Say, I've been working hard, making records and giving concerts, and I got this film coming out! Now you fellas better be watching for it," she scolds.

Further up the avenue, we nearly collide with a swarthy custodian who is taking out the trash.

"Will you look at this?" Midler yelps, tugging me over to the garbage heap. "Do you believe he's just tossing these away? Here," she says, handing me two dogeared, bound volumes of the *Christian Science Monitor*. "You take 1961 and I'll take 1962. Would you help me carry mine back to the hotel?"

As I lug the heavy volumes for the next fifteen blocks, I am convinced there are more of her parents' idiosyncrasies in Bette than she realizes. Reaching the lobby of the posh Sherry Netherland, she thanks me profusely for my gallantry and I leave, my collection of *Monitors* under one sore arm, determined to deposit them in the nearest wastebasket.

Somehow, I wind up taking the strange burden all the way home and sit up until early morning, thumbing through a brown-edged ledger of the early Sixties. I come upon a lengthy article touting the abundant business and investment opportunities to be found in "the nation's newest state." "PROSPERITY BLOOMS IN HAWAII," boasts the headline. The story explains that "the people of Hawaii . . . are showing a single-minded determination to show their mainland cousins just what 'growth' is all about." Obviously, the venerable *Monitor* didn't know the half of it.

"I'm so thrilled with this book!" whispers a frizzy-haired Bette, turned out in baggy jeans, a droopy yellow sweat shirt and no makeup. She's leaning over the galleys of *A View from a Broad* in the small dining room of the rented Los Angeles home she has been sharing for the last two and a half years with actor Peter Riegert (he played Boon, the social chairman of Delta Tau Chi, in *National Lampoon's Animal House*). "There's something about typesetting that really elevates the written word. Or at least my written words." She gently puts the book away and gives me a brief tour of the happily disheveled house. The place is owned by actor Richard Chamberlain, whose mementos are hopelessly intermingled with Bette's gaudy costumes and Peter's dry cleaning.

Later, we sit on a lumpy couch across from the large fireplace in the living room. She is sipping Courvoisier, openly anxious about the impending premiere of *The Rose*, and I remind her of the request she made of Aaron Russo some seven years past: "Make me a legend."

"I said exactly that," she nods, red-faced. "I was half joking and half desperate. And what I meant was that I didn't want to be just another chick singer. I don't want to go to Vegas and wind up singing other people's stuff. I want to be what I think I can be, which is certainly not a legend. But you know, Aaron loved that stuff. That was like throwing down the gauntlet, dearie. His eyes jut lit up.

"It's insane to let something like that consume you," she says with a sigh and a long sip. "It's good in terms of being creative, but it's fairly hard on the people around you, your family. And you wake up one morning and you don't really know very much except that ambitious, selfish dream you've been in love with all these years. I don't want to be that. I want to grow up. I don't want to be Peter Pan *or* Janis Joplin.

"With a certain amount of introspection, triggered by age, plain old maturity, you find that it doesn't hurt so bad not to be in the eye of the hurricane. I don't have that desperation anymore, 'cause I know I can do what I do. A lot of people insulate themselves and refuse to feel that kind of pain. I find myself suffering from the same problem—of really loving to be with people but fearing that maybe they won't like me, you know? And isolating myself, because of a funny fear.

"I used to phone my parents every time something came up. Of course, being so far away from each other, everything always has a distance to it— you know, death, sickness. They used to not tell me a lot of stuff about sickness, and I never told them the bad parts. Until real desolation set in, like when my sister died. What happens when you leave home is, you turn around to watch and see how your folks are doing and they're the same."

Bette becomes agitated when I tell her how affected I was by the phone-booth scene in the film.

"They took something very lovely out of that scene that really burned my ass, because I thought it was the most telling thing in the whole film. She [Rose] says, 'What are you watching [on TV]? Oh. She's good. I like her.' Those two or three sentences told the whole story of the relationship between the mother and father and daughter. They'd prefer to watch somebody else, some other girl on a show. It's so mystical, it makes me all misty-eyed.

"I *tried* to say everything to my folks, but they never listened, they never asked for any daughterly advice. I told them to try to have a little more fun, but they couldn't get themselves into that frame of mind. It used to drive me mad, because I could see them wasting away before my eyes.

"My parents—they were a pair of characters, and now Daniel is turning into sort of an amalgam of the two of them. I guess, because he's retarded, all those traits are just so blatant in him. All those things about yourself that you've been hiding for years, everything that you might be worried about in yourself, is right out there in the open with him—only he doesn't give a damn. There's something to be learned from people like that."

"Something your father learned from Danny?"

"God, that's hard to know. He's a strange old bird." She sits pondering the question for several minutes, then slowly nods her head. "You know, maybe *he's* more open now in his own fashion. He went to New York last summer, flew in unannounced and sat on my sister's stoop until she came home. She sees there's this strange man sitting on the stoop with a little knapsack, and she looks and it's pa. 'What are you doing here?!' she says.

"He only came in for a day. Wanted to say goodbye. He's getting ready to kick off and wants to put his affairs in order."

"And how has knowing Danny changed you?"

She stares at me for a moment, then puts her brandy down and touches her fingers to her face, looking away as if gazing into some distant mirror.

"I always wished . . .," says Bette pensively, ". . . that my chest was smaller . . . that my hair was thicker . . . that my eyes were bluer . . . that my IQ was higher . . . that my shoe size was smaller. I never thought I was too pretty most of the time; I used to spend a lot of time turning my nose up in front of the mirror, you know, thinking, well, maybe you *should* have a nose job. Now, I think I can live with it, and like myself a bit more.

"Maybe I just grew out of it," she says, facing me, "but what I can promise you is that I will *never* do that stuff again."

Slaves to the Empire: The Veterans of *Star Wars*

"*I*t's a twelve-ology," *Carrie Fisher drolly assured over lunch in a Mexican restaurant on Manhattan's upper West Side in 1980. It was the eve of the release of* The Empire Strikes Back, *the second installment (after* A New Hope*) in the original* Star Wars *trilogy.*

"But I don't know how many they're gonna do," added the rising 23–year-old actress, insisting she was contracted to appear as Princess Leia Organa in "at least two more" of the ongoing series of science fiction films. "They have 12 on the tables or something. I don't know what tables or who has them in whose home; they're gambling tables."

The engagingly sarcastic Fisher had more than adequate preparation for the harsh and fickle aspects of Hollywood stardom, growing up with brother Todd Fisher, now a television director, under the apprenticeship of actress-mother Debbie Reynolds, and singing father Eddie Fisher, whose frayed relationship and subsequent remarriages were the stuff of fanzine fodder.

"'DEBBIE REYNOLDS AND HUSBAND HARRY KARL HAD A HUGE FIGHT IN THEIR MOUNTAIN HOME,' that's the earliest one I remember," said Carrie, citing a typical scandal sheet headline glimpsed in her youth. "I remember that being very funny. We didn't have a mountain home; they never fought. Harry could barely get his voice loud enough to get the maid to bring his other Scotch and soda.

"As for my father, his favorite marriage was probably Liz Taylor—wouldn't it be yours? If you had to pick between Liz, Connie Stevens, Terry Richards and my mother, you probably would."

Given the vagaries of her formative years, it's not surprising that Fisher's resigned attitude toward their consummate strangeness would carry over into her opinion of a galactic box office bonanza that proved abstract in the making and obtuse in its career-molding aftermath.

"There are certain things that you can bring to a movie that have substitutions in your life; well, you can't do that in this kind of film," said Fisher of *Star Wars*, echoing the feelings of other cast members. "You have to make Kierkegaard's giant leap of faith. On the set I would have to say, 'Don't blow up my planet please!' and all I saw was the assistant director—who couldn't wait for tea break—holding up a cardboard with an X on it. Or you'd be filmed with a matt camera and there's just a huge blue screen behind you where they fill in the special effects later. Like hyperspace—I'd never seen the effect, so I couldn't imagine how they would do it.

"On a soundstage at Shepperton studios in England," she continued, "they didn't have enough soldiers for the first film's last scene (in the Great Assembly Hall of the Rebel base) so they had to matt them up—they shot one group and then reshot it with the group moved up, and they put the negatives over each other so it looks like a massive group. So actually I never saw that hall filled with people who turned and applauded."

Over the course of the three movies, Fisher began to sense that the special effects and the extras were the true stars of the film. The lead players functioned as extras as well as outsiders amongst the old-guard team mentality that made the finished film work.

"During the Cloud Planet stuff in England," she recalled regarding *The Empire Strikes Back*, "I used to stand in the corner with the pig people— English dwarfs and midgets dressed in the pig costumes," she recalls. "So one day I went, 'Hi-ho, hi-ho, it's off to work we go,' and they started to do the little march, because I guess they'd also probably played the Seven Dwarfs at some time in their lives. So I'm this princess character, Snow White in space, right? Which hasn't translated into other jobs."

Indeed, in the interim between the trilogy's initial success and its 1997 pinnacle as the highest grossing film of all time after its reissue in the revised *Star Wars: Special Edition* form, Fisher secured a rather mixed bag of screen employment. Besides her work in *Mr. Mike's Mondo Video* (1979), *The Blues Brothers* (1980), *Under the Rainbow* (1981), *Garbo Talks* (1984), *The Man with One Red Shoe* (1985), *Hollywood Vice Squad* (1986), *Hannah and Her Sisters* (1986), *Amazon Women on the Moon* (1987), *When Harry Met Sally* (1989), *Sweet Revenge* (1990) and 1991's *Drop Dead Fred*, *Soapdish* and *This Is My Life*, Fisher also recounted her trials with drug addiction in a best-selling book, *Postcards from the Edge*, which also became a movie. Since then she's written two other well-received books, *Surrender the Pink* and *Delusions of Grandma*, and has become a highly paid Hollywood script doctor, working on *Hook*, *Sister Act* and *Lethal Weapon 3*.

Mark Hamill, who portrayed Luke Skywalker, got film work afterward in *Corvette Summer* (1978), *The Night the Lights Went Out in Georgia* (1981), *Slipstream* (1989), *Black Magic Woman* and *Midnight Ride* (both 1991), *In Exile* (1992) and as the voice of the Joker in the animated movie *Batman: Mask of the Phantom* (1993), as well as a featured part in *Children of the Damned* (1995). Since then he's toiled as a top voice talent in over 400 cartoons, including *Wing Commander Academy*, and on CD-ROM games, and is developing a film based on his own comic book, *The Black Pearl*.

Anthony Daniels, the Englishman inside the noisy metal exoskeleton of C-3PO, assumed the same role in the National Public Radio versions of *Star Wars*, and reprised his character in the 1985–86 ABC-TV series, *Droids: The Adventures of R2D2 and C3PO*. Daniels also did voiceovers for the animated *The Lord of the Rings* (1978), and acted in the hit British TV serial *Prime Suspect*, as well as appearing in George Lucas' 1992–93 ABC-TV series, *The Young Indiana Jones Chronicles*.

Kenny Baker, better known as R2D2, had roles in the films *Time Bandits*

(1981), and *Amadeus* (1984) and now tours Great Britain in a one-man comedy stage show.

Peter Mayhew, who played Chewbacca, returned to his job as hospital porter at the Mayday Hospital in suburban London, but occasionally acted in other fantasy films like *Sinbad and the Eye of the Tiger* (1977).

David Prowse, the former professional weightlifter who embodied Darth Vader, established the Dave Prowse Fitness Centre in London. He also landed parts in such films as *The People That Time Forgot* and *Jabberwocky* (both 1977) and in the TV series, *The Hitchhikers Guide to the Galaxy*.

Billy Dee Williams, the rogue turned heroic ally known as Lando Calrissian in *The Empire Strikes Back* and *The Return of the Jedi*, has since acted in the movies *Nighthawks* (1981), *Marvin and Tige* (1983), *Fear City* (1985), *Number One with a Bullet* and *Deadly Illusion* (both 1987), *The Impostor* (1988), *Batman* (1989), and *The Pit and the Pendulum* and *Driving Me Crazy* (both 1992).

Harrison Ford, after portraying Han Solo, has been a leading man in over two dozen other films, including *Raiders of the Lost Ark* (1981), *Blade Runner* (1982), *Indiana Jones and the Temple of Doom* (1984), *Witness* (1985), *The Mosquito Coast* (1986), *Frantic* and *Working Girl* (both 1988), *Indiana Jones and the Last Crusade* (1989), *Presumed Innocent* (1990), *Regarding Henry* (1991), *Patriot Games* (1992), *The Fugitive* (1993), *Clear and Present Danger* (1994), *Sabrina* (1995), *Air Force One* and *The Devil's Own* (both 1997), and *6 Days, 7 Nights* (1998).

Other than Ford, the professional fates of those who starred on either side of the otherworldly struggle between the Galactic Empire and the Alliance to Restore the Republic seemed to be foreshadowed in 1980 by the comments of Carrie Fisher: "The monsters steal the *Star Wars* movies, because the monsters are extremely human, and the humans, well, they didn't give them too much dimension." Or, as George Lucas put it that same year: "The Force has two sides. It is not a malevolent or a benevolent thing. It has a bad side to it, involving hate and fear, and it has a good side, involving love, charity, fairness and hope."

THE INTERVIEW

"THERE'S NO PLACE for personal triumph in a film like this," says Harrison Ford dryly, referring to his return to the screen as mercenary adventurer Han Solo in *Star Wars'* monumental sequel, *The Empire Strikes Back*. Although Ford shares star billing, he is painfully aware that he and the other featured performers are mere pawns in a projected nine-part series of sci-fi films, cartoonlike components with little more dimension than the hapless androids C-3PO and R2D2.

Star Wars, the creation of writer-director-producer George Lucas, is the largest-grossing film of all time—over $400 million at last count—and *Empire*, directed by Irvin Kershner, looks to be its nearest box-office rival. Yet the cast of this spectacular saga seems almost lost in an interplanetary shuffle.

"The star is the movie," says Mark Hamill, a.k.a. Luke Skywalker, and his cohorts sadly concur. Indeed, Harrison Ford has learned so little about his own character that he cannot explain why Solo is being pursued by bounty hunters throughout *Empire*.

"There's no, er, I don't know *why* that is." He shrugs, red-faced. "I can imagine, but basically, I just work here, you know what I mean? In fact, I didn't get the script to the second picture until three weeks before we started shooting. [Some of the actors in *Empire* were given only partial scripts to ensure the secrecy of plot twists.] I haven't gotten the script for the third one, *The Return of the Jedi*.

"One of George's real strengths," adds Ford, "is not giving you all the information you need, yet at the same time not denying you anything essential. You have a feeling that you want to know more at all times.

"I have heard frequently," he continues, "that there is a certain kind of disappointment with the ending of the second film. I've heard people say, 'There's no end to this film' or 'I can't wait to find out what happens.' But they *will*, and that's exactly the effect intended by the ending."

To feed the seemingly insatiable appetite for news about *Star Wars*, Twentieth Century-Fox and Lucasfilm (George's production company) have mounted a promotional onslaught whose scope resembles a rock & roll world tour. Over the last few weeks, the film's stars have been hustled from Los Angeles to New York to Washington to London to Japan and then on to Australia to sit for literally hundreds of newspaper, radio and television interviews. The effort is further supported by a multimillion-dollar ad campaign and a glut of aggressive merchandising schemes that include everything from a soundtrack album to a proposed Yoda doll, the gnomelike Jedi master.

The films' principals were not often together on the sets—especially during the shooting of *Empire*—and the same goes for their promo tours. While they get along well with one another, there's little sense of a shared experience. And as for the actual creation of the film fantasy, vivid anecdotes are rare: Carrie Fisher, who plays Princess Leia, admits that the actors had to "pretend a lot."

"On the set, I would have to say, 'Don't blow up my planet, please!' and all I'm doing is looking at a board with an X on it, held by an assistant director who couldn't wait for tea break.

"There are certain things you can bring to a movie that have substitutions in your life," she adds. "Well, you can't do that in this type of film. I had never seen hyperspace till I saw the finished films, so I could never imagine how they would do it. You just make what Kierkegaard called the 'great leap of faith.'"

"I felt curiously detached watching *Empire*," says Hamill. "I sound like my therapist, but you do start taking these things to heart, thinking, 'Yes, you are a terrible actor, and it was *only* the special effects that made it all memorable.'"

It is perhaps a sign of the times that the biggest entertainment phenomenon in history is also a wondrous cliffhanger that is as mesmerizing as it is manipulative. At this rate, we will have to wait until sometime around the year 2000 to see the final episode of Lucas' cinematic fairy tale, while the actors, who were paid sizable salaries (and, in the case of *Star Wars*, a reported bonus cut of Lucas' own profits), may never derive any great satisfaction from the most celebrated roles of their careers.

The man getting the most personal gratification from this project must be Lucas himself, who, after miraculously surviving a car crash at the age of eighteen, decided. "I should do something positive with my life because I was spared for a reason. Maybe I was here for *Star Wars.**

None of the actors are apologetic about their part in this unfolding drama, but one gets the feeling that they would relish a greater comprehension of, and control over, the science-fiction serial that has assumed such power over their lives and careers. (Ford, Hamill, Fisher, Billy Dee Williams and most of the other costars are signed for *The Return of the Jedi*.)

"The Force is what you perceive it to be," Lucas notes, "and it is always changing."

---

*For the benefit of anyone in this galaxy who is unaware of the *Star Wars* plot, the epic concerns Princess Leia Organa of Alderraan, the lovely leader of the Alliance to Restore the Republic, and her struggle to mount a successful rebellion against the evil Galactic Empire. Formerly a noble federation guarded by the righteous order of Jedi Knights, the massive republic eventually decayed from within, thanks to the power-mad efforts of a wicked self-appointed emperor and his strong right arm, fallen Jedi Darth Vader. The first film found Leia soliciting allies for her courageous quest, including aging Jedi Master (Ben) Obi-Wan Kenobi; adventurer Han Solo and his Wookie comrade, Chewbacca; droids C-3PO and R2D2; and Skywalker. *The Empire* is essentially a nonstop battle, the action built upon all the lore thus far implanted in the imaginations of millions of fans. *The Return* is its finale.

"George tells me that the wisest thing I could tell anyone is that I'm retired," says Mark Hamill, 28, only half joking as he nibbles nachos in a sunlit Malibu eatery called Alice's Restaurant. "Then I would have the best of both worlds. There's no pressure to put out a product, and if you do get a part, you can say, 'The role was so good it lured me out of retirement.'

"Who knows," he says in exasperation, "I think he's probably right."

Hamill views his contribution to Lucas' work-in-progress as "the classic thankless role. I'm the straight man, the earnest storyteller.

"You know," he offers with a hard swallow, "thirty years ago, the studios would have built our careers. We're all freelancers now. I'm finally looking like a grown-up, after all these years. I always got the 'Hey, dad, can I borrow the keys to the car tonight?' parts. That's why I'm waiting. I really have a feeling *Empire* is going to help me.

"I've got one of the best collections of *Star Wars* memorabilia," he suddenly volunteers, "but it's all put away because I'm a serious collector."

"How valuable to sci-fi buffs is the Luke Skywalker doll?" I ask.

"I've been marked down in price," he moans. "But it doesn't look anything like me, anyway. My wife and I went into a Toys 'R Us store awhile back, and they had all these kids' costumes. They'd made a bunch of *Star Wars* ones; four of 'em, and I was one.

"They had sold out Darth Vader, Chewbacca and C-3PO," he murmurs, "and I was the only one available. There were just boxes and boxes of me."

The son of an itinerant navy captain, Hamill grew up in Virginia and Japan, and became absorbed in acting while in high school. Although he has had extensive TV experience, including a short-lived series with Gary Busey called *The Texas Wheelers*, he confesses that "one of the best things I think I ever did was Snoopy in *You're a Good Man, Charlie Brown.* I was embarrassed to mention it before, because it was in high school in Japan."

Hamill's anxiety about landing choice roles was tragically accelerated when his BMW ran off the freeway in 1977. *Star Wars* had not yet been released, and his face was sufficiently ravaged that he wondered whether he would be able to retain any part of his angular good looks, let alone fulfill the remainder of his three-picture deal with Lucas. That mental anguish was only intensified when the film proved to be an international smash.

"It's the crux of my dilemma right now. For an actor to have massive facial surgery is *traumatic*. I thought it jeopardized everything," he admits, wincing when I note that a small lip scar is still visible. "I thought it could possibly be pretty much over for me, unless. . . ."

Since *Star Wars*, Hamill's only other film stints have been the role of "an emotional hard-luck case" in the obscure *Corvette Summer* and the slightly meatier part of a fragile young infantryman in Sam Fuller's *The Big Red One*, a World War II story filmed in 1978 and only now being released.

"After I came back from filming *Empire Strikes Back*, my first job offer was to walk on nails and swallow fire on some celebrity circus in Las Vegas—whatever *that* was. It's so bizarre. Here I am a grown-up and this is how I earn my living. What's my son gonna think of me? All of a sudden there are so many elements that aren't in your control. You wind up almost being another one of the public watching this 'public' you.

"I'd work for scale for somebody willing to take a chance with me, because it's real frustrating to be in something this big and popular and not really feel you're stretching yourself. I met Milos Forman yesterday on an interview [for the film version of the best-selling novel *Ragtime*], and I would kill to work with that man!

"I was dying to get a script reading on *Midnight Express* 'cause I thought for them to use that squeaky-clean image of Luke and then have that [drug imprisonment] happen to him would be great dramatically.

"You keep saying to yourself, 'Don't worry, you won't get trapped.' I can stick it out," he decides, "as long as I'm careful with my money."

He changes the subject, speaking with enthusiasm about his wife, Marilou, their infant son and the house they've just purchased in Malibu. I wonder whether his wife knew of his interstellar alter ego before they began dating.

"I didn't think so," he says, "but since then I've discovered that she knew. But then again, I don't think she was impressed by it. Seriously, from being a dental hygienist in Westwood, she knows more people in the business than I do. That's how I got invited to a recent Eagles concert—she knows them from doing their teeth!

"A lot has happened to me since the first movie," Hamill confides wearily. "And you feel that to go cross-country on these promotional tours is sort of a waste. They're hard, real hard. One of the reasons I feel so empty and lacking when I talk to interviewers is because you ask me these questions and I don't know, I'm searching for the answers myself."

Do you want to see the scars?" asks Anthony Daniels, the suave, soft-spoken British actor who animates the gleaming gold hardware known as C-3PO, *Star Wars'* fussy butler of a robot. Seated next to Hamill on a long couch in a suite at Manhattan's Sherry Netherland Hotel, the delicately handsome Daniels unbuttons his tan silk shirt to reveal a gruesome network of old wounds.

"The whole first film was a miasma of pain," says Daniels. "It was the metal pieces of the suit shoving me about, meeting with another piece of metal to pinch me horribly. It was like sticking your fingers in an electric socket, again and again.

"Fortunately, it was much easier for *Empire,* because the costume was redesigned. It's slightly more flexible. I even tap-danced recently, did a metallic soft-shoe on *The Muppet Show.* What makes it bearable is that, between us, we make up a somewhat beautiful piece of sculpture." Daniels frequently discusses C-3PO in terms of "we."

"In the end, I turned him from an American version of a robot programmed to be a servant into a swishy British twit, but he's quite nice.

"I think a psychiatrist would enjoy being in there with me," Daniels observes, "because you can really watch people, and watch people's reactions to me. It's fascinating. Sometimes I would be standing next to the costume and people would come up and say, 'That guy must be incredibly *stupid* to do this part.'"

He then relates the mortifying experience of nearly being expelled by security guards from the backstage area of the 1977 Academy Awards ceremony because he was, of course, out of costume.

"I'd forgotten my ID badge." He shrugs, rolling his eyes. "I literally had to beg them to find the guy who was looking after me. There's not a lot of dignity involved in being in these *Star Wars* films; I have no dignity left whatsoever. I mean, if I've got an itchy crotch, somebody has to scratch it for me. I actually can't do that—my hands don't go that far."

"He's one of the most famous characters in cinema!" Hamill exclaims, jumping up and stalking about the room like an exasperated press agent. "Yet no one would recognize him on the street!

"Just to show you how famous *I* am," Hamill offers, "a lady came up to me after a reception and said, 'Are you the skinny guy in the gold robot suit? I know he's here someplace and you're the skinniest person here.' I said, 'Okay, I'll sign an autograph,' and wrote: 'Best wishes always, the skinny guy in the robot suit.'

"I took the *Star Wars* trivia test and failed," Hamill says to Daniels impishly. "They asked who your former owner was and I couldn't remember."

"Somebody in Tower Records on Sunset [Boulevard, in Los Angeles] recognized my voice one day," says Daniels, striving to cheer himself up. "All I said was, 'I want to buy a record. Can I have this please?' And he said, '*You're Anthony Daniels!*' I was really shocked."

"The first day we got here, we had a press conference at nine in the morning," says an exhausted Harrison Ford, rubbing his eyes as he lifts his stocking feet onto a coffee table in New York's Plaza Hotel. "And then from about 9:20 a.m. to 1:30 p.m. we met a gross of journalists around a dozen tables, twelve at a time, and moved from one table to another, and so we did about 150 interviews in four hours. An hour off for lunch, and then we came back and did fifteen five- to ten-minute television interviews in four hours and then went back to our rooms and passed out. The next day we did twenty-seven television interviews, and on into Sunday. This morning I've done the *Today* show and, uh, about four or five interviews with print media."

In his eyes, I see murky bog pits on the planet Dagobah.

"The last time we were on tour together," Mark Hamill had told me earlier, "Harrison was the publicity sheriff. He would give us report cards: 'Humility—B. I like what you said about not being in the business for money—A for that.'"

Right now, Ford is too fatigued to grade anyone, himself included.

"I had no experience with science fiction beforehand," he says weakly. "And I didn't go to those Buck Rogers matinees, either. In fact, I have never been much of a film fan."

The son of an advertising executive and the grandson of a vaudeville trouper, Ford did a little summer stock in Wisconsin before flunking out of college three days before graduation.

"That's when I first considered being an actor for money, and I knew I had to go either to L.A. or to New York, and damned quick, 'cause it was starting to snow in Wisconsin. So I flipped a coin. It came up New York, so I flipped it again so I could go to L.A. I wasn't gonna starve *and* freeze."

Ford was fortunate enough to quickly land a seven-year contract with Columbia.

"I did a year and a half and got kicked out on my ass for being too difficult," he says, laughing. "I was very unhappy with the process they were engaged in, which was to re-create stars the way it had been done in the Fifties. They sent me to get my hair pompadoured like Elvis Presley, all that shit, for $150 a week."

Ford had a wife and child to support, so he went into freelance carpentry, rebuilding his own home for starters, then constructing a $100,000 recording studio for Sergio Mendes. He took film work whenever he deemed it "decent" and wound up in *American Graffiti*, Francis Coppolas' *The Conversation*, the TV movie *The Court Martial of Lt. Calley*, *Star Wars*, *Heroes* and *Force 10 from Navarone*, the last of which kept him in Yugoslavia while the sci-fi spectacular was exploding across the nation.

Ford says, quite convincingly, that *Empire* "is the first time I've ever seen anything I've done that I'm happy with." He then states that he does *not* enjoy watching himself on the screen.

I suggest that one of the most engaging moments in *Empire* is the tense few seconds before Darth Vader sends Han into a potentially fatal carbon freezing chamber to subdue him.

"I love you!" the forlorn Leia divulges desperately to her hero.

"I know," Solo replies with a crowd-pleasing arrogance.

With a little coaxing, Ford admits that "to a certain degree," Solo's cocky cachet is his own. "In the script," he explains with a smirk, "it read, 'I love you too!' But that was too much on the nose. If you didn't have something else there at that point you would not get your full payoff in that scene. You know, there's a sense of dread and mystery there, and there's no satisfying conclusion in 'I love you too!' I wanted the moment to have another complexion. Kershner agreed, and that's the way we shot it.

"People who are expecting a repetition of the emotional experience of the first film are not going to find exactly that. The audience that saw the first film is more sophisticated now, three years later, in the same way the techniques are more sophisticated. And the demands upon them are slightly more than they were in the first film.

"This film is much more emotional, and some of the emotions are extremely difficult to deal with. The accomplishment of saying something true about those emotions is great.

"What's also great for me," he adds with a wink, "is to watch the kids watch that love scene [in the *Millennium Falcon*, when Han and Leia kiss] and they don't go, '*Yucky*.'"

The Return of the Jedi will begin shooting in the summer of 1981 (in addition, the BBC plans a radio serial), and most of the regulars will be back, the chief holdout currently being Anthony Daniels.

"Well," he demurs, "do I feel that I want to do it today? *No*. Definitely not. But let's leave it for a bit and possibly . . : It will be all right."

Actually, the most enthusiastic of all the cast members seems to be newcomer Billy Dee Williams, who signed on for *Empire* as Lando Calrissian, a con artist and former sidekick of Solo's. Williams loves the character, whom he views as a "Burt Reynolds kind of charmer" who complements Han's hotheadedness.

"It's more than pure entertainment," he says of the whole enterprise over tea one rainy afternoon. "I see it from at least three levels: a philosophical level, a real level and a cartoon level—and they're all great.

"The introduction of Lando is a good one," he says firmly. "I talked to George when *Star Wars* came out and I was very candid. I said, 'Look, there's Darth Vader, the dark, *black* fear, and there's Alec Guinness playing the *white* knight, Ben Obi-Wan Kenobi. Here we go again, perpetuating that same old stuff.'

"And now, by having Lando [who slowly becomes an ally of Leia's cause and vows to rescue Solo], we're gonna have to put aside the old point of view. Now, we're talking about *symbols—darkness* as averse to *clarity*. Black, white, red, we're all included in the human dilemma, and Darth is scarier this time, because now we learn he's *human*—he's not a mechanical monster."

All of this notwithstanding, a certain, more specific meeting of the minds with director Kershner helped cement Williams' decision to join the project.

"Kershner and I sat down at my house in California and we talked about Eastern philosophy," Williams says. "He's into Zen, and I've been into Zen since I was about twenty-six; now I'm forty. Kershner said, 'I wanna introduce some Zen here, because I don't want the kids to walk away just feeling that everything is shoot-'em-up, but that there's also a little something to think about here in terms of yourself and your surroundings.'

"And that's what Yoda, who's a Zen master, is saying: Before you enter the temple, you have to live out all your desires—the body is the temple and it houses your better self, and your better self is your mind. And that is what this wonderful little character is talking about.

"I tell my son Corey that the greatest teacher is the teacher who says, 'Don't follow me, follow yourself. Because within you there is that kingdom, that life, that force.'

"Boy," says Billy Dee, his face suddenly flushed with a diversity of emotions. "I guess I sure can't describe my concept of these films any better than that.

"People will say, 'Why did you do *Star Wars* after doing all those other things? This doesn't seem to be important for you.' That's really what they're saying. But it is important, because it's part of my growth.

"Power is a very peculiar thing. It's like the ego. The ego's only there to keep you above water. Once we realize something good about ourselves, we have a tendency to abuse the gift. That's what this film series is about: truths *and* consequences. As my wife says, '*Bachi atari.*' That's Japanese for 'What goes around comes around.'"

"I was nineteen, chosen at random, and told to lose weight, which at the time was a problem," says pretty, petite Carrie Fisher, 23, curled up in an over-stuffed chair in her New York apartment. "This time around, for *Empire*, I was told to *gain* weight. The only film I'd done before *Star Wars* was *Shampoo*. But they decided to go with me anyway, a strong girl with a low voice and self-righteous nature."

Sardonic would be a better word. Fisher's flippant outlook on life may be the result of a childhood spent enduring mother Debbie Reynolds' two celebrated divorces ("She's a Texas chain-saw survivor; she's real great") and the gossip-magazine prattle that plagued father Eddie Fisher ("He's a little shellshocked from thirteen years of doing speed, but he's real friendly"). Her quick-witted style, heavily influenced by the blasé-just-before-the-gallows banter of *Saturday Night Live* alumnus Michael O'Donoghue (who's a close chum), contains traces of Joan Rivers, Bette Midler and a dollop of Dorothy Parker.

"I liked whenever Harrison and I yelled at each other," she giggles, recalling her favorite scenes from both films. "And whenever Darth Vader came in, a lot of the scenes were funny, because he was physically depicted by David Prowse, this muscle man from Cornwall or Devon. [Vader's eerie, wheezing voice was dubbed in by James Earl Jones.] And 'cause he had this Devon farmer's accent, we used to call him Darth Farmer!

"In the first film," Fisher adds, "I had to wear that white dress and I couldn't wear a bra. Everything was bouncing around, so I had to wear gaffer's tape for three months to keep my breasts down. A new crew member used to come up every day and get to rip it off—only kidding!

"Lucas always had to remind me to 'Stand up! Be a princess!' And I would act like a Jewish princess and lean forward, slouching, chewing gum."

Fisher laments the fact that several exotic scenes never made it into either film. "In the original script, I was captured, and when Mark and Harrison found me, I was hanging upside down with yellow eyes, like in *The Exorcist*. They shoulda just gotten Linda Blair for it. Some form of radar torture was done to me and I was in a beam, bruised and beaten up, suspended in midair. The reason it was cut from the film was because I was unconscious and the Wookie would have had to carry me for, like, the next fifteen minutes. But I loved the idea of having yellow eyes and being beaten and carried."

The talk shifts to Leia's romance with Han Solo in *Empire*, and Carrie slyly speculates that "if she had her wits about her, she would have fallen for the big, strong Wookie. She's not that experienced, but because she's a princess, she would have some kind of problem with whomever she dated. Like, 'She can't marry out of her solar system' or something."

Her notion of an X-rated sequel to *Empire* makes her howl with laughter.

"Nude scenes with the robots!" she envisions. "They could do *anything*. And Darth Vader having an affair, making the princess do awful, kinky things. Then afterward, you could shoot a scene where you see her sleeping contentedly and have him lying there, smoking a cigarette."

Gazing around her apartment, crammed with antique toys, dolls and the whimsical knickknacks one might expect to find in a little girl's bedroom, I realize there are few *Star Wars* souvenirs.

"They sent me everything at first, as if I had some child lurking about, but I gave most of it away. On Halloween, I had no candy so I gave two children in the building something, and then the whole building descended on me, and I gave a lot of stuff away."

"You know," she says in a mock stage whisper, "they send me *Star Wars* sheets. I just gave the last ones away to some of the *Saturday Night Live* writers. They called me back and said, 'You don't have them for *double* beds, do you?'"

"The merchandising, it's very funny. Harrison used to get so upset: 'Mark gets to be a *puzzle*, why don't I?!' Those kinds of arguments. And we'll go, 'Wait a minute! Why don't I get to be on the pencil box for chrissake! I mean, if I'm gonna be in this and I'm gonna end up being two sizes of dolls, and a belt, and a cookie, and a hat, then why don't I get to be on an eraser, too?'"

"*I*," Fisher boasts, "was on a Princess Leia eraser."

"Do the kids who buy these erasers come up to you in supermarkets," I wonder, "and ask you about the *Millennium Falcon* or Jawas or . . .?"

"No! They come to my home. I swear to you! I sometimes find them in my home, and there are a lot of little girls. One girl named Yolanda sat here and waited for me. That's when I started locking my door. One night—this is great—some *real* strange guy with crossed eyes came up here and said he had bought my address for twenty dollars. Peter Aykroyd [Dan's brother] was here and chased him down the block.

"Weird," she says with a shudder. "You know, I remember falling asleep one day on the set and dreaming about half-robots, half-people. You're hanging around the set for three or four months and you're going to lunch with midgets and giants every day; eventually it permeates the brain. So I had these violent nightmares, dreams where you keep trying to impose *your* reality and you can't. It gets you crazy."

Fisher has since awakened to another, equally unsettling fact: Her involvement in these films has not made her more in demand in Hollywood.

"Not at all." She nods with an even smile. "It hasn't translated into jobs, into other work. It's not an actor's performance. You have fun doing it to a degree, but I'm famous in this weird way because I'm this children's cartoon character.

"*Balls*, people recognize me more from *Saturday Night Live*! I mean, people know who I am, but nothing can be bigger than this movie no matter what happens. When we all kick off, we will be the princess and Luke and Han."

"How does that make you feel?" I ask.

Her smile vanishes and the color drains from her face.

"Helpless."

Susan Sarandon:
Sex & the Singular Girl

"I've been very disappointed with almost every film I've done," conceded Susan Sarandon over our meal at the Russian Tea Room in 1983, "in that it hasn't turned out to be as I thought it would—in the sense of being jarred by how it was cut and what happened to the 'vision' all the participants talked about.

"Two of my biggest hits, *Rocky Horror Show* and *Atlantic City*, were considered unreleaseable by the studios for over a year. It wouldn't surprise me if other films I've done become cult films down the line. I seem to have a nose for doing things which at the time I never realized would cause a stir."

This capsule critique contains the essence of what makes Sarandon one of the finest acting talents in the world today. In a film industry predicated on star vehicles and their ready exploitation, she believes in the intrinsic worth of a craft that was once at the core of the entire enterprise: story-telling.

Born with a somber but steady gaze and a tender physical beauty that never exuded girlishness so much as a womanly sense of sympathy, Sarandon has the innate frankness of an old soul. And due to her willingness to slip her skin and join with kindred colleagues to animate characters not usually considered surefire fodder for mass entertainment, Susan is able to restore the fundamental components of the dramatic experience: a player able to disappear behind a character in order to dive toward the deeper understanding such feats demand, and an audience attracted to the human scale of secret moments they could never have discerned on their own.

Because such subtle mutual commitments transcend mere escapism, Sarandon reminds all of us of the simple but profound integrity to which her profession once aspired.

Reviewing the film that occasioned this profile of Sarandon, *New York Times* critic Vincent Canby enthused that "What makes 'The Hunger' so much fun is its knowing stylishness. . . . Here is a film that, for once, is appropriately served by fast cuts, overlapping dialogue, flashy camera work, wildly fashionable clothes and decor so elegant that only mythical creatures could sit around in it."

Yet Canby felt the striking look suited the movie's startling substance. "Though 'The Hunger' has all the elements that people who seek out horror films expect," he continued, "it is not, strictly speaking, a horror film. Rather it is a film of visual sensations, not all of which are quite so explicit as the sight of Miss [Catherine] Deneuve making love to the innocent Miss Sarandon, while simultaneously giving her a blood transfusion."

By subverting the exotic context of its surroundings, Sarandon and her collaborators brought an interior sense of exhaustion to the exterior agelessness of the film's undead central characters. Their ultra-insecure sphere of urban sophistication attained a somber believability only hinted at in later, bigger-budget stabs at the theme like 1994's *Interview with the Vampire*.

As for Sarandon, she later admitted an additional, private allure on projects like *The Hunger*: "The reason we all did it was to work with each other." The many honest satisfactions offered by most of Sarandon's movies have rightfully made them cult favorites, the devotional word-of-mouth that accompanies them building her following in a way no promotional hardsell could possibly effect.

The bulk of her movies after *The Hunger* boasted Sarandon's customary meld of exceptional performances and unconventional subject matter: *The Buddy System* (1984), *Compromising Positions* (1985), *The Witches of Eastwick* (1987), *Bull Durham* and *Sweet Heart's Dance* (both 1988), *The January Man* and *A Dry White Season* (both 1989), *White Palace* (1990), *Thelma & Louise* (1991), *The Player* (1992), *Bob Roberts, Light Sleeper,* and *Lorenzo's Oil* (all 1992), *Little Women* (1994), *Dead Man Walking* (1995), for which she took the Best Actress Oscar, *The Long Kiss Goodbye* (1996), and *Twilight* (1998).

As if condensing all the convincing dramatic conjure she brought to the trusting victim in *The Hunger*, the nurturing Marmee in *Little Women*, the distaff road warrior in *Thelma & Louise*, and the forgiving Sister Helen in *Dead Man Walking* into a personal credo, Sarandon concluded in 1983 that "I chose to do something in life where I didn't have any guarantees of my security, and I still don't, but I believe something happened when we got rid of superstition and completely went toward science. Parents started telling their kids, 'If you do *this*, something will happen. Study hard and you'll get a good job. *This* is the explanation for *that.*'

"Well, there's no justice in the world. All that matters is what James Cagney said: 'Following your heart.' Then, at least, you're doing something you're passionately connected with."

THE INTERVIEW

"GOING TO BED with Catherine Deneuve wasn't a power struggle, the way some sex acts can be," the stunning redhead at the corner table announces brightly. A hush falls over the restaurant and a nearby patron almost chokes on her chicken Kiev. "I think women have a tendency to sexualize someone they love or admire, whereas men tend to love someone they've sexualized. Women probably admire each other into bed, and it was easy for Catherine and me because we're friends. There wasn't the sense of one person trying to dominate the encounter."

Whether on *The Tonight Show*, a movie set or at the best table in a fashionable bistro, when Susan Sarandon rhapsodizes, people love to listen in. Indeed, she gives us all an earful.

In this case, she's thinking out loud about her explicit love scene with Deneuve in *The Hunger*, the slickly violent and sex-steeped horror film that also stars David Bowie. Susan plays a scientist engaged in research about the aging process, and Catherine is cast as Miriam. A 2,000-year-old vampire, she is seeking to seduce a new victim now that 200-year-old John (Bowie) is abruptly withering into a decrepit shell of his formerly suave self.

"In the book [by Whitney Strieber], the scientist is drugged when Miriam entices her, but I disagreed with that," Sarandon says. "Catherine is very attractive, so why should my character have to be *drugged* to go to bed with her? I suggested rather vehemently we forget that aspect of the story and it was agreed to. The set was closed for the nude scene, but after five days of shooting it, even the cameramen were bored. Still, Catherine was the most considerate person I've ever had to kiss on the screen.

"Unlike women," Sarandon continues," I suspect men don't talk with each other too intimately when they're buddying or slapping each other with towels in locker rooms. One reason there are no effective films about men and women in contemporary circumstances is that nobody knows what the hell men and women in contemporary circumstances are about. Talking like astronauts about not wanting to "threaten each other's space," we're in outer space as far as relationships are concerned.

"My feeling is that when the time comes when women are defined—especially in their own minds—not as the opposite or the complement of males but rather just as human beings, it will take the pressure off both sexes to compete."

Up close, the 35-year-old Sarandon's features are angular, the high cheekbones and pronounced jaw give her face a determined cast, but the warm brown eyes dart mischievously and the delicate mouth is prone to generous grins that precede flat-out cackles. Susan Sarandon is a classic screen minx for the emotionally cluttered '80s—say, a shrewder Rita Hayworth in hand-me-down overalls. Frankly, she has a reputation for being a first-rate flake, clambering in and out of trysts, sparking comically impassioned debates with her various directors, showing herself to be acutely bright and disarmingly brazen. It is these qualities that have somehow conspired to make her a magnet for things flamboyantly accidental and oddly—often *very* oddly—right for her, especially her acting career. She "just fell into it" one day in 1970, five days after moving to New York City with actor-husband Chris Sarandon, whom she had met while they were both students at Catholic University (they are since divorced).

There was an open audition for the film *Joe*, which she wandered into on a whim, and she landed a part. She's been falling upward ever since. Shortly after *Joe* she was making $1,000 a week on an ABC soap called *The World*

Apart. A few largely unmemorable films followed, among them *Lady Liberty* and *The Great Waldo Pepper,* but each contained what most critics conceded was at least a kernel of believability in the offbeat bravado of Susan Sarandon.

Then came her part in the cult classic *The Rocky Horror Picture Show,* a film that was originally considered unreleasable. "Eventually, it was leaked to art houses and college campuses, and it caught on first with the gay community. In the years since, it's made millions, without ever really having had a formal release. But what a legacy it's left me with!" she adds, exultant. "To be most famous for running around with a transvestite ghoul, dressed in a half-slip and a crooked bra!"

While working on *Pretty Baby* during 1977–78 with director Louis Malle, she began a three-year affair with him (he is now married to Candice Bergen) and a professional relationship that also resulted—after another string of box office bombs—in the acclaimed *Atlantic City.* This earned Sarandon an Oscar nomination. Suddenly, the zany siren of the B-movie circuit was being taken dead seriously.

"In terms of vehicles, my career has been made on Chevys, not on Rolls-Royces," she concedes with a laugh. "I don't think I've ever done a film that's been worthy of me yet. My role in *Atlantic City* wasn't really a good part, when you think about it. And my role in *The Tempest* was so horrible that I cut off all my hair during shooting in a fit of rage. I've never had a *Sophie's Choice,* a *Frances,* a *Norma Rae,* a *Private Benjamin*—one of those pictures where your character's name is in the title and it's all about you and you really get a chance to dig in."

Sarandon's not afraid to let the studio establishment and her colleagues in on her strong opinions, as evidenced by her backstage rhubarb with the contentious film press last April at the Academy Awards. After presenting the Best Supporting Actor award to Lou Gossett for *An Officer and a Gentleman,* she found herself running the obligatory press gauntlet, fielding aggressive questions concerning the first Oscar accorded a black actor in many years. Her answers were not what everybody wanted to hear.

"They asked me if I thought Lou Gossett deserved the award," she recalls with obvious disgust. "Can you imagine someone asking me that—after I'd just presented it to him? How tactless and downright stupid can you get! And there was all this back-patting and hot air taking place about his being a black, and wasn't the Academy liberal? Who's kidding who? Lou just did a good job. Period. I mean, how do you even define being black? Ben Kingsley is half Indian and no one makes an issue of that. Such hypocrisy and nonsense!"

Small wonder that Susan Sarandon is rapidly becoming known as a symbol of feistiness and independence in the '80s, an "accidental star," as she puts it, in the best sense of the phrase, being ruled by heart, conscience and intuition rather than blind ambition. Besides work in films and Off Broadway (most recently, in *Extremities*, she won raves as a potential rape victim who overpowers her assailant), she has formed an improvisational study group with other New York-based actors, including Carol Kane, Richard Dreyfuss, Peter Boyle and Andre Gregory. Beyond acting, she is extremely active in the nuclear disarmament movement, and she does volunteer work with schizophrenics at Mt. Sinai Hospital.

Born Susan Abigail Tomalin, the daughter of a Welsh-English father and an Italian mother, Sarandon grew up in Edison, New Jersey, the eldest of nine offspring. From the start, she was a probing, questioning child in a markedly conservative environment, daring, for example, to debate what she perceived as glaring inconsistencies in the Catholic education she was receiving.

Not surprisingly, organized religion no longer occupies a central place in her world. "While I was doing *Waldo Pepper* in San Antonio, I worked with social workers during my time off, taking care of 1,500 kids of sharecroppers. Their houses had no bathrooms, but tons of religious pictures. I can't endorse that approach to life."

The most eye-opening experience of Sarandon's personal development was the "psychological unraveling" she experienced in 1976 after contracting pneumonia during the aftermath of *The Rocky Horror Picture Show*. As a result, she couldn't eat and her weight fell to 85 pounds. Thus debilitated, she began to suffer severe psychosomatic disorders. She lost her hearing, could not keep track of time, had frequent fits of uncontrollable crying and suffered hallucinations in which she saw herself outside her body.

"I went through a huge re-evaluation of the world that almost cost me my sanity," she recalls, her familiar grin vanishing. "I used to believe that love was all-powerful, which is one of those very dangerous myths. You can love somebody in absolutely the right way, but that doesn't mean love will prevail. In other words, there's no fairness in the world—you can do everything right and still get a brain tumor. It was a devastating realization.

"I set myself up for a bad trip and I was committed to an institution, although not for very long. They thought I was schizophrenic, but once you commit yourself to having a breakdown, it's over fairly quickly, unless you've become involved in drugs, which I hadn't. I had never been in analysis before, since that was never thought of in my family, but I had to grow up! I was extremely fortunate to stumble on a very practical therapist who was quite wonderful."

In retrospect, Sarandon feels that the waking nightmares of the past have made her humbler and stronger in the here and now, and more intrepid as an actor. *The Buddy System*, her new film with Richard Dreyfuss, is a case in point. She plays Emily, a stenographer who got pregnant in high school and elected to raise her son in her mother's house. Emily meets a man (Dreyfuss) who works as a security guard at her child's school, and they tumble into bed but find the encounter unfulfilling. A strained, argumentative relationship eventually blossoms into friendship, however, and then love. It is an often-poignant treatment of so-called ordinary lives, and the intertwined themes of the rewards of motherhood and the risky process of loving have a deeply personal resonance for her.

"The film was supposed to be a romantic comedy, with my character being kind of dippy, but I took a chance and played Emily with more intelligence and strength. I just feel that it's important these days in film for role model-type characters, good or evil, to have their human dignity. And so *The Buddy System* is funny but not Neil Simon; serious, but a drama."

In other words, it's another quirky, tough-to-target chapter in the Susan Sarandon Method for winning fans and influencing people.

"The movie made me think a lot about the men in my life, and having kids. I've had a few miscarriages, and there was a time when I left a relationship because I wanted a child and the man didn't. It's something very much on my mind, considering my age. The problem is, if you're a woman who's independent, creative and has a lot of freedom, a great deal of the energy that would go into raising a child goes into your work.

"It's a waste," she frets, "because I'd make a great mother. I enjoy loving, have a good sense of humor, don't think all children are terminally cute and I'm a good listener. But if you don't need a relationship that would engender a family, aren't seeking security, financial support, a direction in life, and you're having a good time, what do you take in exchange?"

It's obviously a nagging dilemma for Sarandon, who says that she has come to "accept loneliness and pain as part of the human condition. Where I used to get irate, now I just feel these things indicate the extent to which I may someday feel joy."

Extremities provided what was the most harrowing role of her convoluted career. A physically violent play, it left her in a neck brace, with splints on her fingers, fractured wrists and the temporary plague of recurrent, grotesquely abstract nightmares.

"Physically and psychologically, I think I got out of the part just in the nick of time," she says. "After being almost raped on-stage every day for the past five months, I had put much of my conscious appreciation of myself and my sexuality on hold because I felt too vulnerable. Also, I had gravitated toward the masculine side of me. Acting, by definition, uses a lot of what we consider to be feminine characteristics. Very rarely is a woman asked to move toward the masculine side. Rather, it's frowned upon; it seems ugly and is upsetting."

As the after-lunch coffee was served, Sarandon looked out the window of the Russian Tea Room, hesitated at the thought of hurrying out into the chilly early-winter Manhattan afternoon, and suggested we keep talking until the caffeine bolstered her courage enough to face the elements.

How did Extremities *affect you?*

I was going to a physical therapist at least two times a week. The producer of *Extremities* said he was paying more for my doctor bills than he was to me. There's no physical female equivalent of that kind of violence. I mean, when you do those kinds of things it reads as being very masculine, very macho.

Has the role left you walking around with a lot of residual psychic armor?

Yes, perhaps, but it's not aggressiveness or self-protection you feel as much as rage, alienation. It's written in the play that she takes on certain violent physical acts in order to control the situation. It's about power, and they're mostly acts—like most macho acts—of bluffing. It's a certain kind of dance.

Describe the recurrent dreams the play inspired.

Besides the usual paranoid dreams, I had dreams of big wasps; the insect is a metaphor throughout the play. That was expected. I knew that to be as alienated as this woman was—since she almost dies, and nobody takes her side, and she's fighting her roommates—would be traumatic for anyone who played her.

I think that a lot of our personality develops from habitual behavior, and I think that when you do something that difficult and ugly for a period of time, it can really start to affect you, no matter how healthy you are.

Before I found a good physical therapist, I was in such pain all the time. I couldn't sleep. But there's something about it being that difficult that initially attracted me to it. But if I had really known what it entailed I'm not sure I would have had the courage to do it. I know the violence was choreographed but it wasn't as controllable as it should have been.

And the audience felt compelled to stand up and scream, and got very involved—a very primitive reaction to seeing a woman with a hammer get the better of a guy, tie him up and put him behind a barrier in the fireplace.

My mother saw, but my father was in Maine and couldn't get in to see it. My mother liked it (*smiling*). My brother, who's twenty-one, he came to opening night and was visibly moved and upset, even though he knew what it was about. He said it was every nightmare he'd ever had about something that might happen to one of his sisters.

What point do you think our culture is at in terms of men and women shaping a society that's mutually fair-minded?

You don't define an apple by saying it's the opposite of a pear, and yet that's often what goes on between the sexes. I think, ideally, we need to be more like brother and sister, or neighbors, comrades, or the guardians of each others' solitude. I mean, I don't think that when two people get together they're meant to give up everything and become one. There are always spaces between you, and the differences between people are to be respected—and guarded, if anything.

What part do you think the women's movement currently plays in this?

Any movement is always a little too serious to begin with, and then it lightens up. We're just now getting to the phase where it's lightening up. I can see why men are confused. But in the end it should allow men to be more of everything, instead of under these strict rules. It's much harder on men because everything in Western society is male-dominated right down to the language. Women can get away with more because they're not under so much surveillance.

But do you know that there are primitive tribes, according to Margaret Mead, where women are the hunters *and* take care of the children and the house—and the men still fight among themselves?! The thing that scares the shit out of me is that the women who are rising to political positions are now adapting the worst characteristics of men in order to become successful and powerful.

Normally, men tend to be more black and white about making decisions. Women tend to be more circumstantial, and possibly wiser in certain ways.

I started to have women's dinners with about ten people, where the men could come for dessert or to pick up their wives or friends. It's funny because there are so many women's lunches but very rarely women's dinners. In the beginning, everyone was kind of self-conscious about it: "What shall we talk about? The guys, 'cause they're not here?"

These people, they weren't all actors and they weren't all artists; I mixed it up. It wasn't like a sorority, everybody didn't know each other. There were older and younger people, and not always the same ones.

We'd end up talking very little about sex or boyfriends. The most positive things most of us could say was that we were hipper to our own games now that we had turned thirty. That we'd made a little bit of progress. But mainly we talked about lightweight things like the meaning of life, what you want, what's important, dignity, excellence, is it really possible to love somebody for a lifetime, death, and having a child.

Are you still considering having children?

It's something that's still very much on my mind, being thirty-five.* If you've raised a lot of kids, and I have to some extent as a big sister in a family of nine children, you're spared the naivete of thinking children stay like puppies and you know how much time, energy and responsibility it takes.

A lot of women I know have had children to doctor something in their lives. It's probably a valid reason, wanting to fill a void. But my parents had no choice because my mother was Catholic. "Sometimes an unwanted pregnancy," she'd say, "but never an unwanted child." As for my siblings, at this point one sister has four children, another sister has one, a brother is divorced, and the rest are younger and unmarried.

Let's talk more about your family and upbringing.

I'm an Italian Catholic. (*Grins*) In third grade I was already having problems with the exclusivity of the Catholic Church. The nuns said, "Only if you're married in the Church are you really married. Any other religion doesn't count."

I said, "Well, then how could Mary and Joseph be married if Jesus didn't make the sacrament of marriage until he got older?" I would be sent out into the hallway as punishment for the question.

I liked the theatricality of the Mass and the message of Christ in its purest sense, but I feel the religion hasn't grown with the times. I do think that the Catholic Church, which is incredibly wealthy, has caused an incredible amount of poverty by teaching an acceptance of things. If they're so

---

*Sarandon would later have a daughter with Italian director-screenwriter Franco Amurri and two sons with actor/writer/director Tim Robbins.

pompous, they should get off their ass about world peace. Thank God some of the bishops got involved with nuclear disarmament.

But personally, there was a point when I was a little where I prayed to become a saint, because I was told that when the communists came over, they would hang us all on crosses. The nuns asked us, "Would you have the courage to still say you're a Catholic and be hung on a cross?" So I would pray very seriously about being a saint, because I figured the boats with the invading communists would land any day.

Later, when I was first went to public high school, I was exposed to the absolutely astounding fact that people of the Jewish persuasion were not at all apologetic about it. That was a real eye-opener and a stumbling block. Then when I went to Catholic University in the late 1960s, and all these incredibly gorgeous priests were leaving the seminaries and dating coeds on the campus.

If you're going to lose your religion, go to a religious school, because you learn so much about it you immediately realize it's not practical.

The film industry is filled with fallen Catholics. There's something about transubstantiation—changing water into wine—that is very akin to acting. I bought that concept as a child and I thought that I could grow up to be a wave in the ocean if I wanted to be.

And yet you also grew up to experience a serious nervous breakdown.

(*Nodding somberly*) The notion that pure love will make the way had to get thrown out of my belief system, almost over my dead body. It was a devastating realization, a major turning point in my life akin to accepting that there's no Santa Claus. I also had to accept that people are evil.

I was committed to an institution in 1976. It's the fighting off of those situations that keeps you in pain. They thought I was schizophrenic; I talked about myself in the third person. Even though "breakdown" is not a medical term, it's a shortcut in describing what happened to me.

If you're going to have a nervous breakdown (*sly smile*), it's very important to get pneumonia, which I did. So then you've lost a lot of weight and are barely there, anyway. Not sleeping or eating will set you up for a trip that is well worth not taking.

I was living in upstate New York, but sort of between places and relationships. I had never been in analysis before. It was never anything that was even thought of in my family.

But it makes you humble, makes you stronger, just as acting is a humbling experience. The more characters you play, the more situations you expose yourself to that you never thought were possible, the harder it becomes to judge people, and be as quick with your pronouncements. You realize that, given certain circumstances, you'll do and say and feel things that you *never* thought you could.

What's your philosophy today regarding both your career and your personal life?

My philosophy is to go toward those things, those parts or whatever, that frighten me. Because then I know I can't repeat myself, and I'll have to do something extraordinary or fall flat on my face. Because I'm basically fighting inertia all the time and need to be threatened in order to rally.

When you hit thirty, you have a sense of finiteness. Some of your friends starting dying prematurely—usually over the question of whether to take responsibility and live life, or just say that it's too much for them. Over the last two years I've had so many people in my life die.

I've been lonely all my life, but I don't think it's another person's duty to dispel that loneliness. When you have friends or a lover who sees things the way you do it's an enormous consolation. But my sense of humor is my saving grace. Even back in 1976, when I was nuts, I could crack myself up at the absurdity of my hallucinations. It's the only way I've survived.

As for my work, it's not that I'm a workaholic who has to be on stage all the time. I turn down a lot of work, I work with schizophrenics at Mt. Sinai Hospital, I do a lot of political work. People say I have a lot of energy, although I don't feel that. I'm just incredibly curious and greedy, but I'm not quite neurotic enough to be lazy.

I crave a lot of stimulation, high emotional situations, but not necessarily negative pressure. I'm terrified to audition, though, and when I saw competitiveness when I was younger I couldn't bear it. I'm competing against me.

My brother called me today from Florida, and he read something somewhere that listed me as one of the "Real Women Who *Would* Pump Gas." I thought, "This is great!"

What are your thoughts on fame, as a fact and fantasy?

It's wonderful being famous; I enjoy it. Since success in the business goes hand in hand with visibility, I don't mind it at all when people recognize me on the street. It makes me feel I'm doing something right. The drawbacks are privacy and sometimes safety. At the same time, I feel a responsibility for what I put out there as an actress and how it's interpreted. All that matters is what James Cagney once said, "Follow your heart," doing something you're passionately connected with. But I'm not surprised that I've become famous because it's always awarded in such an arbitrary way.

Merit may be a factor in fame but it's rarely the main criterion.

True. Meanwhile, the seductive thing about acting is that you never figure out why you're good. I should never have stayed in *Extremities* as long as I did; I wanted to break the back of that fucking play, but it just kept breaking me!

There was one night when, at the end, I would wail, couldn't stop crying, and the audience just sat there, didn't even know whether to applaud. Then I'd run offstage and shut myself up in my dressing room. I certainly got better with the play itself, but there were psychic leaps in it that I never figured how to accomplish.

What you learn onstage is much more applicable to real life than what happens in films, because it's all about holding your own, and at the same time being generous enough to give people their focus when it's their time.

My whole theory on what's wrong with films today is that there are no stories that are built *through* the actions of people, only stories built around or without them. *Atlantic City* was successful because it was a film about dreams and people who wanted to connect. You couldn't tell if it was a comedy or a drama. It had about three different acting styles in it. Its supposed bad sides were its pluses. Nobody had the faintest idea of how to sell it! But audiences found it. I have a history of movies like this.

And you're always good in them.

I certainly try. Hollywood is an incredibly corrupt business. But it's also a lesson in flexibility, as I'm constantly being forced to change in the midst of being scared shitless, constantly being forced to adapt to strangers. What better lesson in a world that may be gone tomorrow than to be forced to live in the moment?

But I believe totally in magic. I believe in grace. I believe in the supernatural, I believe in enchantment. And they have all figured very heavily in my life. I don't want to figure it out or explain it all. I just know and feel that to be true.

Acting is a matter of survival, trying to be more than an overnight success turned into an overnight has-been, trying to remain human. [*Smiling faintly, sipping the last of her coffee*] It's an Outward Bound of the soul.

Bill Murray's
Rumpled Anarchy

"I got into acting to be among the living," stated Bill Murray on the last day of filming in March 1988 for Scrooged, *the contemporary update of Charles Dickens'* A Christmas Carol. *"I needed direction and a way into the world."*

Murray would find what he needed by transforming his customary outsider status to his advantage, assuming the self-appointed role of guardian angel and/or jocular protector of all the equally timid souls within his purview. The cast and crew on the Paramount lot quickly learned that a surefire way to charm the *Scrooged* star in his off-duty moments was through shy youngsters. Just prior to final shooting of the horrifying funeral segments Murray's modern Scrooge shares with the Ghost of Christmas Future (who traps him in a flaming coffin), a deeply grim Bill was becoming a source of concern for director Dick Donner. So, during a camera break, he encouraged one of the technical crew to approach the tense actor with her bashful 8-year-old.

"Bill, this is my son James," she ventured warily.

"Hello James," said the lanky Murray, absently extending his large hand. The boy grasped it and Murray suddenly wheeled the boy around, tickling him into hysterics as Billy yelped, *"I'm so sorry we can't get to know each other better, James old buddy, but I've got this dopey work to do!!"*

The boy and his mother moved on, thrilled with the compliment of Murray's coltish prank, and the star sat down on a packing case, biding his time until the cameras were ready for him again. He reached into his back pocket and pulled out a black and white mimeographed flyer with a crude map stapled to it, the top sheet reading:

ALL WEEK WE WORK. ALL WEEK WE WORK HARD. WHEN FRIDAY COMES WE'RE GLAD. NOW WE MUST CELEBRATE! DAN AYKROYD, BILL MURRAY INVITE EDDIE MURPHY TO: AN AFTER WORK PARTY . . . FROM THE TIME YOU WRAP FRIDAY (AROUND 9 P.M.) UNTIL THE POLICE ARRIVE. JUST OUR FRIENDS AND FAMILY. IT'S A BLAST FOR US!

The shindig it announced was planned for that night and Murray seemed as worried that there would be enough food and "good dance music" at the gathering as he was about the costly movie project he was only hours away from wrapping up. But then such innate nonchalance was the keystone of the Bill Murray-type attitude that many of the comedy-savvy male actors (Tom Hanks, Bruce Willis, Michael Keaton) in Hollywood were then straining to acquire. Pity was, they were probably arriving far too late in the game to catch up.

"A couple of years ago," Murray said, "I went to this New York psychic who read my hand and said, 'You learned everything by the time your were 14.' I thought it made perfect sense." Confronted with Murray's adolescent on-screen worldliness, most film critics concurred with his self-assessment. *The New Yorker*'s Pauline Kael later praised *Scrooged* as "a triumphant parody of Yuppie callousness," and it went on to be one of the most successful

Christmas movies of all time, subsequently taking its place as a modern holiday perennial here and abroad.

In the years since, the always cautious Murray would grow even more selective in his film roles; among his few, largely lauded projects have been *Quick Change* (1990), *What about Bob?* (1991), *Mad Dog and Glory* (1992), the instant classic *Groundhog Day* (1993), his small part in the acclaimed cult homage to a notoriously dreadful B-movie director, *Ed Wood* (1994), and *The Man Who Knew Too Little* (1997).

Murray also made some hard choices in his personal life, parting amicably with first wife Mickey, and starting another family with second spouse Jennifer Murray, with whom he had three boys—Cal, Joseph and Cooper—bringing his total offspring by both marriages to five sons.

Whether as an actor, a parent, or a friend, Murray retains his uniquely equanimous temperament, although his self-effacing style can sometimes give way—as it did at the star-studded gala wrap party back in '88—to a keenly perceptive playfulness.

Late in the party, Murray sauntered past a cluster of cigar-smoking colleagues just as sometime Academy Awards host Chevy Chase slyly offered Eddie Murphy $100 if he'd announce the wrong winner of the Best Picture Oscar during Murphy's scheduled appearance on April 11, 1988, as a presenter. The tableau was a study in post-*Saturday Night Live* hierarchies, with Chase the seasoned cynic, Murphy the earnest young showbiz purist and Aykroyd the randy referee.

"No way!" Murphy told Chase. "That stuff is too serious to mess with." Then, relaxing as he hugged his pretty date, Eddie coyly added, "Aw, but you know sometimes how serious you get, how you don't even smile when you make love!"

"Actually," Aykroyd deadpanned, "sometimes I've laughed my butt off in that situation, Eddie—but then I'm a lot older than you."

Catching a faint scent of self-importance hovering around the group, Murray paused in the doorway and peered at them with a mock-awed, "Ooooooh, look who's in conference," meekly asking permission to enter "the Billion Dollar Room" in which the trio was enthroned.

That well-timed crack took the hot air out of his comrades' sails, and in short order Billy had guided them all back to the dance floor.

Slipping a James Brown disc on the CD player, Murray turned to face the smiling respect of his guests.

"Billy," observed actress Laraine Newman, "makes a good grownup."

THE INTERVIEW

A S HOLLYWOOD PARTIES GO, the one in full swing this past spring in a handsome, Georgian Revival home off Sunset Boulevard was an anomaly. No agents circulated, no studio executives haunted the hallways. The food was lasagna and fried chicken; the beverages, Mexican beer and bottled seltzer—with the seltzer proving the more popular. Instead of dizzying references to "gross points," "back-end deals," scripts "in turnaround" and multimillion-dollar movie deals, the talk concerned the fortunes of Chicago sports teams and New York rock bands, and the only "creative products" under scrutiny were baby pictures.

If any aspect of "the industry" was being bantered about, it was the return to the employment ranks of the party's co-host, Bill Murray, who had, earlier that day, finished filming for *Scrooged*—an outlandish adaptation of the Dickens Christmas classic that will be released on Wednesday. Coincidentally, three other film comedies featuring other former *Saturday Night Live* regulars were then nearing completion: *Coming to America*, starring Eddie Murphy; *Caddyshack II*, starring Chevy Chase, and *My Stepmother Is an Alien*, starring Dan Aykroyd. To celebrate this serendipitous event, Murray and Peter Aykroyd, an actor-composer who is Dan's younger brother, had decided on this first-time-ever gathering of *Saturday Night Live* alumni.

A picture of genial abandon in rumpled khakis, football jersey and sneakers, Murray was urging Dan Aykroyd, Laraine Newman and Chevy Chase to drop their "reserves of cool" on the dance floor and "get down!" Murray's warmth is disarming. Chase, for instance, once considered Murray a rival, and the feeling was mutual. Murray was hired at *Saturday Night Live* in January 1977, just five weeks after Chase left for a movie career. The pressure Murray felt in trying to supplant his predecessor flared into backstage fisticuffs when Chase returned as a guest host for the third season of *Saturday Night Live*. Now, the two are thoroughly at ease with each other. Even Eddie Murphy, a *Saturday Night Live* late-comer whose box-office magnetism eclipses that of most of his associates, is meek in Murray's presence.

"Come *on*, man," Murray brays, coaxing the bashful Murphy into the vestibule dance area. "Show us what you got!" Thus persuaded, a grinning Eddie and his date hit the boards as the last lingering bystanders also grab partners. And Murray leads the gleeful group as a Prince record is played, singing "'Tonight we're gonna party like it's 1999!'"

Bill Murray is considered by his colleagues to be a man who has made peace with any private demons he might have had, someone who has brought his personal life and his career into enviable concord. Slightly disheveled and projecting what Richard Donner, the director of *Scrooged*, calls "a woolly Zen wisdom," Murray acts as a kind of father figure to the *Saturday Night Live* alumni.

Reflecting the skepticism of a generation that grew up on television, Murray's humor has always brought wryly heroic dimension to everyday nonconformity. His performances on *Saturday Night Live* were not known for their subtlety, but they ultimately hinged on his forte: discernment. Gilda Radner won a following with her lucid little-girl pathos, and Dan Aykroyd was an instinctive satirist, a craftsman who disappeared behind deft depictions of, say, a huckster on television. But Murray—who occasionally wrote his own material, as did most of the *Saturday Night Live* regulars—was always starkly personal.

Whether he was a lavishly inept lounge singer on *Saturday Night Live* (warbling "Star Wars, nothing but Star Wars, gimme those Star Wars, don't let 'em *ennnnd*") or a benignly anarchic camp counselor in his screen debut, *Meatballs* (1979), the quintessential Bill Murray portrayal has the actor simultaneously immersed in his role and commenting drolly on it.

Unlike any other actor on *Saturday Night Live*, Murray would permit viewers to see the actual process of assuming a character's essence—and the nakedness of the effort was startling. If his viewers had doubted for one instant the completeness of Murray's investment in the role, his attempt at commentary would probably have lapsed into insolence.

Although Murray's sketches on *Saturday Night Live* endeared him to a generation addicted to irreverence, it was his 1984 role in *Ghostbusters* that established him as one of the most interesting comic film stars in a generation. Dan Aykroyd, who created the characters for *Ghostbusters*, wrote the first draft of the movie with his then-sidekick John Belushi and Bill Murray in mind.

Besides being one of the most successful film comedies in history (grossing more than $300 million), *Ghostbusters* won Murray critical raves for his goofy-gallant depiction of a spirit exterminator—a portrayal that demanded he be convincing as a heroic protagonist, romantic leading man and comic foil for an array of special-effects hobgoblins.

"The broad strokes kept 'em in their seats, but it was the tenderness toward his comrades and the *vulnerability* of his howling he'd been 'slimed' that hooked the crowds but good," notes Michael O'Donoghue, the former head writer of *Saturday Night Live* and a guest at the party. (With Mitch Glazer, O'Donoghue is co-screenwriter of *Scrooged*.)

In the four years since *Ghostbusters*, Murray and his wife, Mickey, have been raising two boys, ages 6 and 3, and leading a stable family life. He is one famous funny-man who rarely agrees to be interviewed and has a strong aversion to the "false fuss" of the Hollywood publicity mill. He has also maintained a first-rate box-office reputation, and was able to command a $6 million fee for *Scrooged*.

"I'm a sucker for hero roles, the big brother parts, especially super-heroes—providing they have flaws," says Murray one early spring morning, seated in his trailer on Paramount Pictures' Hollywood lot.

In *Scrooged*, Murray's miserly crank of the 1980s is Frank Cross, president of the International Broadcasting Company, the youngest network chief in the annals of the industry. A man who loathes Christmas for everything but its commercial uses, Cross churns out such holiday programming fare as *Howard Cosell at the Sistine Chapel* and *Bob Goulet's Old Fashioned Cajun Christmas* in between quiz shows like *Guess My Disease* and *Run for Sex*.

"I've seen TV from behind the scenes," Murray continues, "so I draw from that a bit to expose its hypocrisies. As with Frank, most of TV's programming ideas come from the afternoon edition of the *New York Post*. He's a crumb, a pig, yet audiences who know the story know he's gonna change."

Prior to Frank Cross, Murray's most flawed movie hero was Larry Darrell, in a 1984 remake of Somerset Maugham's novel *The Razor's Edge*. Darrell is a spiritually hungry World War I aviator from Chicago who, after seeing his best friend killed, adopts a mystical Eastern gospel of non-attachment. The movie quietly sank into oblivion, many of those who did see it deciding that Murray was ineffective when playing against type and not being funny.

Early screenings of *Scrooged* have garnered varied reactions. During sneak previews this summer, 93 percent of those surveyed found the movie "very good"—the highest positive rating Paramount has ever received in a survey of this kind. More recently, the responses at press screenings in New York have ranged from ovations to disgruntlement.

The obvious question of whether Bill Murray can shine as someone other than himself is inevitably intertwined with the issue of who Bill Murray is. Murray himself explains that both his choice of material and approach in playing a contemporary Scrooge are rooted in the surreal emotional vocabulary of a kid raised on video.

"I didn't grow up reading a lot of Charles Dickens, although I got a dose of *A Tale of Two Cities* in school," Murray emphasizes, slouched in a director's chair. "Most folks will tell you the best dramatic version of *A Christmas Carol* is the 1951 Alastair Sim movie on the late show every Christmas week, but my own favorite is the animated Mr. Magoo's Scrooge. Maybe it's just me," he concludes with a chuckle, "but I thought there was a lot of truth in the exaggerated vulnerability of the near-sighted little cartoon guy."

While friends like Dan Aykroyd and Chevy Chase have lately drawn criticism for making too many movies, Murray has raised eyebrows in the film industry for making too few. All told, he has starred in only seven features since 1979, while filling cameo roles in four: *Mr. Mike's Mondo Video*, *The Jerk*, *Little Shop of Horrors* and, most notably, *Tootsie*.

"Billy has been very discerning, very instinctive," says the producer Sydney Pollack, who cast him in *Tootsie*. "These days, when people can jump too readily at big deals, his are distinguishing traits. It's funny, but I initially resisted putting Billy in *Tootsie*. Dustin Hoffman and I met him at a party in 1982, enjoying his affable nature, and as we were leaving Dustin turned to me and said, 'Gee, I think he'd be a great roommate for my character.'

"My initial opinion was that Billy was just a strong sketch player. It wasn't until I screened his films at Dustin's urging that I saw what a satisfying actor he could be. Even when those around him are merely filling their parts, Billy always gives a very sustained characterization. There's reality and candor, plus scene-to-scene growth. . . . He's got a complex and original range that puts him in a special category—a completely believable comic illuminator."

Given the phenomenal success of *Ghostbusters*—and the financial independence that afforded him—Murray, was able to do what he wanted during the four years between that blockbuster and *Scrooged*. He took his wife, Mickey, and baby, Homer, to France for a year, and his second son, Luc, was born while they were living in Paris. When they resumed residence in a renovated farmhouse in the Hudson River Valley, Murray would regularly disappear into his tiny office to read historical fiction and the novels of Irish writers.

Sporadically, though, Murray was lured from his lair to take small acting parts. He appeared in several public readings in Manhattan organized by the playwright-director Timothy Mayer, and in a production of Bertolt Brecht's *A Man's a Man*, at Mayer's Hyde Park Festival Theater in upstate New York. But the rest of his sabbatical was devoted to his family, caring for his mother during a protracted illness, and spending time with his far-flung siblings—five brothers and three sisters—with whom he remains extremely close. More than once, Mets fans were startled to encounter Murray and his older brother Brian, also an actor, on the subway en route to weekend games.

Murray plowed through dozens of proffered screenplays, but he couldn't bring himself to accept any of them. "For each year that Bill didn't work, his fee probably went up—until he could ask for and get $6 million in cash for *Scrooged*," says the producer Art Linson. "That might sound like a lot of money, considering he received more for *Scrooged* than the producer, director and cast combined. But when it costs a studio $15 million to $20 million for publicity and prints just to open a major picture, it might just be a bargain in Billy's case—because his name across the marquee will sell over $10 million worth of tickets in the opening three to four days. The only two actors, serious or comic, who can guarantee that degree of turnout in 1988 are Bill Murray and Eddie Murphy. That factor is the source of Billy's power in Hollywood. Not that he plays on it. Normally, unless he's giving input on his own pictures, he ignores it."

Murray himself feels that *Scrooged* was well worth waiting for, since the movie permits him to deliver a substantial theme in a whimsical package. "For now," he contends, "the goal is to cut through the glamour—which has its place, I guess—and give the public a little food for thought. . . . There are moments in the Dickensian morality of *Scrooged* where you have the creepy chance to contemplate your ruin—the bottom of your future."

Up close, Murray's rough visage is not conventionally handsome, yet there is something in the solidity of his gaze that often makes it so. His musical burrs and thoughtful mein reveal a man accustomed to the darkness and the light.

Beginning next month, Murray will be shooting the sequel to *Ghostbusters*. He is pleased with the script "because after four drafts it returns the story to a human scale, with subtlety and no silly explosions at the end. Like *Scrooged*, it's a story about innocence restored, and good values, and the power of faith in ordinary people. It sounds corny but I'd like all my stuff from here on out to be things you wouldn't be afraid to let your kids' kids discover decades from now. Like I discovered *A Tale of Two Cities* or even Mr. Magoo."

Mickey Kelly, a former talent coordinator on the *The Tonight Show* and *The Dick Cavett Show*, is a self-assured brunette. She and Murray were married on Jan. 24, 1981, at 4:30 a.m. in a Las Vegas "elopement"—engineered by the actor—that had begun as a spin through the San Fernando Valley to find a Mexican restaurant. As the drive turned into a puzzling tour, Mickey Kelly's stomach grumbled and her mood grew grim ("I thought he was trying to drive me insane").

These days, in a village by the Hudson, Mickey Kelly runs a custom furniture shop while Murray tends to his "screen thing." On a recent autumn afternoon, she is off running errands while her husband splits luncheon and babysitting chores with the housekeeper.

With son Homer still at school and his sibling Luc dispatched for a nap, Murray commandeers the gleaming, country-style kitchen to prepare a highly touted risotto con Champagne. As a splendid sun advances upon the luxuriant back lawn of his home, he sets a table on the veranda with linen placemats and ceramic dishware. The meal is tasty, the herbal tea flavorful, and the conversation meditative as Murray reviews the quirky milestones that helped mold the man he has become.

He was born on Sept. 20, 1951, in the Chicago suburb of Wilmette, to Edward and Lucille Murray, both descendants of Irish immigrant stock. Edward Murray, a lumber salesman, was a diabetic and died when Billy was 17.

"I feel a little different from the rest of my family," the actor confesses as he seats himself on the porch and breaks off a piece of brioche. "Having the big success made me feel different. I ended up doing my father's job in some ways.

"Because of the diabetes, my father was an interesting combination of a thin, fragile man and a disciplinarian. With a lot of kids, you always feel there's a party going on, but obviously we needed to be reined in for sanity's sake. At the dinner table, he was very dry and quiet, but always triggered to laugh. It was just very difficult to figure out what would do it. It had to be good. It was like he was waiting, and he'd wait forever if need be."

In the meantime, bread had to be won and household expectations kept within strict bounds. Christmas came to exemplify the Murrays' necessarily austere disposition.

"I never asked for toys," Murray recalls. "Asking for toys was out of the question; they were low priorities. It's not that we were denied anything so much as the fact that we knew not to make requests. For Christmas you got essentials: school clothes. Whenever toys surfaced at all, they were pretty much inherited."

Neither Billy nor his siblings possessed the means to bestow decent gifts of their own. "The closest any of us ever came to an allowance was finding change under the couch cushions, so I used to shop each Christmas with a single dollar, getting everybody something that cost a dime. Once Brian had all these significant-looking presents in big crisp boxes under the tree, while ours resembled badly wrapped body parts. Turned out he'd gotten scrap wood from Dad's lumberyard and nailed it into a bunch of big blocks.

"The worst year in my case was the one I bought two pounds of peanuts from the corner drugstore, and I wrapped them in tinfoil. It was a terribly lazy move for a 10–year-old to pull. And I kept going in each day before Christmas and taking a few nuts from each package, so by the time the day rolled around the matter had grown disgraceful."

Now settled into a comfortable country house, Murray relates these stories with a mixture of giggles and shudders. He grows grim, however, when he touches on his 13th Christmas.

"That was my 'unloved year,'" he recalls. "I got everything I wanted, which was really only a clock radio, but I was in some sort of a state, going through a phase. They say the middle kid gets the least attention, but that can be accentuated in a house overrun with them. They gave me all these things, and I just sat there with a puppy-dog's long face. Then I got even more attention because I wasn't happy. *Then* they got angry." He shrugs. "See, I was crying for help."

He read voraciously, his favorites "were biographies for children of American heroes, all the guys like Kit Carson, Wild Bill Hickok and Davy Crockett. I read them over and over, 'cause they were all poor kids when they started. The book that made the biggest impression was the one about Crockett, because he ran away from home as a kid, pulled it off, and his parents missed him when he came back." He gives a huge smile. "That's the kind of happy ending that sticks with me."

He began taking summer jobs in his early teens to pay for his tuition in a Roman Catholic high school. Following in his brothers' footsteps, he made $3.50 a bag caddying at the luxurious Indian Hill Club in nearby Winnetka. Much later, he was able to pour his impressions of the job into his 1980 movie, *Caddyshack*, which his brother Brian wrote with Doug Kenney and Harold Ramis.

"The movie was knowledgeable about golf," Murray says, "but it should have had more about the stratification of country-club life. The kids who were members of the club were despicable; you couldn't believe the attitude they had. I mean, you were literally walking barefoot in a T-shirt and jeans, carrying some privileged person's sports toys on your back for five miles."

The 1960s were a difficult time for him, Murray suspects, not only because of the financial straits the family was in. There were the illnesses as well. Because they were seldom openly acknowledged, his father's diabetes, a sister's polio and his mother's several miscarriages heightened his anxiety and his compassion.

"My sister limps slightly now," he says quietly. "The last time I was home, somebody had developed these old home movies that had her walking with braces when she was 2. God, it was breathtaking. . . . Sitting there and watching it with her, it was like there was a jack on the inside of my brain that was spreading my skull apart."

With that, he gets up and clears away the dishes, hurrying into the kitchen. When he returns, his mood is lighthearted, and he launches into reminiscences of the minor mischief he got into as a juvenile, ranging from accidentally totaling a neighbor's car at 13 to getting punished the following year for heavy petting with an older girl.

He began to focus his energies in increasingly public ways, becoming the lead singer in a rock band called the Dutch Masters, and taking part in high-school and community-theater dramatic productions. Dropping out of college, he gravitated toward his brother Brian's bohemian flat in the Old Town section of Chicago and joined Second City improvisational workshops, eventually becoming a full cast member.

Scrambling to make ends meet, Murray was convicted at age 21 of selling marijuana and was placed on probation. He managed to get his drug-related mistakes out of his system early on, and latched onto acting as a vocational anchor.

In 1974, John Belushi, a friend from Second City, got Murray signed on as a regular on *The National Lampoon Show*, a comedy revue. Lorne Michaels, creator of *Saturday Night Live*, visited the show several times while scouting talent for his program, but passed over Murray in favor of Belushi. In 1977, after Belushi and Dan Aykroyd began straying from the late-night showcase to seek their movie fortunes, Murray was finally summoned to New York to fill out the lineup.

He remained "the new guy" for the longest time—until he stepped into his Manhattan shower one morning in 1978, just prior to the last show of the season. He picked up a Christmas present Belushi's wife, Judy Jacklin, had given him—a microphone-shaped bar of soap on a rope—and suddenly he improvised an addled script about a husband who invites his unfaithful wife and her lover into the shower stall for a mock *This Is Your Life* nightclub routine. A sensational bit of homespun surrealism, it hit the airwaves with a wallop that weekend and instantly transformed Bill Murray into the program's freshest star.

The afternoon is abruptly chilly, the waning light turning Murray's wooded backyard into a tangle of shadows. He rises to pace around the porch.

"The last two years have been incredibly exciting and incredibly draining," he allows as Bark, his golden retriever, bounds out of the bushes toward him. He chases Bark around the yard a few times, displaying the rambunctiousness of a person half his age. Whether at home or on the set of *Scrooged*, Murray seems happiest when the child in him is tapped. There is a flip side to his exuberance, and it surfaces when someone attempts to abuse his openness.

"As the *Scrooged* production was beginning," recalls Mitch Glazer, "Billy asked O'Donoghue and me to go with him to this Mexican desert resort for a little male bonding. We did a lot of swimming and hiking, and Billy was really sweet to all the other guests, who loved meeting him. Unfortunately, there was this one Beverly Hills woman, a Rodeo Drive type who wore furs in the blazing sun, and she insisted on treating Billy like he was some ornament to her vacation.

"On her last day, she was pressing him for autographs and things, and Billy always complied. Finally, she cornered him for yet another autograph and he calmly said, 'O.K., but I'll have to have something in return. I get to throw you in the pool.' She laughed, saying, 'Sure, you do that,' as he signed—and then he went for it, escorting her toward the deep end of the pool. She dropped to the deck, gaping, but Billy reminded her that a bargain was a bargain, and he slipped his hands under her, rolling her—furs and all—into the water."

As Bark disappears back into the underbrush, Murray ambles to the porch and reflects on the concerns he has wrestled with since *Ghostbusters*.

"You know, the *Ghostbusters* mania also coincided with my mother's retirement," he begins evenly. "She's had this clerical job since my father died, and she took an early pension. But she had no sooner tried to finally enjoy life when she found she had cancer of the lymph nodes and needed massive chemotherapy. My mother is a real character, a talkative soul who can make friends with anyone, and she'd always been a massive influence on me. She's so animated, I even used to tape phone conversations with her in order to steal material!

"The idea of her being gravely ill really threw me hard." Murray's voice falls to a near-whisper. But, he continues, his mother's hair loss, a result of chemotherapy, "brought out her inner beauty." His hazel-blue eyes gleam and glaze slightly. "I loved the way the light caught her head when she moved, and how you could almost see her thoughts etched on her skull." (After a brief recovery, Lucille Murray succumbed to cancer early this month.)

Suddenly, the housekeeper calls out from inside the house. "Luc is up from his nap!"

"Fab-u-lous!" Murray answers. "Does he wanna go for a walk by the river with Pop?"

"No!" she replies. "He is watching TV in the den!"

"Huh? What's so swell on TV that he can't fuss around with his father?!"

"He's watching the *Ghostbusters* cartoons!"

Murray scratches his thinning hair. "Damn," he mutters darkly. "Just when you finally figure out what you're doing in the world, you have to start worrying about what you've done."

Acknowledgments

The journalism assembled herein spans several decades. For their assistance, I would like to thank the editors at the publications in which these revised works originally appeared: Peter Knobler, Greg Mitchell, Robert Smith, John Swenson, Mitchell Glazer and Jon Pareles at *Crawdaddy*; Jann Wenner, Harriet Fier, Barbara Downey, Bob Wallace, Peter Herbst, Maryanne Vollers, Terry McDonell and Hans Teensma at *Rolling Stone*; David Hirshey at *The New York Sunday News Magazine*; J. Curtis Sanburn at *Harper's Bazaar*; Guy Flatley and Roberta Ashley at *Cosmopolitan*; and Ken Emerson, Margarett Loke and Edward Klein at *The New York Times Magazine;* and most of all, my incomparable *Rolling Stone* photo-journalist colleague, the visionary Annie Leibovitz.

Much of what I've learned about reporting came during my early years in the New York Bureau of the Associated Press, so I thank my primary teachers and cohorts: Lou Boccardi (who first hired me as a copyboy), Murray Rose, Frank Brown, Dick Joyce, Wick Temple, Craig Ammerman, Hal Boch, Ken Rappaport, George Vecsey, Sr., Mary Campbell and Will Grimsley. Thanks also to my agent Jim Stein and lastly, to my Billboard Books editor, Bob Nirkind.

Bibliography

Information regarding previous publication (in order of their appearance in the text) of the material herein is as follows:

"James Cagney: Looking Backward," *Rolling Stone*, February 18, 1982.

"Theater's First Couple: After 31 Years as a Theatrical Team, Jessica Tandy and Hume Cronyn Have Become the Stuff of Legend," *The New York Times Magazine*, December 26, 1982.

"Dracula: The Warmblooded Revival of the Debonaire King of the Undead," *Crawdaddy*, June 1978.

"Dudley Moore Is Not Always Funny," *New York Sunday News Magazine*, December 12, 1982.

"Andy's Kaufman's Broadway Bout," *New York Sunday News*, April 3, 1983.

"The New Julie Andrews: A Sexy, Sly Surprise," *Cosmopolitan*, July 1982.

"Avé Marie: Win a Date for the Apocalypse with America's Immaculate Sex Symbol," *Crawdaddy*, August 1977.

"Johnny Carson: The *Rolling Stone* Interview," *Rolling Stone*, March 22, 1979.

"In Search of Alan Alda," *Attenzione*, January 1982.

"Is America Ready for Mr. Mike? Trapped in a World He Never Made, Michael O'Donoghue Only Laughs When It Hurts," *Rolling Stone*, July 26, 1979.

"Walter, We Hardly Knew You," *Rolling Stone*, February 5, 1981.

"A Hard Act To Follow: As Walter Cronkite Steps Down, Dan Rather Contemplates His Arrival at the Top," *Rolling Stone*, April 2, 1981.

"I Am the Master of My Destiny: From Old Kentucky to Kinshasa, the Legend of the Louisville Lip," *Crawdaddy*, February 1975.

"Raquel: The Hard Times and Bittersweet Dreams of a Red-Hot Anachronism," *Crawdaddy*, May 1978.

"B-Movie Blues Brothers: Jake and Elwood's Secret Life," "Dan Aykroyd: Messin' with the Kid," *Rolling Stone*, February 22, 1979.

"The Homecoming: Bette Midler Conquers Hollywood in *The Rose.*," *Rolling Stone*, December 13, 1979.

"True-Grit Tenderfoot: John Travolta Learns to Separate the Dancer from the Dance," *Rolling Stone*, July 10, 1980.

"Goldie Hawn: Private Goldie," *Rolling Stone*, March 5, 1981.

"Slaves to the Empire: The *Star Wars* Kids Speak Up," *Rolling Stone*, July 24, 1980.

"Unconventional Sarandon: An Irreverent Actress Speaks Her Mind," *Harper's Bazaar*, July 1983.

"The Rumpled Anarchy of Bill Murray," *The New York Times Magazine*, November 20, 1988.

Index